Published by ST Publishing, Inc.
364 Fair Hill Drive, Suite F
Elkton, Maryland 21921

410-392-5867
www.st-publishing.com
sean@st-publishing.com

Graphic design and layout by J. Kevin Titter

Printed in China

 • ISBN 0-9702560-2-7

THE BEST OF

The SARATOGA *Special*

Saratoga's Daily Newspaper on Thoroughbred Racing

2001
2002
2003
2004
2005

By Sean Clancy and Joe Clancy Jr.

Table of Contents

Introduction

First we bought 10 folding tables from Staples. Then metal folding chairs, the ones that look more suited to a pancake breakfast at the local church than a newspaper. Joe showed up in his Subaru with two computers, a printer and a fax machine. Paul brought the T-shirts and a case of Stewart's soda.

The year was 2001 and The Saratoga Special was open for business.

Bedded down in an out-of-business gym at the end of Broadway, The Special had much to do. Our biggest advertiser had committed to buying the back cover for the season. We quickly learned the difference between verbal commitment and written commitment. Somehow, we couldn't get them on the phone. It wouldn't be the first time we muttered, "We must be crazy" during the next six weeks.

Zero down and 35 issues to go. Gulp.

It's funny to write these words, now, five years later. This book is a celebration of those five years – from the daunting days of 2001 (when we did think we were crazy) to the anticipation of 2006.

The idea then was to create a publication that Thoroughbred racing would embrace. We would write, live and breathe the summer meet, hopefully make an impact and hopefully not lose our bank accounts. Sean long dreamed of the idea. Paul needed something to do. Joe kept the wheels on the ground. Somehow, The Special made it through that first year – it wasn't pretty and it was rarely on time – but we proved a point and came back for more in 2002, 2003, 2004 and 2005.

Now, the idea remains the same but some of the desperation has gone. New computers helped keep The Special a reality, making deadlines realistic goals not Everest-like climbs. New thinking helped bring more business. We also like to think the quality of the product pushed everything along and made people realize we meant what we said – that we cared about the racing, the town, the horses, the people. And most of the tables and chairs are still around.

Five years down, many more to go.

Thanks

In celebration of our first five years. Thank you first to our families – the myriad Clancys out there (Ruth, Joe, Sheila, Sam, Ryan, Jack, Nolan) provided support, thoughts, gifts, transportation, encouragement and a Sallee van full of intangibles. None of it could have happened without you. A huge thanks to Paul Wasserman, Sean's college roommate and longtime friend who became all but part of the extended family through The Special. Thanks also to a varied cast of staffers and contributors. Their roles were many, their pay was little, but somehow they believed along with us – Tod Marks, Dave Harmon, Pete Fornatale, Frank Scatoni, Kevin Titter, Barbara Livingston, Jamie Santo, Travis Stone, Quint Kessenich, Dan Burns, Brendan Wilmot, Susie Alexander, Liz Ronk, Bruno Zalubil, Jen Brasser, Ben Meyers, Adrian Bacolo, Shelly Chase, Dave Martin, Jim Mulvihill, Christine Paska, Vic Zast, Emily Kobel – and everyone at Staffield Printing in Clifton Park, N.Y. Surely there are others we have missed, and the list of thank yous would not be complete without a nod to the advertisers. Some bought into the concept from the start, a few (Sam Slater, Iris and Mike Freeman) supported us without hesitation. Others took more convincing, but they proved none the less valuable.

Premiere Edition – Wednesday, July 25

The Saratoga Special

Price: $1

Year 1 • No. 1

Ready, Set, Go

Gate springs open on racing's heaven for 133rd season

BY JOE CLANCY JR.

SARATOGA SPRINGS, N.Y.

Out of the gate and into action – the racing starts today at Saratoga Race Course.

Inside

■ See OPENING, page 3

The Saratoga Special's Inaugural Year

Saratoga 2001

Saratoga returned again – in all its glory. The Saratoga Special arrived in all its infancy. Arrival would probably be too strong a word. We were crawling, at best. Daily publishing looked like a grand idea on paper. In reality, we had pulled the elephant into the room and had no idea how we were going to get him up the stairs.

Point Given blew into town. Allen Jerkens won the Ballerina with Shine Again. Bobby Frankel dominated a weekend with Flute and Aptitude. Jerry Bailey took his seventh Saratoga jockey crown while Bill Mott secured his third straight trainer title and eighth overall.

As for the Saratoga Special – we saw just enough glimmers of hope to want to do it again.

Day after day.

Set after set. Horse after horse. Story after story. Race after race. Summer after summer. This right here in your hand has been in my head. The Saratoga Special, a daily newspaper covering it all for the six weeks at Saratoga.

It's been in there, rocking and banging needing to get out. And now it's out.

Will it work? I'll tell you in six weeks.

It will work if passion counts for something. If good journalism still matters. If horse racing recognizes a good thing. And it doesn't rain . . . the phones get hooked up . . . we get to sleep an hour or two a night . . . the ads keep rolling in . . . the readers flock . . . it will work. It will work. It will work. I'm taping it on the tops of my shoes, the mirror of my car, the backs of my hands. It will work.

Today is day one of the greatest race meet in the world and day one of a roiling six-week adventure of writing, selling and convincing from this corner of the office. I didn't say corner office.

We're the kids who started a lemonade stand because they were thirsty. Now we'll see if our lemonade sells.

I'll be here every day – writing what I see, what I feel, what I hear in Saratoga. This paper is brand new, this column is working on its third year. I wrote my first journal in 1999 and turned it into the book Saratoga Days (still available in stores and out of my car trunk). Last year, I managed a half journal after breaking my ankle in a steeplechase race. This year, it's strictly journalism as I retired in November and dove straight into this project.

I'm sure I'll always be classified as a steeplechase guy but don't let that lull you into thinking this column, or this newspaper for that matter, is about steeplechasing. I'll get a plug in for the jumping sport from time to time but this is everything and everybody from Albert The Great to Zen and the art of picking winners.

Today, I introduce myself. Tomorrow, I let you live Saratoga from morning to night. From saddle to bar stool. From binoculars in the stands to hooves in the dirt. This is life in Saratoga – through my eyes and hopefully into your hands.

In this first issue, we try to give you an idea of our vision. What we're here for and why. After today we proceed with the vision. Every day we'll try to captivate you, entertain you, inform you. We believe we can do it. We're better writers than sellers. This isn't some corporate conglomerate with divisions and departments, protocols and agendas, board meetings and shareholders.

"Let's start a rock band," is something you'd hear around our office. Dreamers, probably. I was told the other day, it's OK to be a dreamer, just be careful living in a dream world.

This column, a daily journal from Saratoga, will be as close to a dream world as you'll get. Saratoga isn't a bad place to be in a dream world, that I know. Come here every day, sit back with a cup of coffee, a grandchild, a hammock, an open mind, and enjoy a day at the Spa.

I know I will.

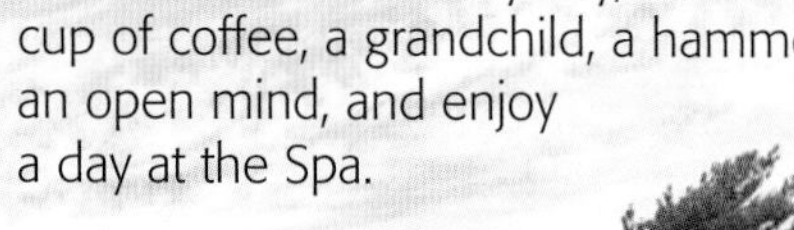

So there we were minding our own business....

....delivering the inaugural issue of the paper and wandering through Clare Court when hell broke loose in front of us.

The clack of metal horseshoe on road, that's as bad as fingernail on chalkboard.

The horse was bounding down the hard road, head down, and ass up. The rider was coming off, it was just a matter of time. His feet were out of the stirrups like dangling lines from a young angler, his legs were raking the horse better than Ty Murray on Sunday nights, and his reins were as long as the handle numbers on opening day.

In a flash, the horse gave one final buck and the rider was simply flung. It was in slow motion, like throwing a wet scarecrow off the back of a pickup truck. The horse ducked the tree, helmet went flying off in mid-air, and the rider went head first into the tree. The horse jumped the rail and the rider just lie there. Paul Wasserman, the business manager for the newspaper and neophyte to horse racing, let out an "Isn't anyone going to help him?" We were already running.

The exercise rider was tangled at the bottom of the tree, scraped from head to foot, blood pouring out of the right side of his head. Goggles lay crumpled, helmet cover was buried in the dirt and grass, bandana looked like it had been used to mulch the lawn, and flak jacket looked like the front of Pete Rose's jersey.

Boy, there is nothing like blood spouting. Drip, drip, drip onto the grass.

The Pinkertons were still standing on Nelson Avenue as we tried to call for the ambulance. They had the walkie talkies which were about as useful as two tin cans and some string. Paul ran to Mike Hushion's barn for a rub rag while I pretended to be Florence Nightingale. We held a rub rag to the guy's head while he lay bent over at a 90-degree angle. A set of Mike Freeman's passed five feet from us and I started to wonder if "anyone was going to help him." The ambulance still hadn't shown. My man was conscious, it was like he was drunk, late at night, looking at you with no expression or reaction. Man, was he dirty.

Paul ran for the ambulance following the directions, "Go diagonally, remember where we gave the paper to Neil Howard."

The ambulance finally came and took over. Of course the back board and neck brace came out – protocol is such crap. We rolled up all the belongings and put them into the helmet that went AWOL when it was needed most. Why exercise riders and jockeys undo their chin straps is still a wonder of the world to me.

They strapped him down to the board doing a "standing stationary" or something, just strapped him down vertically and turned him horizontally. He shook my hand, asked me if I'd go talk to his sister at Joe Aquilino's barn.

I asked his name. In a quiet voice he answered, "Julio. Thank you my friend."

I know Julio has a headache tonight and wonders about his career choice. The boy got pummeled into that tree. As for Paul, he hasn't recovered yet.

Tough people, these exercise riders. The day before I was driving through the stable area when Loretta Lusteg at John Kimmel's barn looked into my car while riding her pony. I said good morning and she said, "Morning. Hey you're wearing a Mariana T-shirt." It took me a moment until I looked down and saw the Anna Rushton painting with the words Mariana Makarova Foundation. Makarova was paralyzed in a morning exercise accident a few years ago and they sold shirts to raise money. I bought five after a good day riding winners at Fair Hill.

I looked down the road and yelled a question to Loretta, something like 'How's she doing?'

She just looked at me with a nahh expression and some trying-to-say-something-positive words.

Julio will be all right.

"Your paper is like sex. It can be great but if you're not getting it, it doesn't matter."

– Richard Hutchinson, on distribution problems

"Can I get back to you on that?"

– Number one response from a jock's agent to a trainer

SEABISCUIT

Seabiscuit, An American Legend, a New York Times bestselling novel by Laura Hillenbrand, captured the imaginations of readers (in and out of racing) in 2001. The amazing life story of "The Biscuit" and the people around him made a great subject that helped Thoroughbred racing reach a broader audience.

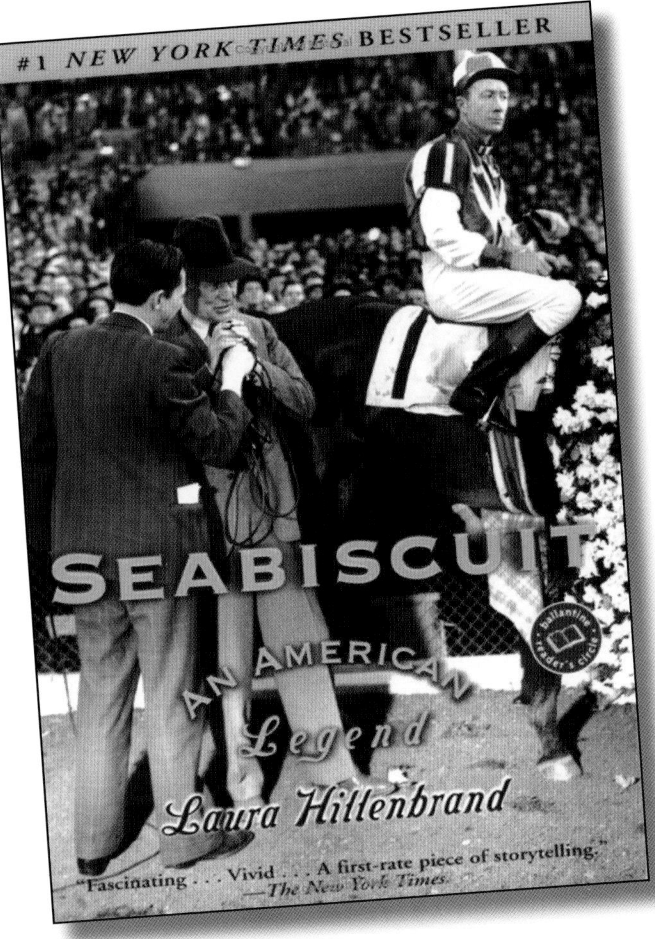

The Special's Pete Fornatale interviewed Laura Hillenbrand for an exclusive question-and-answer session.

I noticed Seabiscuit's last two races before he came to trainer Tom Smith's barn were at Saratoga. He won both. Do you recall any specific stories that didn't make the book about Seabiscuit in Saratoga?

It was hard to find information about Seabiscuit's time at Saratoga, because he was still a high-level claimer, so people didn't take much notice of him. So everything I learned about his stay there is in the book.

When I say "Saratoga" to you, what images does it conjure up? Have you ever been to Saratoga?

Because I am disabled, I have never been able to make a pilgrimage to Saratoga. Most of my familiarity with it comes from the wonderful writers who have chronicled their days there and the history of the place. It is racing's hallowed ground. It is perhaps the only major sporting venue which is most identified not with a great victory but a great defeat – Man o' War's storied loss to Upset in 1919. That is the image that comes to mind most readily when I think of Saratoga.

Is there any horse in training now that reminds you of Seabiscuit?

Seabiscuit is a singular athlete with a singular story; to say any horse is "a lot like Seabiscuit" is for me a stretch. But one horse now in training appeals to me in large part because of the attributes he shares with the Biscuit; John's Call. Here is a horse who, like

SEABISCUIT

Seabiscuit, didn't discover himself as an athlete until later in life, and his tenacity is proving stronger than the deleterious affects of his age. I fell for him last year at Saratoga, when he became the only 9-year-old other than John Henry to win a Grade I race. It wasn't the fact that he won it, it was the way he won it; running with alacrity, obviously taking immense pleasure in speed. After the race, his jockey (Jean-Luc Samyn) reveled in the joy the horse was taking in burying his opponents. My affection for him deepened in his narrow loss in the Breeders' Cup, when he fought to the wire with horses easily young enough to be his sons, ears flat to his head, utterly defiant. For me, much of the lure of racing is the vicarious pleasure to be had in watching creatures perfectly engineered for their task drawing deep satisfaction from what they do. As I wrote in the book, racehorses are nature's ultimate wedding of form and purpose. John's Call is the epitome of the racehorse.

What current trainer/jockey combination would do the best with Seabiscuit? Why?

I'm a historian, not a trainer, so I balk at the idea of assessing the abilities of comtemporary trainers. It seems apparent, though, that he would not fit the kind of trainer who shapes his stable towards the classics and the races suited to precocious horses. I guess if I had to put my hands on Seabiscuit now I would try to get him into the barn of someone who lets the horses dictate where they want to go and what goals to set, instead of trying to fit them into a mold that might not suit them. I would also want someone who could be flexible in dealing with an animal with unusual idiosyncracies. The trainers that come to mind immediately would be Bill Mott, Ron McAnally, Jenine Sadahi and Neil Drysdale.

If, in the middle of your writing process, someone had asked you what the fate of your book would be, what would you have guessed?

It is so hard to know, because so much of it is not up to me. Because I am disabled, I knew I wouldn't be able to do a book tour, and I was afraid that this would doom it. I thought it was realistic to think I could sell 5,000 books, and hoped for 20,000, which is an excellent showing. I can't believe sales have now exceeded a quarter million and are continuing to be strong.

At what point did you know your book was going to be a best-seller? Do you remember how that felt?

I knew almost immediately. Five days after the book was released, my edtor, agent and publicist phoned me on a conference call and told me together that the book was already on the New York Times bestseller list, debuting at No. 8. I let out quite a scream. At that moment, I felt like my subjects – Tom Smith, owners Charles and Marcela Howard, jockeys Red Pollard and George Woolf – were there in the room with me, cheering me on. It was a beautiful feeling. A week later, we hit No. 2; a week after that, No. 1. We stayed at No. 1 for six weeks. It was incredible. The book is still on the list 20 weeks later.

Personally, I think it's clear your book has had a very positive impact on the sport, creating interest, causing more people to pay attention to the track. What else do you think racing needs to expand its fanbase?

I think racing needs to recognize and tap into a female audience, and take steps to appeal directly to it. A lot of young women become interested in this sport for the reasons I did – not for the betting angle, but for the aesthetic. I'd love to see ads that play upon the speed and beauty

SEABISCUIT

of the sport. I think the sport needs to market its top athletes – the jockeys and the horses – to familiarize the public with their personalities and create more of a sense of continuity between events. Ads showing how thrilling the sport is are great, but why not run some ads showing Point Given running in slow motion while talking about who he is? Point Given is an arresting individual with an arresting personality, and I would like to see more of the public come to know and care for athletes like him so they have an emotional stake in tuning in. This was the way it was in Seabiscuit's day, and I think the sport should emulate it. One other thing; I think the sport underestimates how many fans are driven away by breakdowns. In my experience, this is especially true of female fans. I have been impressed by the sport's efforts to remedy the problem since Go For Wand's horrific death, but it could do better and I think it must.

Obviously, Seabiscuit achieved his fame as an older horse. Do you have any ideas how racing can create stars of its older horses in this day and age? On a related note, what do you think of the fact that so much racing coverage is 3-year-old centric?

I think racing is trying hard to focus attention on races for older horses, which are for me the best events, showcasing the animals' talents in fullest bloom. The sport is handicapped by its participants, who tend to retire the best ones early to maximize stud value. Racing is a business, and I understand the need to profit off the horses, but it sends a dagger through my heart every time we see a horse like War Chant, who was simply astounding in the Breeders' Cup Mile last year, retire so early. I'm not sure where the answer lies, but I think if we focus our marketing on the horses themselves, the best individuals will become major celebrities, and the races for older horses will thus become more prestigious. Perhaps in this case, their owners would have more incentive to keep them in the game. Seabiscuit stayed in racing, through age 7, because his owners loved the public adulation that he received when he ran, and because the races for older horses carried immense prestige. Charles Howard wanted to win the Santa Anita Handicap more than anything else, and Seabiscuit had a very long career because of it.

Have you given any thought to what your next project is going to be?

I will probably turn my book into a children's book, by popular demand. We are already speaking with a prominent illustrator and brainstorming about how to shape it into a good read for 9- to 12-year-olds. That's when I was hooked on racing, and I think that's when a lot of kids are.

When I see.... When I hear....

I used to ride – morning exercise and afternoon jump races.

Sure I miss it.

Sure I don't.

When I see Beautiful Pleasure walking around the stable area, I miss it. When I see her gallop like the original runaway train, I don't miss it.

When I wake up to rain like Thursday morning, I don't miss it (actually laugh a little staying dry under the kitchen awning). When the sun, ah glorious sun, came up Friday morning, I miss it.

When I see Express Tour, or at least who I think is Express Tour, I miss it. When I see some loose horse bucking down the outside rail and the rider running after him in boots, I don't miss it.

When I hear the instructions, "jog him til he warms up," I don't miss it. When I hear, "ride him like you find him," I miss it.

When I see a set of draw reins and a horse's head bowed down to his chest breathing like a lineman, I don't miss it. When I see Gary from the secretary's office riding around on Sidney the pony, I miss it.

When I hear him tell Angel Cordero and me that Sidney probably took us to the start one day, I miss it. When I think of my left foot being jammed into the pony on the way to the start, I don't miss it.

When I see the paddock, I miss it. When I see Chip Miller come to the paddock after the sauna, I don't miss it.

When I can see the exercise rider thinking, "if I move, will it help or hurt this situation?" I don't miss it. When I see a horse of Dale Romans reaching for ground down the backside, I miss it.

When I see the set after the break on the Oklahoma, I don't miss it. When I see the first set at the break of dawn, I miss it.

When I hear, "last set," I miss it. When I see a tack hook full of bridles, I don't miss it.

When I see Jody Petty's saddle slip, I don't miss it. When I see the exultation of Michael Cooney after winning his first Saratoga race, I miss it.

When I see an extension blinker, I don't miss it. When I think of a horse who would never need a set of blinkers, I miss it.

When I hear, "I got one for you," I don't miss it. When I see Gaviola walk to the track, I miss it.

When I listen to stories from Billy Turner about the old days working for Burley Cocks, I miss it. When I think of the all the times I got run away with for Burley Cocks, I don't miss it.

When I look at a 2-year-old schooling at the gate, I don't miss it. When I see the winner galloping out after the wire, I miss it.

When Bill Mott says about Hap, "he'd be a good jumper. He'd be handy, he'd be able to punch between that next to last and last fence," I miss it.

When I think of all the horses who couldn't punch, I don't miss it.

When I hear a trainer say, "Oh boy, she went around there seven times, he couldn't do a thing with her," I don't miss it. When I see one go around there twice with a loop in the reins, I miss it.

When I think of never running out of horse, I miss it. When I think of running out of holes on the girth, I don't miss it.

When I think of trying to get on and off the Oklahoma turf gap, I don't miss it. When I think of breezing a good horse on good ground, I miss it.

When I hear the exercise rider ask, "you want me to go from this pole to . . . uh . . . the quarter . . . uh . . . where . . . ?" I don't miss it. When I watch some big strapping bay colt of Mark Hennig's bounce off the track, I miss it.

When I remember the way my foot felt when it was balanced just right in the stirrup, I miss it. When I recall the feel of a knee rub the first time in the shower, I don't miss it.

When I think of talking to the stewards, I don't miss it. When I think of talking to an elated groom, I miss it.

When I realize all I'll ever do now is write about it, I miss it. When I think all I'll ever do now is write about it, I don't miss it.

"You have to pick your islands, sometimes they disappear."

– Trainer Carl Nafzger
negotiating the muddy Clare Court track crossing

You know the Big Red Spring, the 17-minute bell and the Travers Canoe. But here's one more for you.

For the past 15 years or so, there has been a get-together at Gus Williams' house every Sunday for the six weeks of the meet. This party began as a way for a small group to socialize before the races. Each year, the Sunday morning party grew and got more organized – and includes owners, trainers, jockeys and grooms.

Williams, Jack Knowlton and Lou Titterton are members of the Sackatoga Stable. Started in 1995 by six high school friends from Sackett's Harbor N.Y. and now comprised of eight partners with ties to Sackett's Harbor and Saratoga Springs (hence the name).

The stable started with a horse named The Sackett Six, and now includes three horses. Sunday's stable starter Bail Money looked like the ultimate hunch play. The 5-year-old mare wound up fifth while competing in a race named after her dam Bailrullah (must be a first). Purchased in October by Sackatoga, Bail Money has a win and three seconds this year for trainer Barclay Tagg.

The day may not have ended up as the men of Sackatoga Stable had hoped, but it won't get to them.

There are five more Sunday get-togethers and two more prospects in the stable to root for before the meet is over.

What is it? You can see it but you can't touch it. You can feel it but you can't hold it. You can write it about it but you can't get it.

What was in City Zip for the six furlongs of the Amsterdam?

We call it many names. Heart. Guts. Courage. Bravery. Will to win. Intestinal fortitude. Mettle. Grit. Determination. And there is no better form of this mysterious element than the Thoroughbred horse. Not all Thoroughbred horses. Only the rare ones can make the hair of your neck stand up when you're not riding them, training them, even betting on them. Only the rare ones turn you to their corner for no other reason than awe.

City Zip opened the valve and let it all go in the Grade II Amsterdam. The son of Carson City broke sharply and went after the lead. A determined Speightstown went for the lead as well. It took just over 21 seconds for the two to know neither was backing down. City Zip and Jorge Chavez on the inside and $2 million Speightstown with Jerry Bailey on the outside. At about the quarter pole they bumped several times, Chavez rocked in the saddle and City Zip dug down a little deeper, scraping and chipping at it. Speightstown finally cracked and City Zip had his fourth career victory at the Spa.

The crowd saw the whole race like this.

"Look, Chavez went right into the speed duel."

"If I got anything left, I'll close on this."

"They can't close."

"How does no one close on that speed?"

"He's that good."

City Zip is fast, for sure. He's talented, absolutely. But it's that thing we try to count, or hold, or understand. The human will never know it, we have limits and we sense when we're about to reach them. The horse keeps scratching at what a human believes is reached.

City Zip won the Amsterdam for his third straight stakes score and seventh in his career. The $9,000 purchase is now eight for 18 with over $600,000 in earnings. Trainer Linda Rice tried to explain what's in her horse.

CITY ZIP

"He's courageous. I have more confidence in him than any other horse I've ever had. But I never have any confidence that you're going to be in front at the finish when you put up a first quarter in 21 and 3," Rice said. "When he went that fast, pressured, then they roughed him up on the turn . . . he's just tough. He's hard to intimidate."

Chavez agreed: "He's very game. Big heart. The little bump made him upset and he started going more. I think the outside horse came in a little and my horse came out a little. It worked out good for him because it made him mad," Chavez said. "He showed me guts today. I got pressure from when they open the gates. He showed me big guts. He finished after going that fast, bumping. It was like he bumped and said, 'I gotta get there.' "

And that would be the official motto for heart, determination, courage . . .

Hall Of Fame

Romance isn't dead. History still counts. Emotion is alive and well.

Hall of Fame Day, Saratoga, 2001. The stoic giants cried on August 6, 2001. And it felt great.

Horse racing is a tough game, everyone involved knows that. Horses get hurt, dreams get dashed, hours pile up, gut checks come in bunches. There are days when you wish you were anywhere but bombarding down the game of Thoroughbred racing.

Then they induct six legends into the shrine on Union Avenue. Tom Smith, the late great trainer of Seabiscuit. The weight carrying, colt beating Maskette. The Agentinian blur, Paseana. The smoke-colored, smoke-moving Holy Bull. The indomitable worker, Earlie Fires. And the technician, Richard Mandella.

The Humphrey S. Finney Pavilion is packed with everyone who loves the game; from Mike Kelly, the jock's agent, to Bob Baffert, the trainer, to Penny Chenery, the first lady, to the relentless fan without a say in the sport hoping to bump elbows with a hero.

And they're everywhere.

Navy blazers with Hall of Fame emblems decorate the front rows. Walter Blum, Allen Jerkens, Braulio Baeza, Mikey Smithwick, Tommy Kelly, Don Brumfield, Jerry Fishback, Dooley Adams, Scotty Schulhofer, P.G. Johnson, Jimmy Croll, Jerry Bailey, Pat Day, Bill Mott, Ron McAnally and a few more we're probably forgetting. All sitting there like regular people. Listening.

An outside-the-sport writing legend captivates each and every person. A letter about oldtime horsemanship is read and consumed. A grown man imitates a horse (dialogue and all). One Hall of Famer leans on a cane and talks about a new one. A boot-tough jockey cries after one line.

Dreams are mentioned. Mentors are thanked. Horses are revered.

Emmy and Eclipse Award winning author Frank DeFord bantered back and forth from comedy to satire to editorial in his opening address. All of it, enthralling.

From busting on Bobby Knight to remembering Ruffian to railing handicaps to regaling the Hall of Fame, DeFord was as good as they get.

The day drifted back to Tom Smith's era of training horses and not worrying about people. A letter written by Laura Hillenbrand brought Tom Smith and Seabiscuit to life. The trainer was a true horseman without the distraction of socialization. He talked to his horses and that's all that mattered. His plaque now hangs in the Hall of Fame.

Hall Of Fame

Maskette, a 2-year-old of 1908, stepped through the gates next. She won 12 of her 17 races, carried 127 as a 2-year-old. Did they make horses differently back then?

Sid Craig decided the best way to accept Paseana's award was to become the race mare. And he pulled it off. The relationship between horse and trainer and jockey was eloquently related by Craig in Paseana's words. A new approach and a good one at that.

Jimmy Croll came next. The old gentleman balanced on a cane and talked in a low voice. The crowd leaned out of their chairs or over their balconies straining to hear what the Hall of Famer had to say about a horse who was given to him and who gave to us all everytime. When he said, "good friends" he really had us.

Earlie Fires walked to the podium and instinctively pulled the microphone down a foot. He started in on a middle of the road speech about being a jockey. He made it one line. In an only-Arkansas twang, Fires, paused after his opening remark. When he started on the second line, it was all over. There was a man who has survived 35 plus years of riding races crying over a tribute. "It's a little emotional for me and I'm sorry for breaking down," split thank yous to his brothers, his horses, his trainers. Old names were thrown out like confetti. "I love the business, I love the horses more than anything," Fires said. He finished with a "thank you y'all." Then he swiped his left hand across his tearing eyes. He had us all.

Allen Jerkens introduced Richard Mandella. "We were all OK, until Earlie got up here," is how Mandella started. He thanked his father, his wife, his son, his first bosses. He told stories about being an exercise rider and dreaming of having his own brown and white webbings. Can you imagine, Richard Mandella galloping horses and wishing to be a trainer?

Later in the day, the Hall of Fame Stakes was run across the street. Two Hall of Famers, Mott and Bailey, teamed up to win the 3-year-old turf stakes with Baptize. Nothing was lost on Mott, Bailey or the two newest Hall of Famers who presented the trophy.

Mandella stood in the winner's circle, a little bit uneasy. It's usually the other way around, getting the trophy not giving it away. He managed all right.

"It was a great day. Walking around and being in the Hall of Fame with all those great horses and trainers and everything, you kind of wonder, 'how do I fit in here?' I wouldn't trade it for anything.

"Oh, I've had a couple of pretty good days but this would be equal to anything. The difference is, this one will last. You can win a big race and it's over tomorrow. You do this and you get to wear it all your life. I guess with that, it could be the best day, never thought about it that way.

"Yesterday, we got a tour and saw some of (the Hall of Fame). Some stood out but I wouldn't want to say which ones, how could you pick? Some of the older ones, I have a hobby of reading old books, you know Sam Hildreth, John Madden. Being in there with them just doesn't seem possible."

Fires talked with old friends and new fans. The jockey swiveled around trying to see and feel everything while the jockeys crossed the scales after the race and the horses headed home.

"It was a great day, got a little more emotional than I thought I would, but it was a most beautiful day, something we all strive for in this busi-

"You just hope you stay healthy for the rest of the meet . . . the rest of the year . . . forever."

– Jockey John Velazquez
after winning eight races in two days

Hall Of Fame

ness, I finally got there. It's just a great day for me all together.

"Yeah, it's the biggest highlight of my career. Everything is big to you in different categories in your life but this is probably the top echelon of what we all strive for.

"I was put up a lot of times and because I didn't make it, I wasn't sure I ever would get in, but everybody probably has that in the back of their mind. It's really the height of our career."

Mott took care of business with Baptize after the race. He shook Bailey's hand like always, checked his horse like always, did a Jan Rushton interview like always. But it was different.

"It is more special being Hall of Fame day. I wanted to win it for that reason. Actually, this morning, I almost cried when Jimmy Croll got up there, then Earlie, they had me crying. It was touching because I know how touching it is to be up there. I was sitting with Pat (Day) and he said, 'you know there's something about being up there, at that podium,' It puts you in a, I don't know, a weak spot. It's very touching to be up there, you're honored by a lot of your peers and that, I think, is the most important thing in this game. The most meaningful thing to me in the business is to just have the respect of your peers. The guys you work with, if they think you do a good job, that's the most important thing.

"It's pretty special, it really is. It's a good bunch of guys, you look around and they're the kind of people you really want to be associated with. I've been through (the Hall of Fame) but I've never taken enough time to really visit everything that you can visit. I need to do that."

It was another stakes victory for Bailey. Already this season, Lido Palace has won the Whitney, Scorpion the Jim Dandy, Hap the Bernard Baruch. Baptize was another notch in that most impressive belt. It also had plenty of significance for Bailey.

"Especially with Earlie. I came up with Earlie Fires. I had the bug in Chicago when he was there, he was the man. He helped my transition to Florida, got me a valet, found me a place to stay. He was very instrumental in my emotional evolution early in my career.

"He was a good guy to follow. A very honest man, just a good example. He's not the emotional type of guy. I've never seen that side of him; I've seen him do nice things for people, especially to me but I've never seen him get that emotional, made me cry. He started out so matter of fact . . . for me, I remember, you get up there and look around and realize all the people who are there and the people who helped you . . . "

Bailey tailed off into reflection. Not a bad place to be on this day.

"Thank you, y'all."

– The closing of jockey Earlie Fires' Hall of Fame acceptance speech

17

– Saratoga Special T-shirts found in one editor's dirty clothes pile

---

"Let's go to Siro's."

– 8-year-old Ryan Clancy after hitting a show parlay Monday

"I was in everybody's pockets but my own."

– Pat Day after a rough trip

"That could be my rat."

– Trainer Leo O'Brien as two bettors screamed, "Pass that rat," in an Ellis Park simulcast

---

NAMES OF THE DAY:

Under The Rug (eighth race)

By Lord At War out of Sweepings.

Joe Can't Quit (third race)

Back on the office theme here. Co-editor and publisher Joe Clancy this one's for you. You can't quit, my man.

Horses are just like people, you have smart ones, dumb ones, honest ones, lazy ones . . . come meet 20 horses all in the same barn all at the same time, about 9 o'clock in the morning. By the stall number but certainly not numbers.

Stall 21. The chestnut gelding stands in the back of the stall scraping his teeth on the wall. Back and forth, back and forth in an arc. He notices the observer but doesn't care enough to stop rasping his teeth. Ah, to be perfectly entertained and content.

Stall 20. Stake horse lets out a sigh and walks to the front of the stall like duty calls. Stretches his head like he's cracking his neck, ears up and teeth out. Come back here he seems to say.

Stall 19. Small bay strides into his home from the treed walking ring, sneaks a bite to eat from the pulled back hay net.

Stall 18. Empty stall. Bedding's matted down, shank ready for returning horse, whoever he or she may be.

Stall 17. Sleepyhead. Big chestnut at half mast leaning over his webbing. Peaceful. The slumbering giant.

Stall 16. Light bay horse bounces his time away, doing a half weave. Not full-fledged nervous but itchy. Wants to be somewhere else and no one will let him go there.

Stall 15. Hello long tongue. Dark bay stands looking out of the stall with his front legs wrapped tight in a pair of Velcroed ice bandages. Tongue waggles.

Stall 14. I see nothing, I hear nothing, I want nothing except for this flake of alfalfa hay in the back corner. There is nothing else in this world. Nothing.

Stall 13. Empty stall. Remnants of last night's bandages litter the stall which awaits fresh straw. Blanket, chain shank, and snap leather shank await in the pulled back webbing.

Stall 12. Big bay done up in ice boots, secured by a rubber tie at the end of a screw eye, eye high. Hay in the hay net is good but I'd rather have that notebook. Lean over here, will you?

Stall 11. Tail knotted up out of the groom's face, a raise of the hind leg, just a reminder of the allowance being given to the little man at the back of the horse with a bandage wrapped halfway around a cannon bone.

STALLS

Stall 10. No hay, straw will do. Munching, munching, munching, where's my hay?, munching, munching, munching.

Stall 9. Day is done. Four legs secured in white flannel, masking tape wrapped taut around each leg. Exercise is over for today, be asleep in minutes.

Stall 8. Best horse in the barn. Big bold bay with that eye. That eye which looks into yours like your father before he grounded you. You are simply a person in the king's presence.

Stall 7. Empty stall. Last set of the day, needed a good track, out there going through the motions, trainer watching, boom, boom, boom . . . the stall simply waits.

Stall 6. The rubber tie keeps the 1,000 pounds off the floor. Ice boots cooling old bones. Don't cut the tie or the world will thump.

Stall 5. A hot air balloon blaze between the wide eyes. Hay grinds between shaded teeth.

Stall 4. Three bandages with one more to go, green liquid rubbed deep down to the bone. Nose pressed into screen of the back window looking out to the grass.

Stall 3. My world goes this way. The only horse standing perpendicular in the stall, right smack across the stall. Barns have angles and rhythms whether it be the curved tack hooks, the long slope of the roof, the pattern left by a rake, then one horse strikes it all in half. She didn't seem to mind.

Stall 2. The last one in the line (stall one's the tack room), a fitting ending. Asleep, dropped down dead asleep. Head under the buckets, hay stalk across his eye, legs frozen in running motion. Goodnight from the horse.

"Yeah, but I go long."

– Groom responding to boss' comment, "You didn't break too sharp today."

"You're no cowboy."

– Assistant trainer Seth Gregory to a former jump jockey looking quizically at a western saddle

The establishment asked us why we print all our subscribers names on the front page.

The establishment then proceeded to tell us the number was embarrassingly small. The establishment then told us it didn't make sense. Then the establishment gave us grief for spelling one of the readers' names wrong. The establishment wanted to know why. The establishment had the bottom line in mind, we could see it in their narrow eye. The establishment was thinking 'why waste a column of space on a bunch of people's names' instead of dropping an ad in there or cutting pages or whatever else establishments do.

We ain't the establishment.

We're here to have fun. We're here to liven up the place a little. Celebrate the sport. Celebrate the color. Celebrate the life. And to preserve it. That's what we're here for and if we want to print the names of each and every subscriber then hell yes that's what we're going to do. And, you know what, when that number gets so big it takes up 100 pages, we might keep on running it, make it a center spread insert.

I feel like I'm marching to the capital now.

Sorry, but the comment got me riled up. Like Frank Stronach's declaration that he wants NYRA had Terry Meyocks wound up around the backside this morning, comments from the establishment usually send me to the keyboard.

Like it wasn't impressive we only had 63 subscribers. Maybe not to the establishment. But we're proud of it. Considering we're working on year one, issue number 15 as I type.

The questions we get the most are why did we start the paper, when do we sleep, and what are we going to do in the fall.

We started the paper because we believed in the concept of bringing the life of Saratoga to the readers. Basically we were tired of reading nonsense about our favorite town. Well, that's why Joe and I started it. Paul, the business manager, just needed a job after his last employer went bankrupt, establishment they weren't (or were they?).

About sleep. Well, our motto when we started was "we'll sleep in September." We're sticking with it because we sure as hell aren't sleeping in August. We don't sleep. Just skip it for now.

We'll be back next year and all the years after that. Or that's the plan anyway. We're never short of ideas so look out.

My favorite part of the project is when I see someone looking for the paper. Around the sales, it's cool to see that, in three days people are looking for it, wanting it. Sales increase every day and advertisers are calling us (which is good because we don't have an advertising department yet).

We're a long way from the establishment and that's probably the way we like it.

See the problem with the establishment is they haven't invented, written, designed, delivered and sold their own project for so long they can't get past their own establishment.

Do me a favor, if we ever look, sound, or think like the establishment, shoot us.

And subscribers, we love you.

WITH ANTICIPATION

George Strawbridge and Jonathan Sheppard have been together a long time.

The owner and trainer could plaster the Great Wall of China with win pictures. And all kinds. From the country hunt meets of Tennessee to the charmed grasses of Keeneland. From the 1960s to the 2000s. From jumpers with Strawbridge in the tack to flat stakes winners with Julie Krone. And they still don't have the congratulations down.

Sheppard stood just inside the rail of the winner's circle as Strawbridge bounded down from the boxes after With Anticipation upset the Sword Dancer Invitational Handicap.

"Well done, George."

"Well done, me? I haven't done anything."

Whoever did it . . . it was done. Maybe just give the credit to With Anticipation who galloped a strong field into oblivion in the Sword Dancer. The 6-year-old gelded son of Relaunch grabbed the race by the feet from the start. Pat Day guided the fourth choice from the 10 hole to along side Slew Valley near the lead. Feel-good story John's Call sat behind that duo with favorite King Cugat bouncing around the back like a bad story.

By the time they reached the stretch, With Anticipation was cruising while Slew Valley was faltering. John's Call had packed it in and King Cugat had too much to do. With Anticipation hit the line in front by three-quarters of a length with King Cugat gaining ground to no avail.

John's Call came back to only-in-Saratoga applause. With Anticipation came back to a crying groom and to the veteran pair of Strawbridge and Sheppard trying

With Anticipation

to explain how a 6-year-old homebred gelding had turned into a Grade I Saratoga winner.

"It was a heck of a day," Strawbridge said. "When you have a homebred win a Grade I stakes at Saratoga. Thrilling is such a trite word but . . . "

With Anticipation is no motley homebred. He's by Relaunch out of Breeders' Cup Juvenile winner Fran's Valentine.

Sheppard, with a National Steeplechase Association button pinned to his left lapel, walked to the paddock for the 10th (which he won) and tried to explain the horse he's had since he was a baby and why he came to life (well, more life) three starts ago when he was switched to the turf.

"It's extremely rewarding when it all comes together, it's very humbling. He's always acted like a horse who could do this kind of stuff but he's been erratic. If he didn't get in the clear almost as soon as the gates opened on the dirt he wouldn't put out," Sheppard said. "It's a long hard struggle if you put the clock back to trying to jog them on a lunge line and put the girl up for the first time in the stalls to winning Grade Is."

Sheppard liked the horse from the time he came from his Pennsylvania neighbor Derry Meeting Farm.

"When that particular batch of yearlings came over, all they could talk about was Crowd Pleaser, they said, 'you're going to love this horse, he's a super horse,' " Sheppard said. "Naturally I was a little defensive, I don't particularly like people telling me what a horse is going to be before I've even put the tack on it. Strawbridge came over and was going on about didn't I like Crowd Pleaser. I said, 'I do, but I'm not sure this gray horse isn't better.' They both turned out to be extraordinarily good horses. How could you imagine, two yearlings sent to you, going on to earn $1.5 million or whatever they've earned."

Crowd Pleaser won the Virginia Derby for Sheppard and Strawbridge and now stands stud in Maryland.

With Anticipation is on his way to the turf classics this fall.

FLUTE

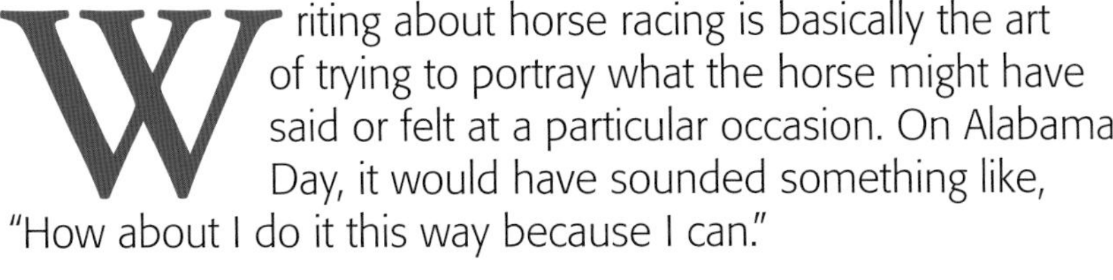

Writing about horse racing is basically the art of trying to portray what the horse might have said or felt at a particular occasion. On Alabama Day, it would have sounded something like, "How about I do it this way because I can."

That's what Flute would have said to her trainer Bobby Frankel, jockey Edgar Prado and anybody who happened to get in the way of her Saturday afternoon stroll.

Flute decimated the $750,000, Grade I race. She won by almost five lengths while leading at every call. The daughter of Seattle Slew, owned by Juddmonte Farms, broke like everybody else and before you knew it was on the lead. In her five previous starts, she never got a call in front until the stretch. Announcer Tom Durkin said Flute with everything but a question mark as she took the field past the stands for the first time. She wasn't supposed to be in front. Not that she cared. Flute made it her race and liked it that way.

The issue was never in doubt. Prado gave her a couple of smacks for insurance but all he had to do was take a look at the wobbly chasers. Exogenous finished second through default while Two Item Limit was third.

Frankel unabashedly puts Flute at the top of his list. And that list, just the weekend list, included The Seven Seas in the Beverly D., Senure in the Arlington Million, Skimming in today's Pacific Classic and Aptitude in today's Saratoga Breeders' Cup. Frankel had the whole world in his hands this weekend. At least the racing world.

Of course he looked more like he was hiding from that world before the Alabama.

Camped out in racing secretary Mike Lakow's office, Frankel came out for a drink of water. Then went back into seclusion. He walked to the paddock to saddle Flaming West in the eighth and went straight back to the bunker before they called, "Rider's Up." All by himself, he moved like a thief, from cover to cover. Things were on his mind, races to be won and horses to be accounted for.

Flute did all the accounting the trainer would

FLUTE

need on this day. Frankel has a refreshening connection to his stable star.

"If you were around her you'd see that she knows what's going on. Everybody thinks I'm nuts but she's reincarnated," Frankel said. "When I go to her she knows exactly who it is. I can stand there and play with her for an hour, as soon as I go away, she gets depressed over it. She's like a little kid when they see their parents leaving and they don't want to see them go. That's the way she is with me. From the day I met her. I really realized it because I has so much time on my hands at Churchill Downs and I started hanging around with her. Thats when I realized it. She's my favorite."

Frankel talked about Flute while watching Flute on the replay inside the trustees room. A flute (no kidding) of champagne in one hand, a video of Flute in his pocket and a feeling about Flute which would make anybody want to be a horse trainer.

"Look at her ears. She's got one ear back, the left one flapping. She's not even extended. Just clocking them," Frankel said. "I don't know who she beat but Fleet Renee would have had a tough time with her today. I don't think Fleet Renee can fight it out with her. I know if they hook up turning for home, I know what would happen. This filly, they aren't getting by her."

Flute has never met Fleet Renee, arguably the only 3-year-old filly in the land within shouting distance. Michael Dickinson didn't enter Fleet Renee in the Alabama.

Frankel stood with Prado's agent Bob Frieze, had a conversation with Lakow, held his glass for a refill, gave about a dozen one-line replies to well-wishers, ("She's a superstar, She's got more in the tank, I left it up to him, I need to make reservations for dinner, I wasn't worried, She's never let me down."), took congratulations from Indian Charlie, Don Orlando, Barry Schwartz and answered questions about his favorite thing in the world.

Did you think about going someplace else today?

"Never a question. Never a question. Not even a doubt. Not even a second thought. I never thought about going anywhere else. That's why I'm here because of Flute," Frankel said. "She's the greatest. And I'm not saying that because she won the Alabama. I said that before she won the Oaks."

Have you ever had one like her?

"No. No. No."

Why's she so special?

"Why? I don't know," Frankel said. "I believe in reincarnation. I don't know who she was but she's been here before. I don't know who. Coulda been a woman, coulda been anybody. I don't know who she was but she was here."

Believe him. He's drop-dead sincere. Who or what could she have been? Someone or something special, that's for sure.

A cell phone is thrust into Frankel's hand.

"Hello . . . Proud of her? Proud of her . . . Isn't she great? She's what I thought she was . . . thank you . . . When's it going off? OK, I'll go watch it."

Frankel heads for the door to watch some race from somewhere else.

As he's walking through the clubhouse, he gets stopped for an autograph. He hands the champagne off to a reporter and signs a program, right over Flute's name.

One more question. What about tomorrow with Aptitude?

He's the favorite for Sunday's Saratoga Breeders' Cup. But he's no Flute.

"He's going great. Really doing great," Frankel said. "He's a horse. You know what I mean? He's a nice horse. But he's a horse. I've seen weaknesses in him. But I've never seen a weakness in her. I've seen weaknesses in Lido Palace. Understand? But I've never seen a weakness in her."

Understood.

Bobby Frankel.

Take two.

The trainer had a good Saturday, his favorite horse Flute won the Alabama. Sunday made Saturday look like a trip to the dentist.

Frankel won the Saratoga Breeders' Cup with Aptitude right here at Saratoga. He stood in the winner's circle, smiled, shook a few hands, had his picture taken.

"One more to go," Frankel yelled as he declined an interview with Jan Rushton. Through the gate, under the clubhouse, past the mutuel windows, by the autograph seekers, over the stroller, through the Italian ice line and back to his couch in racing secretary Mike Lakow's office.

Frankel watched Skimming wire the $1 million Pacific Classic. He took an elbow from Jorge Chavez's agent Richard DePass at about the wire and shook some more hands. The journalists were piling up outside.

"All right, let's go," he said to three of them in a circle. "It was exciting . . . "

Back to his couch after the usual questions were asked. His phone rang again and again. "Do me a favor, Call me back 5 1 8 5 8 4 6 2 0 0. Ask for Mike Lakow's office," Frankel yelled into his blue cell phone.

You know you're at ease when you're giving out someone else's phone number. Frankel stayed in his newly claimed office while the rest of the world looked for him.

"Did Bobby Frankel come in here?" said one frantic writer. Yes.

"Is he still here?" asked another. Yes.

"Is he coming out?" asked the first one. I don't know.

"Did you talk to him?" asked the second one. Yes, but not about that.

They were off in a flash.

"It was exciting . . . "

Finally Frankel came out to answer the phone at the front desk of the racing office. "Doc Danner? No, he's not here."

Back to his couch.

"Todd Pletcher sat here and won two. Wayne Lukas got up from here and lost. I'm 3-for-3 from here," Frankel said.

He waited for the seventh at Del Mar. Battle God went to the lead, fought off about three challenges and wound up fifth. Frankel watched and talked.

First about Flute.

"I paid a lot of attention to her this morning. She doesn't like sweets but she likes the attention so we paid a lot of attention to her this morning," Frankel said. "Came

Two days ago I was intimidated by Bobby Frankel....

The New York accent maybe. The Hall of Fame plaque, partly. The constant look in his eye that says he's got something else to think about or somewhere else to go, perhaps. I think there's a rap there somewhere. Or at least a preconception on my part. In a lifetime of horse racing, I had never officially met him.

I walked by his barn to see Flute and was glad he wasn't there. Allowed me to spy a little on my own. I needed to do a preview about the Saratoga Breeders' Cup, where he had the stone favorite Aptitude, I procrastinated until it was damn near post time for the race.

A friend offered to introduce me, I wavered again. Finally after Flute annihilated the Alabama and I was faced with using quotes that every journalist/writer/stone-slab chiseler had I went to meet Bobby Frankel. And am I glad I did.

I came home Saturday night and wrote my heart about Flute and Frankel. I thought it was a pretty good piece of reporting and writing.

A day later, Frankel won the Saratoga Breeders' Cup and the Pacific Classic and I'm back on the task again. I followed Frankel back to the racing office and waited for a good moment.

I said, "Well, it looks like I'm going to get to know you pretty well by the end of this weekend."

He said, "You made one mistake in your article. You said Flute had never run against Fleet Renee. You know what I'm talking about? You said they never ran against each other. The Oaks. She beat her in the Oaks. Otherwise, it was a good article."

He just said it, matter of fact as, "Do you want cream and sugar?" Then he walked away.

I was so mad. I pulled out yesterday's Special. Yup, right there in black print, "Flute has never met Fleet Renee . . . " My first article about the guy and I come out with something as wrong as oil drilling in Alaska.

I tried to regain any semblance of confidence while Frankel answered his phone. Fire the fact-checker, I thought. No, no, hire a fact-checker, I countered.

Frankel walked back into the main racing office and invited me to watch his last two runners of the day.

"Damn, I'm mad about making that mistake," I said without thinking about it.

"Don't worry about it. Ah, that's all right. It's not like it hurt my feelings. Everybody makes mistakes," Frankel said.

Here's a guy who was about to win his fourth race of the day, including three stakes, telling me everybody makes mistakes. It was comical.

"That paper, it's a stepping stone," Frankel said from behind Mike Lakow's desk with a dialed phone in his hand. "You can make mistakes and the whole world doesn't know about 'em yet."

by three or four different times and spent a lot of time with her. She acts like she never ran. She was alert, she wasn't tired."

Then about motivation.

"The whole thing is . . . I gotta get this monkey off my back with the Breeders' Cup," Frankel said. "The Triple Crown, that doesn't bother me. I haven't run but two horses, maybe three horses in it. That doesn't bother me. But hey, if I don't do it, my career has been pretty good."

Then what makes him a good trainer.

"I just think I take good care of the horses and I adjust to situations," Frankel said. "You know it's a good time for me to brag 'cause when I'm doing bad I'll tell you I'm the worst trainer in the world. I'll drive home sometimes and say, 'What am I doing in this business? Why do I got to aggravate myself to death?' I tell myself how bad a trainer I am. I beat myself up."

Then about how fortunate he is.

"That's what you're living for, days like today and yesterday. I'm having a tremendous meet here, having a great meet at Del Mar. It's unbelievable," Frankel said. "A lot of people never experience these things."

Then about training.

"On days like today, I think I can train. Other days . . . I keep changing my training. I don't train the same way all the time. This game changes so much you gotta keep changing with the young guys coming up," Frankel said. "When you're not doing well, you keep going over and over everything, you confuse yourself. When you're confident you just go with it. I've changed my training methods in the last two years. Well, it's, it's, I don't want to give away my secrets. You know. Not like it's a secret. I've realized . . . well, it's probably the horses."

Then about Aptitude.

"He's a good horse, Aptitude. He was unlucky not to win the Derby. He was 50 feet off the rail going down the backside – 50 feet," Frankel said. "It's very exciting because people got to knocking him. He's a stallion now. By being put up in the (Hollywood Gold Cup) and winning this one, he's a stallion. He's worth a lot of money now."

Then about money.

"I don't do it for the money. I swear to God, I don't," Frankel said. "The money's good for the money title at the end of the year. But I don't think about it as money that I have to spend. I don't care about the money to spend. I got money to spend. It's not going to change my lifestyle. I still got to get up in the morning and go to work. I'm not going to take a vacation or anything. I got to keep on top because if I'm put in the Hall of Fame and don't do any good afterward, then people say you don't deserve to be in the Hall of Fame. To be put in the Hall of Fame and you're still active (Frankel was elected in 1995), if you don't do any good, they say you're lucky and forget about you right away."

Nobody was forgetting Frankel on this day.

Old friends Richard and Tony Dutrow came into the office. They sat around and waited for the Finlandia Handicap at Del Mar.

"I got a shot here. You don't think I can get lucky enough to win another one do you?" Frankel asked.

In unison, the room said, "You can."

Frankel laughed.

About that time, Tates Creek and Kent Desormeaux broke from the gate.

"What are you doing Kent?" Frankel said as Tates Creek went to the lead.

"Why don't you let that other filly drop over on you?" Frankel said as they went around the first turn. "I don't like the way he's riding . . . " Frankel said halfway around the final turn.

Then Tates Creek took off at the head of the stretch, opened up five and won by herself.

"What a ride," Frankel yelled.

Frankel jumped up, high-fived everybody in the room and said,

"Let's go."

Bobby Frankel

POINT GIVEN

We don't need studies. We don't need committees. We don't need advisory boards. We don't need commercials. We don't need round tables. We don't need junior committees.

> **"The nice thing about him is you can switch him off when you want and he'll give it to you again. Any time."**
>
> – Gary Stevens on Point Given

We need stars. Simple as that.

Point Given is here and the world has followed.

Think of this Travers without him. E Dubai would be favorite? Come on, E Dubai? I've watched the horse train every morning. He oozes class but favorite for the Travers? Dollar Bill, A.P. Valentine, Volponi . . . all good horses but road-trip attractions they're not.

There is nothing else to talk about around Saratoga this weekend. And they talk like it's more than just a horse.

"I have a date with Point Given at 3 o'clock today."

"Is there any way you could get us over there to meet him?"

"He has a way of staring."

"Have you seen his forelock? It just hangs over his eye like James Dean."

James Dean, I like that one. He's got the swagger. The glare. The appeal. The air. All down pact. And he better because he's the one headlight on racing's bus at the moment.

Racing has a tough hand to play. The owners and trainers will never be stars. They can be quoted or showcased but they don't literally play the game. It's the same reason Bear Bryant was a cult hero but he never made a cereal box. You can have one hell of conversation with Bobby Frankel but he's not going to fill the seats.

The jockeys are the only stars who actually talk but the average fan has trouble relating to them. First of all, they're five feet tall and weigh a sandwich over 100 pounds. All well and good, but most of us blew past that in fifth grade. And they ride horses. The closest thing to riding a Thoroughbred most average Americans have experienced is what? Driving the grocery cart as a teenager? Pony rides at the cousin's birthday party? Falling down the steps?

So that brings it all back to the horses. And Point Given. He's the one for now. It's a good thing he has massive shoulders. It's a whole big world. You can feel the desperation in people as they clamor for a piece of the Big Red Train. It's like seeing a shooting star almost. They've felt this way before and we're left holding nothing but an old Blood-Horse magazine or a losing ticket or a just a short glimpse of something great.

They know Point Given will be gone before they got to know him. That's the problem with horses. It's also the great thing. The fragility is awing. We need John Henrys, Foregos, Kelsos who last entire childhoods or at least entire college years. But those Victory Rides, Flanderses and Arazis were rockers just the same.

Imagine Point Given coming back to Saratoga for the next five years. Now that would be something. You could compare him through his maturity process. See how his demeanor changes through the years. See if his muzzle goes white. See if he recognizes you or at least the place. You could collect each year's programs. Hang the photos in a row on your wall. Compare the growing process of your own children to his.

But then again, a lot of times, the first view is the best. Enjoy it while you can.

The highest of highs and the lowest of lows. And all the variations in between. Pompeii supplied the variation by winning the Personal Ensign Handicap over Beautiful Pleasure.

After the race, owner/breeder Robert Clay looked like he just gave away his child, trainer John Kimmel couldn't decide if he should laugh or cry, and assistant Loretta Lusteg wiped tears as she sponged down Pompeii.

That's what happens when a tough little filly wins her first Grade I and is scheduled to leave the next morning. Clay sold the daughter of Broad Brush to WinStar Farm on the day of entries. She ran in both their names, in Clay's silks and in all their minds.

Clay and WinStar's Kenny Troutt stood next to each other after the race waiting to do an interview with Jack Whitaker. "It never gets dull," Whitaker said to nobody. Small talk was tough. Richard Migliore was a few feet away in Pompeii's green and yellow silks for the last time. Clay looked like he was sleepwalking.

"It's really a tough day for me, she's a homebred," Clay said. "It's really a bittersweet day watching her come down the stretch but I'm in the business and sometimes you have to tear your emotions away from a business decision. A little bit like (handing over a child). I have her sister and we'll bring another one up here. We're thrilled she won but . . . I wish I still had half of her anyway but that's the way it goes."

Clay was stoic. So was Kimmel. Even Lusteg did her best. They must have taken after Pompeii.

The Personal Ensign was her eighth victory in 16 starts. She's never missed a check. Her worst race of her life was when she finished fourth in her second career start. See why they were crying?

Photos were taken, interviews were conducted and emotions were checked – hard. Pompeii and Lusteg walked home together for the last time.

Two hours later, the Kimmel barn was going about their business like any other Grade I winning night. Kimmel put away the scope that said she was clean, Pompeii dove into her hay net in the corner stall, and a round of "Only after Grade Is" Moet Chandon was served. They watched the replay on the news and tried not to think about the emotional side of racing. A lot of "it's a business" answers were being thrown around. Understandably, for sure. Not truly believed, though.

HIGHS & LOWS

"The gambit of emotions can run from the highs to the lows in a matter of moments," Kimmel said. "It takes me back to the Go For Wand when Hidden Lake won. Here you are thrilled with emotions, my horses run one-two in the race and I look up the stretch and I don't see the filly coming back. The next thing you see is Migliore's taking the tack off and you don't know what to think. You go from being all excited to 'Oh my God the filly could be hurt.' Today was maybe not as big a swing in emotions but it certainly was a bittersweet kind of thing."

Pompeii continued to chomp hay while a couple of cases of beer for the help were set down on the picnic table. Kimmel talked about the decisions that brought Pompeii to the Grade I victory.

"She's consistent and she's shown tremendous courage. It's nice to be around those kind of horses that improve with age. Here's a filly that worked real hard all winter and got to the top of the group in New York. I said 'Robert, she's a nice filly but if we have any chance of doing anything big this summer, let's take her to Fair Hill and kick her out, give her a good 60 days. They did a great job. Now here she comes in her third start of the cycle and she wins a Grade I race. When you make plans and they work out, it's something you can reflect back on and say 'hey we probably did the right thing.' "

Tomorrow, Kimmel won't have to worry about doing the right thing for Pompeii. He scoped her for the last time, she was done up in Kimmel bandages for the last time and her Kimmel feed tub was about to go up for the last time.

"In this game you have to temper your emotions a bit," Kimmel said. "I'm real sad to see her go, she's nice filly. But I've been around long enough to see them come and go. That's the part of the game that's hard to take sometimes. I just hope for the best for her and the connections. "

At 9 in the morning, trainer Elliott Walden will come over and pick up Pompeii from the corner stall.

Devon Heights, a Mt. Livermore filly of Juddmonte Farms ships up from Fair Hill and will be in the stall by noon.

Gary Stevens walked out of the jocks' room on Friday agitated.

First he did a television interview where he answered more dumb questions than a kid after a high school dance. Then he tried to call his agent, his wife, anybody and couldn't get service on his Nokia cell phone. In the middle of all this, three fans asked him to sign a couple of programs and a poster.

Ask him about Travers favorite Point Given. Go ahead, ask. There's nothing like being carried away by a good horse. Sit down on the top of a picnic table under the trees at Saratoga and listen.

It starts simply.

What do you think about the Travers tomorrow?

"There's been a lot of questions, from the naysayers, about the Haskell. That it wasn't impressive and he's wheeling back in three weeks. This horse has thrived on being drilled. The more he runs the better he gets. (Trainer Bob Baffert) had to stop on him after the Belmont because of the hind foot, he walked for 24 days and we really weren't planning on running in the Haskell.

"We kind of had to do a rush job. The Travers had been the goal, they bumped the purse up and it was like 'boom you're running.' I felt like if they were going to beat him they were going to beat him in the Haskell. Bob was real uptight before the Haskell and it made me uptight. I think we both knew in the back of our heads that he wasn't wound up 100 percent.

"I know publicly he's said in the last seven, eight days that we were going to run but privately we've known since he came back from Jersey and we saw what he did when he got home that he was going to run. But we wanted to make sure all systems were go. I feel very very confident. I'm excited.

"The Haskell, I was like, 'are we all right here? Are we all right?' But he got the job done. He's come back home and he's thrived. When I saw the picture of him getting off the van and he had his ears up, I was like, "Oh yeah, we're all right." I feel very very confident. If he shows up the way I think he's going to show up then it's going to take something really, really special to beat him."

Stevens is rolling. The agitation gone. He's a boy talking about a horse.

"People ask me all the time what makes him so special, why do I think he's such a great horse? He gives me an overwhelming feeling of confidence when I'm riding him. When I turn down the backside, I blow up, like, 'how good is this?' I smile to myself. I've ridden some great horses that have given me a feeling like that. But I've never ridden a horse that gives me a feeling like he does when he's on his game, I feel like I can beat anybody. It's just a great feeling of power."

Getting chills? Yeah, they're going around. But who is Point Given? We see a giant horse winning everything but we're in the stands. His personality?

"He's just like his old man. Thunder Gulch has stamped his offsping. I've ridden quite a few of his babies and they're their own man. There's a fine line between asking them to do something and telling them do something. You don't tell these horses to do anything. And with his strength and his size, he's a little different to handle than some of them. If you ever got him upset you could do some serious damage. What he does in the morning is game time. He's playing. We're all fearful he's going to hurt himself playing. But he's not doing it in a mean way, he's not trying to hurt anybody. If he ever decided he wanted to hurt somebody or got mean then shame on everybody."

OK, but where's that come from?

"Thunder Gulch was like that. I remember early in his 2-year-old year, he was lugging in all the way at Aqueduct. He won by a head and I never let him run. He was basically running off with me. Then I went to Hong Kong and Mike Smith was riding him, he'd win by a head and he was constantly leaning on horses. Seemed like he was doing anything to tease the competition and just get up and win. Point Given has that same kind of temperament. It's all a game to him. Bob and I both feel like he still hasn't put it all together. Thunder Gulch put it all together on Derby Day, he turned into a man that day. Point Given is so gifted to me I don't think we've seen the best of him yet. Not that he's not a true racehorse but when he decides to go on and do what he's supposed to do, that he truly doesn't want to toy with the field anymore, it's going to be scary. Like the Belmont, what he win by 13 lengths or whatever? And trust me the last eighth of a mile he was not running. He had his ears up and was

POINT GIVEN

fooling around. I felt like if he beared down and given everything then he could have done a Secretariat, winning by 25 lengths or whatever. That's the kind of horse he is."

What about him? Does he know.

"Yeah, I think he knows. Good horses have a certain presence. They get used to the cameras. This horse has turned into a ham. He'll stop and pose for pictures. John Henry was the same way. Silver Charm got like that. I think they know they're special. I really do. People ask what's the aura with these horses that you talk about. Well that's the aura. Unless you've ridden those kind of horses you don't know. You can't explain it to people, they're like all bull. Well it's there."

Back to tomorrow. Is there any way for this horse to get beat? How can this horse get beat?

"I've got to get him beat or the horse has got to beat himself in some way. That's my pressure, in knowing how good he is, but he's so adaptable when he is on his game. I don't think he has to be 100 percent tomorrow because I don't think we've seen 100 percent of him yet. I expect to see a much better Point Given than we did in the Haskell. And really that's not even running through my mind, I'm not seeing him getting beat. Every scenario I see has him in front and I don't really want to go anywhere else."

Wow, visions. How often?

"Every race I ride buddy. It doesn't always turn out like that but I have to truly believe I'm going to win or have a chance to win every race that I go out there. I have to make up some type of scenario of how I can win that particular race. Fortunately with this horse I don't have to make up that many scenarios, it's just there."

We're just bettors or fans or casual observers. To ride the favorite in the Travers . . .

"You feel like a marked target. Everybody does know where you're at. You have to take that into consideration when you put yourself into a certain spot in a race. The good thing about this horse is he's so big and so intimidating that nobody wants to get in a bumping match with him. And he's going to win every bumping match that he gets in. If you get in a spot that you need to get out of, you point him a little bit and the horse next to you is intimidated. I truly believe that horses do intimidate other horses. When he looks them in the eye, they know. Winning Colors had that, even though she was a filly. Silver Charm had that. And this horse has it."

Does he know who you are?

"I've been around two horses that I won't go around their stall. Period. Point Given and Winning Colors. They hear my voice and they get antsy. I think that's a good thing. They associate me with running in the afternoon, not a morning workout. That's part of why I don't work him in the morning."

OK, the million dollar question. If they blindfolded you, spun you around and gave a leg up. Would you recognize him?

"Oh yeah. Definitely. From his stride. His balance. His size. Just how fluid he his. He wastes absolutely no energy at all. Mainly his size. His withers and shoulders are so wide, I drop my stirrups three inches longer on him. I don't ride that short but I don't ride long either. With him, I drop them down three inches and when I see pictures it looks like I have them jacked up to my chest. That's just his size."

So that's what it's all about?

"He's one of kind for me. When you're a kid growing up you imagined yourself riding Secretariat or Affirmed or Seattle Slew. This is my Secretariat. This is what I waited for."

"And don't get me wrong I've ridden some great horses but this one is special."

Honor it. Accept it. And most of all enjoy it.

Point Given is the greatest horse in all the land. Forget the Derby defeat, the Haskell scare, the bar shoe, and all the rest. Point Given. That's all you have to remember.

The Travers was the latest court for him to hold. The giant red colt played with eight rivals (or victims) and won the $1 million race by 3 1/2 lengths. It could have been 103 1/2. E Dubai finished second with Dollar Bill third.

Point Given stalked the solid pace of Free Of Love and E Dubai, just cruising along like a big ship. Gary Stevens was sure to keep him in the clear about three off the fence.

Stevens was motionless. John Velazquez was all over A P Valentine. Jorge Chavez had been at Dollar Bill for a quarter mile. And Jerry Bailey was about to get inhaled aboard E Dubai. Point Given came off the turn and collared E Dubai. The two battled, or at least appeared to battle. The problem was E Dubai was giving 100 percent and Point Given was barely past preheat. Stevens finally yanked him to his right lead at about the eighth pole and he pulled away with ease.

"I don't know what percent it was but we didn't get to the bottom of him," Stevens said. "I came into the stretch and I thought Jerry had more horse left than he did. I thought he would carry me to the sixteenth pole and I'd get my horse to accelerate with him. All of a sudden I found myself in front without asking him to run. It was a lot like the Preakness. When he finds himself on the lead without me chasing him, he tends to fool around with me. He was having a holiday from the sixteenth pole home. He was just having fun, playing around a bit."

That's what the racing world can do with the big float it's

been handed. We have a star. He's ours now. Just climb on and go with the greatness. Play around a bit. The horse has a little bit for everybody. He's got a playful side. An aggressive side. A goofy side. A magical side. A natural side. Which do you want?

He's won his last four starts; the Preakness, the Belmont, the Haskell and now the Travers. The parade is underway.

"He was just dragging me throughout the race. Basically I felt like the race was over with from the time we entered the first turn. I didn't have any doubts. He was traveling really really comfortable," Stevens said. "I could have opened up at the three-eighths pole and he probably would have won by eight or ten lengths like the Belmont. He toyed with these horses today."

Nobody knows that better than Velazquez who rode A P Valentine.

"You look over at him and he's just galloping while I'm riding my horse just to stay with him," Velazquez said. "They just can't keep up. That's when they get intimidated. Oh, they know when the other horse is going better. Believe me they know. You break their heart, that's it. Like Alydar and Affirmed. How would you like to have been in the same race with them? It's pretty much the same with Point Given. All this bull about him having problems and traveling. Yeah, that took a lot out of him. You could take him back and forth 10 times and he'd still go around there and win."

Point Given brought out over 60,000 fans. And made every one of them walk home with a bigger heart. It was one of those races that made you want to go for a run when you got home. Owned by the Thoroughbred Corporation and trained by Bob Baffert, Point Given simply took over Saratoga for four days. He's as good as we've seen in a long long time.

Time to enjoy him and all his exploits. He simply dazzled the place. From his poise and presence to his speed and stamina, it was the Point Given show. And he's the one directing it.

"He took one deep breath after the race and surveyed the racetrack. ESPN was interviewing me with the outrider and we walked for about 100 yards," Stevens said. "He was just strolling around checking everything out. The outrider cantered me back and turned me loose. He saw all the cameras and the ears came up. He knows."

By the end of the day the Travers air was waning. The sun had gone down, sprinklers were spraying the turf course, traffic started to move on Union Avenue, women walked down the sidewalks carrying their shoes, aluminum cans were being bundled up, tickets were scooped up off the ground, tow trucks readied their winches for service.

Back at John Terranova's barn, Point Given was simply waiting for dinner. Roberto Luna smooched to him to move over and let him in his stall. He finally adjusted his feet about two inches to accommodate his groom. Luna knelt underneath him and swathed kool-out clay up and down his front legs with a rubber glove on his right hand. Point Given looked as peaceful as any creature in the world. Big kind eye and easy motion, looking and eating, wondering and thinking. He knows.

Exercise rider Pepe Aragon yawned and chased visitors from the front of the stall.

"There, there is OK. Not in front. He spooks," Aragon said.

Mobile phones were being dialed, answered and shaken. Point Given, with the weight of the industry still on his broad shoulders dove back and forth into his packed hay net. His ears went up and back with every passing car and every speaking person. His moist eyes almost made him look sleepy. His braided forelock still clung in place.

"Oh, he's a good guy," Aragon said. "I wish he won the Derby, what, there would have been 100,000 people over there for him."

Finally all his legs were finished for the night. He walked once around his stall, anxious.

"He's waiting for dinner that's why he paces," Aragon said.

Finally you can't take it anymore.

"Can I pet him?"

"Sure, sure. He's OK."

I reach up to his face, like I've never pet a horse before.

And in a way I haven't.

Sunday afternoon....

....Allen Jerkens could have run for mayor of Saratoga, chairman of NYRA, whatever office he wanted – and won.

The 72-year-old trainer upset the Grade I Ballerina, a $250,000 stakes for fillies and mares, with Bohemia Stable's Shine Again and was the center of Saratoga's universe. Jockeys, trainers, fans, children, old women, young women, people in ties, people in cut-off shorts, people in tuxedos stopped to say congratulations. Applause fluttered down from the stands. Phones rang all over the place. From NYRA president Terrry Meyocks' cell to the scales in the winner's circle, all calls were for Jerkens.

He could have been the father of the bride. But he was just a horse trainer – a good one.

Shine Again, a 4-year-old daughter of Wild Again, rated just off the rapid early fractions of Imadeed and pounced at the top of the stretch. The Maryland-bred barrelled through a four-horse opening on the inside of Imadeed and 1-2 favorite Dream Supreme, carried the lead into the stretch and held off Country Hideaway's late run to win by a half-length. Winless in open stakes company coming into the race, Shine Again and jockey Jean-Luc Samyn were dismissed at 21-1, but had the Jerkens factor on her side.

Upsets are routine for a barn known for sending out prepared horses.

"Shine Again is a nice, strong filly," Jerkens said. "We thought maybe if she finished in the money, she'd be Grade I placed for her future as a broodmare. Keep your fingers crossed, she's never run a bad race. We'll see where she goes from here."

Samyn, also Shine Again's regular exercise rider, was overjoyed after returning from a lengthy gallop back. He pumped his fist, talked to himself, high-fived the grooms.

"Winning today was extra special with all the time we've put into her," Samyn said. "To see her score against this caliber of filly is a big bonus. I'm very, very happy for Allen after what he went through this winter. He had some health problems. He overcame that. He's incredible, he's really a genius, let's put it this way. It makes everybody happy when he wins."

Jerkens has been a fixture in New York racing since the 1950s, with wins in countless major stakes.

He's famous for victories over champions Kelso, Buckpasser, Cicada and Secretariat. Even without the improbable, Jerkens would be a legend, however.

"Everybody knows how hard he works, everybody knows that when he wins it's well deserved," said Ralph Theroux, a fomer Jerkens employee and agent for Shine Again's jockey.

The trainer's last Grade I came in the 1998 Jockey Club Gold Cup with Wagon Limit, who defeated eventual Horse of the Year Skip Away at 34-1.

"You get my age, you wonder if it's ever going to happen again," Jerkens said after interviews with ESPN and a pack of newspaper reporters were finished. "When Wagon Limit won the Gold Cup a few years ago, I thought that might be the last one. I'm lucky to be here and I'm lucky to win the race."

A Hall of Famer since 1975, Jerkens began 2001 in a hospital battling pancreatitis. His health is back, and now so are the wins.

The trainer led a small group of happy people – wife Elisabeth and Samyn's wife Antoinette among them – to the Saratoga Room for the obligatory toast after the stakes win. The waiter offered champagne, Jerkens ordered a cold beer, watched the replay a few times, took more telephone calls, talked about Kelso (Bohemia's champion he beat three times), commented on a painting or two.

Fifteen minutes later, he was at the big, red door. Elisabeth went toward the car, Allen toward the barn. Not 10 steps away, he paused as the first-floor clubhouse bartender displayed an emotional thumbs-up.

Jerkens returned the gesture, fixed his straw hat and strolled out the gate –

– on top of Saratoga once again.

Let's go this way.

Away from the action, down past Kiaran's barn along the trees. Now slow down, what's the hurry, my man. You're all right. All we have to do is deliver 25 papers and we have all morning. It's a little past seven, nothing to worry us. Should have worn leggings I guess. This backpack's bouncing like a sack of potatoes on my back. There's Pat Kelly's barn, let's cut in between Cordero's car and the bunk house. Yeah, you're OK. Watch the step. That's right. Phil Serpe's barn to our left. Boy Sarah's having a tougher ride than I, get that head down horse. There's Todd's pony, like he's saying hello to us. Hey old boy, you got a great look my friend. Over to Dave Donk's first, drop off today's edition off at the table in the yard. Morning, there's a paper. Oh this is the way to go. He's pretty isn't he. Great ride, I'll tell you. A Starbright mint for you, look at that. Well, that's what I call them. Think I can hang this bag from the saddle horn? Don't mind do you? Ah that's better. Who's next? Kimmel's. Can you put this paper on the picnic table for me? Thanks. Oh, better get out of here, that bay colt seems to like this paint pony. Let's go, let's go. That's right. Boy, it's slow up here. It's been so long, I forgot the rhythmical beat. Been in a car too long. Clop, clop, clop. Don't kick. Hey Rusty, what about that horse? Over to McPeek's barn, which way? Morning. Past Terranova's and Colum O'Brien's. Here you go. How about that. Now this is the way to do it. Pony Express, right? Two papers to Leo's. Past Pletcher's. Hey guys, here's your paper. Hello Mr. Campbell. Better get out of this shedrow. To Leah Gyarmati's. Stretch and tuck them in the saddle flap. Hey, you want to race that pony? Mine's quick, at least to that fruit truck. Destasio's on the phone, wink and hand him one in silence. That's right, track Chuck Simon down. Jimmy Jerkens, "Nice article on the Chief." Thank you. His son calls him the Chief, now that's amazing. Hey Gasper. Hey Bo. Morning. Good looking pony, eh? Hennig's. Yeah, nice to do it again. Quickest way to Lynn Whiting's. Could you put this in the tack room? Thanks. Over to Al Stall's. And back to Frankel's. Over to Clement's. Better not walk right down the middle of the shed. Go around. Shug and Clement. Good, both by the rail. Morning, Allison. Here's today's. Enjoy it OK. Hennig's. Mint. Oh he'd like that. Who's your friend? Allison. To the Annex. Thought that was you. Ooh, you look bad my friend. Back to the turf. Hey Donna. Cool, isn't he. No mints. Watch your head, my man. Western saddle's like a couch. Feel safe with this horn. Del Carroll's. Lisa Lewis' for carrots. Fresh clover. Now, don't gorge my man. Better get to Asmussen's for an interview. Fresh raking job. Walk lightly buddy. Hi, Steve. Bet you never did an interview on horseback before. Not this way. What about Cashier's Dream? Better get going. Yeah, great band, Burners UK. Not too late. It's just a puddle my man. Don't argue, go around. Walk on home, past Leo's. Keith around? Hmmm. That's OK. I'm off. Horse, Gotta Horse. Thanks. Union Avenue, I'll miss you on Tuesday. Walk. Walk. Walk. Picture? Cool. Back past Elliott Walden's. Be nice to that horse. Chicago? Just moonlighting. Toner's raking up. Moe's. Don't need tea. Keep on walking. There's my car. Past Biancone's desk in the shed row. Tagg's on the phone. Howard's on the phone. Damn, wonder how long I been gone. Time to go back. Nearly home. Most fun I've had in Saratoga. Nearly forgot what it's like. Great ride. Finally. Tomorrow's Cup of Coffee? Probably.

Thanks Charlie

Steve Asmussen walked around the paddock with Cashier's Dream at the end of the leather shank.

The favorite for the Spinaway was rattling the ring bit in her mouth like a baby in a crib. Calm and amused.

They put the tack on her and she came out from under the saddling stalls like a go-go dancer gone wild. Her hind end nearly swung all the way around to Asmussen's coat tails.

Barry Irwin of Team Valor walked gingerly behind the chestnut filly, "I think we're about to see something explode."

Like the rockets' red glare.

Cashier's Dream decimated the Spinaway, winning by six with Donnie Meche crouched behind her head like he was driving in a soap box derby. The Michigan-bred daughter of Service Stripe and the Monetary Gift mare Jerry's Sister banged out fractions of 21.89, 44.96, 1:10.17 and finished the 7 furlongs in 1:23.47. By the time she was done the rest of them were staggering home. Smok'n Frolic did the best, finishing second with Magic Storm third.

Cashier's Dream came to Saratoga with an already established resume. She won her first two starts and was purchased by Heiligbrodt Racing and Team Valor from owner/breeder James Jackson. In her next start she won the Grade III Debutante at Churchill Downs. Sent off as the favorite for the Adirondack, she was upset by You. This was her vindication. And her celebration.

"I'm just very proud for her. She's queen of the world again and she doesn't have to worry about who else is out there," Asmussen said. "I wasn't sure of how she would respond. You walk through the paddock with 30,000 people watching, you recreate the circumstances that basically gutted you the last time. Personally, I'm very glad she won for the way I know she'll feel walking back over here."

Cashier's Dream ought to feel like the best 2-year-old filly in the world. Well, You awaits somewhere down the road, but on this day, Cashier's Dream was the star. She was supposed to win. That's why Asmussen left nothing to chance taking the shank and doing it himself.

"I was disappointed with how she acted in the Adirondack. I just thought she lost some concentration," Asmussen said. "Saratoga is different. There is just so much. Walking over, water coolers dragging, a lot of people. I had schooled her myself and I was confident with how she was going to respond to me. Not that it would be any different any other way but how often are you going to be one to five in a Grade I at Saratoga; 35 years and I may live another 35 before I'm in that shape again."

Asmussen jubilantly walked from the clubhouse to the secretary's office after the race.

"You just go with what you believe," Asmussen said. "I think she's faster than they are. If we didn't feel as good walking over as we did in the Adirondack, then we shouldn't be confident. If they beat her, they did it again, they ran a race I didn't see on paper. She always finds more. You gotta think crazy things."

The crazy things could be anything from the Breeders' Cup to the Eclipse Award. Asmussen might have been thinking crazy thoughts but the talked about the reality of the business just the same.

"Today, I was given the fastest horse. Mr. Heiligbrodt and Barry Irwin of Team Valor bought her. Mr. Jackson raised her and started her. We've just kept the boat in the water. She was that fast when she walked up to us," Asmussen said. "When she won the non-two at Churchill, she made up six lengths in about five jumps. It was breathtaking. We witnessed the race like a thousand others and said, 'wow did you see that?' Barry went after her and Mr. Heiligbrodt came to me and said what about this filly. I said, 'she's unbelievable.' He said what about a Service Stripe, Michigan bred. I said it's a race, it's too late for a catalogue page. She walks in the barn and she wins the Debutante 13 days later. Us get credit? No, we were the

CASHIER'S DREAM

lucky recipients. We have confidence that we can get a horse to run their race but I don't care who you are if it's not in your shedrow you're not going to win. Without the ability we're just another mutt."

Cashier's Dream topped off a huge meet for Asmussen who had never spent a summer at the Spa.

"You've seen a good painting and now you've painted a good picture. It went from your head to the canvas. They wrote it down and put your name on the cup, now drink out of it," Asmussen said. "That's the beauty of racing, the best part of horse racing is when they go by the wire it's over. Everything else is a story."

And this one's only getting better.

You'll remember where you were.

The day, the place, the setting, the mood is locked away. Always there, always on call.

I was sitting in a metal chair two days away from the conclusion of The Saratoga Special's inaugural season. The OTB channel played in my right ear like any other day, that elevator beat with an occasional race call from Finger Lakes, Saratoga or Monmouth. Then the man came on and said, "It was just reported that Point Given has been . . . retired."

And then the air was gone.

Our float, our savior, our poster child . . . off to the hills of Kentucky never to be seen in the moment again. We saw his last hurrah right here at Saratoga in the Travers. See why I want that extra turn around the paddock? The horse of a lifetime only lasts minutes.

Retired due to a "strained left tendon" the big horse has left the building. Seems like a long time ago, that Travers. It was a fun dream while it lasted.

Now isn't it shameful that we criticized his efforts. His Derby loss, the Haskell close call, what a sad thing we ever uttered a derogatory word about the horse. The adage comes back to life once again, appreciate it while you've got it.

A few hours after the announcement, Steve Asmussen walked back from the clubhouse after his Point Given, Cashier's Dream, won the Spinaway by a country driveway.

"You just don't know. There are no guarantees.

POINT GIVEN

Point Given's retired," Asmussen said.

He carried her saddle towel in his right hand and a smile that stretched from the jocks' room to the paddock. He knows one day Cashier's Dream will be retired. One day a groom could ask him to walk in her stall to look at "this." He can feel the clunk in his gut from here.

Think it's hard to be a fan? Be a trainer. Ducking under Point Given's webbing to check that leg. Running your hand over it again and again. Willing the heat that you know is there away. Creating the theory of a wrap instead of a strain. You might not like when Bob Baffert puts a trophy on his head or plays the guitar with Richie Havens, but you gotta feel for the guy when he bent down on one knee and ran his hand down the back of that leg.

How about a jockey. Think Gary Stevens' knees hurt a little more this afternoon than they did this morning? He said it over and over, he's the best, the reason, the ride of his life. Sure, he'll rebound with rides on Red Bullet, Macho Uno and other cadillacs but that pit of his gut is rumbling away. And will forever.

How about an owner. Sure Prince Ahmed Salman is a prince. But every prince needs a good horse. This was his. See him grab that shank in the middle of the track last week? It's not about money. He shared Point Given with us and was prepared to do so again next year. Getting out of bed tomorrow is going to take a little longer.

Reporting's easy. I watched the four bandages go on those legs after the Travers. I can't say I didn't think about his ankles and tendons, knees and hocks. Sure I thought about how long they can last as Point Given stood there with his head in his haynet. Sure I thought about them but not as much as I am right now.

Point Given's retired. Yeah, and Ghandi picked a fight. Can you believe that? All our plans, the showdown with older horses, the Breeders' Cup Classic with Galileo, Tiznow, Albert The Great, Red Bullet. Our bags were packed, sitting by the door ready to go and now the pilot just cancelled the trip – engine trouble. No refunds either. Well no full refunds. There's always refunds in horse racing. The Hopeful, ah what timing, comes today. Another batch to latch on to. Can there be another Point Given? Sure, there was once a Man o'War, a Seabiscuit, a Kelso, a Forego, a John Henry . . . a Cigar. They all retired, too. We'll be back to fight another day. The air will come back in the lungs. Maybe not today or even this fall but again it will come. Maybe we'll feel the way we did on Travers Day 2001 again.

Maybe.

**"Horse.
Big Horse."**

–Pinkerton at the Union Avenue crossing as Point Given headed his way

CAME

They say it's better to sell and repent than keep and repent. But it only applies if you're repenting.

John Toffan, Trudy McCaffery and Paco Gonzalez are rejoicing that they never said goodbye to Came Home.

"That's where he got his name, he went to the sales three times and came home three times," co-owner/breeder Toffan said as the Hopeful winner returned from the test barn, led by a smiling Gonzalez. The homebred son of Gone West out of McCaffery and Toffan's mare Nice Assay had, hours before, won the Grade I 2-year-old stakes over Mayakovsky and Thunder Days

Toffan, McCaffery and Gonzalez made the decision to ship Came Home from California for the Hopeful. As wise a decision as not selling him those three times. The victory pushed his career mark to three for three and made him a legitimate contender for the Breeders' Cup Juvenile.

Came Home broke a little sideways and then ran up to the leaders. Chris McCarron eased him back off the pace of Roman Dancer and waited until Mayakovsky loomed at his boot. The three of them ran past the quarter pole in a line. Roman Dancer was done and Came Home gradually pulled away from Mayakovsky to win by 2, breaking the stakes record in the process. It took him 1:21.94 to become a Grade I winner.

It took walking the length of the stretch for Gonzalez to explain the horse's life.

Came Home went to the Keeneland July Sales as a weanling. The bidding was nearing his $700,000 reserve when he flipped over right there in the sales ring. The bidding stopped. He went back to the yearling sales and didn't reach another reserve. One more try at the 2-year-old in training sales was strike three. He came back to Gonzalez, proceeded to get sick, then eventually work with anything in the barn and win his first two starts with ease.

"I'm very proud, very proud of him," Gonzalez said. "He's a nice horse, not just because he won, I just know he's a nice horse all the time. Today's the first time he hit him and only a few times. We haven't run in seven weeks, too. That's not easy. To win this race, look at all the good horses that won this race."

Gonzalez asked for directions to the test barn three times and kept talking.

"He's got the talent and the heart. He's a tough son of a bitch. All the family is the same way. His sister A.P. Assay was very good, not very sound," Gonzalez said. "They try to sell him three times and nobody buy him. Nobody like him. He was small but he started growing. Now he's worth a little money, huh? I was shaking today. I run so many good horses and I'm usually relaxed. Today, I was really nervous. I don't know why."

All the nerves were gone by the time the horse came back to the stakes barn.

Toffan sat in a chair just outside his stall, sipping champagne from a plastic cup while Came Home dug into a haynet and laughed about the whole affair. It's easy to laugh after a Grade I at Saratoga.

Gonzalez stirred his cooked oats while photographers and friends swarmed around the good looking colt. McCaffery kissed his nose, hugged his neck and covered herself in hay. It's not right to quote a woman talking to a horse.

It was all good you can believe that.

As the Came Home team raved about a day at Saratoga, a rugged looking chestnut marched past the celebration. Finally they had to ask, "Is that Delaware Township?" "Sure is," came from the man at his head.

The Forego winner was breathing easy and looking for dinner as he finished his rounds. Big, strapping son of Notebook, Delaware Town-

HOME

ship had put a Forego-like move on the 7-furlong Grade I stakes, coming from the back and around them all to win his first Grade I. Left Bank finished second with Alannan third. Delaware Township has a resolute eye, a fluid walk and a powerful kick that dwarfed anything else in the stakes barn.

Jerry Bailey wore the purple and black silks of New Farm for his 12th stakes victory of the meet.

"He's a horse that comes from behind but runs his best outside of horses so getting squeezed early and making my way to the outside was the best thing that could have happened," Bailey said. "The track was a little deep, a little gooey underneath, he handled it fine and I think it helped the speed come back a little."

Delaware Township provided one of three wins on the day for Bailey who opened up an eight-win lead (53-45) over John Velazquez with two days to go.

"I'll sleep better tonight than I did last night. It's not over but I'll sleep better," Bailey said. "Johnny's really pushed me, he's a great competitor and a great rider. It's a friendly rivalry but both of us want to win. I really set my sights on trying to win this meet. Being 44 I can't set my sights on winning every meet, it just takes too much work and there's too much competition. It's just as much fun. I try to ride good horses and win big races. (My agent) Ron Anderson is very good at what he does, I like to think I'm OK,

....and you add a guy like Bill Mott in and it's kind of hard to mess it up."

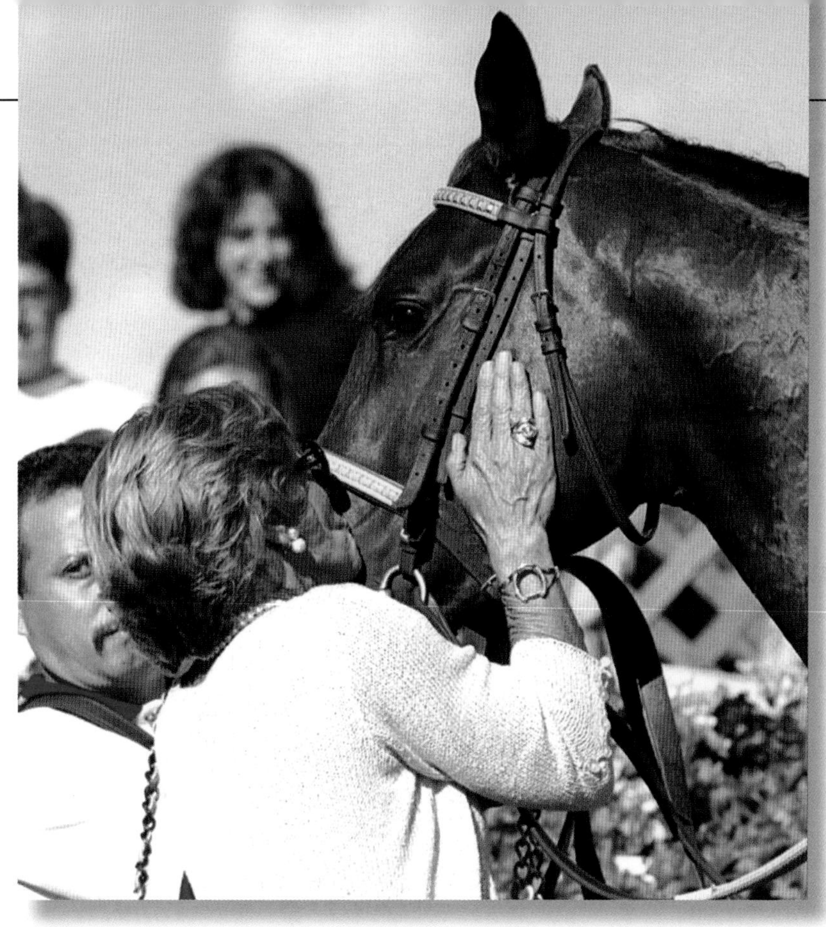

"What a country."
– Trainer Rene Araya seeing Chico the shoeshine man talking on a cell phone

SARATOGA
5
6
7
8
9

SARATOGA 2001.

The Saratoga Special opened for business. Takeout was the talk. OTB was in question. Barry Schwartz was at the wheel. Mike Smith flew off to Del Mar. Mike Luzzi went to the hospital. Jose Santos held his arm. Donnie Meche and Mark Guidry anteed up. John Velazquez and Edgar Prado bombed in from the Belmont cannon. Only to meet Jerry Bailey at his house.

Steve Asmussen pulled up a chair. Ronny Werner along side. Macho Uno ducked his way to defeat. Mayakovski stopped the clock. Touch Love and Buster's Daydream flew Maryland's flag high and proud.

Flute found an allowance race and Hap laughed his way through the Bernard Baruch. Victory Ride did exactly that. Lido Palace broke through. And Red Bullet made up for Macho Uno.

Shug kept his foot on the floor with Serra Lake. Saint Verre found the circle. Two Dancers jumped in the Lake George. Volponi had them thinking Travers. And Snow Dance was on her way.

Top Official made the meet. Big Bambu put Thistledown on the map. Shaun Bridgmohan lost a tooth. Bailey was up by two. Buck Wheat got a plaque. City Zip made us appreciate. Frank McCourt came for a visit.

Scorpion stung Free Of Love. Congaree blew up with a knee. Aaron Gryder got bucked off. Mott led Shug by two. Velazquez won five on a card. Even Dr. Ruth was here for the action. Gryder came back to win three. Five Star Day freaked in the Vanderbilt.

Then it was Hall of Fame Day. Earlie Fires cried. Holy Bull found a home. Tom Smith – better late than never. Richard Mandella got an armshake from Allen Jerkens and a spot on the wall. Paseana came full circle. Maskette as well. And Baptize took the prize.

Sales Week was here already. An Unbridled's Song brought nearly two million. Roger King made another show. The next night Storm Cat took over, $3.3 million over. Bailey and Velazquez were tied. Wayne Lukas crept up the list. The sales finished with records all around.

Irving's Baby splashed around. Jorge Chavez's knee went around. Secret Status came around. Jimmy Jerkens won two. King Cugat lost With Anticipation. Mott and Lukas were even at 10. Penny's Gold was polished. Dreams came true. You, You, You.

Jump Start stepped over a Champ. Ray Ganpath won one for the Chief. Saratoga Sunrise came and went again. Shug sent out two sisters. Paul Toscano lit up the board again. Megantic made Bailey cringe. Thunderello created a gasp.

I'm All Yours won a stakes. Summer Colony made a three-word quote. Raul Rojas won another. Then it was a Fluteabama. Frankel wasn't done. Victory Ride cracked a leg. And Point Given paused it all.

Snow Dance walked the dog. Damned if Saratoga Sunrise didn't come again. Mott reached 13 while Lukas clawed to 12. Personal Pro was certainly that. Velazquez was up by one. Trucking Baron won the Heart Award.

Point Given played around the town. Gary Stevens stopped to chat. The Special reached 28 pages. Pompeii made Robert Clay repent while Kimmel's barn said goodbye. Sky Mist made the paper. Beautiful Pleasure whispered watch out this fall.

Travers day attracted 60,000. Dr. Kashnikow weaved like a loom. Squirtle Squirt got the best of City Zip. And nobody got the best of Point Given.

The Chief Shined Again. Bailey was suddenly up by five. Mott by four. Ransom's Pride chased the duck. It's a Giggle jumped to three at the meet. Cashier's Dream was better than the ATM.

Velazquez squeezed the overnight for the last drops. Came Home in the Hopeful. Delaware Township made like Forego. Velazquez did five one better with Starine but never did catch Bailey.

And The Special was out of words.

And until next year . . . farewell from the Spa.

Thrilling, trying, exciting, maddening, exhausting, rewarding.

The Saratoga Special staff hit the Pick Six of adjectives during its first summer at Saratoga. A year ago, The Special was something we batted around late at night when there wasn't anything else to talk about. Six months ago, it was a maybe. Now, 35 editions later, it's a reality.

Wow!

The staff – Paul, Sean. Susie, Tod, Dave, Dan, Kelly, Grier, Pete and Frank (and a few others) – will forever be proud of the effort we put in, the work we did, the product we created, the readers we involved.

The collection of people – everybody had a talent and no one was more important than anyone else – at 260 Broadway this summer combined to create a product people wanted. Beyond the office, the help included a variety of understanding families (Clancys, Wassermans, Alexanders, Harmons and Markses), the people at Lyrical Ballad, a select few of Saratoga's restaurants, several vehicles and a printer as interested in the product (and not necessarily the deadline) as we were. To top it off, a nucleus of supporters, subscribers and advertisers came through like classy horses on a triple ticket in the ninth.

Take away one piece of that puzzle, and The Special doesn't make it past opening week. From – and to – everyone, thank you.

Highlights of the meet certainly involve racing's stars – with names like Point Given, Flute, Frankel, Bailey, Mott, Velazquez – but our best moments center on people and events of little less grandeur.

The random assortment of fans Paul convinced to buy the paper – they included David Cassidy, Bob Baffert and Corey Brown from Latham who entered NYRA's hot-dog eating contest as The Special's representative (he ate five) and some guys known only as "the veterans." Thanks for reading. We'll see you next year.

The response of Saratoga's horsemen. Grooms, owners, trainers, jockeys, valets were our first readers. They added a new newspaper to their days, liked what they saw and kept on reading. Thank you, for being there if nothing else. And thank you Mary Ryan, Saratoga's breakfast host, for our promotional assistance.

Many assume our daily routine will continue right into Belmont. Others have asked about Keeneland. Sorry, but we really do need to get back to our lives. Like anything worthwhile, The Special was a huge effort. Combined, the staff got plenty of sleep. Taken separately, we're about a month short.

The "other" stories. Any newspaper could cover the Travers, the Alabama, the Hopeful and the stars that participated. But we enjoyed meeting Allen Jerkens, Angel Penna, Raul Rojas, Scott Schwartz, Simon Harris, Scotty Schulhofer, Donnie Meche, Dave Donk, Manuel Criollo, Joe in the boxes, John Kimmel and so many others even slightly off the center of the radar screen.

The volunteers. Vic Zast, Charlie Moran, Bruno Zalubil, Clark Nyberg, Andrea Steiner, Lisa Barnett, Tom Coyle and others wrote articles when we needed them (often before we needed them). Cartoonists Muck and Terry Smith provided a daily dose of humor – with a twist on the equine lifestyle. Thanks for the effort, and the involvement.

The surprises. A bag of Special hats and shirts from Sam Clancy. A tray of food from Buddy and Kate Martin. A shelf of books and other resources from Lyrical Ballad. Flowers, balloons and plants (yes, flowers, balloons and plants) arrived from several sources. Encouraging e-mails, notes, faxes and advertisements arrived without warning – usually when we needed them most.

Early on in this effort, someone asked if we could do it (a daily newspaper). The unsaid rest of the sentence was "with such a small staff." We always knew we could do it – even if there were a few doubts as to whether we would be able to (there's a difference if you think about it).

The right combination of work (lots of work), people, circumstances and subject matter made it all possible.

This is the last drop.

Good to the last drop? Perhaps. I've never been that good at saying goodbye. But here goes.

The Saratoga Special is going to sleep.

In a way, thank all the Gods in the world, now I can watch a race and not think about my lead or my take or my quotes. In another way, damn I can't believe the biggest project to date is over (at least until next year). In another way, my brother Joe needs to get back to his family, Paul needs to get to the jewelry store, Susie needs to use her education, Frank needs to go work on Gary Stevens' book, Pete needs to go find the next Seabiscuit, Dave needs to clean his basement and Tod needs to get back to his real job editing a mainstream magazine.

The trouble with Saratoga is that it marks time. We have to wait another year for another go with the old girl.

We had one goal this meet. Create a good read. It was very simple why we started this paper; the greatest moments in horse racing would happen in the afternoon and by the next morning they were already being knocked around. We missed the old guys who wrote with verve and passion. This year's motto was, "Sleep in September." Next year's might be "Cynics Beware."

Just this morning it happened again. Point Given retired on Saturday and by Sunday morning he already had no shot for the Hall of Fame. Man, can't we celebrate the game for a moment? Can't we just think about how good he was when we last saw him? Why throw cold water on an already cold bath?

Saturday was our last day on the job. The day's events wrapped up the theme of our summer. Made it very simple and clear, right there for us to understand and to remember. First we read about Point Given, then a book was placed on my desk and by the end we were leaning on a barn wall watching another good horse be a good horse.

The book is titled, Race Horses and Racing by F. Gray Griswold, dated 1925. It had a bookmark set in place which led the reader to a passage called "A GOOD Sportsman." It reads:

"A GOOD sportsman is a man who has developed his mind and body in the open air and who has good control over both, who has a keen eye, a level head, and a light hand. He is a man who is kind and considerate to all living things, who has good judgment, who can do no wrong nor suspect evil in others, who does not crow over his own success, and who has learned to accept defeat with a smiling countenance, yet does not accept it until the last breath has left his body."

I'd like to think we're an office of GOOD Sportsmen. Or at least live with that as a goal.

This year was to show you who we were, what we wanted to do, what kind of difference we wanted to make. We love the game, especially the game played in this town. Writing about Saratoga is easy. We want to write about the good stuff and there's no better place for good stuff than Saratoga.

Standing in the stakes barn, as a Saturday afternoon faded into a Saturday evening, while Came Home posed and played for all his new admirers, and horse racing lifers stood around just because they wanted to, was a good conclusion to a long but rewarding summer.

We know our approach is different than what you're probably used to. No controversy, no criticism, no negativity. But we figure you can get that somewhere else easy enough.

Over my shoulder in our makeshift office sits piles of the first 34 issues of The Saratoga Special. Maybe in that pile lies what turned it all around. It's a hell of an idea, anyway.

To all of you who said something positive, bought an ad, took care of a horse, slapped us on the back, answered our questions or gave us a buck for a copy – thanks again.

You are good sportsmen.

Medaglia D'Oro
With Anticipation
Edgar Prado
Todd Pletcher
Pat Day

Saratoga 2002

Shaking off the body blows from 2001, The Saratoga Special returned for year two. It had to get better. And it did. We wisely went to five days a week, caught our breath and doubled our page count.

There was plenty to write about on those pages.

Medaglia d'Oro won the Jim Dandy with ease and then fought off a gallant Repent in the muddy Travers. Edgar Prado claimed his first Saratoga title while Todd Pletcher began his assault of the record book, winning 19 races for his first championship. Pat Day vaulted above any jockey in history when he guided With Anticipation to a nose victory in the Sword Dancer.

SARATOGA

It was a brutal time to start something.

Mare Reproductive Loss Syndrome had ravaged Kentucky, the stock market was taking a beating, and the economy was all over the place. If we did a business profile or marketing survey or whatever big companies do, it probably would have said "Turn back, the timing is not right." Oh yeah! Phooey!

We worked hard and we had fun. Ten days after we left town – September 11, 2001 – the world changed forever and our summer of struggle in Saratoga didn't seem so important.

In 2002, we started with a slightly bigger staff and some bigger goals. We didn't do Monday newspapers, instead doing a double Sunday/Monday edition and an expanded Wednesday edition. The result was a more manageable schedule, a better newspaper – and fewer deadlines.

We still published every day during sales week (Aug. 4-10), and another big edition for Travers Day. Thirty-two editions in all.

As usual, we started with an open mind and a message to readers: "We graciously accept donations, praise, advertising, food, letters, writing contributions, ideas and input. We will accept criticism. But grudgingly."

Bring on The Special, Year II.

Daily Racing Coverage

Wednesday, July 24, 2002

The SARATOGA Special

Year 2 • No. 1

Price: $1

Good Morning, Saratoga

Tod Marks

Inside

Complete entries and expert selections.

Schuylerville Stakes preview.

Calendar of events

Tod Marks

Looking back
Touch Love, Schuylerville 2001.

The Challenge Ahead

Racing's stars line up for storied track's 134th meet

BY SEAN CLANCY

Is it a challenge? "No question about it. Absolutely," said eight-time and defending Saratoga champion trainer Bill Mott as he rode back to his barn two days before opening day.

And finally the last X has been crossed through the last calendar block. Thank the moons, the tides and the Calendar Gods, it's Saratoga time again.

Time for another year of the greatest race meet in the world and time for another season of *The Saratoga Special*. If you're keeping score, it's the 134th time for the meet, and the second for the paper.

If you have ever been to Saratoga, you know what awaits. Competitive racing with energetic players (from horses to fans) in an atmosphere that only occurs at Saratoga.

If you were around for *The Special's* first year, you know what's in store – passionate writing, knowledgeable insight, and a look at Saratoga that you can't find anywhere else. We mean anywhere else.

Is it a challenge? Just like Mott says, "No question about it, absolutely."

We started our daily racing coverage last year, finding a way to grind out 35 issues in 42 days. There was Point Given's Travers of course, Bobby Frankel's weekend of winners, $3 million yearlings, stars like Hap, With Anticipation and Came Home, a six-win day for John Velazquez, and more titles for Mott and Jerry Bailey.

We interviewed Ray Ganpath, Laura Hillenbrand, Frank McCourt, William T. Young, Jerry Bailey, kids at the Ben and Jerry's stand, Joe in the boxes and wrote about anything and everything.

Saratoga is a big canvas and we tried to cover it with as much paint as we could get our brushes dipped into. There were attendance and handle records, track and publishing records and, like always, the greatest of racing.

For the first time in history, attendance climbed past the one million mark, (1,011,669). Records were set for on-track handle, total handle, single-day attendance, single-day on-track handle, single-day total handle, Travers Day attendance, Opening Day attendance, Opening Day on-track handle and Opening Day total handle (there will not be a test on those at the end of this article).

• See *OPENING*, page 4

Saratoga marks the passage of time.

Like a birthday, an anniversary, a new school year, Christmas, an annual physical, tax day, family vacation, or a simple personal tradition that only you know about.

The six-week meet has a life of its own, nowhere do you get more consumed with what you're doing than Saratoga. There is no time or reason to look at your position in the world or the position of the world. You just go, go, go and never look up until it's over. On closing day, you shut the door to one life and open it to another. "Hmmmm, where am I going now, what is going on around me, and what will happen between now and opening day of Saratoga next year? Will I get back here next year?"

On Sept. 3 of last year, we closed shop like we always do at the end of another stay with Saratoga. We packed up the car, the barn, the office, the rental house and headed our different ways.

Different ways. Like a liberal family of 12.

No one could have guessed the ways it went.

The World Trade Center was attacked, the Pentagon too. A war in Afghanistan was started and finished. Rudy Giuliani was a hero. We had a new-found respect for firefighters and police officers. The stock market tumbled around like shoes in a dryer. George W. Bush grew more acceptable while Anthrax got scarier. Airport lines went around the block. It was officially a recession.

Tiznow won the Breeders' Cup and was retired. Eight months later, so was his jockey Chris McCarron. We lost Exogenous, Tempera, Lonesome Glory, Nureyev, Kris S., Spook Express, Cashier's Dream, Seattle Slew, Ogden Phipps, Jane Lunger, Ted Williams, Sam Snead, Daniel Pearl, Katharine Graham, George Harrison, John Mabee, Bob Camac, Howard Battle.

The Yankees lost a World Series. Barry Bonds knocked more out than anyone. The Olympics came and went not without a figure-skating scandal. The Patriots became Super Bowl champions. The Red Wings won and Scotty left. The Lakers did it again. War Emblem became a household name, Ken McPeek too and Prado had a classic. Magna bought some more racetracks. Slots were passed in New York. And Bailey kept on winning. Tiger, too.

Politically Incorrect was canceled. David Letterman was wooed but ultimately stayed. Halle Barry and Denzel Washington broke ground. U2 won another Grammy. A Beautiful Mind was the best. Israelis and Palestinians upped the venom. Pakistan and India continued to glare. Enron blew up, WorldCom followed, and Arthur Andersen was left holding the shredder. Ken Lay had to sell a house while Martha Stewart was investigated.

They tried to hide nuclear waste in a Nevada mountain. Forest fires ravaged the west. Farm subsidies continued to skew the balance. Serena and Venus played in the finals. Alaska was still under threat from oil diggers. The Catholic church was in a crisis. Cars started to become hybrids while SUVs got 14 miles to the gallon. The West Wing was hot. So was the summer, but nothing like Azeri and Astra.

Just another off-season and now it's Saratoga – time to put the daily newspaper (major metropolitan variety anyway) down, turn off CNN, rack up the credit card debt and have some fun again.

September is for thinking.

4

– Where the Test ranked in Sportscenter's plays of the day on July 27.

One is bay. The other dark bay or brown.

One is 4-for-4. The other 6-for-10. One breaks from the rail. The other right next door in two. Both are Grade I winners. Today is the Test.

Carson Hollow and You stand out in the 7-furlong, Grade I, $250,000 Test. Carson Hollow, owned by Frank Stronach, Hemlock Hills Farm and Gabrielle Farm, comes in undefeated and straight off a Prioress Stakes romp at Belmont Park. Edmund Gann's You has already earned over $1 million and comes in off a score in the Grade I Acorn. Carson Hollow stretches out a furlong from her last victory and You shortens up a furlong from hers.

Richard Dutrow Jr. trains Carson Hollow, a New York-bred daughter of Carson City, while Bobby Frankel trains You, winner of last year's Adirondack at Saratoga. They are well aware of each other.

"I wish You would scratch," Dutrow said standing outside Carson Hollow's stall while she enjoyed a massage the day before the Test. "I've already talked to Frankel, he won't take no bribes. I tried that, he's not going there."

Dutrow is probably kidding, and of course he will also tell you he's not ducking anybody.

"Without a doubt this is tougher than the last race. She's gonna have to come forward. She's done everything we ever thought she would do. We always knew she could run but last time she surprised me, she really showed she can run," Dutrow said. "I don't feel any pressure because I know she's coming to the race the right way. If she wasn't eating or her attitude wasn't right then there might be a little pressure on me to make the right decision but she's doing so good, I don't feel like I have any pressure. I don't have to question myself about what is going on with her. I KNOW she's good."

John Velazquez gets a return call on Carson Hollow, who is unbeaten in three starts at the distance, and Dutrow doesn't plan to change her front-running tactics.

"If she breaks good, I certainly won't tell Johnny to take a hold of her. She's rated well on the lead and I don't think we'll change it," Dutrow said. "She breaks good every time but they're not going to just give us the break, she's got to do it again. If she breaks good and gets beat, then she just got beat by a better horse."

That better horse could be You, who should find a perfect stalking spot breaking just outside Carson Hollow.

"She stayed light on me all winter and spring. I thought she'd blossom but finally when she got to Belmont she started doing well," Frankel said. "It could be so many variables; she might like training on this track, could be the weather, the humidity, the cycle. You never know, especially with fillies."

You won the Las Virgenes at Santa Anita in February, the Santa Anita Oaks in March, finished fourth in the Kentucky Oaks in May, and won the Acorn in June. All Grade I. She's run in seven straight Grade I races, winning four.

"The way she ran last lear, I can't complain," Frankel said. "There is a chance I would come back in the Alabama, depends on how she runs. People always think she can't get the distance, but for me, I never thought she was strong enough to get the distance. Now with the way she's training she might be able to but we'll see how she runs.

You can't get too far in front of yourself in this game."

"The first one I win by a nose and everything went right. This one I win by a nose and a lot of things went wrong."

Voodoo Dancer and Tates Creek

Just another day in the charmed life of Bobby Frankel. He saddled Juddmonte Farm's Tates Creek to win the Grade II Diana Handicap. Two races later he saddled Edmund Gann's You (in the same stall) to win the Grade I Test. Jerry Bailey rode both fillies; Tates Creek from her typical stalking position on the turf and You from out the back on the dirt. There's more room across this page than there was between the noses in the photos.

Epics.

Tates Creek sat just off Babae and Snow Dance in the 1 1/8-mile turf stakes, found a seam on the turn, opened a lead and then scrapped all the way to the wire with Voodoo Dancer and Jose Santos.

On the edge of the winner's circle, the photo-finish callers watched the replay. With every stride they called it, "Inside, inside, inside, inside, oohhhh." Tates Creek was the inside horse.

"She's a very agile filly, you can make a couple of moves on her to get position and hold it, that makes my job a lot easier," Bailey said. "Picking my way through traffic with her wasn't a problem. The problem was, because I had kinda taken her out of her game, was she going to have as strong a finish? I know Voodoo Dancer and Jose knows I'm one of the horses to beat and they're not going to give me anything easy. They're going to jump on me as soon as we turn for home. She was very, very game."

Frankel knew this all along.

"She's very consistent, tough, just a competitor. She's winning the photos," Frankel said. "I wouldn't have these horses if I didn't get them from Juddmonte to start with, they validated that I could train these kinds of horses."

Two races later You and Carson Hollow validated all that is good in the horse.

Carson Hollow and John Velazquez blazed away on the lead while You scrambled around the back. She broke adequately but not sharply, her talent had put her in the race leaving the backside but Short Note backed into the path that Bailey had chosen on the rail. Hesitation ensued.

"When you're going down the backside, you can't loop the field," Bailey said. "They're too good of horses to do that so you really have to play the hand that unfolds in front of you."

Around the turn, that hand was about to fold for You.

"I was hoping she would have enough speed to lay just off Carson Hollow but she's just not that kind of sprinter," Bailey said. "Then you have to deal with traffic, there was more traffic than I wanted,"

Spring Meadow and Jorge Chavez lost their line inside Bold World and Pat Day. They veered for another lane and You sneaked through between Spring Meadow's left shoulder and the white of the rail.

"Chavez was trying to go out and Pat kept him in, so he was trying to dive down in and I'm already there," Bailey said. "When they hit your butt like that, the public can't see it, but it knocks them down. Most won't go through there and you can tell about halfway through they won't. With her she got stronger as she got up in there."

Carson Hollow came off the rail and into the 2 path while You kept to her clinging trip on the rail. The duo went to the line in unison with both fillies' heads turned to each other like a stare-down.

"You have to have a courageous horse to weave your way through," Bailey said. "And then to be stuck on the fence, pinned down in there, to fight as hard as she did and the other filly came back again, she wasn't through. It was a great race, I'm not sure I'd want to do it again."

Announcer Tom Durkin came up with the line of the meet, "It's a photo finish that doesn't deserve a loser."

You's dark nose was hidden behind the towering head of Carson Hollow. The photo finish callers wouldn't even try this one.

Velazquez and Bailey were just as lost.

"I asked Johnny if he thought he won, he said he didn't know and I didn't know," Bailey said.

Finally the 2 flashed over the 1 on the board.

Bailey and Velazquez looked each other and shrugged.

"It's tough because I've been on the other end," Bailey said. "It's tough to ride that good and the horse to run that good and not win."

Not a problem for Bailey and Frankel on this day.

Carson Hollow and You

Just one week ago there was a jockey race.

Open minds spoke about a competition between Jerry Bailey, John Velazquez and Edgar Prado. Some even mentioned Jose Santos, Richard Migliore, Jorge Chavez. Now it seems like wishful thinking.

Leaving Jerry Bailey out of a week in review from Saratoga would be like ignoring the sand when describing the beach. Saratoga's defending champion performed at his prolific best. The 44-year-old won 15 of the possible 57 races over the first six days, including four stakes.

Del Mar Show checked off the Bernard Baruch on Friday. You and Tates Creek swept the Test and the Diana on Saturday. Dancethruthedawn dominated the Go For Wand on Sunday to give Bailey four stakes victories in a row.

Bailey used the rest of the condition book – too – winning anything from turf stakes to 2-year-old sprints and even a claimer. Bill Mott and Bobby Frankel provided four wins apiece and the other seven were divided between Gary Sciacca, Pat Reynolds, Patrick Biancone, Michael Matz, Mark Frostad, Steve Klesaris and Frank Alexander.

And on Sunday, they even gave away his bobblehead doll.

Nobody's catching up with Bailey on the racetrack right now, but he slowed down long enough last week to talk to The Special:

Sum up the first week: "Good week. It's the best start I've ever had. I'm usually slow the first two, three days, by the end of the first week I'm in the mix."

So now it's easier? "Heck no, it doesn't make it easier. It means everybody is looking for me now. It's kind of how the cycle falls. A lot of live horses fell this week, which is good because they might be able to run back."

Are you riding by instinct or thought? "I think if something happens during the race that's unexpected – that you haven't thought might happen – then you have to go on instinct and more often then not that will be the right move. If you sit there to think about it, you've probably waited too long to react to what just happened. The more you win, the more the chances are that those decisions will be right. When you're doing things right, you're just doing things right. I don't how it works like that, but at least with me it does.

Do you get in bed at night and laugh? "No, I conk out. I'm tired. I ride eight (in a day). It's hot. I've ridden more horses here in a week than I have in three weeks at Belmont. It's the mental fatigue too, you can't make any mistakes, the horses are just too good. The mental stuff takes it out of you as much as the physical, probably more."

When do you stop and think 'whew, what a day?' "I was very satisfied with what happened Saturday and thought those very words and again (Sunday) night but I know you have to lace them up and go again the next day, especially here because it's a tough meet. Johnny and Edgar aren't going to lay down, they're going to be coming after me and they might win 15 next week, who knows?"

Do you allow yourself a moment of reflection?

"Right after Labor Day."

LEADING JOCKEYS – Through July 29

Name	Starts	1st	2nd	3rd	Earnings
Jerry Bailey	38	15	4	2	$1,080,840
Jorge Chavez	36	6	7	2	$324,410
Jose Santos	36	6	6	6	$363,010
John Velazquez	40	6	4	3	$386,045
Edgar Prado	40	4	4	6	$262,810
Richard Migliore	30	4	4	4	$190,615
Pat Day	38	3	5	3	$244,670
Victor Carrero	34	2	5	4	$134,280
Mark Guidry	13	2	4	0	$75,310
Javier Castellano	26	2	2	6	$109,565

Like a man without a country, today is a day without a stakes.

One of only seven cards without a black-type race during the six-week meet, today's docket consists of one steeplechase, three allowance races, two maiden races, two open claimers, and one maiden claimer. The seventh and eighth are the co-features.

Five 2-year-old colts meet up in the seventh (the male counterpart to Wednesday's filly feature) and the eighth attracted 10 fillies for a 1 1/16-mile turf test. Both are allowance races carrying identical conditions of non-winners-of-a-race-other-than or non-winners-of-two races.

John Velazquez rides seven of the nine races. We caught up with him sitting in a borrowed golf cart outside the Oklahoma training track during the break. We put the Form in front of him and asked him to tell us what he sees.

"First one is a jump race, the second I don't ride."

Third, Smoking Wine, 5-1. "First time for a price, first time Lasix, got a little shot," Velazquez said. "Low numbers."

Fourth, Volkonsky, 2-1 favorite. "Todd Pletcher – Dad. This one has a shot. Never been on him, don't know anything about him. Been working on the grass, by Deputy Minister out of a Stage Door Johnny mare. This horse (This Guns For Hire) will be tough, alone on the lead."

Fifth Race, Assmar, 10-1. "He runs whenever he wants. Ran OK going a mile, longer today."

VELAZQUEZ

Sixth Race, Feather Boa, 9-2. "Todd Pletcher. The first time she broke a little slow, she should improve. Zito, Simon, Lukas. Look at this, (Carson's Girl) worked in 50 here on the training track. She can run, you can believe that."

Seventh Race, Admiralty Arch, 2-5. "This is a nice horse, he'll need more distance but he's quick enough. Lukas is the one tough horse, look who he finished third to (Zavata)."

Eighth Race, Hottentot, 7-2. "Pletcher. I've done everything with her. The filly who won the stake beat her (Nunatall). Tommy Voss, Colonial Downs. Mott's horse. Mark's filly. They must think a lot of Born Something, ran her in a Grade I over there in France."

Ninth Race, Sunshine Dreamer, 6-1. "Klesaris, $40,000. I had her in the middle of the track last time. The filly who won has already run twice since."

"Not a bad day."

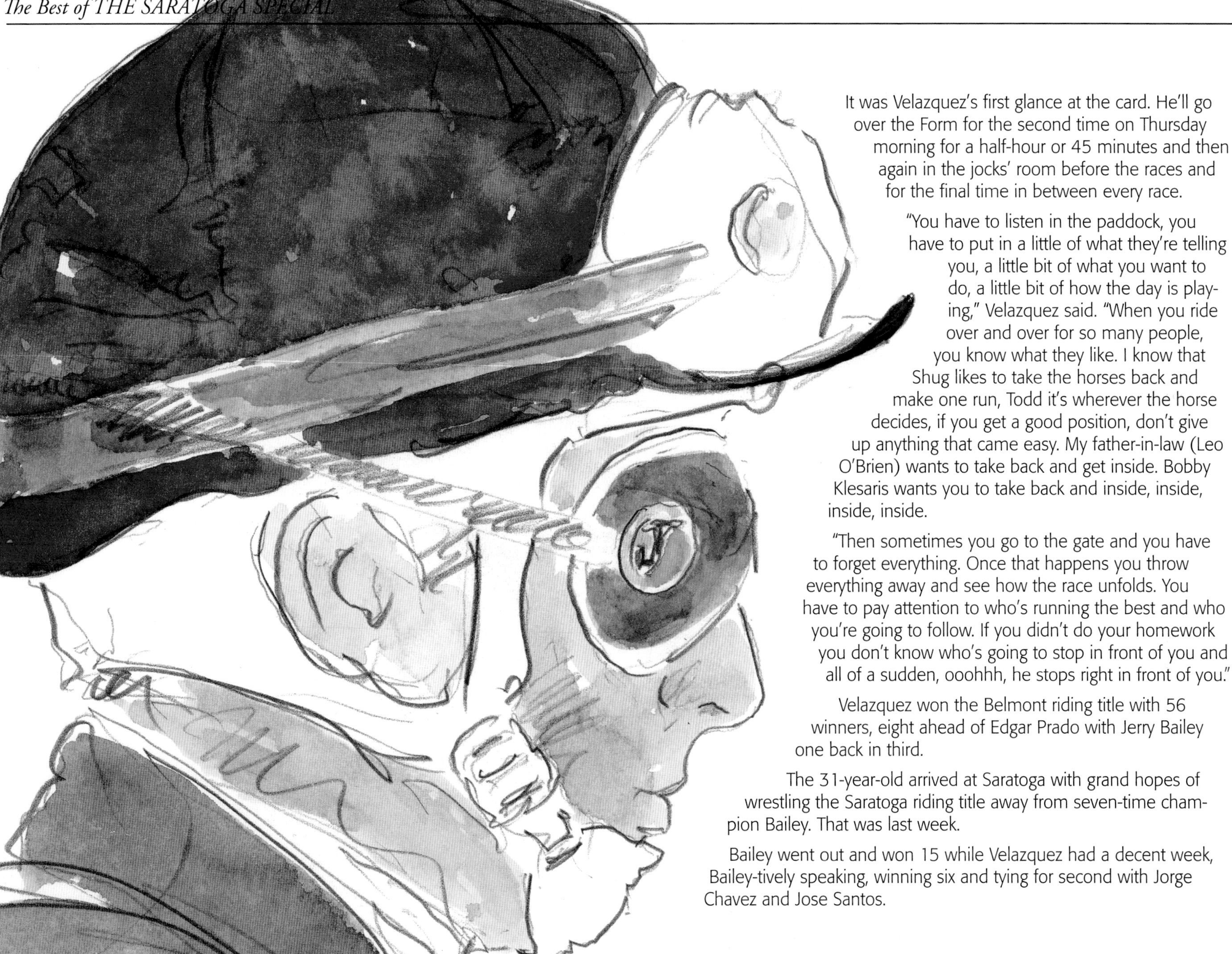

It was Velazquez's first glance at the card. He'll go over the Form for the second time on Thursday morning for a half-hour or 45 minutes and then again in the jocks' room before the races and for the final time in between every race.

"You have to listen in the paddock, you have to put in a little of what they're telling you, a little bit of what you want to do, a little bit of how the day is playing," Velazquez said. "When you ride over and over for so many people, you know what they like. I know that Shug likes to take the horses back and make one run, Todd it's wherever the horse decides, if you get a good position, don't give up anything that came easy. My father-in-law (Leo O'Brien) wants to take back and get inside. Bobby Klesaris wants you to take back and inside, inside, inside, inside.

"Then sometimes you go to the gate and you have to forget everything. Once that happens you throw everything away and see how the race unfolds. You have to pay attention to who's running the best and who you're going to follow. If you didn't do your homework you don't know who's going to stop in front of you and all of a sudden, ooohhh, he stops right in front of you."

Velazquez won the Belmont riding title with 56 winners, eight ahead of Edgar Prado with Jerry Bailey one back in third.

The 31-year-old arrived at Saratoga with grand hopes of wrestling the Saratoga riding title away from seven-time champion Bailey. That was last week.

Bailey went out and won 15 while Velazquez had a decent week, Bailey-tively speaking, winning six and tying for second with Jorge Chavez and Jose Santos.

VELAZQUEZ

"I rode a couple of horses I liked that didn't fire," Velazquez said. "You pretty much know when you'll have a good day but it's still a matter of having the horses run the way you think they'll run. Sometimes they fire, sometimes they don't. You never know. You could look at the Form and say 'wow I have six, seven really good mounts' and you go there and get blank."

Before the meet started, Velazquez talked about what it takes to win the title.

"I think I can win it, I think I have good enough business. Hopefully horses will run the way we expect them to, then we'll have a good shot," Velazquez said. "My business is not quite as good as last year. I had better horses last year. I need to take it as it goes. You want to win it but you don't want to take it too personally either."

The first week tested this mantra.

"I won six races and Bailey won 15, it was tough. I had a lot of second-calls that won including one that Bailey rode," Velazquez said. "If the week worked out the way I thought it could, I would have won 12 races but it didn't work. I have my bad days, everybody does, go home mad, you're so competitive."

Saturday night after losing the Test to Bailey by a nose was undoubtedly one of those nights.

"I was upset Saturday after the race with Carson's Hollow. I won't lie about it, I was really pissed off," Velazquez said. "I didn't like the way I rode her, well I liked the way I rode her until the quarter pole. I was upset with myself. That shouldn't happen. I didn't look inside, somebody come inside and when I saw him it was too late. Opening up the rail cost me the win."

This is the side of a jockey's life that the hecklers don't see.

"I had a bad Saturday but I have to be glad I'm here, I'm healthy. I need to go out there and do my best. When I go out there, I'm going to win, that's how I think," Velazquez said. "I'm not down at all. This is a short meet but look back at Belmont, I won two races the first week, two the second week. Then the third week, almost the fourth, I had the two accidents and I end up winning the title. That doesn't mean I'm going to win this title, but you can't get that down and that depressed about it."

There is no better race than the jockey competition at Saratoga when the best jockeys become better.

"It means a lot. This is the meet that everybody wants," Velazquez said. "It's like everybody wants to win the Derby, a Triple Crown race, a Breeders' Cup race. Everybody wants to win here. It's prestige and everybody's here. The best from the best. You want to show you can compete with the best. For myself, the pride thing. Believe me I don't care what anybody else thinks. I want it for myself. Something you can carry with you for the rest of your life."

But it isn't light. A race like this can wreak havoc with a man's psyche. Last year, Bailey won the title by setting a record with 55 wins. Velazquez won six races on the last day, a record, and finished with 52 which also broke the previous record – but didn't get the title.

"Not to get to enjoy winning six because you were too caught up with not winning the title . . . it didn't sink in until I went home and thought about it, 'I guess it was special.' And I won the stake, it should have been special," Velazquez said. "I wasn't happy at all, it just went over my head. Now I know not to take it personally, you come here and do your best and if it doesn't work, it doesn't work.

"Last year (Bailey and I) had a joke with the Rocky movies," Velazquez said. "Every day, if I won two or he won two, we'd go home and watch the Rocky movie and get up the next day and be ready to fight again."

Ding, ding, ding – five more weeks to go.

Shine Again

Nominations for the Honorable Miss closed July 20.

Weights assigned July 27. Entries closed July 31. The race goes off at 4:45 today.

It won't be until Allen Jerkens lies down for a raceday nap before the Hall of Famer knows what kind of shot Shine Again has in the $100,000 Grade III sprint.

"When I take a nap, I can always tell when a horse is really bothering me," Jerkens said. "I always say if you go seven days a week, you got to get a nap in there even if it's a short one. When I can't sleep, I know I'm really nervous about one."

Shine Again might be better than Vivarin. The 5-year-old Wild Again mare enters off two straight easy allowance wins and breaks from the rail under Jean-Luc Samyn.

"Those two races helped the bank account, $64,000, that's not hard to take, it's as if she won a $100,000 stakes," Jerkens said. "Any time they go out there and don't have to get an ass whipping, it's got to be a benefit. But at the same time, it's a shock to them the next time when they're dealing with someone who's not coming back when the other ones were. That's why you try to do a little something coming up to a race like this to let 'em know it's not going to be easy. A fast work to make sure it's not too big a contrast. She blew out pretty strong the other day, we let her roll the last eighth of a mile."

Shine Again breezed a half mile in 48 seconds on July 30, second fastest of 26 drills over the main track. Last year Shine Again giant-hunted through the Grade I Ballerina, winning by a half-length over Country Hideaway and Dream Supreme and paying $44.20 in the process.

"She's doing good from looking at her and being around her," Jerkens said. "She's always been nice, I guess she's a little more grown up, doing well, does her work, seems to know what's expected of her all the time."

Jerkens knows better than to expect too much.

"I never look at the Form. There's no sense looking at it, you're in there and you hope your horse fires a big race, if they don't fire their big race they're not going to win, that's for sure, especially in there," Jerkens said. "She's a big mare now. Naturally, they always said 5 was mature, absolute mature. If they get to be 5 and keep their desire then you have a really strong horse. If they don't have the desire, it doesn't mean nothing. Just like people, some of them just don't want to do it and some just do it no matter what. The oldtimers used to say a bird that can sing can be made to sing."

So there's only one question left to ask Jerkens.

Are you going to be able to sleep tomorrow?

"Don't know."

He let out a deep sigh, sprayed some more water on the horse path and muttered,

"And another thing, I shouldn't have any coffee in the morning."

BOBBLEHEADS

Do we have to get a bobblehead?

How many do they have? I hope they don't run out. Why can't we go to a shorter line? What are we doing now? Why can't we do it later? I'm hungry. Whoa, it's like a mountain of boxes, Dad. It is a mountain of boxes, Dad.

The boys are back in town, and they went to the races Sunday – Jerry Bailey Bobblehead Day at Saratoga. They paid their admission, dodged the spinners (what's the Beyer par for going through a turnstyle?), got their green tickets from the man in the booth and went to the Big Red Spring – and the dolls. One for Jack. One for Ryan. Open the box, tear off the bubblewrap and start bobbling.

So began a great day, and another chapter in parenthood that included – in no particular order – food, drink, lines, walking (lots of walking), music, television, horses, cars, a museum, a museum security guard and a restaurant.

The bobbleheads were just the start. Ryan had to have one. Jack – the hungry one – came along for the ride. He would have settled for a bobblepretzel.

Two minutes after taking possession of our bobbleheads, we bumped into Joan Ciampi and an NTRA Productions camera crew shooting a segment for that afternoon's Go For Wand Stakes coverage. Ciampi wanted volunteers, and the Clancy Brothers gladly stepped up.

"OK, I want you to hold up the dolls and bobble your heads. Got it?" They got it, and wound up on ESPN2 – bobbling along with the little Jerrys. Aunt Joan, back in Maryland, saw it and so did we (ah, the beauty of tape delay). Jack got a headache.

After our brush with fame, we raced to the Carousel to catch Mary Ryan's interview with Bailey (the real one). Ryan, who no longer calls his favorite jockey Jearly Bearly, had to have an autograph and out-waited a big group to get Bailey's signature across the front of The Special.

Jack was hungry – still. Two pretzels, $6. No napkins, priceless. Hold the mustard, please

Thirty minutes later, little brother Nolan (complete with stroller, juice boxes, diaper bag and snacks) joined us at the National Museum of Racing while Mom went shopping for our Saratoga house (Dad forgot a few things).

We renewed our membership, got our red tags (which were lost shortly thereafter) and went to the theater to see the Race America movie. It's old, low-tech, out of date, but wonderful just the same. MacK Miller calls young horses "orangutans," sounding somewhat like my father. Secretariat the stallion gallops in a field, a young Wayne Lukas directs a workout and an old Claiborne Farm van (where is that yellow truck?) clatters down a driveway.

We toured the museum, watched Is It True upset Easy Goer in the 1988 Breeders' Cup Juvenile and saw Secretariat capture the Triple Crown. The video systems are a big improvement over old trophies. So is the kids room.

I have come to the museum since I was Ryan's age, and don't remember much beyond a room full of silks. In the 2002 version, my children tried on their own jockey silks and flak jackets, rode a wheeled pony and had blacksmith races. Nolan even talked to a stuffed sheep – "Baaaaah."

Our final museum stop was the Hall of Fame Heroes and Seabiscuit galleries. Ryan and Jack loved the scavenger hunt, even if their zeal attracted the attention of security (we're almost done, ma'am, honest).

Ninety minutes killed and a brief rainstorm dodged, we walked back to the track. Nolan smiled, giggled, wandered into a picnic or two, charmed Charlotte from the press office and danced to a Santana song by Bobby Dick and the Sundowners. Jack and Ryan added signatures from Pat Day and Victor Carerro to Bailey's signature on The Special.

By the fifth race, Mom was still shopping and Nolan needed a nap. So we walked home. All the way home. Perhaps we were looking at that "not to scale" map, but York Avenue seems much closer on paper.

Mom (Sam is her real name and she's a candidate for sainthood for even coming to Saratoga with children ages 9, 6, and 15 months) came home with an assortment of staples including fruit – and a box of Trix.

Nolan took a nap, I went to work (briefly) and like all Saratoga winners we made dinner plans. Cliff's by the lake won the restaurant race by a nose over Bruno's and we feasted on steak, spaghetti, mozzarella sticks, chicken fingers and grilled cheese.

Stuffed and satisfied, we returned to Saratoga in time to remember my car. All those hours earlier (to beat the bobblehead lines), we had driven to the racetrack only to walk home. No problem, we'll get the car now and everything will be back where it started in the morning.

Problem. At some point in the night, NYRA security locks the gates. My Subaru spent the night at the track – safe, if a bit lonely.

"Maybe we should climb the fence, Dad," came a small, tired voice from the back of the minivan. "Do you think there are any more bobbleheads?"

Good night, boys.

This is the part we like –

Allen Jerkens

– wandering, visiting, talking, observing, learning, preaching, laughing, reflecting. We try to do a lot of things here, what we do best is walking the beat and bringing that home. We do it by the foot. And on foot.

Our feet fell to Allen Jerkens' barn Thursday morning.

Stopping by Jerkens' barn for a story isn't exactly a novel idea. Writers from Joe Palmer to Jay Hovdey have strolled through for a chat with the 73-year-old Hall of Famer. And it looked the same, sounded the same, felt the same. Jerkens, skimmed down to a T-shirt, standing at the end of the horse path with a hose in his hand, thumb creating a nozzle, spraying down the dust. Onion and Beau Purple come to his mind, Sky Beauty and Classy Mirage are compared, theories about horse sense are put out there and then contradicted.

Water sprays on your pants, Jerkens apologizes to a rider going past, checks in with a vet about tomorrow's entries, and drifts through the sport. You stand back and let the man talk.

First about nicknames.

Jerkens is the Giant Killer to some, Chief to all.

"I don't like the Giant Killer. Everybody's beaten a good horse every once in a while. I can't help what they call me. Got to be 30 years ago, Robert Grayson started calling me Chief. He was my pony rider and he started saying, 'Hey Chief, what are we going to do here?' Somebody heard him."

Girls.

"(Shine Again) is like Classy Mirage, she won the Ballerina too. We got lucky that day, Inside Information fell down leaving the gate, she got to us at the head of the stretch but she had made up too much ground. Missy's Mirage was better than her. She and Sky Beauty are the best two mares I ever had. Shine Again is right behind them. If she was to win another one like the Ballerina . . . but Sky Beauty won 10 Grade Is, that's pretty hard to top."

Longevity.

"When you're a trainer and you've been around a long time, it's the horse that does it, the fact you can keep them going a long time that's your job. That's what you're proud of. If you get great horses, anybody's going to win with them. If you can keep them going for a long time, that's a feather in your hat. It doesn't happen very often. If you keep going, something always happens, leg-wise or they quit trying."

Desire.

"You try not to run them too much or they'll lose their desire. And it helps to run in races where they're not hit too much. I think that shortens a horse's period of desire. If the jocks had a rearview mirror maybe, but sometimes it's so unnecessary to come down there six, seven lengths in front and bang on them, it's such a waste. It's such an injustice to the horse. Here he is doing everything you taught him to do and everything you want him to do and he still gets hit. If he has any brain, he might say, 'jeez what the hell did I do wrong here?' Maybe this isn't so, maybe they're not that smart, I don't know but I've always thought about that. I think if a jockey is a long ways in front, if he just keeps himself in motion just in case there's somebody he can't see making a desperate move. If he's already folded up then I don't think that's too good either because then you have to . . . if you just keep going, and glancing and looking a bit and keep yourself in motion . . . "

(Jerkens crouches over and waves the air with his hand turning back to see if anything's coming, the water from the hose makes like a jump rope).

Jerry Bailey and John Velazquez.

"I've seen Arcaro, Shoemaker, can't say anybody's better than this guy. Johnny's going to be good, another year especially the lesson he got the other day (in the Test)."

Nerves.

"I've been nervous about running a lot of horses. The little horse of my wife's (Spite The Devil) the other day, it's been so long since we've had one that could run. I was nervous when I ran Kelly Kip all the time, I never wanted him to get beat."

Training.

"Picking out the best stock is important, (Bobby) Frankel is so good at that besides being such a good trainer. You have to have the horses but they give the horses to the guys who do good. Just like the jocks, Bailey is the greatest but he rides great horses. If Bailey can't ride one day, you'll see three of his mounts win but he still is the best, he makes right decisions more times than not. The better the rider, the worse he looks when he does (screw) up."

Riding steeplechasers.

"I rode nine of them. I had a horse we bought for $75. Oh La La. 1946. I rode one of the favorites one day but he didn't jump any good that day. He schooled all right on the farm but everything was self-taught. I wanted to work for a jumping trainer but they all said, 'you don't want to be a jumping rider.' Which was true, now. So I rode my own, finished seven times of the nine, fell at the liverpool at Belmont Park."

Victories.

"Nah, finished fourth once in a five-horse field. There was a guy named Les Malen. He was riding a horse one day and he looked back and said, come on up in here, I'm not going anyplace, so I finished fourth, he knew the $200 was good for my father, we were just hustling. It was a good experience."

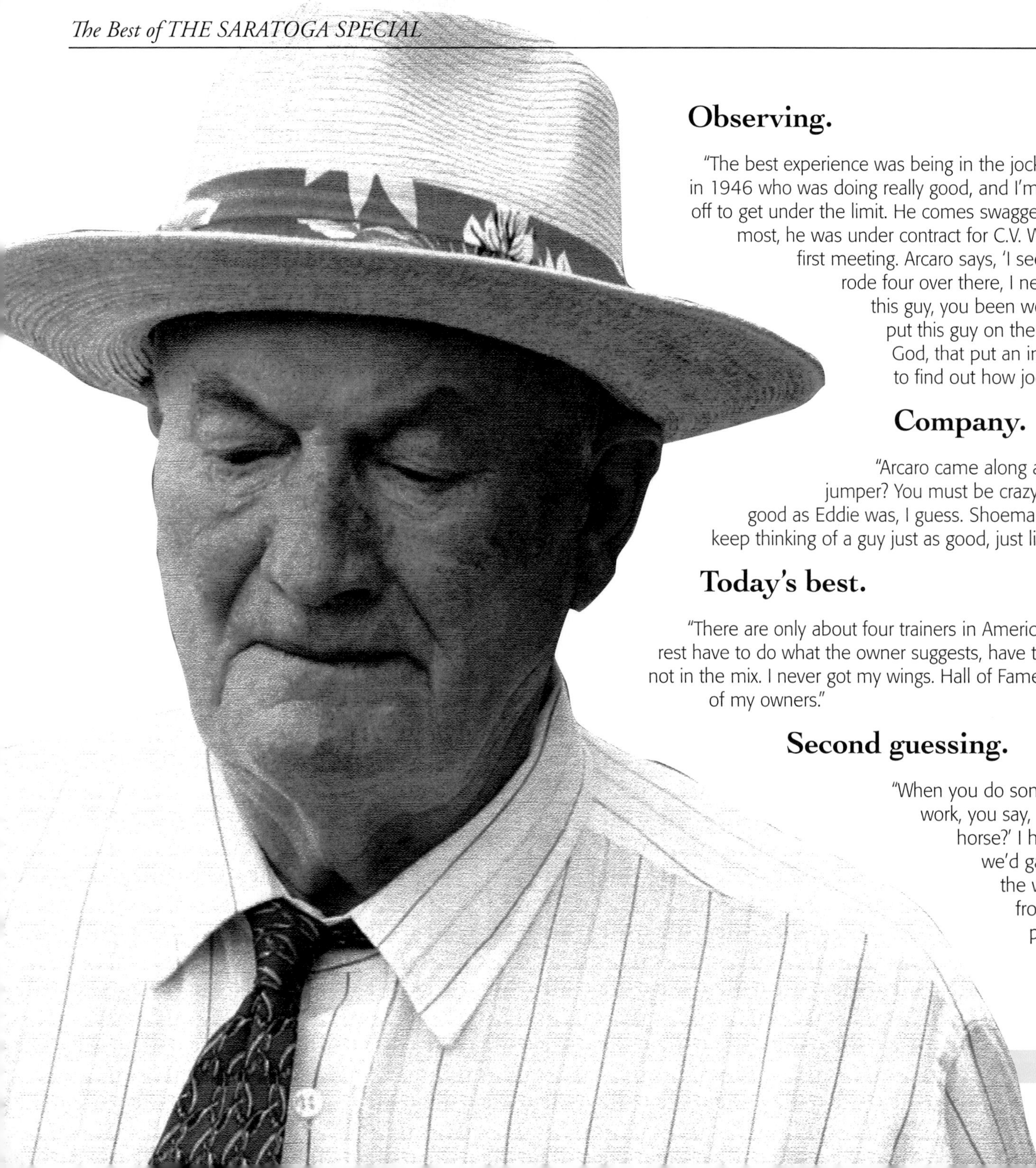

Observing.

"The best experience was being in the jocks' room. There was a guy Paul Miller, a bug rider in 1946 who was doing really good, and I'm sitting in the hot box taking a couple of pounds off to get under the limit. He comes swaggering into the jocks' room, he was 17, 18 at the most, he was under contract for C.V. Whitney. Atlantic City had just opened up for the first meeting. Arcaro says, 'I see you win a stake over there.' He says, 'Yeah, I rode four over there, I never let none of the other ones run.' I said, look at this guy, you been working on your own horses, can you imagine you put this guy on them and he's just going to see how the track was. God, that put an impression on me. I wanted to kill him. But I got to find out how jocks talk in the jocks' room."

Company.

"Arcaro came along and said, 'You're sitting in the hot box to ride a jumper? You must be crazy.' Arcaro was a good guy. (Bailey's) got to be as good as Eddie was, I guess. Shoemaker, of course, Cordero, Velasquez, Baeza. You keep thinking of a guy just as good, just like ball players."

Today's best.

"There are only about four trainers in America who could do what they want with horses, the rest have to do what the owner suggests, have to cow-toe to the owners and keep your job. I'm not in the mix. I never got my wings. Hall of Fame, Eclipse Award, doesn't mean nothing to some of my owners."

Second guessing.

"When you do something the morning of the race. If it doesn't work, you say, 'why the hell did I come out and work this horse?' I had a good white pony in the '70s. Generally we'd gallop around Clare Court once or twice, then jog the wrong way past the wire, then blow them out from the wire to the mile pole. I'd wait at the 7/8-pole and if they weren't getting them stopped I'd grab them with this pony, he could run."

Legends.

"Max Hirsch used to have this barn. I think four guys in the Hall of Fame were in this barn (Saratoga's Barn 7). Him, his son Buddy, Jimmy Rowe and me. Max Hirsch used to have a stove, a cook, everybody used to come back and eat, all the turf people, a lot of owners. The blueberry pancakes. Onion was stabled right over there . . . "

The best.

"Buster Millerick. The guy who wrote the book, Preston Burch. I always put Billy Mott with him, every once in a while someone comes along who can handle the horses real well, their work ethic is great, they can handle the owners, and they can handle the help. Like me, I get too excited to be real good."

Missing parts.

"I haven't won any of the classics, you'd think I could have won one along the way somewhere, something happens, I don't know."

Horse sense.

"We read a lot into horses. Like one horse can take another one's heart away, maybe they could if they continuously did it but I never subscribed to that theory."

Faults.

"I think I'm over-conscious of having a horse get tired. When you come around with guys who want to bet on horses, you always want to make sure he doesn't get tired. You don't want him to lose his money because he got tired. If he's not good enough, that's one thing."

Perspective.

"Sometimes they win despite of us, other times they win because of us."

LEFT BANK
1
LEFT BANK

Left Bank had changed everything. And Demi O'Byrne knew it.

"He's a great horse at 7 furlongs and now he's a great horse at 9 furlongs," O'Byrne said. "He must be one of the best horses in the country."

You could almost see O'Byrne, Michael Tabor's racing manager, writing the stallion ad copy while he stood in the winner's circle after Left Bank won the Whitney Handicap by 1 1/4 lengths over Street Cry and Lido Palace.

"A Grade I winner at 7 furlongs. A Grade I winner at 1 mile. And a Grade I winner – and track record holder – at 1 1/8 miles."

Now that's a stallion advertisement. Left Bank added that ever important last line to his page with a flawless performance in the Grade I, $750,000 stakes. Trained by Todd Pletcher and ridden by John Velazquez, Left Bank equaled Tri Jet's 28-year-old track record of 1:47. He did it in exactly 1:47.04. Not bad for a horse who was known as a 7-furlong specialist, a mile tops, going in.

The six-horse field broke in front of the stands with longshot Saint Verre outrunning Left Bank into the first turn. Velazquez slid Left Bank into Saint Verre's trail and that's where it was won.

"I put him right behind the other horse and the dirt hit him, he jumped five or six strides and right away you see there's a loop in the reins and he was off the bridle. I was like 'wow,' " Velazquez said. "I didn't think it would be that easy. When we reached the backside, I was just holding him from the mane and he didn't go anywhere."

Riding Left Bank for the 15th time in a row, Velazquez knew what to do.

"With him, I just put my hands in the middle of his neck and give him enough rein for him to be comfortable," he said. "I just kinda hold them tight with his mane and his neck and then he pulls me himself, that way I'm not in his mouth. I let him pull me and not me pull him. The longer he goes, the more quiet I am in the first part of the race. Obviously he likes it."

For Pletcher, the Whitney erased a defeat in the Met Mile May 27.

"Any time a plan comes together it's great especially when you put yourself in a situation for people to say, 'you've got a great sprinter why are you trying to run him long?' That made it all that much better. One of the reasons Mr. Tabor kept him in training at 5 was to try this," Pletcher said. "When you look at Street Cry and Lido Palace, we were trying it against the very best, it wasn't like we were picking a soft spot somewhere. It was all there. Nobody can say he stole the lead with soft fractions. He did it on a very level playing field."

Pletcher tried to explain how his sprinter became a router.

"He's one of those special athletes," Pletcher said. "He's just got a little something extra."

That might work on the stallion page too.

8 The Saratoga Special Saturday, August 31, 2002

Saratoga Results

Friday, August 30
Weather: Clear. Track: Muddy. Off Turf.

1ST, 1 1/8 MILES. F&M 3&UP. ALW. PURSE $48,000.
7 Wishful Splendor Prado E S 8.40 3.80 3.20
2 Clear Destiny Day P 4.50 3.80
3 Magic Peak Guidry M 5.80
Finish Time: 1:53
Ch.f.3, Smart Strike-Kaylem Ho, Salem
Bred by J.M.J. Stables Inc. in KY O: John Manganaro T: Nick Zito
$2 Exacta 7-2 Paid $37.60 $2 Trifecta 7-2-3 Paid $319.00

Tod Marks
Wishful Splendor

2ND 1 1/8 MILES. F&M 3&UP. MSW. PURSE $46,000.
5 Treasure Beach Santos J A 6.70 2.60 2.30
2 Alluring Velazquez J R 2.40 2.20
3 Venetian Glass Carrero V 2.90
Finish Time: 1:53 3/5
Gr./Ro.f.3, Silver Deputy-Winka, Waquoit
Bred by Green Willow Farms in MD
O: Eugene and Laura Melnyk T: Carl Domino
$2 Exacta 5-2 Paid $13.60 $2 Quinella 2-5 Paid $5.30
$2 Trifecta 5-2-3 Paid $40.60 $2 Daily Double (7-5) Paid $29.60

Dave Harmon
Treasure Beach

3RD, 1 1/8 MILES. 3&UP. MSW. PURSE $46,000.
2X Single Rainbow Prado E S 12.00 4.10 2.90
6 Addicks Day P 2.70 2.30
1 Tama Chavez J F 3.30
Finish Time: 1:52 1/5
Ch.c.3, Thunder Gulch-Pleasant Sunshine, Pleasant Colony
Bred by Elia, Simon, Wallace, White in KY
O: Dattt Stable T: Phil Serpe
$2 Exacta 2-6 Paid $25.20 $2 Trifecta 2-6-1 Paid $89.00

Tod Marks
Single Rainbow

4TH, 1 1/8 MILES. 3&UP. CLM 75,000-65,000. PURSE $46,000.
2 Pleasant Divorce Chavez J F 8.00 4.10 2.80
5 It's So Simple Carrero V 3.70 2.60
1A Top Bunk Luzzi M J 3.20
Finish Time: 1:51 1/5
Ch.g.4, Pleasant Tap-Divorce Testimony, Vice Regent
Bred by Edward Evans in KY O: Daniel Borislow T: John Scanlan
$2 Exacta 2-5 Paid $22.00 $2 Quinella 2-5 Paid $11.40
$2 Trifecta 2-5-1 Paid $105.00
$2 Pick Three (5-2-2) 3 Correct Paid $123.50

Dave Harmon
Pleasant Divorce

5TH, 1 1/8 MILES. 3&UP. ALW. PURSE $52,000.
5 Giving Noreen Castellano J 32.00 14.00 3.50
6 Reina Blanca Velazquez J R 9.30 3.30
1A Indy Glory Chavez J F 2.20
Finish Time: 1:53 4/5
Dk.B./Br.f4, Valid Wager-Eloquent Leader, Mr. Leader
Bred by Mockingbird Farm Inc. in FL
O: WinStar Farm T: Elliott Walden
$2 Exacta 5-6 Paid $216.00 $2 Trifecta 5-6-1 Paid $621.00
$2 Pick Three (2-2-5) 3 Correct Paid $604.00

Dave Harmon
Giving Noreen

6TH, 7 FURLONGS. FILLIES 2YO. MSW. PURSE $45,000.
5 Feather Boa Velazquez J R 32.00 13.00 3.30
7 Cold One Chavez J F 8.90 3.10
1A Bonay Prado E S 2.10
8 Holiday Lady Carrero V 2.30
Deadheat for third. Finish Time: 1:25 2/5
Ch.f.2, Saint Ballado-Runaway Spy, Mt. Livermore
Bred by Ramona and Victor DiVivo in KY
O: Peachtree Stable T: Todd Pletcher
$2 Exacta 5-7 Paid $192.00 $2 Trifecta 5-7-1 Paid $251.00
$2 Trifecta 5-7-8 Paid $434.00
$2 Pick Three (2-5-5) 3 Correct Paid $953.00

Tod Marks
Feather Boa

7TH, 1 1/8 MILES. 4&UP. ALW. PURSE $56,000.
6 Pleasant Breeze Carrero V 7.50 3.70 2.60
2 Full Flow Prado E S 6.50 3.40
1X Ground Storm Bailey J D 2.60
Finish Time: 1:50 4/5
Dk.B./Br.g.7, Pleasant Tap-Sleepy Time, Turkoman
Bred by Robert Masterson in KY
O: William Cliffton Jr. T: James Bond
$2 Exacta 6-2 Paid $51.50 $2 Trifecta 6-2-1 Paid $122.50
$2 Daily Double (5-6) Paid $121.50
$2 Pick Three (5-5-6) 3 Correct Paid $1,149.00

8TH, 7 FURLONGS. FILLIES 2YO. STAKES. PURSE $200,000.
THE SPINAWAY (GR. I)
1 Awesome Humor Day P 8.40 4.30 3.60
9 Forever Partners Velazquez J R 3.90 3.60
7 Midnight Cry Perret C 9.70
Finish Time: 1:24 1/5
Dk.B./Br.f.2, Distorted Humor-Horns Gray, Pass the Tab
Bred by Dr. Naveed Chowhan in KY
O: WinStar Farm T: Elliott Walden
$2 Exacta 1-9 Paid $31.40 $2 Trifecta 1-9-7 Paid $479.00
$2 Pick Six (2-2-5-5-6-1) 5 Correct Paid $1,065.00

Dave Harmon
Pleasant Breeze

Saratoga Leaders

Through Aug. 30

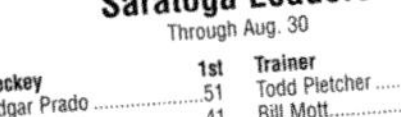

Jockey	1st
Edgar Prado	51
Jerry Bailey	41
John Velazquez	37
Jorge Chavez	25
Jose Santos	23
Pat Day	22
Richard Migliore	20
Shaun Bridgmohan	14
Mark Guidry	12
Javier Castellano	12
Victor Carrero	11

Trainer	1st
Todd Pletcher	18
Bill Mott	17
James Bond	9
Bobby Frankel	9
Claude McGaughey	9
Nick Zito	9
Gary Contessa	8
Richard Dutrow Jr	8
Dale Romans	7
Linda Rice	6
Elliott Walden	6

Tod Marks
Awesome Humor

9TH, 7 FURLONGS. 3&UP. MSW. NY BRED. PURSE $41,000.
11 Indougherty'shonor Espinoza J L 42.80 12.40 7.80
4 Senor Mac Prado E S 3.60 3.10
2 Oatka Justa Prince Carrero V 6.70
Finish Time: 1:26 1/5
Ch.g.3, Anjiz-Premiere Revue, Premiership
Bred by Susan Feather in NY O: Susan Feather T: John Gross
$2 Exacta 11-4 Paid $191.00 $2 Trifecta 11-4-2 Paid $2,157.00
$2 Superfecta 11-4-2-6 Paid $7,317.00
$2 Daily Double (1-11) Paid $277.50
$2 Pick Three (6-1-11) 3 Correct Paid $892.00
$2 Pick Four (5-6-1-11) 4 Correct Paid $28,760.00
$2 Consolation Daily Double (1-5) Paid $8.50

Saratoga Attendance: 17,209 Mutuel Pool: $2,748,354.00

Dave Harmon
Indougherty'shonor

How We Did

RACE 1: Our third choice, WISHFUL SPLENDOR, returned $8.80 to win.
RACE 2: We had the $13.60 exacta here with our second choice TREASURE BEACH ($6.70) and our top pick ALLURING (who let us down as the heavy favorite). The Double came back $29.60.
RACE 3: Our top selection, ADDICKS, finished third.
RACE 4: Our third choice, IT'S SO SIMPLE, was second.
RACE 5: Our second choice after scratches, REINA BLANCA, returned $9.30 to place.
RACE 6: FEATHER BOA, our second choice after a scratch, came home by 2 1/2 lengths and lit up the board at $32 to win.
RACE 7: The only one of our four picks remaining after scratches, FULL FLOW, paid $6.50 to place.
RACE 8: Our third choice, FOREVER PARTNERS, finished second as the favorite and paid $3.90 to place.
RACE 9: Top choice Senor Mac came up short in the stretch and finished second, paying $3.60 to place.

– Pete Fornatale and Frank Scatoni

RESULTS PAGE FUN

Some of the best feedback we've gotten all summer came from Saturday's "every-winner" results page. The idea was an on-deadline whim, but has a base in fact and history. Other Saratoga publications – back when The Special's editors were pups – used to do the same thing, but gave it up. We'll keep trying to fit them all, but won't make any guarantees. Anybody know a sponsor?

Thoroughbred Retirement Foundation

Walking around the Saratoga sales ground looking at high-dollar yearlings falls at one end of the horse racing equation. The high end.

Sitting down and talking to John Stuart about the Thoroughbred Retirement Foundation sits at the other end. The low end. Pure potential here, and spent product there. Polar opposites with the racetrack sitting right in the middle. All three are getting closer.

Stuart, a consignor, owner and lifelong horseman, joined the TRF and later became its president after executive director Diane Pikulski convinced him to get on board. Stuart deals in the stallion season and share business – the TRF's main fundraising tool.

"I always wanted to get involved in a horse charity and this was the first time I was asked so I signed up," Stuart said. "I worked a little in the fundraising, got really interested and they asked me to put together a committee and some fundraising to start a farm at the Blackburn Correctional Facility (in Kentucky)."

The TRF accomplished that goal and started making more.

"It's the fastest growing charity in the horse business. It has the second largest endowment in the horse business, behind (the Grayson/Jockey Club Research Foundation)," Stuart said. "Now a lot of the establishment organizations like Keeneland, Churchill Downs, NTRA are looking at us to see that the money is spent wisely and the public feels like the horses are being taken care of properly."

And that's the mission. To keep horses from slaughter and to see them grow old, whether as riding horses or pasture pets.

"The TRF has done a great job in the awareness of the problem. Our founding chairman, Monique Kohler, is an advertising person and she's got a real gift for it," Stuart said. "No charity in the horse business has had the articles like we've had in the New York Times, the Globe, USA Today, GQ. Those are places the racetrack doesn't get to."

How important is it? Ask the people who make a living off the motion of their wheels.

"It's good because there are so many horses with nowhere to place, it's good they find a home for them," trainer Bobby Frankel said. "I just gave three horses away. They were really good racehorses, they were stallions but nobody wants them unless they're by Mr. Prospector so I had to give them away. They're going to make them riding horses."

Frankel trains over 100 horses, finding the old-timers a place to go is tough.

"I got one now, Martini Quais, he's running at 9 years old. He's won like $600,000 and he's still a horse. What do I do with him? They're all good horses and I won't drop them down. I end up keeping them until I find them a home, it costs me a lot of money sometimes. The three I gave away, I probably had them for six, seven months, just feeding them at Santa Anita. Finding them homes is the toughest job I have, what hurt them is the duel hemisphere breeding. I used to be able sell these kinds of horses to different countries."

Frankel obviously deals with the high end of the equation. He rarely has geldings anywhere in his California or New York barns. The TRF tries to make a difference for the geldings and the retired broodmares sliding down the chute.

"The ultimate goal is to for the racetracks to provide a safety net," Stuart said. "A couple of stalls on the backstretch where they can go, a local committee who will call the TRF, and some fundraising to provide for the horses that come from those racetracks."

Since its creation in 1982, the TRF has involved correctional facilities. Prison inmates cared for the ex-racehorses, and learned a new trade in the process. New York's Wallkill State Correctional Facility was the TRF's first home, and the program expanded to include Maryland's Charles Hickey School (a youth correctional facility), the Blackburn Correctional Facility in Kentucky and the Marion Correctional Institute in Florida.

The next step will involve other facilities and a new focus.

Horseman John Hettinger gave the TRF a farm, now called the Exceller Farm, in upstate New York. Exceller houses 30-40 retired horses in training for other careers under farm manager Michele Oren. Stuart envisions other similar facilities, and announced the pending creation of farms in Montpelier, Va. and at the Kentucky Horse Park.

"The prisons are great places to keep the horses but they aren't a very good place to adopt them out of, so we have two new facilities which have something in common – they get a hell of a lot of tourists," Stuart said. "We're going to build a new facility at the Kentucky Horse Park where we'll have our headquarters too. There, we'll always have horses available for adoption. We're going to have another facility like that at Montpelier. It's awaiting Montpelier's final approval. We'll have a couple of 100 acres there and have 100 to 150 horses there always available for adoption."

Montpelier has a long history in racing. Once the home of U.S. President James Madison, the National Historic Trust property hosts a steeplechase meet every year and was at one time the base of legendary owner/breeder Marion du Pont Scott's Montpelier racing and breeding stable.

"We have the retired guys who are permanently done at the prison," said Stuart. "The guys that have a chance for a new start will go to the Exceller Farm in New York, the Kentucky Horse Park and Montpelier. We'd probably have 100 to 150 in training at any one time."

Training means taking a racehorse, getting it sound and then turning it into a pleasure horse.

"We think there are 6,000 Thoroughbreds being slaughtered a year. Maybe half of those have to be euthanized anyway so the idea is to get them euthanized without going to the slaughterhouse," Stuart said. "The rescue groups around the country can absorb the other 3,000. When we get this thing running at the max in a year or two we'll be able to absorb that many through our adoption and retirement homes and working with other groups. In Kentucky and the east coast we're making good progress. I don't think many are falling through the cracks.

The people who participate don't want to see that.

"The horses are the primary ingredient, none of us would be here without them, given that fact, it's only right that we treat them with a little respect when they retire," said jockey Pat Day. "I'm happy for the efforts that are being made to insure that they don't wind up at the killer, that they grow old gracefully in a nice lush paddock with a little TLC and some attention."

Frankel agreed: "I like to reward them for rewarding me."

PAT DAY

You know a guy's had a good career when a calculator doesn't have enough digits to tally up his career earnings.

Pat Day's career paycheck totaled $263,877,888 before he won the Amsterdam with Listen Here at Saratoga on Saturday. Not that Day's ever pulled out the counting machine.

The 48-year-old jockey quietly chips away at the all-time earnings record set by Chris McCarron who retired earlier this summer. Through Saturday's racing, Day trailed by $329,910, not that he knew it while giving Listen Here another patient ride.

"Out there after the race, (ESPN television reporter) Jeannine Edwards told me I was within a half-million or somewhere around in there. I didn't know that," Day said. "Believing it comes to pass it will be a tremendous accomplishment. I don't gauge by where everybody else is or what everybody has done, I just merely reflect on what the Lord has blessed me with."

Horse flesh for one.

Wild Again, Easy Goer, Awesome Again, Theatrical, Unbridled, Summer Squall, Flanders, Dance Smartly, Cat Thief and on and on. From Brush, Colo., Day joined the Hall of Fame in 1991.

"I have to pinch myself, it's like a dream. It's been an incredible ride and continues to be an incredible ride," Day said. "I thank God for directing my footsteps into the horse racing industry. When a horse responds like Listen Here did it's great fun. I'd be lying to you if I said I get all excited about coming in here and riding eight or nine every day."

At Saratoga, Day quietly comes to work and does his job away from the direct focus put on Jerry Bailey, John Velazquez, Edgar Prado and others.

"Day in, day out I still enjoy it tremendously," Day said. "Obviously not like I did 20 years ago but the enthusiasm is still there and the desire to compete and participate and certainly the thrill of victory is ever so sweet. I think it might be sweeter today than in years past because I recognize, realize that somewhere in the . . . well, I'm sure I'm closer to the end than the beginning of my career. Knowing that, you don't know which victory might be the last so it makes each victory that much sweeter."

With McCarron retiring at the top of his game, Day churns on.

"I know Chris had some serious injuries through the course of his career and he also had to watch his weight. I've been so very fortunate with regard to injuries. I've had few injuries and spent minimal days on the sidelines. I've never had to watch my weight a day in my life. I've been very, very fortunate in all regards and continue to be blessed with opportunities to ride good horses."

Day knows that he's fortunate to be riding good horses on the A circuit.

"I heard someone ask (Angel) Cordero one day, "What's the first to go, your knees, your back . . . ? He said, "Your stock." You know what I mean? So as long as I'm healthy, feeling good and able to get on good horses, then I hope the Lord will allow me to stay in and participate."

Check the results from Monmouth Park (the Haskell is worth $600,000 to the winner) and grab the calculator because....

....Day may have passed McCarron Sunday afternoon.

HALL OF FAME

Same shade, different meaning.

How can a navy sport coat be so nondescript in the paddock and so sentimental at the Hall of Fame induction? It's all in the patch.

Every Hall of Fame member receives a navy sport coat with a Hall of Fame patch on the left lapel when they're inducted into racing's shrine on Union Avenue.

Once a year, they come together.

There's trainer Tommy Kelly, steeplechase jockey Jerry Fishback, D. Wayne Lukas across the way. Mikey Smithwick eases in without his blazer. Jerry Bailey sits down near Bill Mott. Pat Day wears an American flag tie and takes up the same row as Mott. Braulio Baeza checks his watch while Allen Jerkens tries to forget his horses back at the barn. Ron Turcotte, ah Ron Turcotte, smiles from the aisle. Jonathan Sheppard laughs with Charlsie Cantey talking about the old days in her keynote speech. Bobby Frankel, in a tweed blazer, slips in halfway through the ceremony.

Welcome to the tailor's needle Noor, Jack Westrope, Serena's Song, Bud Delp, and Cigar. Cantey was flawless in her opening speech, taking the audience through her career in horse racing and in so doing recalling the ever changing face of horse racing. The five inductees certainly span the timeline.

Noor rode in on the horse of yesteryear ticket. He belted Citation four times, winning 12 races from 1947-50. Colonel Mike Howard accepted the award on behalf of his great grandfather Charles Howard. In a rare presentation from the presentee, a scrapbook on Noor, compiled by Charles Howard's wife Carmela, was given to the Hall of Fame.

Westrope was described as "a jockey's jockey." Is there any other way? He rode 2,467 winners over his 26-year career and died doing it. Westrope was killed in the 1958 Hollywood Oaks when King Ranch's Well Away bolted into the inside rail. Westrope, from Baker, Montana, won his first race when he was 12 and won the national riding title at 15. His widow Terry Chafee and daughter Pamela Westrope Donner accepted the honor.

Wayne Lukas instantly picked the program up when he presented Serena's Song's award to Bob and Beverly Lewis. Like always, Lukas was flawless as he pounced on all the right words and spoke three octaves higher than anybody else on the card.

His description of Serena's Song included the line of the day, "She had the elegance of Grace Kelly, she had the moves of Ginger Rogers, and she had the charisma of Marilyn Monroe. For you people that are a lot younger and don't have a clue as to what I'm talking about, she had the moves of Janet Jackson and the charisma of Britney Spears."

Not often you hear those five names in the same sentence, especially at Racing's Hall of Fame.

Bud Delp came next. The Maryland trainer won more than 3,500 races and conditioned Spectacular Bid to three championships. The 70-year-old trainer talked about his entire career from his first winner in 1962, to driving Bill Shoemaker to the airport after Spectacular Bid set a track record at Delaware Park.

Fittingly, Cigar finished it all off. Owned by the late Allen Paulson and his wife Madeleine, Cigar was horse racing in the 1990s. The son of Palace Music won 16 in a row, tying the modern record set by Citation.

C.V. Whitney couldn't have dreamed about today's Hall of Fame Day when he presided over the opening ceremonies in Congress Park in 1951. It's a day to celebrate the sport.

Nobody did that better than Pat Day.

The Hall of Fame jockey (1991) pulled on his navy blazer, listened to the speeches, reflected about his career and then went out and won the National Museum of Racing Hall of Fame Stakes on Quest Star for trainer Elliott Walden.

"It's extra special to be a member of that unique group of individuals, man and beast alike," Day said. "Certainly to participate as a Hall of Famer in the induction and a little bit in the autograph signing, then the icing on the cake was to win the stake named after the Museum and Hall of Fame."

Nothing was lost on Day.

"I think Charlsie Cantey got it kicked off on the right foot. It set the tone and stirred up some old memories," Day said. "Her reflecting on her beginning caused me to reflect on mine. I just sat there very appreciative of where I am. I covered a lot of ground from humble beginnings to my first victory at Prescott Downs to Wild Again to the Derby of '92.

"It's the epitome of anyone's life in any sport to be recognized and inducted into the Hall of Fame," Day said. "This isn't a job, this is my hobby and I'm able to make a living at it. I've always looked at it like that, if it ever became a job, job . . . it's not the same today as it was 10 years ago but I still enjoy it, certainly days like today just fire up the enthusiasm."

After the race, Day stood with Walden and Delp. The jockey was wearing yellow and brown silks, but the blue jacket wasn't far from his mind.

"Oh, I keep it hanging in the closet. It's got its spot, you know right there," Day said reaching for air in front of him.

"It just goes with me. Going to Saratoga? Gotta take the sport coat."

As you know,

....this is a family newspaper and we'll be the first to say we probably run too many personal columns. By the time you're done reading the season's worth, you'll know about every horse I ever galloped, every car I ever crashed, every friend who's sleeping on my floor, and every crazy thought that came through my head during these six weeks and pretty much my whole 32 years.

I don't necessarily think this is what you want to read, it's just the only thing I can come up with when it's all crashing down around me. That's what happens when you get desperate. You go to what you're comfortable with.

So I took my nephews, Ryan and Jack, to the Hall of Fame induction. They were cooped up in a rented house with their mother, an aunt, a cousin and their 15-month-old brother. They wanted to go to the Hall of Fame, how hard can this be?

"It's hot. It's hot. It's hot," both of them tell me when they climb on top of 500 newspapers and a week's worth of clothes in the back seat. Jack pulled a shirt from the pile and pulled it across his waist like a seat belt. Sam (their mother) stood on the sidewalk, arms folded across her chest.

"Don't look," I plead with her.

"Just drive carefully."

No problem.

We zip over Lake Avenue across town and make a parking space across the street by Barn 6.

"Uncle Sean, can we park here?" asks 9-year-old Ryan.

"Yes, it's fine, just get out."

I check the sign and measure the distance my bumper hangs into yellow paint. No time to worry, we zip across the street and to the sales grounds.

"Dad says he's going to bring us to the horse sales," Ryan says as we scat through the crowd and toward the pavilion.

We walk upstairs and look for a seat.

"It's too high up here, can't we go downstairs?" one of them asks.

OK, back downstairs and into the bottom level.

We find three seats just off to the side of the Hall of Fame member section.

"Yeah, this is better."

Tom Voss walks through the seats with a stopwatch hanging from a pocket.

"Hey, there's Mr. Boss. He's in the Hall of Fame?" Ryan asks.

"Uh, no, he's here for the festivities like us."

"Huh," answers Ryan. The 6-year-old Jack hasn't said a word since the "Hot" remarks.

I point out Ron Turcotte to Ryan.

"Whoa, that's Ron Turcotte."

Jack twists the plastic name tag on the back of Ryan's seat and kicks the woman next to him.

"That triangle thing up there is kinda like the scoreboard?" asks Ryan looking at the, well, I guess it is the scoreboard. No numbers will flash until Tuesday night.

"Hey Ryan, there's D. Wayne Lukas. See him?"

"Where? I can't see him."

"Over there on the other side of the stage."

"The guy with the really dark glasses."

"I like it, this is good. I read it last night too."

– George Steinbrenner, on The Saratoga Special.

"Yeah."

"Is he blind or something?'

I fall on the floor while Ryan tries to figure out what's so funny.

Jack is oblivious as he wiggles in his seat like a discovered earthworm.

"Ryan, see Pat Day?"

"That's Pat Day? I've never seen him like that before."

The coat and tie throw him off.

At some point, Dick Hamilton welcomed us, John van Stade told us about the museum, Ed Bowen introduced Charlsie Cantey and Cantey told us stories. Noor's plaque went up, Serena's Song, Jack Westrope, Bud Delp and finally Cigar became official Hall of Fame members.

My boys were in the Hall of Fame of boredom.

Ryan borrowed my note pad and scribbled, "I can tell Jack is bored." Jack had twisted his shoelaces, poked his brother, crumpled the program into a telescope.

"When does it end?" Jack asked again.

Soon, Jack, soon.

Finally the Cigar team posed for photos and the closing remarks came and went. We bolted for the door and a parking ticket.

"What did you think boys?"

"It was better than school," Ryan said. "But, I kinda wish they brought Cigar."

Last year's quote of the meet was "Don't tell your boss" from trainer Allen Jerkens as he dumped a scoop of oats into the feedtub of Buddy, trainer Jimmy Picou's lead pony.

A year later, the feedshare continues.

"I said to him the other day, 'I know this is you. You had a lot to do with this,' " Picou said as Buddy bounced home from the track full of energy.

"Oh, did he get high?" Jerkens asked, innocently.

"I think he gives him one going and coming," Picou said. "He goes past with the wheelbarrow and scoops it out each way."

About that time, Jerkens strolled up on his pony.

"Oh, we only give him a little alfalfa and a little oats," Jerkens said. "When you don't have something for him, he pins his ears."

I like what I do more than I dislike getting hurt. You know what I mean?"

MIGLIORE

Yeah, Richard, I do.

Richard Migliore hit the ground on Sunday, caught up in a collision in the Jim Dandy stretch while riding Iron Deputy. He was back on his beat Tuesday morning. In sneakers and a ball cap and ready to fight again. His right arm was sore and swollen, his ribs sore to the touch.

"I love riding horses a lot more than I worry about the consequences," Migliore said in between good wishes from Ray Ganpath, Filiberto Leon and a car full of grooms. "And that won't change. The day that changes is the day I'll ask you for a job writing a newspaper."

Well, that's exactly why I write a newspaper. That day came.

For 13 years, steeplechasing was all I cared about. I knew I had had too many head injuries but I wanted to ride races more than I worried about my head. Eventually I was worrying more about my head than I was enjoying riding races. Then, retiring was a very easy decision to make. Before that I couldn't figure out how I was ever going to stop. As it starts changing, you start to understand it.

Migliore isn't at that stage. Chris McCarron was. Blythe Miller might be.

Migliore won his first race in 1980 on a horse called – Good Trip. It's certainly been that for the Brooklyn native who has won over 3,500 races. With those trips to the winner's circle come trips to the hospital. Like rent or taxes or jury duty, it's the payment for the luxury.

McCarron retired this summer after winning more money than any jockey in history. It had changed. Miller suffered a concussion here last week and it very well could be time for the active leader in steeplechase victories. But I don't know. Deciding when it's time for somebody else is like deciding on whom someone else should love. She'll know, just like I knew, and McCarron knew and Migliore will know some day.

"You have to ride every horse, every race with the same desire and the same focus, your focus can't be 'I gotta get around on this one' it's got to be 'how am I going to get him to win?' " Migliore said. "At Aqueduct this winter, I had four horses break down with me in a 10-day span. That starts playing with your head. This time, I'm just anxious to get back on."

Getting back on seems easy when you want to get back on. Every jockey knows the danger and knows the stress the career choice puts on family and friends. Even fans. If you looked around Saratoga after Iron Deputy stumbled on Sunday, you know what I mean. The crowd was stunned like it always is when a jockey goes down. And Migliore's family wasn't even there. His wife Carmela, sons Joey, Philip, Luciano and daughter Gabrielle were at home.

"Joey was all excited to watch the Jim Dandy, so they all sat down and ooooooohhhhhhh. They're down there (home in Floral Park) and my wife gets all shook up. When I got loaded in the ambulance I told the guy 'someone has to call my wife and tell her I'm talking, I'm banged up, but I'm OK.' So they got Father Romano who I've known for years, he got hold of her and then Rick Violette, Mike Hushion, everybody was handling it.

"When I got out of the cat scan I called home and talked to my wife and got her calmed down. She said, 'please talk to Joey,' so he got on the phone, he's crying and you know when kids cry, I wanted to cry. I said, 'I'm OK, it's part of the job . . .' He said, 'I just want to see you.' Like ripping my heart out of my chest. He used to always talk about being a jockey until the day I broke my arm (in 1999). He was watching that, he still likes the horses and loves the racing but he doesn't talk about being a jockey anymore."

Like they say, it's not a sport for the faint of heart.

"I'm sore, I'm bruised. As far as I know, nothing's broken," Migliore said. "On Sunday I felt like I had been run over by a train. My ribs are sore but at least I'm getting my air now. When I stopped rolling, I thought I had broken my arm because I couldn't feel my hand but I had searing pain in my forearm. When I tried to move it, my fingers were so thick and swollen already, I thought, 'I broke this arm again.' By the time I got to the hospital I started to get some sensations back in my fingers. I still don't know how it swelled up so quick. I just assume because of the plates, there's no give so maybe I jarred it just right."

Migliore's arm looks like a balloon you get at the fair, the kind a clown could twist into an animal shape. Lines and dents, bulges and swells. He flexes it and feels it with his other hand.

"(Sitting out) stings, especially in Saratoga because you look forward to riding up here all year," Migliore said. "I feel like I'm riding really well and you just don't want anything to mess with my momentum. I took yesterday off and chances are I'll take off Wednesday but hopefully by the weekend I'll be riding again."

He's had plenty of help getting him back to the jocks' room.

"It's been incredible. I can't even say enough things about the people who showed up at the hospital, the phone calls . . . it makes you realize how many people care about you and how many friends you really have," Migliore said. "It was overwhelming. I guess at one point at Saratoga Hospital, they brought out a cart with cookies and coffee for all the people in the waiting area."

And his wife and kids weren't even in town yet.

"The lady told me, 'Boy, you have a lot of cousins, and brothers, and sisters, and sister-in-laws, and brother-in-laws," Migliore said. "Shaun Bridgmohan (from Jamaica) told them he was my nephew, the lady looked at him and said, 'you sure don't look alike.' "

Migliore doesn't expect to feel any tepidation when he does get back to it.

"It's not like I've missed a lot of time and it's a big traumatic thing," Migliore said. "It's one of those things; you take a tumble,

...you make sure all the parts are working and you go again."

Nothing like walking in for the feature and finding out who won all the early races.

Sometimes it's good, sometimes it's bad, well not ever bad but sometimes dull or disappointing, you know if Bailey wins four, Velazquez wins two, Prado, Chavez and Santos . . . they're my boys but after a while, they see you coming and start reciting the lines . . . he fired when I asked him . . . it's easy when you ride that kind . . . well Sean, he was the favorite . . . you better ask them . . . no, I wasn't nervous . . . you're the writer . . .

Yesterday Dennis Carr won the seventh. Now that's cool. Carr was around Red Terrill's barn back in the early 1990s. There was a slew of us there, Orlando, Dave, Tim, Red . . . some crew. Dennis was riding races, his dad was working in the jocks' room, he was doing OK, never dominating but holding his own. He packed it all up and went to Northern California for a better shot. Following him was easy after knowing him here.

Carr came home this year and has been riding the New York circuit for about five months. I caught up with him standing outside the Oklahoma track the other morning. One thing about Carr, he tells it like it is. He's realistic and entertaining all at the same time.

"I went out there at the beginning of '95 for a chance to ride more horses. I always wanted to try California, southern California. I went to Del Mar meet in 1997. It was a brutal seven weeks. I went 1-for-65 for the meet but that might be good compared to what this meet is going to look like."

Longshots in the last have been the jockey's staples at Saratoga before he won the seventh Thursday on Private Port for Carlos Martin.

"It worked out in the long run because after the Del Mar meet I headed back to Northern California and I had gotten on a lot of horses down there. I rode probably 90 percent of those horses when they shipped up north to run on the grass. I won a bunch of stakes and allowance races on the grass just because I went down there so it went from what I thought was a total disaster to a great move in the long run."

You can almost see Carr's mind, thinking somehow coming to Saratoga in 2002 will land him some live horses down the road, whether it's Belmont in the fall, Aqueduct in the winter, or going out of town for a stakes.

"It was a good run for me going out there but all my family and friends are back here, it still didn't feel like home. Every holiday is a long-distance phone call or a long-distance trip if you want to see anybody. This place is one of the major things that brought me back. I've always

Dennis Carr

SPECIAL OCCASION

loved this place, like home, my dad was born and raised here so we always had family and friends here. It always felt like home."

Not a bad home and certainly not a bad spot for the summer.

"Out there in the summer time, we run these fairs from mid-June to the beginning of September. Every two weeks you're in a different spot, bouncing around the Bay area. Some of these tracks, you come in and say 'wow, it's time to really suck it up and do what you have to do.' On top of it all, some of the jocks' rooms are probably no bigger than that van but we get the simulcasts from Saratoga and it's like, 'Oh, man I can't believe it.' That's when being homesick really kicked in."

Regrets don't seem to be in Carr's thought process.

"The whole experience out there was great. I loved the area and met a lot of good people. You go one way and you go to the beaches, go the other way and in three hours you're up in Lake Tahoe or Reno in the mountains but this is home."

Home doesn't always mean easy.

"Business is tough, I'm not going to sugarcoat it, it's been brutal. That might be the easiest part knowing it was going to be tough. You've just got to keep pushing. Push long enough and one of those doors will open, and maybe you'll land on a nice horse. Being out there, I rode a lot of horses and won a lot of races, about 1,000 races out there in the seven years I was there. I think it gave me a better foundation to come back and give this another try.

"This is basically a working vacation. As much as you want to be out there you can't force things to happen. I have to look at it as a working vacation and try to get into some outfits and be able to ride more when we get down to Belmont. The biggest thing is to try to not let it get to me. As much as I want to do well here, win a couple of races, but the more I let it bother me, the tougher it will be."

Carr was 0-for-9 going into Thursday's card after winning 11 races earlier this year. Private Port was his first official winner at the meet but don't think Carr's been idle.

"I met my girlfriend Alisa Leone up here, 11 years ago. We went out for a couple of years and then went our separate ways. Just recently in the last year and a half we've been together again.

"Friday (July 26) was 11 years since we met. The first night we ever went out, we went to The Waterfront. I stopped in and said, 'Listen I don't know if you need reservations but I need to reserve a table.' They didn't really want to do it so I said 'I want to reserve a table out on the patio because that's where we sat the first time. It's a special occasion.' They made sure I had my table.

"I told her I had a little surprise for her but we had to get through dinner. The first thing I ever bought her was an ID bracelet, it had her name on the front with an engraving on the back. So after dinner I pulled out a box and she could tell it was a bracelet. It had her name on the front and an engraving on the back again. So I said, 'you know I got you one 11 years ago and I thought it was time for a new one.' I know she's thinking 'man, OK, another bracelet,' she's probably about to hit the ceiling. I say, 'I just got a different engraving on the back' so she flips it over and it says "Will you marry me?" Her jaw just fell in her lap. While she was reading it I pulled the ring out of my jacket pocket.

"She had no idea, I didn't tell my parents, her mom, anybody, there was going to be no leaks whatsoever. I just told her we were going to get something to eat, dress casually. I got through it and all the waitresses I guess were talking. They told everybody in the place. When they realized she said yes, the whole place started clapping.

"We're going to try to do it next year on the same Friday. We met on the Friday, engaged on the Friday, I think we should get married on the Friday.

"The first Friday of the meet."

OLD MAN

Jonathan Sheppard's barn has everything.

"Brandy, you're a fine girl . . ." playing on two radios. Two little girls rubbing ears and scratching muzzles. A cat. Several steeplechasers. And – arguably – the best turf horse in the country.

With Anticipation lounges in Stall 12, ignores a hay net, and dozes while a fan stirs the air.

Perhaps he's dreaming. Maybe he's visualizing his run vs 10 quality opponents in today's $500,000 Sword Dancer Handicap.

But he's surely turning back time.

The nearly white 7-year-old gelding had arthritis as a 2-year-old, survived Kentucky Derby aspirations as a 3-year-old, lost the Grade I Gulfstream Park Handicap by 55 lengths last March and reinvented his career when he switched to the turf 16 months ago. The Augustin Stable homebred boasts $1.5 million in career earnings (80 percent of it since April 2001).

"There was never anything major – no fractures, no surgery – but he had soundness issues with his ankles and things," said Sheppard. "He would be gimpy and have problems. He and (graded stakes winner turned sire) Crowd Pleaser were in the same crop and were both good 2-year-olds. We actually thought – maybe – Derby, you know?"

To get Sheppard, who wrote his ticket to the Hall of Fame with steeplechasers and turf horses, to think Kentucky Derby must have taken some horse. Changing that goal saved the horse's career, however.

"When he was showing warning signs, we didn't keep hammering. We gave him some time to work through it," said the trainer. "When a horse is at the track and people have high hopes for him, it's easy to just keep pushing and hope he gets better if you see a sign to back off a little bit. I have the luxury of understanding owners and a farm. With our set-up, you are much more likely to keep horses going as they get older."

With Anticipation tries to become the first horse since El Senor in 1989-90 to win back-to-back runnings of the Sword Dancer, and is the 5-2 morning-line favorite against a field that includes three other Grade I winners (all but one of them – 8-year-old Cetawayo – younger). Denon, a neck behind With Anticipation at Monmouth July 6, looms as the most dangerous foe along with Volponi, Cetawayo and Startac.

The 1 1/2-mile turf stakes looks perfectly tailored for an older gelding trained by Sheppard, even if the horse is bred to be something else.

For years, Augustin owner George Strawbridge has longed to introduce something other than turf pedigrees into his broodmare band. That's why he bought broodmare Fran's Valentine (who was disqualified from first in the inaugural Breeders' Cup Juvenile fillies) and bred her to Relaunch (sire of Met Mile winner Honour And Glory and Breeders' Cup Distaff winner One Dreamer).

"We've always been top-heavy with turf horses in the stable and I would tell George it's not surprising you get a turf horse when you breed a turf horse to a turf horse," Sheppard said. "So he bred a dirt horse to a dirt sire and still got a turf horse. I don't know why."

Sheppard pointed to With Anticipation's stride as a reason for his success. The horse covers ample yards with each step, and transfers that to a devastating gallop in long-distance turf races.

"We broke him as a yearling, and I wasn't the first person to get on him but I've been on him," the trainer said. "He's always been a little stubby jogging, but he has a wonderful gallop. He always has, really. It just took me five years to figure out he needed turf."

And time.

Nothing like a choice. The Sword Dancer produced stories better than an old fisherman. And they were all true.

You decide. Was it With Anticipation, a white 7-year-old gelding winning his second Sword Dancer in a row? Was it the race itself with Denon getting through on the fence, With Anticipation coming around and both landing together on the line. Or was it Pat Day becoming the all-time richest jockey.

Any of the three, all of three – this is why horses run and people watch.

Day walked into the paddock for the Sword Dancer needing $70,711 to pass Chris McCarron at the top of the all-time money won title. He would have eclipsed the mark with a win or a second. With Anticipation's long white head decided the ceremony. Trainer Jonathan Sheppard greeted Day on the track, owner George Strawbridge Jr. walked his homebred into the winner's circle, Day saluted the heavens twice, NYRA handed the "Congratulations Pat Day" sign to the jockey while he was on the back of With Anticipation. The crowd went crazy. Day pulled his tack off and planted a kiss on With Anticipation's shoulder.

Maybe all that pull upstairs does work. If With Anticipation loses the photo, Day still wins the title and what? – they give him the sign back in the jocks' room or he waits for Denon, Edgar Prado and Bobby Frankel to go through the moves and the crowd goes home.

Nah, that's not how the best of the best do things. They win when it counts.

"I was worried early because he wasn't really caring for the ground. He warmed up great, acted great, broke well but just wasn't handling it," Day said. "You can't whip on them with a mile left to run, you try to keep them in contention and keep them happy and hope they'll respond when the racing starts. When we got some racetrack in front of us and he eyeballed that horse, he went after him with a vengeance. Like he knew where the wire was, like he knew what he had to do and he was gonna get it done."

At the head of the stretch, Prado punched Denon through a hole on the fence and opened up quickly. With Anticipation slipped to fifth with a little more than a furlong to run. He was outside and in between horses while Denon was streaking home.

"I got to overriding him a little bit, you'd think after 30 years . . . about the sixteenth pole I had to slow down and wait on him just a touch. He kinda looked over his shoulder at me like, 'come on jock, relax.' I was riding him like some 2-year-old I guess," Day said. "He was giving it to me and knew what he was doing, the best thing I could do and the only thing I should have been doing was helping him, not whipping on him."

You can be sure Day helped more than he hurt; just like he's been doing since he won his first race at Prescott Downs in 1973 earning $347.

"When I eased on over to the backside, it came over me, thinking about not only winning the race but getting the title," Day said. "It was an emotional moment. A couple of times, it got kinda tight in my throat. I was glad that he was willing to come back nice and easy to give me a chance to collect myself."

Sheppard had collected himself by the time he reached the winner's circle, but he was a long way from collected while he watched With Anticipation toil in the $500,000 stakes.

"I just couldn't quite put my finger on it, I didn't know whether I had him quite sharp enough, his last work was a second or two slower than I actually hoped it would have been and that was my fear," Sheppard said. "You start second-guessing yourself but Pat's kind of tricky because sometimes you think he doesn't have much horse and actually he knows what he's doing and he has more than you think."

This time at least.

With Anticipation seems to be as good if not better than last year. The Hall of Fame trainer knows old horses.

"Being associated with jumpers I'm kind of used to it. It's not such a big thing in my mind as it is in other people's," Sheppard said of the horse's success at a seemingly advanced age. "If you take care of your horses and give them a little break from time to time I don't think it's so bizarre. Of course he is a gelding and they're normally easier on themselves. The stallions tend to get a bit more temperamental as they get older. When you think of the great old horses, they're almost all geldings; Forego, John Henry, Kelso. Not that he's quite in that category....

....though, he's getting up there."

WHY?

I knew something was odd, not odd, odd's for describing mismatched socks, this was sad, I guess.

Yeah, sad but with tension, too. Almost surreal, though I'm never really sure what that means. Not quite secretive but definitely guarded. You know the feeling, a little like you just objected at a wedding, cursed during Thanksgiving dinner and missed your cue to exit the stage. All with a pall.

I stopped by Todd Pletcher's barn Tuesday morning. Whitney winner Left Bank's life was on the line after colic surgery on Saturday and Warners and Balto Star won for fun days earlier so I thought I should check in to see where it all stood. Pletcher wasn't there so I popped my head in the office and said hello to assistants Seth Benzel and Maggie Sweet. It was like I broke up the final hand of Texas Hold Em.

I asked if Todd was around, they told me he was at Belmont. I asked about Left Bank and they gave me the company answer. I wanted to know, more because I was rooting for the horse who impressed me with his heart in the Whitney and less about writing an update for the paper. I've known Seth since he worked for Bill Mott in Florida in 1998. We're friends. But I'm also the press. Tough conversation. Seth needs to do what he has to do to protect the barn's interests (and there are many). I need to do what I need to do to serve my readers. He's a reader, I'm a peer, he's a horseman, I'm a horseman, we're friends. Tough call.

Little did I know Schuylerville Stakes winner Freedom's Daughter had been put down the day before. Tougher call. Boy, do I feel sorry for the Pletcher barn. Yeah, it happens and you carry on but it never rolls off you. Horses are your pride, your projects, your friends.

That explains the conversation I had with Pletcher's employees. When I asked about Left Bank, they looked at me like I had no heart. It wasn't for the paper. I just was thinking about the horse, like a friend asking a friend about a friend. But they didn't know that. They were going through the motions of work after a 2-year-old filly vanished, gone, and a 5-year-old horse who had been there since he was 2 was fighting hard to stay alive.

Tell me Monday and Tuesday weren't brutal days at work for every person on the team. Freedom's Daughter succumbed to Colitis X which killed her in less than 36 hours and Left Bank was at Tufts University in Massachusetts.

A day later, the question of why the press wasn't alerted sooner about Freedom's Daughter's death was brought up to me.

Who knows why? Could be 100 reasons: from the owner Padua Stable needing to be told first to simply not wanting to talk about something bad. Think about the last death you dealt with, alerting the press wasn't at the top of your list.

That's where the difference lies between working with horses and writing about horses or watching horses. I'm probably too sympathetic, too naive about what goes on around me at the racetrack. I root for the horse, believe the trainer, side with the help. That's the way my heart works. That won't change.

I'll miss Freedom's Daughter and pray for Left Bank.

Why? Because I've known ones just like them.

It was visible to the naked eye. Farda Amiga turned to walk out of the winner's circle, pricked her ears and let out a long, deep sigh. And no wonder.

The 3-year-old filly just needed a moment of peace after another rousing performance by her and another rousing performance by her Brazilian connections.

Farda Amiga won the Kentucky Oaks in May, setting off a celebration which you had to see to believe. Saturday, it was Saratoga's turn.

Pele never had a kick like these Brazilians. Owners Marcos Simon, Julio Camargo, Jose DeCamargo, trainer Paulo Lobo and what seemed like all of the South American country were in the winner's circle after Farda Amiga ran down Allamerican Bertie to win the Grade I stakes.

The American flag was waved, the Brazilian flag was waved and a one-lyric song, possibly the Brazilian version of The Police's "Roxanne," rang down. "Fly Farda Amiga, Fly Farda Amiga, Fly Farda Amiga," you get the jist. It was one of those winner's circle celebrations where everyone from Ray Paulick of The Blood-Horse to Barry Schwartz of NYRA just stood around the edge and watched the spectacle. This is not how the Phipps family or the Whitneys celebrate a win.

But what the heck, it's been a couple of months since Brazil's World Cup win. Its beleaguered currency, the real, has shed nearly a third of its value so far in 2002. A Leftist could be elected president in October and eventually push the country toward a default on its burgeoning $250 billion public debt.

That's where Farda Amiga comes in. She has Brazil abuzz.

"My wife is with my cell phone to Brazil," Paulo said. "After the Kentucky Oaks, I received 35 messages from Brazil in 10 minutes."

Pat Day rode the 3-year-old daughter of Broad Brush. The jockey isn't one to get swept up in emotional outbursts but he's certainly aware of them.

"It's contagious," Day said. "You can feel all the enthusiasm in the winner's circle. I was out at the barn a couple mornings ago and they were all, well not quite as enthusiastic as after the race, but they were very, very keen, excited, enthusiastic. Enjoying the game."

Any thoughts about going to Brazil for a celebration?

"I don't think I could keep up with them," Day said.

And nobody can keep up with Farda Amiga. The Alabama, on paper, was a marquee race with seven of the best 3-year-old fillies in the country entered for the $750,000, 1 1/4-mile stakes. Neil Drysdale scratched Bella Bellucci because of the wet track. That left six with Allamerican Bertie at the head of the line.

The Churchill Downs shipper led You and Smok'n Frolic while Nonsuch Bay, Farda Amiga and Jilbab were having their own race in the back. Farda Amiga inched closer leaving the backside and around the turn, gradually collaring Allamerican Bertie who was game until the end while finishing three-quarters of a length back. You settled for third.

Lobo was the most subdued of the Brazilian gang, but just as proud.

"I have been (in the United States) since January 2000, this is my first time to Saratoga," Lobo said. "It's an amazing race. With the Kentucky Oaks, it's the most important on the dirt for 3-year-old fillies. I left Brazil with my father, I had 70 horses there. We have 12 now, we brought half of them from Brazil. I think a farther race is better for her. I was very worried about it. After the Kentucky Oaks, we kept her in the stall for 30 days. She's an amazing filly. I am very proud. It is very hard in America, the competition is impossible."

Impossible?

Lobo smiled, "Well not impossible. You understand me?"

Nobody has endured a meet like Todd Pletcher.

Freedom's Daughter won the opening-day Schuylerville and Left Bank stretched his speed all the way to win the Whitney Handicap. In a matter of weeks, both would be fighting for their lives.

Owned by Padua Stable, Freedom's Daughter died of Colitis X on Aug. 12. Michael Tabor's Left Bank is recovering from emergency colic surgery, his racing career over in hopes of life as a stallion at Kentucky's Ashford Stud.

I caught up with Pletcher in his tack room at the end of Saturday morning. One reporter left and another came, the phones rang non-stop and the 35-year-old talked about what it's like to be a horse trainer.

"We've had some real bright spots and some real real real down points. Every year before the meet starts, people say, 'Do you think you can be leading trainer, think you can do this, think you can do that?' When I come up here, I have very realistic expectations. Every time you enter a race, you think you're entering a horse who will be 5-2. Then you get the overnight and you say, 'Man, where did this horse come from or where did that horse come from?' It happens all the time, people come here and they want to do well so they'll drop a horse down in condition, or down in claiming price.

"Any time we can come up here and be competitive and win some races, we're happy. To be lucky enough to win the Schuylerville and the Whitney, those were real high points. Then the same two horses . . . with Left Bank, to have a horse as a 5-year-old get to the prime of his career, to win a race like the Whitney at a mile and an eighth, you're a couple of races away from the Breeders' Cup, maybe a championship for older horse, you just don't get to that level very often. To lose it to a colic surgery, that part is hard to swallow. But the fact that the horse is OK makes it a little easier to take, if he wouldn't have made it through that surgery, that would have been crushing.

"The filly just gives you such an empty feeling. Here you have one who gallops a mile and a half in the morning, that afternoon she's sick, and less than 36 hours later she's dead. You just can't . . . you can't do anything to stop it, you can't do anything to help her. You try to trace back to what we could have done differently. Sometimes Mother Nature just kicks your ass and there's nothing you can do about it.

"They're tough situations on the realism of the game we're playing. I don't know. I'd by lying if I said it didn't take some starch out of you. You want to feel a little sorry for yourself but we're fortunate that we have other horses to train, other good horses. We have obligations to those horses and our clients to pick our heads up and do the best we can. That's all you can do, keep going, your choices are keep going or quit and I'm not ready to quit at this stage. All you can do is keep your head down and keep plugging.

"Like (Pletcher's former boss) Wayne Lukas said, 'You knew this when you signed up.' I would say out of anybody I know who handles adversity well, he's got to be the best. He's the eternal optimist, no matter how bad a day he has, he's the first one there in the morning. Try again. Whether or not you learn that from someone but you can certainly see it in him. For anybody who's been as high in the game as you can go and who's had some down time, he's the perfect example. He's a stayer, for sure.

"A lot of people have been very sympathetic. A lot of people stopped me and told me they felt bad about it, we got some nice E-mails and phone calls. The industry as a whole has been very supportive. I think the one thing that everybody in this industry can identify with are the bad times. It's a very competitive business, you want to win every time you run. But when things like that happen to people, when horses get hurt or horses get sick, the one thing everybody in this business has in common is they all love the animals. You might not like some of the people involved but everybody feels bad for the animals. There's been a lot of support.

"With a horse like Left Bank, he's been in our barn since he was a 2-year-old in March. The only two times he's ever left our care was the colic surgeries. Once as a 2-year-old and since he came back he's never left our care until the other day. A: He's a big beautiful horse that everybody just loves to look at. B: He's got a lot of personality and C: He's world class. Put that all together and plus he's been in our care for four years, those kind everybody gets attached to. Everybody's majorly concerned about his well-being. Everybody's going to miss him. Like I said, we do what we can. The fact that he made it through the surgery and it looks like he gets to go home on Monday that's the primary concern.

"It goes to show you how fragile the whole situation is, from a physical standpoint you could match him up with any horse. Every horse and every person is susceptible to some illnesses or ailments. That was his weakness, he was susceptible to colics. In this business, you try to control all the things you can control because there are some things you can't, those are frustrating. To get him to that point, as a 5-year-old, physically at his prime . . .

"With Freedom's Daughter, our biggest concern was 'Did we have something that could possibly be contagious?' That was our major concern, so we sterilized her stall and left it open for three or four days. We do have other horses at Belmont and other horses that are running . . . you try to learn from everything and be more aware of something down the road or react more quickly the next time something happens or identify something sooner. You try to learn from everything but on the same token you can't dwell on it, you have to sure yourself up and go on.

"Left Bank, at this stage in the game was something you really looked forward to in the morning, especially the way he came out of the Whitney. He was training so good. To watch him train in the morning was a main focal point. As long as he's OK and gets to go breed mares then it's a great thing. When I go to Kentucky for the sales, I'll get a chance to see him. Retirement situations work both ways, when you have a horse like More Than Ready or Trippi or Left Bank or Graeme Hall, whoever it is, it's a great thing that they get to retire and go to stud. You feel like you accomplished something to get them to that point but you also know they're gone.

"With Left Bank there is absolutely nothing we could have done differently. I think the whole staff identified it so quickly. The filly, we identified it very quickly, the only thing I would have changed is I would have sent her to the clinic sooner. But you can only use your judgment and your veterinarian's judgment. Obviously if we'd have known it was as bad as it was, we'd have sent her over there 12 hours sooner than we did. My guess is it probably didn't matter. We were in a no-win situation no matter what we did. During the course of the year, how many times do you have a temperature that you treat, 24 hours later the horse is perfect and you're back on the track in three or four days? That's really the only thing, in retrospect, we would have changed. We didn't think it was life-threatening at that stage – 36 hours after her temperature was 1:01, she was dead.

"This is the worst in terms of the quality of horses and the succession of it. We've had horses get sick before, we've had horses die before, we've had horses break down before like everyone else,

....but to get a double dose like this was tough."

So there I was standing with a stack of 100 papers (issue 16, if I remember) in the parking lot outside our office on Broadway and Phila.

It was past midnight, I actually had made it to the Glass for two beers with the Walsh brothers, when a thief came fleeing past me. He was flying, with what looked like a pie plate tucked under his arm, shirt billowing around him, and an O.J.-on-the-run look in his eye.

Ever have an urge to do something stupid? I nearly threw the bundle of papers at him. I just wanted to. Not sure why, just felt right. If I knew then that it was a real live cat burglar, I would have heaved the papers, tripped up the scofflaw, tied him up with the paper bands, called the cops and collected a reward. Instead, I tossed the papers in my trunk and never thought any more about it.

Until I was nearly arrested five minutes later. A Saratoga police officer rode up on his bicycle. A radio crackled from his hip, a flash light searched me and my car and he informed me there was a breaking and entering report (it's my car, I was thinking). I didn't get exact quotes but it went something like – "And the description matches you. What are your reasons for being here?"

You want the short version or the long version?

"Well, Sir, I started this newspaper with my brother and my old college roommate . . . it's night number 17 on a 32-night voyage or hell-run depending on who you ask . . . I have 1,000 newspapers in my car and I was trying to arrange them so I could fit tomorrow's edition somewhere other than in my seat . . . why I'm doing it tonight is because I'm even less coherent in the morning . . . granted it looks like I'm up to no good with both doors and the trunk open in the middle of the night . . . but I always need a moment to unwind after deadline is reached . . . but I can assure you the only thing I'm guilty of is over population of a Honda Civic . . . and oh yeah . . . he went thataway!"

That's the long version. The short version would be, "I have no idea what I'm doing out here and he went thataway!"

So where did he go? Well, if I was a burglar on the run I would try Congress Park, bolt through the carousel, hide the evidence with Spit and Spat, run around the Casino and up over the date bush at the end of Union Avenue.

Then zip across Empire State College (that won't take long) and get to one of those alleys back near White Street, hang a right to Five Points making sure you miss the red light that seems to catch all five ways before yours. Once you get there, you have two choices; hide in the cemetery right there behind AJ's Cleaners or go straight on to the track. The cemetery has got to be the quietest, but the track would be a safe haven if you made it past the Pinkertons. Considering how many times the Travers Canoe has left in the middle of the night, the track could be the way to go.

If you made it through the night, maybe holing up in a pony stall or in the Stonerside woods, you could probably slip in as a hotwalker for Allen Jerkens in the morning. They call it organized chaos over there, perfect to use as a thief blind. Walk the horse from the left side and don't yell back or you'll blow your cover. If you suspect they're looking for you, hop on the coffee truck and ride right on out the front gate. If you think you've given them the slip, get a job as an agent (sorry boys, it just fit so perfectly).

I did hear a man was arrested – and accused of robbing Graham's Restaurant – the next morning after hiding in Round Lake (didn't think of that one).

Evidently it had nothing to do with newspapers or coffee trucks.

QUOTE:

"He's finally settled into a good pony – at 18. This is his 15th straight Saratoga, he broke his maiden up here as a 3-year-old. Doesn't even need a bridle, he knows every path here."

– Trainer Tom Voss, about his lead pony Mickey Free, who won the A.P. Smithwick Memorial Steeplechase in 1987.

Stopping for a break between working horses in the morning, Edgar Prado looks you dead in the eye. "I'm on a mission."

And what a mission. Prado went from being four down in the jockey standings to four up in two days. Now that's a mission.

Jerry Bailey opened up a huge lead in the jockey's race by winning 15 races the first week; Prado has been chipping away at it ever since. Over the weekend Prado capitalized on Bailey's decision to go out of town. The seven-time Saratoga champion won the Arlington Million with Beat Hollow on Saturday and finished sixth with Include at Monmouth on Sunday.

"Saratoga is such a short meet, people are very interested in the jockey title," Prado said. "Winning it is important."

Bailey knows that better than anyone. He's won the title seven of the last eight years. He rides more races in a day at Saratoga than anywhere else. And wants to win another title. Prado is looking for his first Saratoga title.

The son of an assistant trainer in Peru, Prado opted at an early age to pursue a career in race riding.

"I was going to train to be a lawyer," he said. "I didn't get really far in school because I started riding when I was 16."

By 17 in 1984, he was leading jockey in his native country and was so successful that he leaped at the chance to try his skills in North America. Prado arrived in the United States in 1986, contracted to trainer Manuel Azpurua, and soon was a winner at Calder Race Course.

He then moved north to become Maryland's dominant jockey of the 1990s.

"Laurel and Pimlico were like a trampoline for me," Prado said. "It helped me get noticed, but nothing can compare to riding in New York."

In 1997, Prado made 536 trips to the winner's circle to become only the fourth jockey to ride more than 500 winners in a single season. Two years later, he switched his tack from Maryland to New York in time for Saratoga.

His victory total diminished, but his reputation grew.

"My favorite rides are when I come from off the pace and have to weave in and out of horses," Prado said.

Over the last week only one thing's been hotter than Prado. The air.

"In Peru I lived near the coast, it was bone dry, but only hot three months out of the year," Prado said. "I don't like it hot. Getting on horses in the morning and then in the afternoon can be very tiring in the heat."

Not that you can see that in Prado's demeanor. He says hello to everyone with an infectious smile. He chats in Spanish with grooms at the food truck and English to trainers at the gap.

Like every jockey, Prado has a routine. He dives into the Racing Form every day and assesses the human side of the equation.

"I'll get to the jocks room at 10 or 10:30, sit in the sauna and stretch out. I'm rarely able to take a nap. I'll get the scratches and start preparing my program," he said. "I always watch the replays. The head-ons are so important. You learn little things every day. I study the trainers and the jockeys. You have to know which trainers encourage their riders to run on the pace and which jockeys are likely to send on their own. Not many trainers really give instructions. Some want to talk to you about how the track is or if speed is holding or the inside is no good."

If Bailey goes on to win the riding title, Prado will point to four consecutive race days (July 27-31) where he went without a winner, but won't dwell on it. Life is good in New York.

"I miss the pace of life in Maryland, but riding in New York you get a lot of incredible horses who put you in the spotlight," Prado said. "After I finish riding I go to enjoy my family and get ready for the next day. Whatever happened today is history.

I start thinking about tomorrow."

Loose Horse Record

Everybody has a loose-horse story (like the one last week that wound up in someone's backyard next to the pool), but nobody can top Dennis Brida's.

"I hold a record for that," he said outside his wife Juliane's Horse Haven barn last week. "The police found my horse at Exit 12."

Top that.

Brida's horse, Saratoga Belle, was training early in the fall of 1985 when she spooked from the noise of a chainsaw. The filly ran twice around the Oklahoma track, back to Brida's barn, out/over/through the Union Avenue stable gate, down Union Avenue, into the Yaddo Gardens, through a lake to Ballston Spa.

True story.

"I was a young trainer and to me she was the greatest thing in the world. She had a cough so I was being real cautious and wanted to make sure she was completely over everything before I started training her again," said Brida. "She was probably too fresh, but some guys were taking limbs off the trees outside the barn – in the morning – and she got loose."

Fully tacked, Saratoga Belle covered all that ground with Brida, two outriders, the Saratoga police and – eventually – state troopers in pursuit. The police found her on the Northway, bleeding badly, in shock, with the saddle under her belly. Veterinarians gave her oxygen, and used 180 stitches to close the wounds.

Saratoga Belle eventually went back to training, and won her first start back – July 1, 1986 – at Rockingham Park.

Ears up. Alert. Dead still while the trainer gets another girth to fit. No sweat. No jig or dance. Everything forward. Strong, determined. No fuss. Looking out for no one. Straight ahead. No distractions.

Summer Colony

THE LOOK

That's a game face. And that was Summer Colony in the paddock for the Personal Ensign Stakes.

The massive 4-year-old filly owned and bred by Ned Evans made it a race face too, winning the Grade I by 4 1/2 lengths. Trained by Mark Hennig and ridden by John Velazquez, Summer Colony went right with second-choice Dancethruthedawn from the moment the gates parted. The two fillies locked on each other like a pair walking onto Noah's boat.

Jerry Bailey had Dancethruthedawn on the rail while Summer Colony eyed her from the outside. The others were inconsequential.

Midway on the far turn, Summer Colony moved on, first by a half-length, and it widened all the way to the wire. The game was over.

"I gained a lot of confidence when we walked in the paddock. She had her game face on," Hennig said. "She's just been doing everything right. It's easy to have confidence in one who goes out there every time and gives 110 percent like she's been doing since last August. She loves this racetrack, she just brightened up so much when she got here. Jerry is always tricky, you never know what he's thinking and I was happy we had her inside of us. I think Johnny was patient leaving there and made Jerry commit. As long as we were stalking her, when it came down to the stamina of a mile and a quarter we'd be able to beat her."

Summer Colony has more stamina than a clock. The daughter of Summer Squall is undefeated in four starts at a 1 1/4 or farther. The Personal Ensign was the 11th start in a row where she finished first or second (nine wins) dating back to her maiden breaker, by 32 3/4 at Saratoga last summer. Velazquez has been aboard for most of them.

"I needed a good horse like that to pick my head up. She's the best horse around, that's all it is. The whole way, she had one ear up and one ear down. She'd go a little bit, look a little bit, go a little bit, look a little bit," Velazquez said. "She was there for me the whole way. She never did anything for me to lose my confidence in her. From last year, I told Mark she's going to be a good horse. Even when she won by 32, she wasn't there mentally yet. Little by little, we took our time and she's done it the right way. She's as good as she is now because they gave her the time she needed."

Time, talent, whatever, Summer Colony could be the best older filly or mare in the country on dirt.

"Right now she's the best filly around. You can do whatever you want with her now. You can take a hold of her, you can put her on the lead. She lets you do that. She's serious, all business. She just has to stay sound," Velazquez said. "They were galloping along but the other filly wasn't going anywhere and she opened up little by little, when I put a half-length in front of the other horse she wanted to lay in on her. I wanted to make sure she kept going and her mind kept going. Right away she knew, she put her head down, her ears down, she knew then it was time to rock and roll."

Velazquez gave her successive pats as she crossed the wire.

"I get along with her, I know her real well," said the jockey. "We always knew she could run, but mentally she was not there. Sometimes they come out of it, sometimes they don't. Hopefully they'll use that talent eventually. Now her mind is there with her talent. She's just that much better."

It all goes back to that face.

One was carrying the meet's leading rider, one was was carrying the man in second.

One was coming off his best race, the other was coming off his longest layoff. One had stalked the pace the whole way, the other hadn't been within shouting distance. One carried his head high, the other stretched his head low. One was shiny bay, the other mud brown. Both were splashing hard through the Saratoga slop. There had to be a winner.

Medaglia d'Oro beat Repent in the 133rd Travers. It wasn't quite Jaipur and Ridan or Holy Bull and Concern but it was better than it was supposed to be. Medaglia d'Oro was touted as the 2-5 morning line favorite. It was his race to lose.

Trainer Bobby Frankel wasn't worried.

"I don't see the scenario changing. All he has to do is break," Frankel said beforehand. "Let him run out of there and don't worry about who's the speed or who's not the speed. He rates himself. If they're going to go too fast, he'll be off them, if they go slow he'll be in front. I don't think they can go too fast for him."

Medaglia d'Oro was coming off a 13 3/4-length romp in the Jim Dandy while Repent was making his first start since finishing second to War Emblem in the Illinois Derby in April. Medaglia d'Oro was meant to win. Repent was meant to be found out somewhere along the 1 1/4 mile.

Instead they made it another Travers to be savored.

Ridden by Jerry Bailey (the man in second), Medaglia d'Oro stalked Shah Jehan with Saint Marden also stalking from the outside through 23.14, 46.82, and 1:11.53 splits. Repent and Edgar Prado were settled back in sixth.

Shah Jehan and Saint Marden backed up and Medaglia d'Oro moved to the lead at the half-mile pole. Quest made a run on his outside while Puzzlement and Repent began to rally from well back. Quest faltered, Puzzlement hung and it was down to Medaglia d'Oro and Repent.

Medaglia d'Oro never wavered while Repent never backed off. It was a half-length difference.

It may as well have been a mile for Ken McPeek. Repent's trainer stood on the edge of the winner's circle while Frankel walked into the center of it. McPeek stared off at the center of the infield and let out a couple of damns, just loud enough to hear. He finally got the attention of his assistant Helen Pitts. They both knew how close it was. He snapped his fingers like a man does when he's just missed pulling off an achievement nobody thought possible.

"He's a very, very, very, very good horse," McPeek said.

Give one more very for Medaglia d'Oro, at least on this day.

Frankel knows this better than anyone. The Jim Dandy was easy, the Travers tough. They're all the same to the trainer.

"Sometimes horses will give everything they have no matter how easy it looks," Frankel said. "I have a feeling he's one of those."

MEDAGLIA D'ORO

By the end of the day, both horses looked a long way removed from the Travers. They live about 50 yards from each other near the Oklahoma training track. Two Spanish grooms sat in the tack room, five stalls down from Medaglia d'Oro while one lone groom sat and had a Sprite in the tack room next to Repent.

A blue feed tub still hung outside the stalls in Frankel's barn. A piece of duct tape with Medaglia written in black marker designated the one horse in the barn who still needed to eat. His forelock braid hung between two big sideways ears, his head went back and forth with the hay net and the remaining foot traffic. His legs were still open, two grooming buckets to the edge of the stall ready to go when ready.

Repent rattled his door when he put his whole head down into his hay net and rooted like a vacuum cleaner in a couch cushion. King Of The World shook his head at his neighbor. A thin glaze of brown sat like eyeliner under Repent's eyes. His long blaze a bright white. A blue play ball hung limply at the back of the stall. Repent didn't look tired.

Back at Medaglia d'Oro's barn, the grooms answered any question in unison, "Travers."

"Now since there's four days in between, I ship on the second day after it's over. Years ago, we only had the one day, Sunday. Everybody had to move on Sunday. We didn't run on Sundays. Mr. Fitzsimmons had his own van, he used to ship one van every night for a whole week. In those days, you didn't have the Thruway so it would take eight hours to get home."

– Allen Jerkens, on shipping out of Saratoga

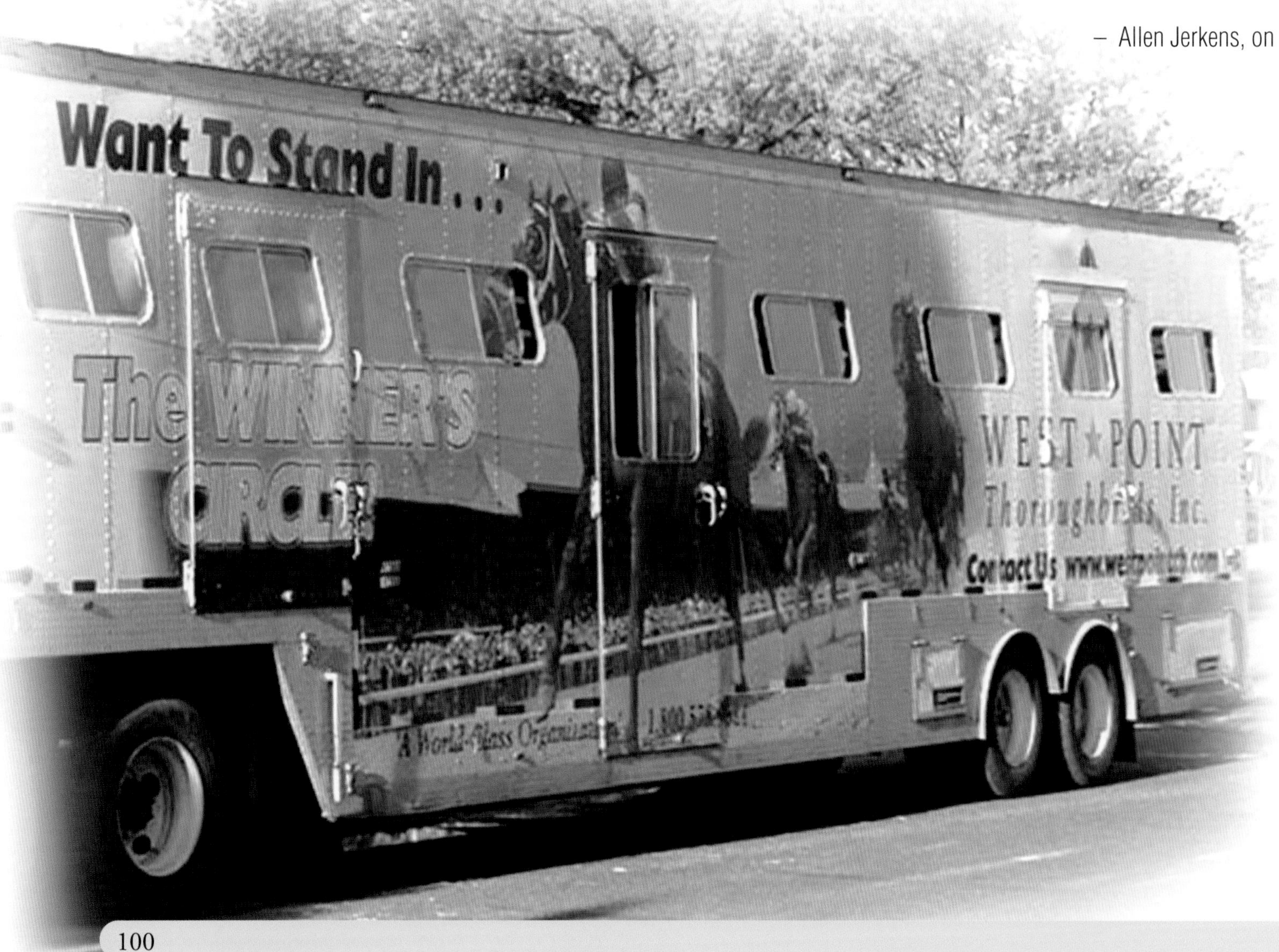

Finally we're able to solve world peace. Crank up the Travers reruns, turn on a little rain, crawl under a tree and see the world get along.

They closed the track Saturday morning at 8. It rained and rained some more. And we stood under a tree and watched Arts And Letters, Loud, Bold Reason, Holding Pattern, Jatski, Willow Hour, Wise Times, Sea Hero, Point Given . . . it was the best morning at the track this summer.

Nobody told us the show was coming, we just looked up from our cups of coffee and started watching races on the TV at the edge of the Morning Line Kitchen's roof. The first ones were black and white, no sound, and everybody turned to Allen Jerkens to know who we were viewing. I think he was too busy watching Shine Again on the track to give it much thought but he did throw out Annihilate 'Em when we needed him (1973) most.

Racing fans, what a breed. By the time the 1980s came, there were 16 of us under a tree picking out trips, guessing riders, telling stories.

"I was right there on the turn, that's me jumping up and down."

"Sam Maple, God rest his soul."

"Oh, Chief's Crown, he killed me."

"Cordero, I asked why he didn't go around, 'Papa, I had him down in there.' "

"Look at Mike Smith, Quarter Horse'n him home."

"No way it's been 20 years since Runaway Groom."

"Eddie Maple's wing."

"Here it comes, here it comes . . . 'there is cause for Concern.' "

Holding Pattern held off Little Current in the mud again. Honest Pleasure stretched them out again. Affirmed came over on Alydar again. Willow Hour got up in the mud again. Forty Niner gutted it out again. Rhythm circled the field again. Holy Bull was true again. Thunder Gulch went to his knees again.

We watched them all.

It's an answer to a bad joke. How do you keep racing fans out in the rain? Turn on Travers' reruns.

Jorge Chavez was there, sitting on a picnic table watching himself go from chopping Robert Perez longshots around to eking out one with Will's Way. Ronnie Ebanks stood stone silent with Affirmed and Alydar, now that's saying something. Jim Cornes nearly twisted in a knot when Forty Niner was sparring with Seeking The Gold. Half the West Point syndicate was there marveling with every finish. Tony Micallef choreographed Angel Cordero's ride on Brian's Time.

Not sure where all of us should have been during the hours we spent watching but there was no work being done. Cell phones were turned to mute and chores were postponed.

Racing brings out all kinds. Everybody is a fan. They'll watch replays of the Travers in the rain under a tree for hours bantering back and forth about who was better, who should have won, what price they went off.

Just to watch the old days again with Marshall Cassidy's calls, the old light bulb numbers along the bottom of the screen, the trees on the far turn, the old wooden rails, the massive steeplechase fences on the inner turf, the railless inner turf, the tail-finned cars in the background, the billowing breeches of the jockeys, the running W of King Ranch, the finesse of Braulio Baeza . . .

Turn them on today, I'll meet you under the tree.

Hey, Pony Boy

You're an Australian groom waiting for a lead pony to take your steeplechaser for a few spins of Clare Court. The lead pony is late.

What would you do? Ask somebody, of course.

"Excuse me, can you take our horse? He needs to do three laps of Clare Court."

The man on the pony leans down, "You can. He's pretty old, but he'll probably do three laps for you."

The man on the pony was Allen Jerkens, Hall of Fame trainer. The two blokes in need were Merrick Staunton and Kevin Burke, Australians in Saratoga with New York Turf Writers Cup hopeful Zabenz.

The Chief didn't end up taking the pony job – he found someone else – but did make time for the Australians and trainer Robert Smerdon.

"Burkie will talk to anyone and he just walked over and asked," said Smerdon. "Merrick has a far better global knowledge of racing. He's on the net and things and knows people. He saw the initials on the saddle towel and was pulling Burkie's sleeve. 'I think that's Allen Jerkens. Get away from him. He's a legend.' "

A few days later, Zabenz aired in the Turf Writers. Jerkens was there for the race, and for Smerdon.

"The day after we tried to borrow his pony, I went over to his barn for a talk," said Smerdon. "He thinks like a horse, he does. He asked about my horse, got all of the information and said it would be interesting to watch. Amazing – you ask a man to pony your horse, and then you have the most informative 30 minutes of your life as a horseman."

Editor's Note: A lacrosse columnist, television personality and owner of Quintessential Productions in Baltimore, racing fan Quint Kessenich found The Special via e-mail, and came to Saratoga as a volunteer. "Maybe we'll find a spot for something you write," he was told. In short order, Kessenich was everywhere.

No TV. Not one nap. What day is it? My car is trashed from 120 coffees and 40 Snapples. My body is confused. I've got a worried Mom, an ex-girlfriend who doesn't understand; and a new one who does.

Saratoga is racing's version of The Masters, tradition and idyllic conditions. Earthy smells, angular light, pine trees, the smell of liniment, Spanish chitchat and coffee con leche with sweet and lo. Sweat. Mud. Sun on my face, sore feet, and an everlasting voucher.

Living in three different places at once. Chicken scratch notes that I can't decipher. Sipping a Bloody Mary at the Jim Dandy bar on a Monday.

Watch a vendor pick up used cups from the picnic area, as nobody seems to notice. What is she doing with them? I hope it's not what I think, but if it helps buy a few more outfits at The Gap, so be it.

Observe the guys at the Oklahoma turf course managing the traffic. Watch a hotwalker on the harness side punt a colt in the stomach. Find a Derby horse on the overnights. Notice that the stewards don't seem consistent and never rode a race. Watch a friend without credit bid a colt to $250,000 at Fasig-Tipton. Shake your head at the mockery of Hip No. 152.

I've been in the Baltimore Orioles lockerroom and watched Cal Ripken work his craft. He's no Edgar Prado. Not even close. Listened to Brian Billick pontificate after a Ravens victory. He's got nothing on any trainer.

Listened to Burners U.K. They talk too much. Play music, please.

QUINT

I used to read the newspaper and think the writers were experts.

Aaron Gryder tells us a story about making weight, a lifelong battle which haunts so many of these guys. The next day he loses an excruciating photo. I've never rooted harder. Was it the pound?

Your day is good when winners and smiles surround you. Dodie Duys, Ronny Barber, Yonis Lasso. Obscure trainers like Treveille Carty, Jonathan Buckley and Kate DeMasi. Kingpins like Linda Rice, Richard Migliore, Bill Mott, Jorge Chavez, Jimmy Bond, John Kimmel and Prado. You don't forget the class of a Carl Nafzger, Wayne Lukas, Phil Gleaves, Jimmy Picou, and the steel blue eyes of Lisa Lewis.

Every day, a new hero. Rick Violette. The Judge, a real southern gentleman. Cellphone Dana. WinStar's Traci and Stefani. Liz Ronk's photo album. Watching Susie work herself to death. Listening to Bobby's dreams. Ken McPeek. Shoe men Cousin Joe and Bernie. Gary Contessa and Frank Amonte. Sit and try to comprehend what Todd Pletcher must be feeling. Angel Cordero. The dapper Anthony Mormino. Leon Blusiewicz. Bob the Usher. Anya the Labatt's babe. Nancy from O'Shea and French. Ian, Peter and Mara, and Rob. Ralph Theroux. Steve Ropitzky the clover man. Jay Longton at the equine pool, photographers Dave Harmon and Tod Marks. Got time for a tale from Sean?

Storm Cadet, Shine Again, Zawzooth, Roaring Fever, This Guns For Hire, Saint Marden, Capsized, and Gold Play.

Missed the Travers. Drove slowly out of town, sped back. You don't realize how tired you are until you get away.

Saratoga is summer camp for adults. I broke 100 for the first time at the golf course on July 23. We're off the turf; I haven't had a moment to play since. Ate three scallops for $14 at Siro's. I was on the set of The Sopranos at Sergio's. Bumped into fellow Baltimorons: Magna's Ted Mudge, John Angelos of the Orioles, Ted Bauer, Dave Cottle and my best friend Bob Shriver. All jealous.

My hosts were Denise and Jack Kalinkewicz. Didn't see much of them. Denise is a saint, a teacher; she did my laundry and never complained that my sneakers stunk. Debbie and Steve O'Shea are my Saratoga link. Painted their house on Cottage Street a decade ago, it may as well be a B&B with nightly barbeques and endless guests. I'm very lucky.

Thank you Sean and Joe Clancy. You've labored to create something distinctive and positive. Your energy is infectious, your skills and talents are immense. I felt the pride when Mark Hennig abruptly stopped talking to the paparazzi and told them he's got to go talk to the guy from The Special. You know you've arrived when Ron Anderson asks you if today's races are on the turf.

Meet me by the tree at 3 o'clock. Meet you under the Six Oaks. Let's watch a turf race from the roof. Not used to asking questions, accustomed to providing answers. Refreshing to look people in the eye and actually listen. Sleep like a 12-year-old. Maximize every day. I thought I loved racing before. Now I really love horse racing.

Ever leave your real life for 40 days and do something you've always dreamed about? It was even more than I wished.

It's time to go home. I miss my dog.

– Quint Kessenich

Bobby Frankel needed an exercise rider on Friday morning. His horse was tacked up on the ring, his scheduled rider had one more to get on and, like every morning, time was of the essence.

And like so many times this meet, Edgar Prado was there.

"Hey Edgar, you're not doing anything," Frankel said. "Hop on this horse for me."

Prado finished his conversation about what else, cameras, without ever answering Frankel. He turned and walked into the courtyard for a leg up on Sumitas for a spin of the Oklahoma track.

Prado was everywhere this summer. From taking pictures at sunrise, to winning the Hopeful with Sky Mesa, to being the swing exercise rider for Bobby Frankel; The jockey was in the right place at the right time.

With two days of racing still to play, Prado is on his way to his first Saratoga championship. The 35-year-old led Jerry Bailey by 10 wins and John Velazquez by 14 with 21 races to go. Prado's booked for 10 mounts on Sunday and is slated to ride Harlan's Holiday in the Pennsylvania Derby at Philadelphia Park on Monday.

Bailey's record of 55 winners, set last year, is in jeopardy.

"It's been an excellent meet. I'm very proud. I worked hard for it but no matter how hard you work, if you don't have opportunity nothing will happen," Prado said. "It's all combined. If you don't have the talent, you can't be lucky. I have a better chance riding a bad race on a good horse than riding a super race on a bad horse. It's all about the horse, luck and opportunity together."

Bailey won 15 races the first week and seemed to have won the title in the first six days of racing. Prado scraped away at the margin by winning on anything from New York-bred maidens like Go Going Gone for Carlos Martin to stakes like the Honorable Miss with Mike Gorham's Mandy's Gold. They piled up.

"The best of the best come here. My agent (Bob Frieze) did a super job. Things came into place. The barns we ride for did not get sick, that was a plus," Prado said. "A lot of the barns, Mark Hennig, Todd Pletcher got sick, that slowed Johnny and a couple of riders. That was a minus to them and a plus for me."

Prado left the safety of Maryland in 1999 to try Saratoga. He's gradually became one of the go-to riders on the circuit. Slowly, better horses and more opportunities have come his way.

"If you don't come to a place and think you'll do good then you might as well stay where you are. You have to look at it in a positive way and try as hard as you can," Prado said. "If you win one race, then you try to win two tomorrow. Not because you want to be greedy but because you want to be competitive. You want to do the best you can for the people who are helping you."

Consider that done.

Prado won for everybody, stakes to claimers, sprints to routes.

"I haven't won it yet but if I do win, I'll dedicate it to all the backside

Edgar Prado

people. The grooms, the hotwalkers. They put a lot of work into it and nobody ever mentions their names," Prado said. "They're the underground people. They spend more time with the horse than anybody else. They do the job. I'm on the horse for a minute and a half and I get the winner."

Combined with riding the most winners, a jockey must mentally win the battle of Saratoga. Prado is as good as anybody, going about his business day in, day out.

"I'm very competitive when I'm riding. When the race is over, what are you going to do about it? It's over," Prado said. "I tip my hat off to whoever wins. I always believed in that. It could be you or someone else, when the race is over, forget about it. That's my philosophy, if I follow that, I'm really happy."

Prado followed it all the way through the meet.

"What was my best winner of the meet? Even though I didn't win the Travers, Repent was a great race. He overcame traffic, mud, he was game, he was trying to win the race. Whywhywhy overcame a speed track, he was determined. You could mention Owsley, she won nice and easy. And Wonder Again impressed me. And a lot of babies are running well. Every horse has a territory, they all ran good. From the Travers winner to the $25,000 claimer, they're all very important when you're head to head for the meet. Every win counts."

Fifty-two of them – and counting – by Sunday.

I missed more races than I saw. I rode more waterslides than horses. I slept less than I needed to. I wrote less than I wanted to. My fingers hurt. I think I have mouse elbow.

But I still lived Saratoga 2002. On the way here back in July, I made a list (though I can't find it) of things I wanted to do. I think I accomplished half.

Naively, I thought I might write more this summer than last, but the time evaporated at about the end of Week 1, and my job quickly shifted to layout, editing and steering the ship from blank computer screen to what you are holding in your hand.

That's why you don't know my face.

Back to my list, I did get to Cooperstown (though it would take a weekend to fully appreciate the place instead of half a day). I did have some wonderful dinners with my wife Sam downtown (we hit the 43 Phila, 1 Caroline, Sperry's trifecta box). I went to the drive-in for half a movie. Toured the museum (and completed the scavenger hunt). Found time to make a facial appointment for Sam – then found time to let her keep it. We took Ryan, Jack and Nolan to Great Escape. If you go, take a 16-month-old (borrow one if you have to) and ride the wave pool in an innertube – all day. The Lincoln Baths have nothing on the relaxation that sweeps over you, though it helps to go without sleep for 12 days prior. I saw the geysers. I toured the car museum.

That paragraph sounds like a vacation, but be assured that those were moments carved from six weeks of work.

The rest of the time I worked. I spent most of Saratoga 2002 in a 400-square foot office somewhere near the top of the Arcade Building. I didn't write many words for The Special this summer, but I read them all. My job involved planning (a little), computers (a lot), headlines (Alotta Zavata and Mud Fight were my favorites), photo editing, story editing, caption writing.

The best part was the creative process. Though we should probably plan ahead, most editions of The Special start out as empty as an artist's canvas. Then we add paint – ads, photos, articles, headlines, captions, lists, dates, names, numbers, quotations. By midnight (sometimes earlier, sometimes later) the painting was done – for a day.

Sean and Quint supplied most of the articles, and that's where The Special grew the most from 2001 to 2002. We covered more ground. Quint Kessenich talked to everyone from Wayne Lukas to Treveille Carty, and that made a huge difference in our product.

Outside of the office – I did make it out a few times just to prove that I was not the Invisible Man – my Saratoga highlights included everything yours did, horses and wonderful moments.

I listened to Jonathan Sheppard talk about riding With Anticipation, then watched Pat Day ride the horse to a win in the Sword Dancer. Might be the best race I ever saw. Ryan and Jack were there, got a pat on the head from Pat.

I interviewed Edgar Prado, and got a funny look when he heard me say Joe Clancy. No, I'm not Sean. They let me out every once in a while. I'm the guy who wrote the caption under the photo of you taking a photo of the sunrise. He talked about blowing two rolls of film, then talked about Owsley and then rolled the "mouse running away from a lion" quote off his tongue. Fabulous stuff. The next day, the meet's leading jockey pulled up next to me in the stable area and asked "Joe, do you need a ride somewhere?" 'No, Edgar, I don't have far to go but thanks anyway.' I should have jumped in and gone wherever he was going.

I interviewed Lisa Lewis and Jose Santos after Capsized won a sloppy Fourstardave on Travers Day. The trainer looked relieved, maybe as tired as her horse. Santos knew it all along, and said Capsized would have won on turf or dirt that day. I met Capsized the next day at the barn. Classy horse, and a new favorite to watch for. I interviewed Bobby Frankel after Surya won a three-horse mudfest. Quick, matter of fact, to the point, not nearly as intimidating as everyone would have you believe. But I didn't get to watch the Travers with him. Didn't matter. He would have had to come to my office instead of Mike Lakow's anyway. Maybe next time.

Ryan, Jack and I collected two autographs for a six-year-old photograph of Cigar. First, we walked to Stonerside and visited with Bill Mott. He talked about Cigar, asked Ryan and Jack how old they were, and signed the Mass Cap photo for us. If I ever go back to working in a barn, I want it to be at Stonerside. I was once a 50-cents-a-horse hotwalker (had to work off a Rawlings baseball glove) and cooled out 80 horses during a summer at Delaware Park. I'd pay 50 cents a horse to walk them at Stonerside.

Later that day, we staked out Jerry Bailey. He just won the Arlington Million, but there he was walking through the gate – about 30 seconds after someone told us we missed him. Ryan scrambled, Jack dropped the acorns he was organizing and I laughed. Bailey paused, shook some small hands, said hello and signed. Thanks Jerry. Now I can finally get this photo framed.

I walked into two phenomenal stories: Dennis Brida and his loose horse that went "through the Yaddo" on its way to Ballston Spa; and Australian trainer Robert Smerdon, whose assistants unwittingly asked Allen Jerkens to pony their steeplechase horse around Clare Court. After nearly making the pony deal, the Aussies figured out Jerkens was in the Hall of Fame and had a good laugh at their innocence. A day after Smerdon's horse Zabenz won the Turf Writers, I set up an interview with the trainer and Joe Hirsch and needed an explanation. "He's the Allen Jerkens of reporters," I said. Smerdon understood.

Eventually, everybody's reason for being here, goes back to horses. Or at least it should. I saw some wonderful horses – Iron Deputy working, Owsley dragging Prado to the front, Capsized begging for carrots, It's A Giggle jumping in the morning, Jubileo ripping it up in a Port-A-Pad one day after winning a race, Point Given's sister bucking around Oklahoma, Jimmy Toner's turf fillies.

Thanks guys, I wish I had time for more.

Cup of Coffee By Sean Clancy
Barbara D. Livingston

Well, it's 11:22 p.m. and this is the last thing left to be done.

Issue 32 is 23 pages completed, only the last Cup of Coffee still to fill. I wish I felt up to the task. Wish I could give you one final hurrah to wrap it all up and send us on our ways. Somebody once told me not to apologize in my writing. OK, here goes, I'll do my best.

It's just Joe and I left. The office is quiet. The band from Hurricane Sam's or somewhere down the street can be heard just over the air conditioner. They say the streets are packed, we wouldn't know.

But we wouldn't have it any other way. I've written close to 100,000 words in the last six weeks and loved it. I didn't say they were all good words, but they were written. I hope you read most of them. Joe designed 600 some pages and loved it, well, he tolerated it. I didn't say they were all good pages, but they were close.

Like a good Oscar speech, I'll say this; the individuals who helped us are too numerous to mention. I'll never forget you though. All you had to do is say a good a word along the way or offer encouragement. Believe me, I know who you are. I'd like to write each of you a thank you note but I'm tired of writing. This will have to do.

This paper can't work without our passion and your acceptance. We're here to make a positive difference in the sport and celebrate Saratoga. Yeah, we're an office full of dreamers. Nothing wrong with that.

Was it a success? Sure it was a success. We wrote, you read. We'll be back next year.

Am I glad it's over? Well, I'll be glad to watch a race and not worry about who's winning, what my lead will be, how I'll get fresh quotes, if I saw the dramatic moment of the race, if I know how to spell the owner's name . . . yeah, I just want to watch a race again for fun.

It'll be relaxing to speak to people again and not be hoping they say something funny or functional for "Here and There in Saratoga." It'll be relaxing to know 5,000 papers aren't sitting on the porch every morning and 20 pages aren't waiting to be filled every night.

It won't be so great knowing there is no chance to see You and Carson Hollow, Medaglia d'Oro and Repent, With Anticipation and Denon, Tates Creek and Voodoo Dancer in an average day at home.

What will I miss? You asked.

I'll miss stepping over the tongue ties on the ground. I'll miss the seagulls that fly over the paddock at the end of the day. I'll miss my friend who opens the paddock gate and says goodbye to me every evening.

I'll miss seeing horses like Summer Colony. I'll miss watching Janet Reed check nighteyes. I'll miss walking to the Test Barn with John Ward. I'll miss the smell of marijuana (from far away) on my walk home. I'll miss laughing at the looks on people's faces when they step out of valet parking at Siro's. I'll miss a cold Anchor Steam at the Glass.

I'll miss Edgar Prado's work ethic. I'll miss spotting Jerry Bailey's positioning on the turf. I'll miss the hot cups of tea at the kitchen. I'll miss walking down the alley next to White Street on the way to my house. I'll miss climbing out onto my roof at 48 Union Avenue. I'll miss hearing a good quote for the paper. I'll miss seeing the horse's reactions to big things. I'll miss seeing people ask for the paper when I get out of my car in the morning. I'll miss the lead ponies. I'll miss the occasional breakfast at Beverly's. I'll miss Ken Ramsey's enthusiasm. I'll miss Sil Celeb's gait. I'll miss Bobby Frankel's quotes. I'll miss the OTB show. I'll miss it all.

I'll have to come to Belmont this fall but it won't be the same. Forty-six weeks to go until Saratoga 2003.

I'll say goodbye now. Thanks for reading.

Ten Most Wanted
John Velazquez
Empire Maker
Todd Pletcher
Ashado

Saratoga 2003

In our third year, The Special moved next door to the Saratoga Chamber of Commerce and, wow, did things seem smoother.

Probably, nothing like what jockey John Velazquez and trainer Todd Pletcher were feeling. The duo combined to set records for most wins in Saratoga history – Velazquez pounded in 61 victories while Pletcher dumped 35 of his own.

Ten Most Wanted shipped in from California to take the Travers while enigmatic 3-year-olds Empire Maker and Funny Cide never got to make it happen on the racetrack.

Let's get a few things straight.

Trainers, I love all your horses. Jockeys, I know you can outride me and all my readers any day, any time. Grooms, assistants, hotwalkers, I admire and respect what you do. Owners, I know you pay the bills and take all the risk. NYRA, I know it isn't easy rowing a thousand-oar canoe in choppy water.

Now let me ask you a question for a story I'm writing but please, please don't raise your hackles and don't think I'm questioning your horse, your honor or what you do.

I'm just writing a story.

Every once in a while, I manage to phrase a question wrong. Like I did yesterday morning to Jimmy Toner. Thinking about the Diana Handicap, I saw him standing by the training track, grabbed my tape recorder, scrambled out of my car and fumbled my first question like a rookie running back in the rain. It went something like, "How's Wonder Again? She's been a little disappointing this year, do you think . . . "

That's where I blew it.

"Disappointing?" He looked at me like I had keyed his car and ripped his favorite ballplayer. Which in a way I did – Wonder Again is certainly his favorite ballplayer. But that's not what I wanted to do. I'm not ripping Wonder Again or the year she's having. Two tough losses without a spot of luck does not alter how you look at a stakes-winning filly who does nothing wrong.

I meant to say, "With a little luck, her year could be perfect. Has it been disappointing to have her run so well but not win?" And then we would have gone from there.

Like I said, I love Wonder Again. Big bay filly with resolute eyes, broad shoulders, conviction in every move. She galloped past on the Oklahoma as I was trying to climb out of the hole I had dug myself simply by getting the words out wrong.

Her deliberate stride cut through the sticky going of the Oklahoma, her ears laid back across her head, her eyes focused on each impending stride. Toner watched her, a cross between a proud father and a helpless air-traffic controller. His eyes watched her while his mind wandered to the lands that only trainers know.

She pulled up from her gallop and we tried to get back to talking about a

Jimmy Toner

QUESTIONS

good filly. Which we did, but it took awhile. And thank the gods of journalism that I botched it with Toner who's as easygoing as they get on the backside. He always has time for your questions and always answers as honestly as he can. Usually, it's like talking to my father about a horse. This time, it eventually got there, it just took a few minutes for me to make sure he knew that I still respected Wonder Again.

Now mind you, Toner wasn't hostile, just understandably defensive about his stable's star. Which made me mad that I had caused such a reaction. I want to talk to confident trainers about good horses and great performances.

Like Toner and Wonder Again. Like Del Carroll and Tap The Admiral. Like today's stakes winners, and tomorrow's, the next day's . . .

I'll try to get the questions out better and trainers, you keep the answers coming. Because evidently we're in this together.

The day before I unintentionally slagged Wonder Again, Steve Young asked me about the newspaper business.

I told him that it's great except that I wonder if the business plan makes sense with all the overhead, the risk, the capital investment, the travel and the hours. Young gave me an unsympathetic look, and awaited a "Duh!" from my mouth.

When it didn't come, he took up the lead.

"You're talking to me about an unsound business plan? About capital investment? About travel? About risk? Sounds like training horses."

I think I'll stick to newspapers.

SARATOGA

It's where bad days go to die.

It's where romantics go to pursue their daydreams. Saratoga is the boundary between the world you know and the one you can only imagine. Come on in and spoil yourself.

In an age when Thoroughbred "Racinos" resemble senior daycare centers, Saratoga is a summer camp for adults. It's super-charged with youthful energy and hope, without the noisy slot machines, oppressive cigarette smoke and degenerate ticket-ripping jockey-cursing slime. Openly carry the Racing Form down Broadway, debate about the merits of the Ragozin or Thorograph sheets and banter about the horses well past last call. Every day is a special day.

Of course, special is in the eye of the beholder. Upset and Jim Dandy no doubt still laugh about their time at the Spa; Man O'War and Gallant Fox only mutter something about a graveyard. Far from it – every horse at this meet is live. If horses have talent, they're probably here. Last summer, three equine athletes possessing a wicked combination of beauty and brawn summered here. You remember Volponi, Orientate and Storm Flag Flying. Who's the next superstar?

It's easy to be impressed by the well-oiled mega-stables. They're all here and their regally bred stock will win the majority of the races and become familiar faces in the winner's circle. Yet sometimes fate has other plans. We root for the boutique barns. Their stories are usually more interesting anyway.

You don't need a passport to soak up international flavor – horsemen and women from all over the world converge to run for the huge purses and acclaim. Jockeys become headliners and we watch in awe as their bravery, honor and self-reliance are tested every day. The colony is an eclectic mix, grinding out a legitimate 12-hour day, six or seven days a week, which is unique in the world of professional sports.

Appreciate their craft and ask yourself . . . What would Edgar Prado do? It's easy to be impressed with the way he interacts with trainers, owners and patrons. Prado is reliable, courteous and dependable. Now there's a suitable role model in an era of sports jerks.

Characters and personalities abound. We'll remind you that the experience isn't entirely about nailing the late double. Last summer, The Saratoga Special brought you Jay Longton at the equine pool; TV analyst Anthony Mormino; jockey's agent Ron Anderson; trainers Eddie Miller, Treveille Carty and Ray Cameron; Missing Miss, the one-eyed filly; Sam the Bugler; starter Bob Duncan; Philadelphia-based trainers Michael D'Amario and Kate DeMasi; Tracie Smith rider, trainer and owner; Finger Lakes-based trainers Charlton Baker and Jonathan Buckley; jockey Dodie Duys; the giant poker game they call the Fasig-Tipton yearling sales; and Steve Ropitzsky, a local farmer who's been delivering clover, carrots and corn to the backside for 32 years.

One million fans will hustle through the turnstiles this summer. Most get sucked into the herd mentality created by the Saratoga paparazzi. Each afternoon the races are analyzed and scrutinized to death. Ironic considering that many sharpies pari-mutuelly prefer Aqueduct's frozen tundra. Instead, take a deep breath, exhale and enjoy and behold Saratoga racing for what it is. Golf has the Masters, tennis has Wimbledon, NCAA basketball has March Madness and racing has Saratoga. It's a feast for the horse lover and the senses, the beautiful landscapes and beautiful bodyscapes, exquisite food, the arts, the people, the pines, and the music . . . different in every sense.

Our goal is to expose you to the people, the horses and their stories, to offer new answers to the puzzling questions, to dig deeper and work harder, to be reporters and fans – and to have a great time doing it. We'll shine the spotlight on racing's best, yet champion the little guys and grunts doing the dirty work, whose successes here not only highlight their year but their entire career.

Some say that traveling to Saratoga can bring your life into greater perspective. For us, the best thing about it is that tomorrow we get to do it again. Every day a new hero.

Lights, camera, action.

– Quint Kessenich

Del Carroll

What I love about this newspaper....

....is stopping and talking to a horseman about a specific horse aiming for a specific race. What I hate about this newspaper is sometimes I don't have time to get the conversation out of a tape recorder and into this newspaper in time for that specific race.

With that in mind, here goes. I stopped by Del Carroll's barn Thursday to talk about Tap The Admiral and the Bernard Baruch.

An old-time horseman with an old-time horse.

Carroll leaned on the wooden rail of his barn and wanted to talk horses. Tap The Admiral, a 5-year-old who's made $445,686 (before the Baruch), wanted to get in the conversation too. He leaned over his webbing and looked me right in the eye like only good horses do. He nickered for his lunch. He pawed the ground for his lunch. He implored his trainer, coach, father for his lunch.

No luck, old boy. Still early – 10:03 and chores to be done.

Carroll motioned to his groom down the shedrow.

"See what happened Jose, we went ahead and fed him a few minutes early yesterday and now he thinks every day he's going to get fed when he wants to," Carroll said. "We're not going to feed him early anymore, he's too smart."

Jose understood about a quarter of what Carroll said but Tap The Admiral got it all. Mad, he pawed the ground some more.

"Haaa, Papa," Jose said to the horse's red face, which rocked up and down like an oil derrick.

Del Carroll II is a born horseman. His father Del Sr. trained for many years and died from injuries sustained in a fall while exercising a horse (in the late 1970s). I remember Del Carroll Sr. training horses for Will Farish at Delaware Park. Winter's Tale comes to mind. He used to run over fences at Delaware when I was growing up a half-mile from the track.

There were horses like Tap The Admiral back then and luckily there are horses like Tap The Admiral now.

"He wants to do it. He makes my job easy, makes it fun. He loves to train, loves to run. He's just happy to be here. He's always got that sparkle in his eye, always willing to please," Carroll said. "The best description is he makes us look good because he likes to do it. We all know that that's all we're trying to get these horses to do, do it on their own and hopefully we can get them fit enough."

Tap The Admiral was tired of conversation – it was lunch time.

"Hey, hey, hey. That's enough. Stop it. No, no, no," Carroll said to his stable star.

"He's so spoiled," Carroll said to me.

Tap The Admiral looked each of us in the eye.

"They're all different but with this horse, he's always had the attitude that he's the man, always believed that he could," Carroll said. "Whether it was sprinting for maiden special or maiden 60 early in his career, he thought he could. All I have to do is keep telling him, 'All right, you're the man.' "

Tap The Admiral dug at the ground like he was looking for buried treasure under the rubber stall matt.

Carroll tossed a few pieces of grain at Tap The Admiral's nose. They bounced off. The horse knew the game well, and pawed the ground again.

"I'm hoping he'll stay around. These grass horses can stay around until they're 6, 7. Mostly I'm hoping because he's a buddy," Carroll said. "It's fun to have them around. They come and go too quick. It looks like he'll get enough racing in the northern turf season so I can give him a rest. That helps keep these turf horses around. It's like going to Florida and trying to buy a used boat, it's got 300 hours a year on it. Try to buy one up here and it's got 30 hours a year on it because it's only used seasonally. I'm trying to do that with him."

Finally, the delay grew too much for both trainer and horse to stand. Carroll started to walk down the shedrow to ask his help how they were coming along with lunch.

The last thing he said was so well put that I thought about it all day: "It's all a big game. Once in a while we make money at it, most of the time we lose money.

That kinda summarizes it."

QUOTES:

"Does it hurt when you fall?"

– Stupid Question of the Day
To a retired jump jockey:

"Do you guys practice that?"

– Stupid Question, Take Two
To a retired jump jockey on the art of falling:

"What time is it in India?"

– Trainer Kiaran McLaughlin Saturday morning

"Do you like him, like him. Or like him?"

– Overheard at the sales grounds

"Say 'Bacon, egg and cheese' and she'll look right at you."

– Trainer Rick Schosberg, to a photographer trying to take a picture of his dog

LADY TAK

Steve Asmussen doesn't like to be called a liar.

So he won't tell the truth.

At the Keeneland 2-year-olds-in-training sale last April, Lady Tak was clocked galloping out from a 1-furlong breeze. Asmussen and Bill Heiligbrodt timed the chestnut daughter of Mutakddim. She went an eighth in 10 and one – the official clocker caught that. But how fast did she gallop out?

"Honestly? I wouldn't want to be quoted on that, you better ask Bill," Asmussen said with a big smile, moments after Lady Tak won the Test stakes. "They can think he's a liar."

So how fast, Bill?

"Thirty-two and two but nobody'd believe me," Heiligbrodt said of the freakish time. "I thought I had made a mistake so I went and found J.B. McKathan because I know he times everything. I checked it out with him and he said it's there."

That was good and bad for Heiligbrodt – McKathan buys horses for the deep-pocketed Bob Baffert.

"I didn't think I'd be able to buy her because I thought Baffert would buy her," Heiligbrodt said. "They didn't buy her because she's little bitty and she had no pedigree."

Heiligbrodt bought her for $75,000. In the Test, she may as well have been 18 hands and pure blueblood. Ridden by Jerry Bailey, Lady Tak sat inside Molto Vita while fractions rattled up on the board like an EZ Pass counter at the Lincoln Tunnel.

On the turn, Molto Vita started to feel the effects while Lady Tak picked it up and Kentucky Oaks and Acorn winner Bird Town stalked to the outside. Lady Tak cut the turn and was free when Bird Town couldn't match the acceleration. Lady Tak drew off to win by 4 1/2.

Bird Town, prepping for the longer Alabama, wasn't under any punishment from Edgar Prado. She finished second while House Party picked up the third-place check.

Lady Tak broke the Test stakes record and nearly snapped Darby Creek Road's 25-year-old track record of 1:20 3/5.

"She just went seven-eighths at Saratoga in 1:20 and four," Asmussen said. "If you don't think I'll be sitting in a coffee shop when I'm 80 talking about the fastest Test in history, you're wrong."

The fastest Test in history, that's saying something, especially when you think of past winners like Moccasin, Gamely, Ta Wee, Desert Vixen, Lady's Secret, Safely Kept and Go For Wand.

Of course, Asmussen and the rest of his horses know all about Lady Tak's speed.

"When I work something with her, they usually just give up. If I have to get a good work into her, I work her with an old gelding of my father's, Mountain General. My father won't disown me," Asmussen said. "He won a Grade III at Churchill last time. He gives her a good half and then says, 'I don't care, I don't care.' He doesn't even like to see her on the track."

There isn't a filly in the country that wants to see her going 7 furlongs on the dirt. Asmussen holds out hope that she can get a 1 1/8-mile around one turn at Belmont but knows that today's conditions were ideal.

"I thought this was it all year. She's a small filly so distance wears her out a little," Asmussen said. "That speed comes from inside. Maybe it's like the movie, Seabiscuit; he wasn't very big either."

It was Lady Tak's sixth win from nine career starts. She won her first five including the Fair Ground Oaks but then lost three tough ones in a row. Elloluv upset her in the Ashland, she had a rough trip in the Kentucky Oaks where she finished sixth and then lost the Acorn to Bird Town by a nose.

From the moment she lost the Acorn, Asmussen aimed Lady Tak for the Test. Twenty-four days after the Acorn, she had her first work, 5 furlongs in 1:02. A week later, she blasted 5 furlongs on Saratoga's main track in 59 seconds. A week after that, she went a half in 47 3/5.

Five days later, she owned a stakes record at Saratoga.

Bobby Frankel stands just outside the wooden rail that runs along his barn.

There's something in the way he moves that says it's a big day. He looks like a guy who's waiting for the bus and is afraid he might have missed it.

About that time, Jerry Bailey walks over with a pair of black Nike gloves already on his hands. Javier Castellano is there, helmet on, gloves on, warm but nervous smile. Edgar Prado kneels down at the base of a tree, the most relaxed of anybody. Aaron Gryder shows up wearing a longsleeve pullover on a warm morning.

Frankel leans against a tired flower garland from Wild Spirit's Delaware Handicap win. A big bay horse circles the shedrow, solid and strong. A smaller coiled chestnut walks around in front of him. Antonio Graell pulls his helmet off, through for the day.

Frankel looks around, "What do you want to do?"

Prado seems to already know what he's doing; Castellano knows he'll be told. Bailey says it doesn't matter. "You're the boss." Gryder laughs and pinches the right arm of his pullover, "That's why I'm wearing this."

"OK, Aaron, you work Empire Maker, Jerry you get on Special Rate," Frankel says, turning to the open walking ring where horses are in all stages of their morning.

"Ruben, does Special Rate need a tongue tie?"

Special Rate gets his tongue tied while Frankel shouts for a horse to be ready in 10 minutes. Prado still kneels at the base of the tree while Castellano rises to get on Peace Rules.

"Five-eighths. You're going with the pony. You won't get around there if you don't," Frankel says to Castellano. "Remember, don't fight with him or he'll go in 56."

With his legs still dangling down Peace Rules' sides, Castellano fixes the knot in his reins. The horse shakes his head while energizing himself as he's walked onto the path that leads past the Oklahoma and to the main track. Pure exuberance.

Empire Maker comes next. His now famous black blinkers cover up the broad star between his eyes. He takes everything in, watching like a grazing deer in an open field. Gryder adjusts his stirrups and takes a deep breath.

Frankel follows Peace Rules while Empire Maker and Special Rate amble behind. The trainer turns to see their progress, maybe see their reactions too.

Cooling-out horses halt as Frankel's threesome crosses through the stable area and makes its way along the parking lot adjacent to Union Avenue. Horses stabled on the main-track side pass horses stabled at Oklahoma.

The guards boom a long deep "Horses" and traffic halts on Union Avenue.

"You sit off him a couple of lengths," Frankel says to Gryder. "If he gets away from you, don't worry, ride it like a race. Twelve, 12 and change."

Gryder smiles like he'll be glad when this is over, but is still supremely confident that he'll do it right.

Empire Maker extends his focus as he gets closer to the track. The gate on the main track is still shut and the horses must mill around for a moment. Miguel, the outrider who will take Empire Maker to the pole hands Frankel a thin leather pony strap. Frankel takes it and walks halfway to Empire Maker.

"Hold on Bobby, do me a favor, take this one," Miguel says handing Frankel a thicker leather strap with a brass snap at the end.

"Need a stronger one, huh," Frankel says, taking the strap and snapping it on the right side of Empire Maker's bit. Frankel holds the shank while the gate's open and three of Todd Pletcher's horses bounce onto to the track. Gryder has his goggles down ready to go. Empire Maker never balks, which he sometimes does, and the three horses jog off the right way.

"Peace Rules going five-eighths," Frankel says to the clocker's radioman at the gap. "Empire Maker and Special Rate, three-quarters."

Frankel walks to the outside rail and stares down the track.

THE WORKS

"It'll be all right," he says as the horses get smaller in the distance.

Frankel's phone rings.

"You're going five-eighths with Epicentre," Frankel says into the phone. "You and Prado. I don't care, either way, either way. Bye."

Two horses come into sight, heading down the long backside.

"Is this them?" Frankel asks. "Yeah, yeah, this is them."

Special Rate and Bailey have a long lead on Empire Maker and Gryder. Steady, they get closer and bound around the turn. Bailey one off the rail and Gryder right on the rail. Both jockeys are motionless, they could be sitting in chairs.

Empire Maker strides by in a high action that's gradually making up ground on Special Rate. Around the turn they go and then winnow away in the distance, joining up near the wire. Frankel watches them all the way to the finish. He says nothing.

His head pivots to the left in search of the red horse, Peace Rules. There he is, visually quicker than the other two. He rolls around the turn with Castellano looking like he's got an angry hornet buzzing around his head. Afraid to move, they go winging past and are gone as fast as they came.

Frankel backs off the rail and takes a look around. Moments pass while he asks the radioman for times on "Bobby Frankel's horses."

Empire Maker jogs past, camel-brown sand marks across each side. Special Rate slows to a walk, head hung low, like a beaten man.

Empire Maker eyes the open gap, jinks a half step in that direction and Gryder urges him past. They agree to disagree without a fight and carry on to just past the gap. They turn in and walk back to the track's exit.

Gryder nods to Frankel. Bailey nods to Frankel.

They all head home.

The official times were Peace Rules, 5 furlongs in 1:00.06. Empire Maker, 6 furlongs in 1:12.03 and Special Rate, 6 furlongs in 1:13.22.

Dance but don't lead.

Smell but don't touch. Strum but don't jam.

Welcome to Mornings by Aaron Gryder. The 33-year-old jockey rides some of the best horses on the grounds. Weekend favorites Medaglia d'Oro (Whitney) and Empire Maker (Jim Dandy) to be exact. But that's where it stops. He works them in the mornings and Jerry Bailey rides them in the afternoons.

Both are trained by Bobby Frankel, who does things his way. Nobody's complaining – especially not Gryder, who has breezed the Belmont Stakes winner at least a dozen times.

"I work a lot of horses for Bobby and a lot of people tell me, 'You're crazy, you're wasting your time, you're wasting your time.' I go around every morning and ask everybody if they need help. If they don't need help than I've at least offered my services," Gryder said. "I'd rather get on a horse for Bobby, even if he doesn't ride me now because if something falls through the cracks, you know it could be a very nice horse. I know when I work his horses, there will be a payday someday."

Frankel named Gryder on Dreamers Glory in today's eighth race, so there's at least a chance for a payday. Gryder jokes with Frankel about riding Empire Maker and Frankel tries to placate Gryder for all the hard work. It's a solid relationship between two professionals.

"The first time I got on him was here last year, a couple of months before he had ever run. Frankel said, 'Do you want to come get on my

Aaron Gryder

THE RIDER

Derby horse?' People always have dreams but there's only a handful of stables in the country that can say that and it might come true," Gryder said. "If I'm going to work horses that I'm not riding, I'd rather it be good horses than horses that are aggravating. It's always more enjoyable to get on good horses."

Funny thing, enjoyment. Empire Maker is a thinker, a horse who watches everything and tests. He's scrutinized by the media and debated by the fans. It's Gryder's job to keep him between the rails (a big thing in his case) and give him the proper work needed to win races like the Belmont, the Jim Dandy and the Travers. This is enjoyable?

"He has his quirks and I know that at some point he's going to try something," Gryder said. "It's not like he's a rogue horse but galloping out he'll stop pretty abruptly within a three-stride period. He usually tries you about the same spot. If you weren't prepared for it, he could easily put you in a compromising position."

Gryder won 11 races at the Belmont spring meet and has won two races so far at Saratoga. He's won riding titles at Hollywood Park, Arlington Park, Churchill Downs and Aqueduct. Riding horses like Empire Maker in the morning puts Gryder in an enviable position. Not riding them in the afternoon puts him in a slightly pitiful position. Or does it?

"I don't get frustrated. Obviously I'd like to ride him in the afternoon, and I play around with Bobby and voice my opinion. I'm still young and I'm going to get my chance," Gryder said. "I've been on some good horses in the past and I need some good horses now. I'm in the biggest lull since I've been in New York but I have no doubts that I'll get back to that point, working for that stable can only help when it starts to click again. I'll get on a roll again."

Gryder's "some good horses" would make anybody's list. Sunday Silence, Bayakoa, Ferdinand, not to mention the countless stars he works for Frankel.

"Ferdinand was a very, very good horse, more of a laid-back horse. Sunday Silence was definitely the most impressive horse. Even in the mornings he was flashy when he worked," Gryder said. "Empire Maker will work as quick as you want or as slow as you want, the way Sunday Silence would work . . . I worked him the last time before the Santa Anita Derby. Charlie (Whittingham) said, 'Just let him run along, that was never riding him, that was just let him run along.' You'd sit on him and at the eighth pole, you'd grab the reins a little and let him take it. He worked in 58 and 4 that day, like 11 and change the last eighth. The way he went from so relaxed with his ears pricked to when I turned the reins, he was explosive."

Gryder rides in the morning for lots of reasons, but one in particular.

"There's no feeling like getting on a good horse. I enjoy that half-hour," he said. "When you let your hands open a little bit and they jump into the bridle, that's a feeling we all want. It's different."

Morning or afternoon.

ALLEN JERKENS

Allen Jerkens: The great contradiction.

He talks about horses like he's one of the breed. He tries to get in a horse's head; how they sleep, whether they clean the feed tub, what makes them run, what makes them tail off and what separates one from the other.

Then he'll tell you none of it matters anyway.

Of course, the man has been winning races since 1950, has a plaque in the Hall of Fame and is banging along at a 25-percent clip this year.

Something matters. Especially when it comes to a mare like Shine Again, who has earned more than $1.1 million under "The Chief's" tutelage. Then again, she's a good pupil. The daughter of Wild Again is 2-for-3 this year with a win in the Grade II Genuine Risk at Belmont. Only a tough trip in her latest, where she was a fast-closing second in the Vagrancy, keeps this from being a shot at four in a row.

Owned by Bohemia Stable, Shine Again finished second in last year's Honorable Miss before going on to capture her second straight Ballerina at the end of the meet. The plan hasn't changed. Much.

Again, there's contradiction. Last year, Jerkens ran her in the Vagrancy; she finished third, then won two straight allowance races. This year, she ran second in the Vagrancy and he gave her a break before going into this 6-furlong dash worth $100,000.

"She's just about the same as last year," Jerkens said. "She seems to know what's going on all the time, she knows what to expect by what you do with her. She knows if she has a sharp work a few days before the race, she knows something's up. I try not to work her too much, but on the same hand, she's a big filly and you have to do something with her."

Shine Again worked 5 furlongs in 1:01 1/5 Tuesday and there's no telling what kind of Jerkens' spin she's had since. Jean-Luc Samyn rides her every morning and will again be her afternoon pilot.

A trainer who once worked for Jerkens said it was tough to learn a lot from him because you could never figure out why he did the things he did. It's all feel with Jerkens. He might blow them out a quarter or work them a mile on any given day. There is no set model.

It's all about getting a horse to respond to the program set out. Of course, it doesn't always work. Horses are different, Jerkens knows.

"Some do care and some don't care," he said. "I've had horses that we've done everything we could to make them happy and we couldn't see a difference....

....and then others it made all the difference in the world."

The Saratoga Special

Succeed is in the house.

He's the big bay horse I ride in the morning, the one I'm slapping on the neck and talking to all the time. The Saratoga Special saddle towel gives it away. It's the return of the pony express, although he's no pony. He's all horse. And if this seems like a repeat column, it is in a way. I wrote that he was coming to Saratoga last year. Now that he's here, I can really wax on about the greatest horse that ever lived.

Just like people, you meet horses along the way that you connect with, ones who see the world the same way you do. What Succeed thinks is funny, I think is hilarious; what he's scared of, I'm petrified of; what intrigues him, mesmerizes me. It's been this way from the beginning.

I met him at Gulfstream Park in 1998 as I walked up Mark Hennig's shedrow on my first day of work. I galloped him while I was there, somehow sealing a bond that would go on for five years – and counting. Eventually he flunked out of flat racing and I convinced Hennig and Lou and Patrice Wolfson (of Harbor View Farm) to make him a steeplechaser. I ran him once, he finished second, pulled his suspensory, and then he looked me in the eye – broken, stranded, looking for a buddy.

Who needs the Thoroughbred Retirement Foundation? No horse around has a better life. He spends more time outside than a mailbox. He does a little work during the week and plays on the weekends. He's got a big belly and a bigger pension plan. Heck, he's spending his summer in Saratoga. How good is that?

He's no dummy, he loves it here. He jogs when he feels like jogging, stops when he feels like stopping, sleeps in the sun when it shines on his back.

He has stuck his head in the middle of the fruit truck, ponied a jumper around Clare Court, watched horses train on the main track, followed amused kids down horse paths, eaten leaves off trees, and even hopped over a drainage ditch into a barn. All just for the fun of it.

This is your favorite horse without a looming test to bend him to the limit. He'll never run in another race. He'll never have his joints tapped. He'll never clang around in a gate. He'll never get his tongue tied down. He'll never get another shot of Lasix. He'll never be asked to lay it all down while a whip slaps off his side. He'll never miss another meal. And hopefully he'll come back to Saratoga every year.

Succeed's good for the soul. Sometimes in this business, you forget why you're in it, why you ever started. I know it's a business, a way to make a living, but for me, it's for the Succeeds of the world. So many horses come and go that you sometimes seal yourself off from them. It's easier to ignore them than care. Occasionally there's one that won't let go. He (or she) ties into you. And usually breaks your heart.

That's what's so good about Succeed. He only lightens my heart. It's good to see a horse enjoy life and know he's never going to be tested again. Imagine training horses if you never had to run them. Just train them – keep them happy, keep them fresh, ease off their legs, feed them so they're high, turn them out so they can roll, rub on them so they look pretty and ride them for the sheer joy.

Take away the stopwatches, toss the condition books; we're going into the pleasure-horse business. Nah, that's not it – pleasure-horse hobby is more like it.

Succeed is the ultimate hobby horse. He's made me believe in breeding. A full-brother to two-time Eclipse Award winner Flawlessly, Succeed has it all when it comes to horses. Clever, supple, great mouth, good eye, sinewy moves, innate stamina – and he shares it with me every morning.

Hopefully he'll share it with you before it's over. I know it sounds like a line from a small-town politician, but part of the reason I brought him here was so the world could see him. Just to know that he's out there. A stoic horse that had more leg problems than Forrest Gump now has a great life.

There's an old Indian legend that says if you save someone's life, you're responsible for it forever.

Sean, meet Succeed. Succeed, meet Sean.

Coming Home

Mickey Preger Jr. spent his life in New York while working for his dad. They teamed up with horses like Fearless Leader, Mairzy Doates, Real Easy, Little Bad Wolf. Preger breaks babies in Camden, S.C. during the winter and spends his summers at Delaware Park where he trains seven horses.

Preger came to Saratoga with two horses to run over the weekend. It's been better than a family reunion.

During the races on Thursday, Preger walked down to the scales at the finish line. The phone rang.

"Mickey, it's the stewards."

"Hello," Preger said. "What did I do already?"

"Mickey, how are you? How's you dad? Everything OK?"

"Sure, everything's fine. Did you want something?"

"Just to say hello, Mickey. It's good to see you."

That was just part of a great trip for Preger.

"At Delaware, you can stand at the rail and train six sets and you never see an Empire Maker go past or a Funny Cide or any horse that makes you stop and say 'Who's that?' " Preger said. "It's fine down there but it's not New York. This is good racing."

"Who don't I miss?"

– Longtime New York-based Mickey Preger Jr., on returning to his stomping grounds

Can't we all just get along? The Whitney was meant to be a horse race – with Medaglia d'Oro and Volponi playing the lead roles. Instead it became a war of words.

P.G. Johnson, trainer of Volponi, reportedly dissed Bobby Frankel, trainer of Medaglia d'Oro before the race. Frankel bit his tongue and waited until Medaglia d'Oro won the Whitney before he said how he felt about it.

It bothered him.

And it really bothers me.

I always thought we were in this together. Trainers, jockeys, owners, fans and especially writers. Yeah, sex sells, and having one trainer slag another coming into a big race makes good copy.

Bobby Frankel

My problem is I like both Frankel and Johnson. And I think they might even like each other if they stopped reading the papers and talked to each other.

Yeah, I'm idealistic, I know. But you either like Frankel or you don't. You either like Johnson or you don't. Why? Because they tell it like it is. They always give their opinions. They have no desire to suffer fools. They go with their guts. They don't care about their images. Sometimes they talk for the sake of talking. And they've been successful every step of their lives.

Go visit the Hall of Fame.

They say opposites attract. Then again, like charges repel. So in that respect, sames deflect. Makes sense then that Frankel and Johnson aren't getting along.

They're horsemen, I know that. They train horses with conviction and confidence.

Frankel gets more bad press than all the other trainers combined. Once a day, there's a letter in the Form ripping him for either winning too many races or not thanking someone who needed to be thanked or doing something negative to the game. He was quoted as saying Barclay Tagg was cracking under the pressure during the Triple Crown. What he meant was . . . ah, it's too late, the damage is done. Sure he was critical of Funny Cide's fast work before the Belmont, but that was his opinion and he shared it. I figure that's why he was asked.

One time I screwed up a story about Frankel. He pointed out the mistake and then told me not to worry about it, everybody makes mistakes, called this paper a stepping stone.

Johnson is old school. He's quick with his tongue and quick with his opinions. The toothpick in the right side of his mouth can move pretty fast when he's talking about training horses.

I once sold two horses for Johnson and when I asked him what he wanted me to do with the money, he asked me if half sounded fair. In the horse business? This was impossible. I sent a check to his owner for half the money and she called me a week later. She started with, "We have a problem . . . " She ended with, "You gave me too much money." Yeah, in the horse business.

Neither Frankel nor Johnson roll out the safe cliches. They tell it like it is – all the time. There is no gray area. Is that good or bad? Johnson might have been harsh about Frankel and Medaglia d'Oro but I can't help but wonder about the context.

So now we're at a standoff. It's the view that worries me. I've been in the crowd when a trainer says something about another horse or person. Then I've been in the crowd when that something gets reported back to the other person.

It's called goading, I believe. How many brothers and sisters do you have?

P.G. Johnson

If you have two, which means there were three of you, then you understand goading. In my house it went something like, "Joey says you stink." "Well, you tell Joey I said he stinks." "Joey, Sean said you stink." And away we would go. My sister Sheila would get to change the channel while Joey and I rolled around the floor trading headlocks.

They have the Jockey Club Round Table. I want to have the Whitney Round Table. I'm inviting Frankel and Johnson to sit down and have dinner with me; just the three of us, it'll be awkward over the appetizers, but then I think we'll get along.

See, I like Bobby Frankel. And I like P.G. Johnson. Personally I like knowing where I stand. If you like me, then good; if you hate me, then too bad. I can't change either so let's move on.

Of course, I still believe in world peace. So where should we eat, boys?

Empire Maker and Strong Hope

Todd Pletcher's getting so good he's making editorial decisions.

And you know what? He isn't too bad at it.

"I hope the story isn't that Empire Maker lost," Pletcher said. "I hope it's about a horse who's won five in a row. A big, strong, beautiful, well-bred horse that's getting better and better and handling every class step and every distance step."

OK, you win.

Strong Hope is still the story. Throw in an Empire Maker sidebar and a Funny Cide footnote and the Jim Dandy/Haskell epic is written.

This was supposed to be the day that prepared the Travers. Empire Maker was meant to win the Jim Dandy and Funny Cide was meant to win the Haskell at Monmouth Park. Last horse standing in the Travers gets the loot.

Ah, the best laid plans of . . . and Peace Rules dominated the Haskell and Funny Cide never got untracked. As for Empire Maker, he was upended by speed and tenacity.

Strong Hope, owned by Eugene and Laura Melnyk, went straight to the lead – where he does his best work. California-invader During tracked him in second while Tafaseel held his own near the lead. Nacheezmo was just behind them and Empire Maker was well off the moderate pace. The Belmont Stakes winner had only Congrats behind him.

By the turn, Strong Hope and John Velazquez were still going strong and Empire Maker was circling the field. With 3 furlongs to run, it was between those two.

Empire Maker never went string-straight in the stretch while Strong Hope fought hard on the rail. He looked home free until Empire Maker finally started to make up ground late.

It was a cringer, either way. Strong Hope had enough left to hold on while Empire Maker roared under the wire, running out of room. Congrats rallied late to pick up third

According to Velazquez, Strong Hope is still learning.

"He still doesn't know that much," said Velazquez. "He's getting better with each start. Every day he gives you a little more. He's a little headstrong the first part and then when he runs, he goes side to side, not straight. He didn't care about the other horse, he was looking where the footprints were."

Hopefully he'll relax a little more the next time. Now he's had a two-turn race so he should be better in the next race.

The Jim Dandy was Strong Hope's fifth consecutive victory. He broke his maiden at Aqueduct in April and then chipped off two allowance races at Belmont before winning the Dwyer. All on the heat.

"He's just naturally fast and it's working – we're not looking to change it. He's such a strong horse that you're going to get in a fight with him to back him up," Pletcher said. "We try to just let him run his race. You wouldn't find a horse any better looking than he is today. He's a beautiful, strong horse with a great temperament. He's just what you're looking for."

It's exactly what the Melynks saw when they bought him at the Saratoga yearling sales in 2001. A cool $1.7 million brought down the hammer.

"So far everything we've asked him to do, he's done," Pletcher said. "To be honest with you he came in and they said they liked him on the farm. It wasn't for a little while that I realized he was the Grand Slam colt who brought $1.7 million. We trained him for a little while and said this colt is all right. We looked a little more and realized that's who he was."

As for the Travers . . .

Pletcher didn't hesitate. "That's why we're here."

I don't know if I can even say a speech. There are so many people to thank. I'm going to start with my first grade-teacher and work my way down from there. I might just have to say, 'Sorry guys, I love you guys and thanks to all of you.' It won't be one of my best but as long as I get that plaque, it'll be OK. It's going to be one of those, 'I need a moment here' speeches."

That'll be fine, Mike, that'll be fine.

Along with trainer Sonny Hine and horses Dance Smartly and Precisionist, Mike Smith will join racing's elite today when he's inducted into the Hall of Fame.

Not bad for a kid from Roswell, N.M. Yeah, that Roswell, better known for flying saucers than flying jockeys.

Following an uncle who trained and a father who rode races, Smith won his first race on Forever Man at Santa Fe. It was 1982. He quickly left home and made his way around the country by racetrack. Arkansas, Nebraska, Illinois, Minnesota, Kentucky, New York and finally California.

His best move was to New York, when he found a permanent box in the New York jocks' room. This is where he would make it. From 1991 to 1993, Smith won more races in New York than any jockey and he won the Saratoga riding title each of those years.

In 1991, Leo O'Brien took Smith to The Curragh to ride Fourstars Allstar in the 2,000 Guineas. They won it in a photo. Eclipse Awards came his way in 1993 and 1994. Smith was the regular rider for Horse of the Year Holy Bull and Champion Older Mare Sky Beauty in 1994. He won 20 Grade I stakes that year.

Then it all came crumbling down. Smith broke his collarbone in March 1998 and broke two vertebrae in his back at Saratoga that summer. He was well on his way to his first Saratoga riding title (and took the Travers aboard Coronado's Quest) since 1993 and lost it on the last day – while sitting in a hospital bed – to John Velazquez.

Smith returned quickly from the back injury but business was lost.

Eventually he relocated to California and discovered the girl of his dreams.

Azeri. She changed everything. The 2002 Horse of the Year gave Smith another big horse to push his ballot through the slot. She won everything and Smith had finished his final primary.

"I've thought all along that she had the ability to be one of the best fillies I've ever ridden and she's come even further than that. She's the best filly I've ever ridden and I have not reached her full potential yet," said Smith, rattling off the names of champions Inside Information, Sky Beauty, Heavenly Prize and Jersey Girl. "She just does things so easy. She's so well balanced, she can make up a length like that. She used to be awkward but now she's matured. She's just so naturally quick that she can leave the gate and open up three."

And more. The 5-year-old mare has won 13 of 14 starts, all with Smith aboard.

"To look at her, she's a basic-looking mare. She doesn't stand out, but when you get on her and take three steps, you know you're on something special," Smith said. "She just carries herself that way. I've always had the utmost confidence in her and with every race she gives you more. Every time she ran, she was there."

Azeri means everything to Smith.

"It's more special because of what I've been through to get here," said Smith., who enters the Hall with 4,258 career wins and more than $157 million in lifetime purse earnings (through Aug. 2). "Now that I'm here, to know that I'm back, it's very special. I'm so relieved, it's a humble feeling."

Humility always worked for Smith. When asked how he rides Azeri, he makes it sound easy.

"I just let her get the job done."

Just like he's been doing for all these years.

MIKE SMITH

Mike Smith speaks his way into the Hall of Fame:

"I was so nervous because I just didn't want to leave anybody out, Jeez, I got so flustered up there that I left the most important people out so I had to run back up and get it done. I wanted to keep some of the important people toward the end and I totally blew Shug (McGaughey) off. I had a big long speech for him and I blew it. When I got to the bottom of the stairs, I said, 'Oh my God, you got to let me back up.' They said, 'No it's over.' I said, 'No you get me back up now.' I'm such an idiot. But it worked out. I'm glad I got to say what I said because he means the world to me."

"He'll forever be my coach."

– On now fellow Hall of Famer Angel Cordero

"If it wasn't for Steve Adika, I would have never made it. Trust me, he'll tell you."

– On his former agent:

There was one sure way to get three Hall of Famers in the winner's circle for the Hall of Fame Stakes. And it wasn't grab a few navy-blazered inductees from the luncheon and get them to smile. The task was up to Stroll. The 3-year-old colt needed to win so trainer Bill Mott and jockey Jerry Bailey could greet their newest Hall of Fame colleague Mike Smith in the presentation line of the Grade II stakes.

One, two, three. Say cheese.

Stroll sat just off the pace set by Sharp Impact and drew off with ease to win the $150,000 stakes by four widening lengths. Urban King rallied for second and Saint Stephen finished third.

It was the third win in a row for Stroll, who's learning how to rate – something which does not come easy for sons of Maid For Walking. Older brother Patrol, also owned and bred by Claiborne Farm, lost this race last year when he wasn't able to ration his early zeal.

Mike Smith

But Stroll's starting to grasp the approach of relaxing early and finishing late.

"He's very headstrong," said Bailey. "He used to be nearly unrateable, but he's learned how to semi rate. All he has to do is relax a little bit around there because he has a tremendous kick. Going into the turn, they always tend to slow down a little bit to change leads. He came out of the bridle just a little bit there and that was enough."

Two years ago, Bailey won the Hall of Fame Stakes on Mott's Baptize. Earlie Fires, a mentor to Bailey, presented the trophy. This year it was Smith, who also has a history with Bailey.

"It's a special day," Bailey said. "As long as I've known Earlie, I've known Mike longer because we came from the same area. I used to work at a place called the Upper Valley Bar that his grandfather and father owned. I used to stack crates and stuff like that. Mike was a young kid then; we went to the same high school, so there's a long history."

Smith and Bailey, like most jockeys, share similar road stories. They both traveled from track to track (Santa Fe Downs, Sunland Park, Hawthorne, Canterbury, Aksarben, among others) before trying the big time of New York.

Bailey arrived in 1982, while Smith made his appearance in 1989.

"Mike came to New York and said he was going to stay the winter," Bailey said. "He was always a good rider so I figured he'd make it but I had no idea he'd go on and do the things he did."

Smith rode winners all winter that year, and never looked back.

Eclipse Awards, Breeders' Cup victories, stakes by the bunches. And ultimately, the Hall of Fame.

"Why'd we make it? I can't speak for him but I just worked hard," Bailey said. "I assume he did the same thing because he's always been a hard worker. I thought he could make it. I came in and was low man on the totem pole. I worked hard, stuck it out and I made it. So there was no reason he couldn't."

Mott's was one of the first big outfits to open the tack-room door to Smith. The two teamed up to win the Jim Dandy with Chief Honcho during Smith's first Saratoga meet in 1990.

"He was always pretty smooth. Good hands; horses seemed to run well for him," said Mott of Smith. "He's always won races. He's a natural on a horse. Absolutely, I'm proud of him. It's a great honor. You're now a member of an elite group of people. It causes you to look around and see who's in there with you."

Monday, Mike Smith stood in good company.

HALL OF FAME

The Hall of Fame committee picked Bill Nack to give the address at this year's induction ceremony. He did one thing wrong when it comes to warming up a crowd before the main attraction.

He stole the show.

Precisionist, Dance Smartly, Sonny Hine and Mike Smith never had a chance.

"I had to put my sunglasses on," sales consignor Kip Elser said.

"I knew I should have brought some tissues," owner Amy Peltz said.

Yes, Nack had them crying at Fasig-Tipton Monday. Of course, he had them laughing too. And everything else in between. He carried the crowd through his early days at Newsday to covering Swaps in the Washington Park Handicap, working with Round Table to spending mornings with Secretariat to a trip around the world with Cigar.

He told his life story in racing without you ever knowing you were getting his life story. It was eloquent, passionate, historical, thoughtful.

"I was attending the paper's Christmas party . . . and I did something that nobody in the history of journalism had ever done before. I mounted the copy desk in the middle of the sitting room and recited all the Kentucky Derby winners from 1875 to the present one."

Aristides to Cannonero.

Next thing he knew he had the job as turf writer for Newsday. Readers were the lucky ones. Nack covered racing for Sports Illustrated for 23 years until his retirement. He still contributes to Sports Illustrated, GQ and other publications. As good a turf writer as he was he blew his calling. Public speaking.

One stanza was better than the next. You didn't notice the chills on your

arms because you got used to them. He confirmed your belief that this is the greatest game in the world. He made you remember why you ever liked it in the first place.

The six-time Eclipse Award-winning sportswriter was asked once why he liked horse racing. He said for the clarity it provides.

"In a world of muddle and confusion as we piddle between those two eternities of darkness, I came to love racing for its clarity. The cloud-parting clearness of the outcomes. Those epic struggles unto resolution. Indeed, I think sports are generally as popular these days because they do offer clarity."

This was a morning for clarity.

And awards. Lest we forget, there were awards to hand out.

Wanda Hooper accepted the plaque for her late husband Fred's champion sprinter Precisionist. She called the horse's trainer, Ross Fenstermaker, to the podium. Ever a horse trainer, Fenstermaker came up with "He was a good horse. He deserves it."

Tammy Samuel-Balaz accepted the award for Canadian champion Dance Smartly and mentioned the four generations of the mare No Class that she was part of under her family's Sam-Son Farm banner.

Writer Steve Haskin presented the award to late trainer Sonny Hine. Haskin once worked in Hine's barn for a story idea. The article got a groom fined for cooking in the tackroom, a barn foreman divorced because of his living arrangements, and Hine lost an owner because of a quote – in a week. Hine didn't care. Hine's wife, Carolyn, made it all the way to "thank you" before she started crying. She did her best to convey Sonny's spirit.

Jerry Bailey introduced Mike Smith with a flare that he usually saves for the racetrack. He called Smith the best storyteller in the room and even impersonated him with perfection.

Smith had a list of horses, owners, and trainers to thank. The list provided the cues but he went off the cuff the rest of the way. It was Mike Smith at his best. Witty, humble, thoughtful, sincere. Early in the speech while he was thanking horses like Sky Beauty, Holy Bull and Azeri he said he wanted to save Shug McGaughey for last. Then he never mentioned him again. Minutes after he said his goodbyes, he returned to the podium. "I forgot Shug . . . you made me feel like Superman when I pulled on those black and cherry silks."

Hall of Fame Day made a lot of people feel that way.

It was a glorious summer. One we both knew would never last. We woke up together every morning. She knew me, I knew her. We'd run together. Communicate. Share good days and bad.

Her name was Strawberry Reason.

We've both moved on now; she's the mother of a champion and I'm the father of a newspaper. I think she did better.

Strawberry Reason gave birth to a dark-bay son who was later named Vindication. Yeah, you know the one. Her latest son, a dark bay colt by A.P. Indy, hit the sales ring last night as Hip 107 – and sold for $1.9 million.

Owned by Virginia Kraft Payson, Strawberry Reason walked into my life in 1996. My friend Holly Robinson came to Delaware Park with a barn full of Roger Atfield's horses. She called me for help.

"Sean, I need somebody to get on some horses."

"OK, I'll ask around and see if I can come up with somebody."

"Ask around? Come up with somebody? Sean, I need help now. Like tomorrow. Be there at 5:30 and don't tell me you have a job. I know better."

STRAWBERRY REASON

Click.

So I had a job. And if anybody knows Holly, you know there was no getting out of it. I showed up at 5:30 in the morning and she put me on 10 horses as fast as I could get on them. I melted out of her barn with a new job and a new Horse.

Strawberry Reason.

Strawberry Reason and I got along. We clicked, which I hate to admit didn't happen that often in my riding days. They say some riders have good hands, others have good eyes, some have a good leg. All they ever said about me was I showed up when I was supposed to.

There was King James, World Cup, Majorca, Homage, Conset Bay, Ginger Beach and – best of all – Strawberry Reason. She was the only one I could ride at Holly's. King James bucked me off and separated my shoulder. Ginger Beach tormented me. I had to get off and tease Majorca with a handful of grass just to get to the track. Strawberry Reason was the respite to them all.

She watched me walk down the shedrow. She was smart. Intuitive. She knew what was expected and knew how to enjoy the routine. She'd jog the wrong way, 2 miles most days, making me ride her well. There are horses that you can't ride well; it's simply impossible. They are intolerant of everything. There are horses that it doesn't matter what you do; you can ride them any way you want and they go the same way. And then there are horses that demand you ride them well. Be patient, don't pick up your hands, sing a little, balance, feel, piano strings from your hands to their mouths. If you do it right then they will do it right.

Strawberry Reason made me ride her well and we had a lot of good mornings.

Eventually, I came to Saratoga for the summer and someone else joined up with Strawberry Reason. She wasn't mine anymore. I lost track of her until two summers ago when I walked over to the Taylor Made consignment and saw Vindication.

I hadn't read the catalogue page. Someone told me the colt would go for a lot of money, so I figured I'd go see him. He stuck his tongue out and looked me dead in the eye. I was taken aback – until I read the page.

Damn, Strawberry Reason. My old girl. Vindication looked so much like Strawberry Reason. They say he looks like Seattle Slew, let me tell you, he looks like Strawberry Reason.

As Duncan Taylor of Taylor Made said of Strawberry Reason's genetic thumbprint, "She puts that head on him, and it's worth a million dollars alone."

Vindication had the same eye, the same presence, the same demeanor, the same look as she did. And wait until you see his brother. Believe me, you'll see him.

He marches when he walks, moving through the crowd like a presidential motorcade. You can't miss him. Great ears, up and over his head. Long powerful walk. Curious. Inquisitive. He looks every person in the eye. Right smack in the eye. He glares at you.

It's all Strawberry Reason. Some horses do things that you just like. They react the way you want them to react.

When it was time for the colt to sell, he walked down the chute to the sales ring with slight apprehension but with conviction too. He stood at the end, turning his head from side to side looking for comfort. When the four Taylor Made attendees stopped moving, he stopped moving. When the door opened for him to enter the ring, he hesitated, peered through the door, his ears forward like two periscopes looking for enemies. Then he followed Judd Newby into the sales ring.

If only I had $1.9 million.

Mike Hushion suggested we write a story on John Nerud, the man who trained Dr. Fager, Gallant Man, Delegate, Intentionally, Ta Wee and countless others.

"Oh, the stories," said Hushion. "The other day he was talking about Ben Jones, Pancho Villa, Dr. Fager . . . you just want to listen. Getting to know him over the last few years is one of the best things that's happened to me in this sport."

I started with one question about Dr. Fager, but didn't need to ask many after that. This was an honor and a pleasure. Nerud ended the interview with a simple "Well, I've given you enough for one day."

What about Dr. Fager?

When Dr. Fager was a baby, I knew he was a good horse. I didn't know how good, but I knew he was a good horse. Dr. Fager wouldn't have brought $7,000 in a sale. He was very straight in his front ankles and he had two club feet but he was an absolute, magnificent machine. No horse has ever lived in the world that could beat him at a mile.

The last time I run him, he did something that will never be done again. He ran seven-eighths in (one) twenty and a fifth with 139 pounds. I tried to get the (racing) secretary to put 42 on him but he wouldn't do it. It wouldn't have made a difference.

He was a marvelous, marvelous horse. Didn't want to be hit. Great, big, strong, masculine horse. He didn't even want you to raise your voice to him. He didn't want you to holler at him and he didn't want to be hit.

He could do anything. Start him, stop him, start him, stop him. He could go an eighth in 11, an eighth in 14, an eighth in 10, an eighth in 14 – whatever you wanted to do with him.

He was very easy to train but very difficult in the afternoon because all he wanted to do was zoom, he's gone. I don't believe you wanted to try to slow him down. He win Handicap Horse of the Year, Horse of the Year, Sprinter of the Year and Grass Horse of the Year. There was nothing left.

Who influenced your training?

Ben Jones told me how to train horses. I took over 40 head of horses one time and I was green. Ben Jones came down to the barn – he trained for the same people. He said, 'Now son, you ain't got enough sense to train these horses and I'm going to tell you what you do. Keep 'em fat and work them a half-mile and they're going to win in spite of you; I made the Hall of Fame doing that.

I never changed. That's all I did. I'd run them. You don't get paid to train them, I'd run them. I'd be getting a horse ready for a race, I'd put him in one of these allowance races. I didn't care if he got beat, I'd get a race in him. Now today, all these guys with good horses get touchy. 'You can't run him in there, he might get beat.' Sure, he's going to get beat.

Be careful what you say.

Pancho Villa used to come to Agua Caliente and Ben Jones was touting him. (Jones) told him one day, 'This horse is going to win today. I'm betting my life on it.' Pancho Villa said, 'You just did.' He scratched the horse.

Have Thoroughbreds changed?

People say this reason and that reason on why horses don't stay sound. We breed differently now. We used to breed to race and now we breed to sell. If you look at the human race, how much has it changed in the last 50 years? Just think about it for a minute. How about the kids that are fat now? People have gotten bigger and they've gotten dumber. Nobody's got any common sense, you have a machine to do that for you.

Horses are growing on land that we're pressuring. We're putting more horses on less land. We're putting fertilizer and chemicals on that land. We're doing the same thing with food we raise for people. I don't think there's any one reason why horses are not as sound as they were. I don't have the answer.

What do you think about today's stars?

Empire Maker's going to stud this year. That's a disgrace, he should go to stud two years from now. If they don't let up on Funny Cide, he ain't going to last. He needed a break. He shouldn't have run in the Belmont.

If I had Funny Cide, I would have skipped the Belmont. He wasn't

John Nerud

training, he was overwrought. I would have made every newspaper in the United States and every racing association would have been mad at me, but I wouldn't have done it. ---- it. It's me and my horse.

Trainers don't have that weight any more. I could do anything I wanted to do with Mr. (William) McKnight. He never knew how many horses he owned or how much I gave for them. He trusted me. I made him about $60 million. I bought him two racetracks, a stable, a farm.

The best on the best.

Ben Jones was the best. I was running Historian against Armed in Chicago, this was right after the war. I got weight off of Armed and beat him. So we went to Washington Park, the next race was 17 days away – we raced horses that often in those days. I trained for a fellow from Kansas City named Mr. Wolf. He said, 'Do you want to run?' I said, 'I'm going to watch Armed and see what Ben's doing with him.' He galloped him 15 days, never done anything but gallop him and graze him and walk him. The 16th day he worked him five-eighths in 59 (seconds) and change and galloped out in 12. He ran him the next day and he broke the track record. What trainer would do that? I didn't run. I decided right then when he worked.

Today, if you worked a horse in 12 the day before the race, they might come get you with the net.

But see, they don't understand a horse. Ben Jones didn't look at a horse; he got inside and looked out. That was the difference. He was greedy, he didn't want anybody to be in the money but him. He might run four horses in a stake and be one, two, three, four. A great horse trainer and a great guy.

Compare today's racing to the racing of the past.

Racing today is probably the best it's ever been. They have more money and we're getting people to come out to the races and more people to bet on the races. People are getting sick and tired of baseball and basketball and those sports. People get tired of the salaries. And they raise the seat prices every day. If you take your wife and kid to a baseball game, it'll cost you $200. You can come here with $50, stay all day and you might have money when you go home.

But we haven't publicized this.

PLETCHER

Todd Pletcher will remember the day the lights went out as the day his record went up.

For the 21,670 patrons on hand Thursday, there was no better place to be during the blackout than Saratoga, ignoring the power outages and celebrating Pletcher's achievement. The 36-year-old trainer has won 25 races in a 20-day period, eclipsing Syl Veitch's 49-year-old Saratoga mark of 24 wins in 24 racing days in 1954.

When Irish Road won the featured eighth race, Pletcher slowly strolled down the clubhouse stairs, stopping to shake hands with just about everybody. When the win was made official he posed with his wife Tracy and children Payton, Kyle and Hannah alongside jockey John Velazquez and the ownership group representing Mount Joy Stables.

"My wife has been bringing the kids out to the races for the last few days," said Pletcher. "We wanted them to share the moment."

Pletcher understood the gravity of his historic accomplishment.

"I'm a fan of the sport," he said. "I read all of the old books. Forty years from now when I'm sitting with my grandchildren in the grandstand and they open the program, the magnitude of the record will set in."

Pletcher also recognized all those who helped him reach this remarkable achievement.

"This record is a reflection of our work ethic, professionalism and our business sense," he said. "We put in an enormous amount of hours managing the operation. It's really a team effort in every sense of the word, starting with the owners all the way down through the hotwalkers."

If not for NYRA's self-contained power, Pletcher's record would have had to wait for another day. The electricity shut down at 4:11 p.m. The race course momentarily lost its TV signal, lights and tote board before the reserve power generators kicked in.

The feature, a $50,000 allowance race, was washed off the turf and run on the main track at seven furlongs. Pletcher's Irish Road did what the blackout couldn't and stopped the timer (at 1:21.94) with John Velazquez in the saddle.

"I'm glad I was the one who broke the record for him," said Velazquez, who leads the jockey standings with 35 victories. "Todd deserves this record –

I'm just lucky to be a part of the team."

A Pinkerton yells to slow down.

A car on auto-pilot slides into an open parking spot next to the big tree. A gray lead pony goes to work. The Special paper rack gets filled to the top. The first cup of tea is made with a single nod being shared. Toadie sets up a Sallee trip through the blackout with "They'll be out of there if they can get out of there." Jose zips a red fleece vest over his flak jacket and adjusts his helmet. Erin McLaughlin gets ready for soccer camp.

Lilah jogs onto the track and two trainers ogle at her size. A Spanish exercise rider does the sign of the cross as he nears the gap. Four tourists walk up to the rail and fold their arms simultaneously. Pat Turner comes off the track on a high-headed bay. The clockers try to get a spelling for that Albertrani horse. Fa . . ta . . da . . al . . ar . . ab.

Mark Hennig's working a pair. The Chief sits under a tree branch. Doc Danner drops seven folded overnights from his book. John Pregman sits on the corner of a picnic table. A Special gets folded and fitted under a leather belt. The first West Point saddle towel goes to the track. Kate Fitzpatrick runs her stirrups up as she crosses the road.

Mineshaft walks intently to the track. An Orseno horse bolts to the outside fence while riders wail in warning. You can't help but think that rider doing the sign of the cross might have had a point. Dave Grening talks about the blackout and writing for nothing.

Rick Schosberg eyes the track while his dog Rafter eyes the coffee stand. Mike Cellito drives his golf cart the other way. Three of Pat Kelly's walk across the parking lot. A white-faced horse of Niall Brennan's goes proudly past. Todd Pletcher and his pony go jogging past.

Mike Lakow

drinks his first cup of coffee while answering his first turf inquiry of the day.

Nancy drops off the papers. The old Pinkerton swings his leg from the back of a pickup. Lorna Vincent gives an "Elloluv" to anybody who makes eye contact. The set of Bond's disperses like water beads on a windshield. Wendy checks on a time. Pete Vestal walks alone.

A pony strap goes on a D-bit. Richard DePass give his first "Hey, Holm" of the day. A chestnut trips over a rut. Billy Badgett's pony wishes for a tail. Mike Freeman shuffles up the horse path. Jen Brasser coaxes a Vinnie Blengs horse through the gap. A bacon, egg and cheese is ordered. Dennis surveys his world.

The Special is analyzed. A gray cat skirts under a parked truck. Barclay Tagg wears Funny Cide stress on his face. A wooden rail is set on the ground. A box of Indian Charlies finds its way on the counter. An old one blows to the ground. The tip cup rattles with another dose of coins. A corn muffin is split in half. Half a coffee gets dumped in the grass.

The gate clangs in place. An outrider canters past. The siren is silent. An old clocker leans against the wooden stand. The latest night at the Glass is rated. An Irish exercise rider wipes his forehead with his shirt sleeve. Peter Pugh talks about old jumping riders. A cup of tea is balanced on the edge of a rail. Mike Hushion quietly joins trainers row. Another badge is checked. Bobby Barbara looks for his set. Angel Penna says one good morning for anybody in earshot. A big bay goes pulling past.

The morning is an hour old.

ISLAND FASHION

"Barclay Tagg gets revenge on Bobby Frankel."

Yeah, yeah, yeah. That's the easy one. The candy-from-a-baby angle on the story. It's also false.

Tagg won the Alabama yesterday with Jeffrey Nielson's Island Fashion. And it had nothing to do with stealing a $2 million bonus from Bobby Frankel, a la, the way Frankel stole the $5 million Triple Crown bonus from Tagg earlier this year.

The Frankel-trained Spoken Fur was poised to win a $2 million bonus if she could win the Alabama. NYRA offered the cash for any filly who swept the Mother Goose, the Coaching Club American Oaks and the Alabama. Spoken Fur had won five in a row, but was facing Kentucky Oaks and Acorn winner Bird Town in the 1 1/4-mile Alabama. Island Fashion was an extra. Nothing but a longshot making her first start for Tagg.

She certainly wasn't anointed as the Frankel-breaker by Tagg. Horse trainers don't have time for revenge. They're training horses, not poking voodoo dolls and conjuring up plots of vengeance.

"I have no rivalry with Frankel," Tagg said. "It's not a hockey game or anything like that. The horses do the running. We don't do the running."

Nobody did the running like Island Fashion. Ridden by John Velazquez, the daughter of Petionville, broke sharply from the rail spot. Eased off the inside and behind Awesome Humor, Island Fashion had a perfect slot in second. Bird Town adopted a spot in third while Spoken Fur was a bit unsettled in fourth. Longshots Halory Leigh and Fircroft were in the back.

Leaving the backside, Island Fashion was the only one running. Bird Town found nothing and retreated while Spoken Fur ran evenly the whole way. It was anticlimactic, at least in the bonus department. Island Fashion scampered home alone. The bonus was history. And so was the Alabama, which was fine with Tagg.

"I've always thought the Alabama was the premier filly race in the United States. Ever. Maybe in the world," Tagg said. "It's a big thrill for me to be able to win the Kentucky Derby, the Preakness and the Alabama. That's about as big a thrill as anybody could have."

That's what this day was about, thrills. Not rivalries, not bad blood; nothing other than horses racing.

"All I want to do is train good horses and win races for nice people. I've said that all my life," Tagg said. "Frankel had a great quote the other day. He said something like, 'I'm not a social director. I don't take owners to dinner. I train racehorses. When I get beat, I get depressed.' Well so do I, Robin can attest to it."

Robin Smullen is Tagg's assistant at the barn and partner in life. She takes his cell phone and answers it while he's being mobbed by reporters. She gallops Funny Cide. She makes sure the little things get done. Tagg knows he'd be lost without her.

"Trainers have to keep up with all the little BS. We've got to have good assistants to help with it all. That's the whole thing, keeping up with all the little stuff," Tagg said. "Make sure you don't give them something that you're going to get a positive (drug test) for. Give them all the vitamins and minerals and crap they need. You monitor their feed, you monitor this, you monitor that. The horses do the work, that's all you can do. If my horse outruns Frankel's great, it doesn't have anything to do with me or Frankel.

It's not about the trainers."

Puzzlement

For two weeks....

....P.G. Johnson touted Allen Jerkens and Puzzlement like they were paying him.

There are lobbyists who say less.

One Hall of Fame trainer talked about another's horse. Johnson declared Puzzlement as the horse to beat in the Aug. 2 Whitney. Well, he wasn't. Medaglia d'Oro took care of Johnson's Volponi with Puzzlement a non-threatening fourth.

Then a day before the Saratoga Breeders' Cup, Johnson climbed on the Jerkens' soapbox again. "I like Jerkens in the race," Johnson said. "He was only 2 1/4 lengths behind me last time and he was closing."

Then minutes before the race Saturday, Johnson was at it again.

"I don't care what anybody says, Jerkens is the horse to beat," Johnson said. "My horse might beat him but I can't out train him. He'll run good today."

One out of two ain't bad. Third-choice Puzzlement upset odds-on Volponi in the $300,000 stakes. Owned and bred by Joseph Shields, Puzzlement finally earned a big check after competing hard in big ones like the Travers, Jockey Club Gold Cup, Suburban, and Whitney.

Puzzlement, a son of Pine Bluff who was making his third start of the meet, was well off the pace early while Volponi tracked Blue Boat in second.

By the second turn, Volponi collared Blue Boat who fanned the Breeders' Cup Classic winner wide. In the middle of the turn, Puzzlement went outside a tiring State Shinto and then steadied for a moment while Iron Deputy aimed for the same hole.

Chavez waited it out before pealing the paint inside Iron Deputy. While all this was going on, Jerry Bailey had Volponi on the lead but there was no pin to offer. He was steady down the lane while Puzzlement lengthened stride. It was over, Puzzlement glided down the rail and drew off by 3 1/4 lengths. Volponi held on for second and Iron Deputy was third. Second-choice Harlan's Holiday never got untracked and finished last.

"I've always thought he was a good horse but things have to go perfect. And it did for him this time. I blew him out just perfect, he had a great trip, he's got a great groom," Jerkens said. "We're lucky to keep him sound this long. That's the hardest part."

After the race, the hardest part seemed to be getting Jerkens to the Trustees Room for champagne. The 74-year-old trainer stopped to shake hands with an old exerciser rider.

"How about that?" he said with a laugh.

He commiserated with his son, Jimmy, who saddled Iron Deputy.

"Where'd you finish?" he said. "Oh, that was you third? He ran good."

By the time Jerkens arrived at the Trustees Room, the replay of the 1 1/4-mile race was on its way.

"I was afraid the pace was too slow," Jerkens said as the field went down the backside. "Where was Volponi, second?"

Yeah, right behind Puzzlement.

Exactly where Johnson thought he might be.

Tony Reinstedler and Mark Guidry....

....had an in-depth strategy session before Sunday's Lake Placid. When you have a filly who refuses to be headed during the early stages of a race, in-depth is relative.

On the back of Reinstedler's hand read the number 48, in black ball-point pen. It was the address of a party after the races: 48 Union Ave.

Reinstedler turned the back of his hand to Guidry, who was about to climb on the speedy Sand Springs, the favorite over nine rivals in the $150,000 turf stakes.

"Give me the first half in this," Reinstedler said to Guidry.

Good thing, the party wasn't at 46 Union.

Guidry got as close to the party as he could, managing the first half in 46.41 while the daughter of Dynaformer opened up by six. She held on strongly to win the Grade II stakes over Indy Five Hundred, who rallied from last. Second-choice Film Maker ranged close to Sand Springs but couldn't run her down and finished third.

After the race, Guidry stopped at the big screen to watch the closing stages of the Lake Placid.

"They're coming," someone said to Guidry.

"They better come with more than that," the jockey replied. "She's got more there, let me tell you."

Take one look at her chart and you can see that. The Willmott Stables homebred won her debut at Saratoga last summer. She came from off the pace on the grass and scored at 7-1. Her next start was in the Natalma at Woodbine, she finished third as the favorite. Next came a disaster in the Alcibiades at Keeneland, her only dirt start, where she was beaten 55 lengths. Reinstedler ran her back 20 days later, she finished second to Ocean Drive in the Green River after leading early. In her final start of 2002, she was eased in an allowance race at Churchill Downs after bearing out on the turn. It was a rating experiment gone awry.

This year, she's been on the lead and in the winner's circle. Guidry climbed aboard for the first time in her 3-year-old debut and they combined to win an allowance race by 7 1/4. Next came a 1-3/4 lengths victory in a second-level allowance race. The Grade III Regret came and went with a three-length score. All at Churchill Downs. The streak was up-ended at Hollywood Park when Sand Springs finally gave in to Dimitrova in the 1 1/4-mile stakes. She finished second, beaten two lengths, in the $750,000 stakes. The Lake Placid, a furlong shorter than the Hollywood Oaks, pushed Sand Springs' earnings to more than $500,000.

Like Sand Springs, Reinstedler got to the party on time.

SAND SPRINGS

It's a timeless question.

How do you make racing fans? Have kids, people. Have kids.

Considering I'm not a parent, I make do with my nephews. (Yes, this is the annual column about Joe's kids Jack and Ryan). So the boys (10 and 7) wanted to go to the track. Hard to say no when it's 7 in the morning and they're looking at you like you have their lives in the balance. Either stay home with 2-year-old brother Nolan and – ugh – your parents. Or go to the track with Uncle Sean.

First, a toasted bagel and chocolate milks at the Morning Line. Then walk, wander, talk and – utter boredom.

"This is what you do all day?" Ryan asked, exasperated.

"What are we going to do next?" Jack whined.

"Can we go play basketball?" Ryan asked for the third time.

"Can we ride Succeed?" Jack asked for the fourth time.

We headed over to the Oklahoma side to watch turf workouts. We met Neil Howard, trainer of Mineshaft. We sought out Tony Reinstedler and ended up meeting Sand Springs. We talked about broken noses with Bob Chapman. We chatted with anybody we met. And the best I get out of my boys was, "Well, it beats being at home with Mom and Dad."

Jack and Ryan scuffled behind me like I was dragging them to a kissing booth. Funny Cide, Empire Maker and the Black Stallion could have galloped past and they wouldn't have picked up their eyes out of their shoes.

Finally, I put them to work.

We needed to do a preview on the Albany so we found Dale Romans sitting in a folding chair outside his barn deep in Horse Haven.

We literally pulled up a hay bale and went to work. I handed Ryan the Form, gave Jack the tape recorder and told them to go to work. Ryan asked the questions. In his first official interview, he came up with three pretty strong questions.

"Who do you think you want to look out for in this race? Did you have a good talk over with Bailey? How about that two horse, he looks pretty good, too?"

Romans never showed Joe Hirsch more respect and answered all Ryan's questions. See the answers on page four.

As Jack (the quiet one) held the tape recorder out like it was a dirty sock, Romans turned the tables.

"You have to ask me one question," Romans said to Jack who hadn't said a word since, "How do you turn this thing on?"

"I don't care what it is," Romans said. "You can ask me my last name, how many kids I have, how many horses I train."

"How many horses do you train?" Jack asked.

"I have 35 horses up here and a lot more at Churchill Downs," Romans said. "When I was your all's age, that's where I started working with horses. That's my favorite track, like your shirt."

Jack looked at his green T-shirt and read Churchill Downs upside down. Suddenly Mr. Romans had life. Jack laughed.

"How hold are you?" Romans asked Jack.

"Jack," Jack said.

"How old are you?" Romans asked again without a change in tone.

"Um, 7," Jack said.

"My son's seven too," Romans said.

"How old are you, 10?" Romans asked Ryan.

"Yeah," Ryan said

"My daughter's 10, too," Romans said.

Jack and Ryan had met a friend on the backside. Their uncle was just a bystander now.

"I was talking to Barclay Tagg and he said he's had two good feelings about horses," Ryan said. "Funny, as he called him, in the Derby and that one horse who won the big race (Island Fashion). He said he bet on Funny in the Derby."

"I think if I ran a horse in the Derby, I would bet because even if I lost, I'd have a souvenir in the ticket," Romans said. "And if I won, I might not cash it. I might just keep it as a souvenir because I wouldn't need it."

"Are you going to bet on your horse tomorrow?" Ryan asked.

"I think I'll bet two dollars across the board on Acceptable Venture. That's a big bet for me," Romans said. "Are you going to bet on him?"

"I don't know," Ryan said. "I might."

"So did you always want to train horses?" Romans is asked.

"It's the only thing I ever knew. I started at your age. My dad trained, he had a big stable. When I was your age, my dad had the barn that I have now at Churchill," Romans said. "I ran my first horse when I was 12. We had five in and no help so the old guy that worked for us tied a knot in the end of the shank and sent me to the paddock."

The boys' eyes were wider than the feed tubs hanging from the poles of Romans' barn.

"He said, 'Listen now, if he goes to hurt you, turn him loose,' " Romans said. "So I got to the paddock and told Dad what he said. Dad said, 'Don't ever turn one of my horses loose.' That was a lesson."

Romans is a racetrack lifer. These boys might be too.

"I thought working all day and sleeping in the tack room was it. Like camping out," Romans said. "We used to work all day, play cards, flip quarters. It was a great life. Can't do that now. If you had a 12-year-old kid running a horse, they'd put you in jail. It was a different time back then."

Somehow it felt like we were slipping back to a time when kids were brought up with horses and the racetrack was their playground.

Ryan and Jack were offered the chance to see Acceptable Venture. They walked down the shedrow like it was their dad's. A horse dove out with teeth bared, they never flinched. They found Acceptable Venture three-quarters of the way down the shedrow. Like any horse he stuck his head to greet them, they touched his head and his muzzle.

On the way back they came across Bojangle's Cat and they laughed that they had a horse named Bojangles in their video game (yeah, it is a different era). We walked back to where Romans was sitting and continued our conversation. Now it was just about watching morning hours go past.

"They're good boys, you can see that," Romans said. "They'll make it."

And somehow, Jack never looked more at ease standing on a pile of hay. And Ryan never looked more at home, sitting on a white Igloo cooler and swinging his dirty sneaker across a pile of ice boots,

....at the end of Barn 53.

The ninth race was over.

John Imbriale was warming up for the replay show, the brooms had already started sweeping and the black phone in the racing office rang again.

"Racing," the voice answered.

Mike Lakow wasn't through yet. The racing secretary had talked on the phone 70 times during a day that started with a walk around the backstretch and still wasn't finished, 12 hours later.

Double-entry Wednesday. The racing office took entries for the Friday and Saturday cards. That means eight staff did double time in the office. Over 300 names funnelled through the entry box. Some races overfilled. Others were scrapped. Ten races were carded for Friday and another 12 for Saturday. From number one in the first race, Cannonball Red to number 16 in the last on Saturday, Special Times – entries were given and taken.

"In most cases I like taking entries for two days because we have the advantage of using extra races wherever we can. We can balance out the card pretty well," Lakow said. "This day is an exception because Travers Day is Travers Day. We're trying to get the best 11, now it's 12, races on the card. We don't do it too often but the horsemen have gotten really good at it. When I worked at other racetracks, we'd have horses entered on the wrong day and all kinds of stuff. Here it works pretty smooth. My crew is tremendous. The people in my office know exactly what to do and they come in and get the job done."

From P.J. Campo to Bill Nemeti to Andrew Byrnes, the staff goes strong all day. It's one of those days when Pat Day's agent Doc Danner comes in with lunch for Nemeti and Lakow downs a hot dog while proofing a New York-bred maiden.

"Disasters? Today, no. Occasionally, yes," Lakow said. "It's always nice to get two cards done and have tomorrow morning to get ready for Travers."

Ah yes, the Travers. The big one with surprises. Derby and Preakness winner Funny Cide has been in and out for weeks. At the last minute, Shug McGaughey entered Congrats and Bobby Frankel put Peace Rules in as a backup to Empire Maker.

"Today was kinda weird because we didn't expect Congrats or Peace Rules to go in the Travers," Lakow said. "We spoke to Shug this morning. He was on the fence anyway but we made sure he was aware there could be a problem with Empire Maker. We also called Chris Clement for Dynever. We made the calls and Shug decided to take a shot."

Of the 300 entries taken, eight had special meaning. Congrats, Strong Hope, Peace Rules, Ten Most Wanted, Empire Maker, Wild And Wicked, Funny Cide and Sky Mesa make up the 134th running of the Summer Derby. The Victory Ride, Ballston Spa Breeders' Cup, Fourstardave, and the King's Bishop top off the card.

It could be the best Travers card ever.

"It's up there. I've been here for 13 years, I can't say it's the best . . . but it's a very competitive card, certainly the fans are going to have their work cut out for them," Lakow said. "The King's Bishop came up a tremendous race. The Travers, if it holds, is tremendous. There are no fillers in the Travers. Great horses. The Fourstardave is competitive. You know, I think it is the best."

"RACING"

That is if it doesn't rain like last year when all the turf races washed away and the Travers was run in near darkness.

"Last year was the worst day in my life in racing. A jock's agent who I respect, Ron Anderson, said it was the best card he had ever been around," Lakow said. "You build up the whole meet to one day and then it falls completely apart."

As Lakow went through the forecast for the next three days (Friday's the question), stakes coordinator Andrew Byrnes cleaned up a pile of papers, jock's agent Mike Cellito walked through the office, and clerk of scales Mario Sclafani eyed up the traffic outside the window.

"It's a beautiful card on Saturday and I think everything's going to hold together," Lakow said. "Six days a week of top racing with all different personalities is tough. What I've become more than a racing secretary is a psychologist. I have to change my tone with different people and calm other people down. This is all new to them and it's such a vast place."

Lakow's job seemed vast as he proofed a program page for the second time, answered a question about Wild Spirit's weight in the Personal Ensign, tried to eke out some information on Funny Cide, and put a call into senior vice president Bill Nader.

"I'm not sure what my job description is. It changes every day," Lakow said. "This place is crazy. The racing at Belmont Fall is as good as Saratoga but here it's different. The region, the neighborhood, the people who live around here think this is the greatest thing in the world."

About then, the phone rang again. Lakow answered it the same way he had 70 times earlier in the day . . .

"Racing."

QUOTES:

"I didn't say no."

– Kip Elser on how he became South Carolina's Thoroughbred Retirement Foundation spokesman

"When I was growing up there were four racetracks in Cleveland. Each had a 44-day meet. When they were over, you and the horses went back to the farm to rest. Life was good."

– Trainer John Hennig

"She's not just a dog."

– Trainer Bobby Frankel about Happy

"I have a black-tie at 7:30."

– NYRA chairman Barry Schwartz

"You're telling me your social schedule? I make your social schedule."

– NYRA chaiman Barry Schwartz's wife Sheryl

All he wanted was a cup of coffee.

Barclay Tagg had made his decision. His greatest horse would skip the Travers and race another day. The horses had all been trained so he went for a cup of coffee with his girlfriend Robin Smullen.

He almost had a regular cup of coffee at his regular place, the backside of a racetrack. He sat on the top of a picnic table, shared part of his danish with Frank Alexander, watched a few horses walk to the track – then the swarm enveloped him.

One reporter needed a quote. Another needed a comment. A camera crew needed a sound bite about the gate, even asked him about the gate trainer. Another crew needed a comment about Funny Cide and why he wasn't running.

"All I wanted was a cup of coffee," Tagg said.

It was a long cup of coffee.

Finally Tagg made his way back to the barn where at least white plastic chains could keep people at bay. Well, partially. Reporters ducked the ropes anyway, still thinking Tagg was going to give something away.

"I'm talking at 11," Tagg said from a chair outside his tackroom.

Tagg looked over his condition book, lined up Javier Castellano for two horses and Jerry Bailey for one. The media started to swirl around the edge of his barn. Tagg never budged.

"It's hard enough to get some peace and quiet with your horse to figure him out on your own," Tagg said. "Then you have all of them scrutinizing you."

Tagg has had a few rough weeks with the media. It was even said that he owed it to the public to run Funny Cide in the Travers. Or tell them he wasn't running.

Tagg had one obligation this week – Funny Cide.

Take care of your horse and the public will be taken care of. It's a simple premise and Tagg followed it to the letter. He said all along that things weren't perfect with Funny Cide. If everything went right then there was a chance he'd run in the Travers. You know, $1 million, and all.

That's what horse trainers do, they make decisions every day. It's not a science, most of it is guesswork. Nobody's asking trainers about the half-dozen or so horses that scratch most days. Nobody's accusing any of those trainers of ulterior motives because they scratched out of the last race Friday. Tagg was being a horse trainer.

Earlier in the week, he breezed Funny Cide and scoped him. Things looked good. On Friday, Funny Cide galloped and then stood in the gate. Would you do that on an already hectic Friday morning if you had no inkling of running? Tagg scoped him again after all that and things were not perfect. So he scratched him.

End of story.

He took care of his horse. That's what good horsemen do and that's what good press should understand.

Tagg is not a media darling. He doesn't try to be, he doesn't want to be and he's never going to be.

The guy got one of his best owners, Earl Pardue, by doing exactly what he did all week. Telling it like it is, being his own man.

Pardue once boarded a plane and saw a guy reading the Daily Racing Form. Pardue struck up a conversation and asked him if the man had horses. The guy said yeah. Pardue asked him who is trainer was.

Barclay Tagg

"Well, it was Barclay Tagg, but I fired him this morning," the man answered.

"Why'd you fire him?" Pardue asked.

"Well, he told me my horse was no good," the man said.

"Could I get his number from you?" Pardue asked.

Pardue and Tagg were a good team for a long time.

Tagg, like any horse trainer, just wants some space to train his horses. He'll do the best he can to tell the media all he can. After that, it doesn't matter. He's not compromising.

"You need good horses and you need to take care of them," Tagg said. "We don't do anything else. We work all day, every day. We don't play golf, we don't go to the swimming pool, we don't go shopping, we don't do anything but take care of the horses."

Amen.

Occasionally a race sets up exactly as it looks on paper.

Aimee Dollase

The 2003 Travers was one of those races. Strong Hope and Peace Rules, both one-way frontrunners, softened each other up and left it for the closers. And it turned out that there was only one of them – Ten Most Wanted under Pat Day.

"It was obvious Strong Hope and Peace Rules were going to entertain themselves," Day said. "I felt like I could be in the catbird's seat."

The son of Deputy Commander drew off to win the Grade I stakes by 4 1/2 lengths for his greatest score. All done with aplomb. Owned by Paul Reddam and a host of others, Ten Most Wanted has a big kind eye. He moves like he's been smoking dope on the way over from the barn, like he's saying, "Give it time and it'll be OK." For a big strong colt, there is no intensity in his actions. Intelligence for sure, but no sense of urgency.

And he gets it straight from his trainer.

Wally Dollase preaches patience. Routes. Time. Nature. It's near the end of August and he hasn't run a 2-year-old this year. And he's not planning on doing so until October. Even then, his babies will run once, maybe twice.

"I've got a lot of patience. That's the secret. A lot of owners don't have much patience and they force their trainers to do things they shouldn't do," Dollase said. "You pass a point as a trainer when they start thinking you know a little about what you're doing. When you reach that point you can take the time and make the horse a good horse."

That's what the 134th running of the Travers was about. Ten Most Wanted becoming a good horse. Officially. Ten Most Wanted had been the near-miss kid ever since he started training like a good thing on the week of the Kentucky Derby. The Derby was a disaster from the start where he was bumped and torqued his back.

Dollase took him home to California and patched him up for a Belmont Stakes try; he ran Empire Maker to a close one. Then he flopped as the favorite in the Swaps, falling a head short of During.

The Travers was another chance for the breakthrough. And it couldn't have worked out better.

After a first quarter in 23.55, it looked like Strong Hope and Peace Rules might manage to stay away from each other. Then the half went spinning past in 46.36. The 6 furlongs fell in a crowd-revving 1:09.98.

On the final turn, Strong Hope was the first to retreat and Peace Rules was on borrowed time. Behind them loomed Ten Most Wanted. Sky Mesa floundered to his outside and well back were Congrats and Wild And Wicked. Peace Rules hung tough but Ten Most Wanted had the race in his grasp. It was over. He was the only one running home.

"He's got such a beautiful stride, and his physique – he's a gorgeous individual. He's got a stride that's effortless. None of this wasted action. You have confidence when you have an animal with that conformation," Dollase said. "He's a lovely horse to be around. He loves his peppermints. He's very smart. Some of them are too smart, they figure out the game quick. He's always been a solid horse. But he proved today that he's a racehorse."

Dollase put blinkers back on Ten Most Wanted for the Travers. He had worn them in his first three starts and without them in his next five. Day has been aboard Ten Most Wanted for his last six starts and had witnessed the maturation process.

"I'm proud of the horse and I'm really proud of Wally and his crew. They've done a great job with this horse. I liked him this spring but I

Ten Most Wanted

thought he was a bit immature, he just wasn't quite there," Day said. "Blinkers and maturity played in his favor today, but he still wasn't really keeping to the task in a drive. He was going through the motions and he had them at his mercy but he wasn't as responsive to my urgings as I would have liked him to be. The competition is going to get deeper from here and I dare say that he's going to step up to the plate when he has to."

That could come as the 3-year-olds meet older horses in the fall. Like anybody with a good horse, the Breeders' Cup – in Dollase's neighborhood, Santa Anita – is the ultimate goal.

"He's still on his learning curve. His future is in front of him and he's just going to get better. Time and maturity," Day said. "But they deserve a great round of applause for the job they've done with him. They've taken their time, not trying to pressure him, not trying to get him to develop or mature quicker than he's capable of doing. They let him dictate it. Whatever they're doing is working. They let him call the shots."

Dollase finds it easy to have patience.

"So many horses run too early in their 2-year-old year and they get hurt. They're really good horses but the owner or the trainer didn't have the patience to wait. That's what I have. I'm in no hurry," Dollase said. "I like horses. I take care of them. I don't abuse them. My kids like them. I had a breeding farm for 15 years and the kids were raised there. We love horses, we love animals, we like dogs, cats, we have all of them.

When you do those kinds of things to animals, they respond."

4

Dave Mathews tickets given away by "Concert King" Tom Voss.

7

Credit card solicitations in a Special editor's mail from home.

27

Men, women and children (and pets) who have stayed in one rented house during the meet, so far.

49

Empty cases of beer behind the bar at the sales grounds on Wednesday morning.

84.57

Gainesway Farm's lunch bill (not including tip) from the Spring Street Deli.

178

Bandages hanging on the clothesline outside Todd Pletcher's barn.

Nothing compares to a track on the day of an important race.

Tens of thousands of people congregate for the same reason. Anticipation wafts in the air like the smell of cotton candy at a fair.

And then there's the backside.

I walked – mostly by necessity (parking troubles) but partly by design (after the deadline from hell Friday night I needed a walk) – through Oklahoma on Travers Day. Call the experience Zen and the Art of Walking Through the Stable Area.

My stroll starts at 5:08 p.m. The guard at the Fifth Avenue gate checks my pass, and I am on my way with a bottle of water and a backpack full of notebooks, newspapers, business cards, pens, a tape recorder, allergy eyedrops, a few hats and a phone book.

Did you know they park cars on the Oklahoma Training Track for Travers Day? I didn't. Better not stay too late at Siro's – you might get harrowed in. Compared to a bustling morning, the place is deserted. Horses are resting in their barns, the dogs are at home. The only people here are those who have to work. Shug McGaughey's barn – Congrats is in there somewhere – looks as neat as an Army base. A plain-clothesed security guard scans for trouble (my coat-and-tie look helps my cause). I see handcuffs, and I'm sure there's a gun somewhere.

Down the path I walk. The sand is loose, not packed down by hooves like it is in the morning, and makes for tough footing. Trainers would probably call it cuppy and scratch me, but I keep going.

Remarkably dry (those homemade drainage ditches really work), the barn area unfolds if you look around. Helen Pitts and Wild And Wicked soak up the cooling breeze in Barn 70, awaiting the Travers. There's another security guard. Helen hollers a greeting and wonders if she'll ever get to the frontside. Me too.

Beyond the people in the barn, there are workers here. A garbage truck rumbles past, stopping at Dumpsters and backing up with the familiar "beep, beep, beep" which drowns out the faint call of the Fourstardave. Sounds like Trademark, but I can't tell.

Here comes Posse. Out of Barn 65 walks Steve Asmussen's runner in the King's Bishop. A white lead pony shows the way, while two men guide the horse's head. A third assistant follows behind with a bucket and some other traps. The horse looks great from back here, but no human ever walked faster than one leading a horse. I find a dust-free zone, close but not too close.

Down the path some more. The barns with no Travers Day runners are as still as geese resting on a pond – rake marks, bandages drying on the line, symmetrical rows of hanging feed tubs, plants swaying in the breeze (Colum O'Brien's look particularly healthy).

There's a domestic dispute brewing at the kitchen (she's mad and about to get in her car; he's sitting on the top rail of a fence, unmoved). A blue NYRA armored truck, No. 103, rests in front of the outrider barn next to a pair of John Deere tractors. What's in it? Do they park it there all the time?

In the chute leading to Union Avenue, Posse – like anyone – pauses a moment to look at a baby in a stroller. The 2-year-old girl, who's taking her tired parents home, gazes back in wonder as if the horse is carrying Santa Claus and the Easter Bunny. Posse never really stops walking, but he eyes up that stroller and what's in it.

At 5:20, we cross Union Avenue. Posse and his posse go first as the "Horse" call goes out from the guards. Everything stops. Cars, conversation, pedestrians all come to a halt for two horses and five people.

And then it starts again. On the track side of the street, the activity redlines faster than a VW Rabbit in first gear. In the latter stage of picnicking, the people spot the horse. After a dozen "Who's that?" questions, Posse's groom slips into his blue No. 3 pinny (5:23) and then the questions change to comments – "Ooh, Posse looks good. Come on, Posse. You gonna run today, Posse? Get it done for me today, Posse."

Though we can hear it, we walk in a cocoon – somehow buffered from the din.

At 5:25, I advance into the paddock. Twenty-three minutes of walking through dirt in loafers will break your ankles, fill your socks with pebbles.

And refresh your soul.

– Joe Clancy

Horse Health

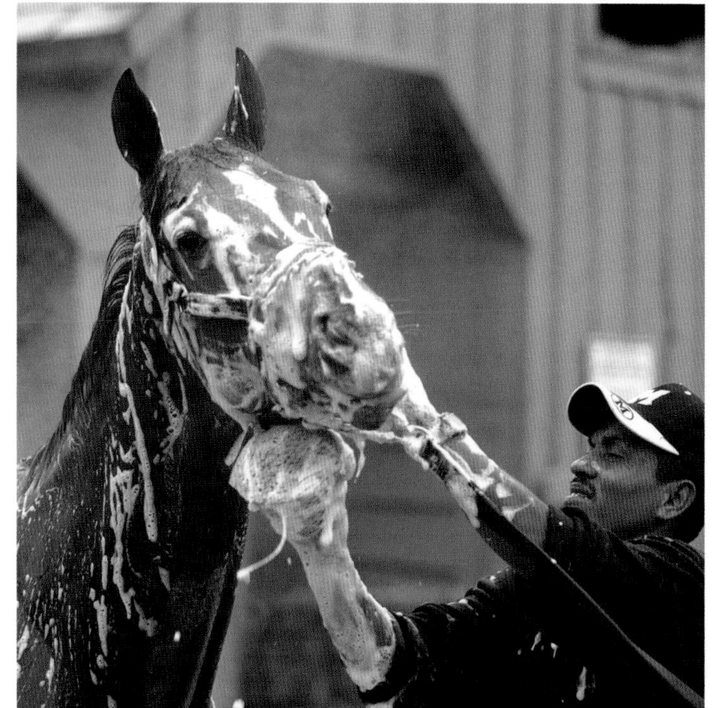

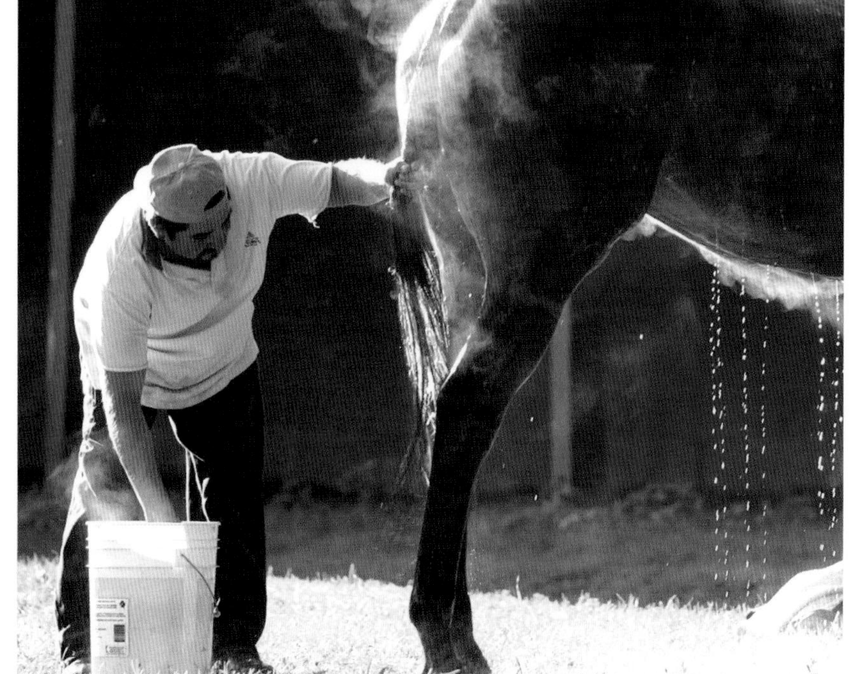

To the horse's health.

Please don't colic. No chips or fractures. May he eat the bottom out of the tub and could the boy just pull him up on time. Don't get too big a run at the pole and no need to gallop out that fast.

Could you take him easy once around? Don't let him drink too much, just seven gulps and then a turn. Heavy sheet or a fly net today? Don't eat those weeds, son. Watch the shank now.

Is it time to float his teeth? What about a five-day Panacur? Do we clip him full or just a trace? How about a jock with good hands and a patient pony for the gallop to the start.

Give him the box stall, it's a long ride. Don't cut his mouth jock. Easy at the gate. Does the kickboard fit? Poultice today and open tomorrow. Two squirts of Red Cell and one of corn oil. Give 'em a mash with some extra bran.

Bandage 'em up tight. But leave room for a finger or two. Do him up dry in front and some Bigeloil behind. Pick his feet and check his frogs. Wash his tail and comb his mane. Don't forget, blow out his eyes and hose his knees.

Don't tighten the girth too close. Lay the saddle towel good and flat. Is that bit too tight? Tie his tongue, but not so tight it turns blue. A full cup or a half? Maybe cheaters for today. Hope the track's not too hard. Oh, I hate sloppy tracks.

You can't jinx a horse with a bet. Watch the outlet by his stall. Turn off the fan at night. Watch the vein. Miss the break and the day is shot. Is that horse sick who just shipped in? Hay rack or on the ground?

Don't learn to crib, bud. Don't walk the stall, girl. Oh, not a weaver to teach all the rest. Don't watch him eat. Don't wake him up. Don't talk too loud. Go home and get some rest – but be back quick.

Off the rail but not too wide. Did he get a gate card? Do his papers match? Is he walking short? Is that a quarter crack? What about the hocks? I swear it's his stifles.

Don't spook him. Don't shake him. Don't baby him. Two patches or one? Blow him out or shedrow him. Five-eighths, gallop out three-quarters, no, no, no, go a half and that's enough.

Carrots are OK. Can he see the track from there? Take his temperature. Write it down. Check it again. Turn him out for the day or lock him up day and night? Put him on the lead or take him back? Did he cough?

His coat looks dry. His eye looks dull. His tail's too short. He's digging again. Get him a goat. She's washing out and shaking scared. The training chart says gallop two. Somebody call the vet. Good God, could it be another tendon?

Grow into yourself. Get it together. Ah, not another late developer. Travels wide in front and narrow behind. Go to the hill and see if he settles. The turf's too hard and the dirt's too deep. Scoped clean but sounded bad. Scoped bad and sounded clean.

Could be his feet but I'm thinking shoulder. Grabbed his quarter. Bucked his shins. Sore back. Hay, oats and water might not work. Call the vet. Bite your tongue. Get ready, he's running soon.

To the horse's health.

ASHADO

Two horses. One pole. And a head full of thoughts.

Ashado and Be Gentle hit the eighth pole together in the 7-furlong Spinaway. Both fillies were embarking on an unknown furlong.

Todd Pletcher, trainer of Schuylerville winner Ashado, was thinking . . . well, she's reserved in the mornings, she's been away for six weeks, her last works were slow, she's only won in the slop.

Not to worry, Todd. Ashado got the job done, inching away from Be Gentle for her third straight victory, her second stakes score and first Grade I tally.

"I thought she was game but she's so idle, so lazy in the mornings, that when it looked like she was in a dogfight, I was like, 'Man, I hope I have enough in this filly,' " Pletcher said. "I made a mistake of working her by herself the first time after the Schuylerville. It was a waste of time, she didn't put anything into it."

Edgar Prado implored Ashado for a final spurt in order to shake the tenacious Be Gentle. Pletcher kept on thinking.

"The next time I worked her I knew I needed company for her and the only company I had was Strong Hope," Pletcher said. "I didn't want to put her head and head with him and go in 58 and change. So I had her follow him around there and that's what she did. He went in 1:01 and she went in 1:02. That was my biggest concern, I just didn't know if I had enough into her."

The daughter of Saint Ballado was on the rail with Be Gentle at her throat. Favorite Daydreaming had stumbled at the start, rushed up and then hung while Ashado and Be Gentle made it a two-horse race. Pletcher was still thinking.

"She hadn't run in six weeks, she's kind of a big filly, she eats well," Pletcher said. "She went over there (the main track) and ran really well twice, but both times it was on a sloppy track so then I'm in the back of my mind going, 'Well, she's a slop-lover. . .' Yeah, all that stuff is going through my head at the eighth pole."

At the wire, it was all gone. Owned by Starlight Stable, Paul Saylor and Johns Martin, Ashado is now 3-for-3. A $170,000 purchase at the Keeneland September yearling sale, Ashado was on the pace from the start and became Pletcher's second Spinaway winner. After the race, all those thoughts at the eighth pole, were nothing but memories.

"Sometimes good horses overcome bad training. The one thing I felt good about was that she's always been lazy – it's not something she developed since she ran in the Schuylerville," Pletcher said. "A couple of times in the morning, in order to get her fit for her first race, we had to get her attention a few times. When we did she would always do what she had to do. But she's not one of those fillies that's going to run away from somebody in the morning and she's probably reserving a little something in the afternoon too."

Pletcher won the first two juvenile stakes at the meet, the Schuylerville and Sanford, then lost the middle two, the Adirondack and the Saratoga Special. He sends out major contenders Chapel Royal and Limehouse in today's Hopeful.

"I'll settle for the first two and the last two," Pletcher said with a laugh.

He was probably even thinking that at the eighth pole.

Shug
Azeri
Birdstone
Afleet Alex
Allen Jerkens

Saratoga 2004

The Special moved to 48 Union Avenue – complete with porch parties – for its fourth year. We still weren't sleeping but our page count jumped again, our advertiser list grew steadily and readers were starting to count on us. John Velazquez and Todd Pletcher continued their assaults on the Saratoga record book while Birdstone won the Travers in the dark.

Shug's 32 Flavors

Claude "Shug" McGaughey III was inducted into the Hall of Fame Aug. 9. He started training in 1979 and began working for the Phipps Stable in 1985. He trained eight champions before his induction. The Special had McGaughey look back at those eight champions plus another 24 (one for each publishing day) of his favorite horses.

1

Inside Information won the Ashland and Acorn in 1994 and the Breeders' Cup Distaff, Shuvee, Spinster and Ruffian in 1995. She was named champion Older Filly or Mare in 1995.

"She was 14 out of 17. She broke her maiden the same day as Heavenly Prize. They split the race at Belmont right after we came back from (Saratoga). She had some bad feet and I didn't run her back until Aqueduct and she finished third.

"Then we kinda piddled around and she won the Ashland, the Acorn way off. I ran her in the Mother Goose, against Lakeway, they went down the backside in 8 and change and she finished third. The Phippses weren't there and I remember walking back with Bill Harrigan and Buzzy (Tenney). They were saying, 'Oh, you know, that was the first time she was ever tested.' I said, 'No,

Saratoga faces its toughest task this year.

Can red-and-white awnings, fast horses and misty mornings override the gloom of security restrictions, ongoing investigations and turnover at the New York Racing Association?

Color fliers advertising the integrity hotline greet racing fans at Saratoga's front gate. NYRA's Senior Vice President Bill Nader gets verbally attacked at the Hall of Fame's open house. Horsemen spend as much time angling for backstretch passes as they do readying their horses.

The times they are a changin'.

NYRA's troubles encompass a budget deficit last year, investigations into money scams among the mutuel tellers and business trouble in general.

The company is in the midst of trying to right the ship. And that's where Saratoga comes in. The six-week meet always provides New York racing – East Coast racing for that matter – shelter from the storm. It's one of the few racing festivals that is still a racing festival. Everybody thinks positive, everybody loves the game, everybody is happy about being in the world of Thoroughbred racing. The best horses from around the country converge for a stakes-a-day season that stands above all others.

But this year, it feels different.

NYRA had to adopt various changes as its business is being investigated, monitored and basically scrutinized from all angles. Security measures at all gates have provoked the most angst. People are troubled. It's been heard that owners' wives will have to pay to get in the gate, special passes must be procured for entrance to the paddock, the will-call gate is nothing but a memory.

Now, I haven't had a problem getting in the stable gate on the three occasions I've tried. Security guards were cordial, while still on the job. They looked at my pass and stepped away from the car. The backside seemed quieter than usual, the Morning Line Kitchen shuttered down like winter – of course, weather had something to do with that.

It will be interesting to see what it's like Wednesday morning.

Will NYRA's troubles shroud the place, squelching the ambience until it feels like Finger Lakes on a Monday?

Doubtful, but how much damage is being done while NYRA takes it on the chin for past indiscretions? How many fans will leave and never come back after being blocked at the gate or made to pay another admission fee or not be able to put a blanket down for an afternoon picnic spot?

I can't help but remember what I was asked as I walked to Sunday's Open House.

"Is this the way to the casino?"

The packed car was pointed down Nelson Avenue toward the harness track where slot machines are spinning and whirling. I winced when I heard the word casino, right here in good old quiet Saratoga. Yikes.

So coins are dropping at the casino down the street and budgets are being tightened around NYRA like an Atkins Diet summer camp.

And now it's up to Saratoga's six-week Thoroughbred meet to make everything right again. The Schuylerville starts it off, followed by the Sanford, the Bernard Baruch and all the other spectacular stakes.

Two-year-olds make their debuts (The Cliff's Edge, Pollard's Vision and Birdstone broke their maidens last year). Stakes horses routinely show up in allowance races (Gygistar, Passing Shot and Ghostzapper won conditioned races in 2003). Stakes races always bring out the best in the country. Grass racing is second to none.

This year it's Sightseek, Pico Central, Storm Flag Flying, Ghostzapper, Eddington, Funny Cide, Azeri, Lady Tak, Seattle Fitz, Lunarpal, Midway Road, Bowman's Band, Roses In May, Friendly Michelle, Yearly Report, Society Selection, Medallist, Request For Parole, Stroll, Wonder Again, Rock Hard Ten, Fire Slam . . .

So we still have the racing. If anything can trim through red tape, it's the Saratoga meet. This year will be a fascinating study in human and corporate behavior. NYRA's blocked in on the final turn; horsemen and fans will feel the pressure. It's up to Saratoga to wave a magic wand to overcome it all.

Have faith.

"He's great – quiet, calm, doesn't get crazy or anything. But he still can't jump."

– Trainer Tom Voss, on John's Call, who occasionally goes foxhunting with the Elkridge-Harford Hounds in Maryland. The horse flunked out as a steeplechaser before becoming a millionaire on the flat.

Shug's 32 Flavors

something happened to this filly today. I don't know what it is, but something happened.'

"She ended up doing something to herself behind, neurologically. I got a guy from Ohio State to come in to look at her. He suggested we put her on anti-inflamatories, a DMSO jug, for 30 days. Then we brought her back for her 4-year-old year, the only time she got beat was when she stumbled leaving the gate in the Ballerina to Missy's Mirage.

"Then she came back and won the Ruffian, the Spinster and won the Breeders' Cup.

"I was a little surprised because she had a hard time winning the Spinster but she had a real good breeze a week before. I always thought Heavenly Prize was better but she caught a racetrack she loved. She ran a faster time than Cigar ran that day. At that time, it was the fastest Distaff ever run. She loved the mud and Heavenly Prize didn't.

"I'll tell you the truth about her, I never knew she could run as much as she could run. When you say she was 14 out of 17 . . . "

Heavenly Prize was voted champion 3-year-old filly in 1994 after winning the Alabama, Gazelle and Beldame.

"Heavenly Prize was a terrific 2-year-old. Won a Grade I in her second start, the Frizette. I took her to

2

California for the Breeders' Cup. She ran against Phone Chatter and somebody else who was good in only her third start. I was kinda concerned about her running around two turns for the first time so I told Mike (Smith) to keep her on the inside going

Jeremy Rose

Afleet Alex

Name of the Day:

***Napster*, ninth race. By *Stop The Music*.**

Jeremy Rose walked down Tim Ritchey's Delaware Park shedrow about two months ago and nearly fell over the straw bale in front of him.

"Who's that in stall 14?" Rose asked Ritchey.

"He's a new 2-year-old we bought in the sale," Ritchey said.

And now he's the best 2-year-old in the country. The horse was – and is – Afleet Alex and he won the Sanford impressively Thursday.

The son of Northern Afleet neatly tucked himself in the middle of the full field while previously undefeated Lunarpal battled longshot Winning Expression on the lead

Around the turn, Rose pulled Afleet Alex to the outside and suddenly the only question was by how many lengths the Delaware Park shipper would win. The horse moved from sixth to first in a quarter-mile. The official margin was 5 1/2 lengths. Flamenco finished second with Consolidator third.

Ritchey picked Northern Afleet out at the Fasig-Tipton 2-year-old in training sale at Timonium in May. Ritchey, a former show rider and a standby on the Mid-Atlantic circuit, bid $75,000 and couldn't believe the hammer fell.

"He was tops on my list, I had four colts picked out and he was number one on the list," Ritchey said. "I didn't think I'd get him bought to tell you the truth. I just waited for him and thought we'd have to go a lot higher than $75,000."

Cash Is King Stable put up the money and instantly had a runner. Rose worked Afleet Alex every time – and liked him more with each passing furlong. Ritchey sent the Florida-bred out June 26 in a Delaware Park maiden race. He won by 11 1/2 lengths.

"He was as lead-pipe a cinch as I've ever sat on. I figured I could get left in the gate, fall off and he'd drag me around there and still win," Rose said. "From the first day, he felt beautifully. He has an eye that you can see there's some thinking in there but not too much thinking. He's always been perfect in everything. He relaxes and finishes."

Sixteen days after his debut, he won an allowance race at Delaware by 12. Again, it was easy work for the stout colt whose limbs look like Popeye's after a can of spinach.

"He's just an easy-going horse. When he ran first time, you would have thought he'd run 20 times," Ritchey said. "He just walked over there and never broke a sweat. He's just a very professional, very mature 2-year-old."

Ritchey had no qualms coming to Saratoga for his first stakes victory.

"Good horses are going to carry you as long as the jock doesn't mess it up," Ritchey said. "He's a good horse – whether he's a great horse or even a very good horse, we'll find out. Right now, he's a good horse."

Rose was a little less reserved.

"He's a beast. Every time I hit him he found another gear, I was like, 'When's he going to run out?' Galloping out, he'll go all day," Rose said. "Coming down the stretch with everybody screaming and yelling, I thought someone's coming to get me but at the same time I know I'm opening up and they're not coming to get you."

This was Rose's second time at Saratoga and by far the best day of his three-year career. Rose won the Maryland Million Classic twice, but never a Grade II at Saratoga. He flew up yesterday and was still trying to find his way around the track after the race. Casually dressed in a pair of shorts and sandals, the jockey threw his tack bag over his shoulder, and went for a lemonade in the picnic area. He needed directions to the stakes barn.

"I'm still lost around here," Rose said. "I was nervous six days ago when Tim said we were definitely coming up. I said, 'We're going to play with the big boys, Pletcher, Frankel, Bailey . . . whew. All I wanted to make sure was that I didn't get him stopped."

It would have taken a mountain.

Shug's 32 Flavors

around the turn. When the hole opened up turning for home, he went for it and she didn't know what to do to go in there. By the time she figured out what to do, of course, Pincay and Delahoussaye closed that hole.

"Then she came back and had a mediocre start to her 3-year-old year. She kinda got untracked up here. I ran her in the Test and she finished third. And I ran her back in the Alabama and I don't think they thought I was doing the right thing, against Lakeville Miss and she won way off. Then she won the Gazelle and the Beldame.

"She came back as a 4-year-old and dominated those stakes up here. She won the Hempstead, the Go For Wand, then the John Morris which is now the Personal Ensign. Then she got beat to Serena's Song in the Beldame. Then we ran her and Inside Information in the Breeders' Cup and she finished second. She was pretty good."

3

Lure was a star without a proper category in U.S. racing. Never a champion, the Claiborne Farm turf specialist won 14 of 25 starts including two editions of the Breeders' Cup Mile (1992 and 1993).

"Lure was one of the most brilliant milers that I've ever seen. Extremely fast. He was a lot of fun to train, really, from day one. He was pretty quick. He won his first start and set a track record on the dirt (going 5 1/2 furlongs in 56 1/5).

"From the time we put him on the grass (in training) up here when he was a 3-year-old, you saw him get better and better and better. We ran him on it and he wasn't where I wanted him to be

Mike Luzzi asked me, "Why'd you stop riding?"

"Well, the last year I was riding, I'd get down to the start, look around and think, 'This is not the most important thing in all the world. That's when I knew it was time.'"

"Huh, when I get down there, it's still the most important thing in the world," Luzzi said.

"That's good. You'll know when it isn't."

That was Wednesday morning. By Wednesday afternoon, Luzzi was careening toward the outside rail on Honey Fritters in an off-the-turf maiden – the most important thing in the world quickly becoming the scariest thing in the world.

Luzzi bailed out and landed on his feet for a moment. That's when mass times acceleration equaled enough force to snap his right femur.

Like that, Saratoga 2004 was over for Luzzi.

Coming off a strong spring at Belmont, the 34-year-old jockey was ready for a prominent upstate stand. With nearly 2,500 wins to his credit, Luzzi has been one of the top 10 jockeys in New York four of the last five years.

Now, he's got a titanium rod in his thigh, vertigo when he stands up, a round of pain killers to down every four hours, a wasted MacGregor Golf Course season membership – and no paycheck in sight.

Wicked game we play. By doing the most important thing in the world, Luzzi (like all jockeys) put himself at risk. Thrill versus pain. Falling, dieting, breaking your leg in two are the prices paid for the thrill.

Expensive tickets.

Luzzi makes a good living as a jock. But any day can be the last day. As a writer or a trainer or a real-es-

QUOTE:

"The ferris wheel is definitely not at the top.

– Peter Pugh on the training business

Mike Luzzi

HURT

tate agent, a day can be a bad one, but it's rare that it ends with an ambulance ride to the local hospital. I've written some bad stories, they never hurt (me) as much as bad rides. I've written good stories, they rarely thrill like good rides.

I've never pumped my fist three times after writing a good story but I've also never been asked, "How many fingers am I holding up?" after a story that went up in flames.

It's strange – when I was riding races, I never knew how I would quit. How I could ever walk away from such a rush. Then there was no choice. It was time to go and I went.

I watched 10 horses jump nine hurdles in Thursday's jump race. I didn't want to be out there and I don't miss it. There was a time when I couldn't even watch a race if I wasn't in it. A time when I didn't want anybody to win the race because I was competitive with all of them. Now, I just hope no one falls and one of the jump jockeys sleeping on my floor wins a race so we can get a free round of drinks at the Parting Glass.

As for Luzzi, he's busted up and ticked off thinking about all he's missing.

Hopefully, he will come back to fight another day. He'll be a little wary when he returns. Then the trepidation will go away and he'll be riding winners, just as he was before he ever met Honey Fritters.

Jockeys have been hitting the deck in rapid fire lately. Alex Solis broke his back in California. Jose Santos broke his arm in the Belmont paddock. And now Luzzi is out with a broken femur.

Gladiators amongst us.

Luzzi's Hummer is still sitting in the jockeys' parking lot – a U.S. Open baseball hat, thrown on the dashboard, Wednesday's Racing Form hanging off the edge of the passenger-side dash, morning helmet and a pullover thrown on the passenger seat. A bottle of Advil in the cup holder and a set of golf clubs in the way back.

He'll need the Advil.

Shug's 32 Flavors

then and he won way off. Some of those figure guys come running down to the winner's circle going, 'Do you know what he just did?' I didn't know what he had done. He had won, you know.

"Then we ran him in the Kelso on soft turf and he was second, I thought that was a great race. Then when I took him to Florida (for the Breeders' Cup at Gulfstream Park). I've never seen a horse keep moving forward, moving forward like he did.

"The day he ran, I got him in the paddock and kinda looked back and said, 'Good Lord, look at this.' You know, we look at them in the stall or they have blankets on. He had the inside post and I told Mike (Smith) to take advantage of this. It was really exciting to see him run that day."

4

Cadillacing won seven of 13 starts including the Grade I Ballerina at Saratoga. As a broodmare, she produced stakes winners Cat Cay, Strolling Along and Lion Hearted.

"Easy Goer's full-sister (by Alydar out of the Buckpasser mare Relaxing), she was a hard one for me to figure out. She ended up being a better sprinter than she was going long. She was bred to go long, by Alydar out of Relaxing. It took me a little while to get a hold of that.

"She won her first start, then she won the Astoria at Belmont. Then she got on the also eligibles in the Breeders' Cup. I thought Mr. Phipps was going to have a hernia. I ran her in the Demoiselle going a mile and an eighth and she got beat. The biggest thing with her was I

Ramon Dominguez...

.... was the leading jockey in North America last year with 453 wins (he was also tops in 2001 with 431). He set a meet record at Delaware Park last year with 254 winners, and leads that colony again this year. Though still based in Delaware, he continues to make forays in racing's larger circuits and often draws comparisons to Edgar Prado, another former Mid-Atlantic star. Dominguez (second in the nation with 225 wins this year) rides six today at Saratoga, including Forest Music in the Test.

Do you set a goal of winning the most races in a year?

"I try not to set my goals too high. Being leading rider at a track, I don't take it for granted and I don't assume I'm going to be leading rider, It doesn't have to go your way – you have to be lucky, healthy and all that. I take it day by day and try to win as many races as I can. Hopefully at the end you can say I had a great year whether you finished on top in the country or not. It's not something you can expect every year."

You left Venezuela at a young age. Was that difficult?

"It was a self-motivation kind of thing. I was a bug rider and decided to give it a shot. I was doing good over there, I always had it in the back of my mind that I could always go back but I was very determined to do well here. I didn't check that as an option. I had to do it regardless."

When will you take on New York full-time?

"I really haven't asked the question because I'm just not ready to leave. I've had several people who I respect a lot bring it up, 'You could leave any time you want.' It's not something I'm looking to do any time soon. Hopefully the offer will still be there and I'll still be riding successfully when I decide to leave."

Have you ever asked Edgar Prado about his decision to leave Maryland?

"I have not talked to Edgar Prado about it, but I'm pretty sure it wasn't a money issue for him. It's more to just move up in your career. There was nothing that Edgar had to prove in Maryland. He did as good as he could do. He proved there was nothing more for him to prove. You leave to ride better horses."

Do you ever wish you were riding the big races?

"I have been lucky enough to ride good horses so I've gotten to taste some success at the highest level. I try not to say, 'I wish I was there,' because it's something I don't think about because I know I'm not planning on doing that right now. I don't think, 'I really want to be in

RAMON DOMINGUEZ

the Derby next year.' If it's something that happens while I'm here, that would be excellent. And whenever I leave this place, I'll be thinking like that. I'll be antsy to get on good horses. I'm very content winning the races I win here and riding the horses here."

What do you think about the Mid-Atlantic area?

"I don't want to underestimate Delaware or Maryland – they are great tracks with history behind them. But the best horses, at this moment, are at different tracks. By going there, it will definitely feel like a big step. And it will be very interesting. Again, I don't want to count the eggs before they hatch, I'm sure it will be exciting and I'm sure I will do well. If I do go, I will work as hard I can to make it happen and hopefully it will happen."

Do you have a timetable?

"I really don't know. I guess when the moment comes. It won't be so much where you want to be but where you should be. When the time comes, I hope I can make that move with my agent. Everybody wants to be in the big leagues but if you're there riding bad horses then there's no sense being there."

Do you remember seeing America for the first time?

"From the very first day, I couldn't believe my eyes. How beautiful things were and how organized things were. The first time I came to the jockeys' room, it was at Gulfstream Park. I couldn't believe the lockers didn't have doors or locks and everything was open. I thought, 'This is great.' It was a different experience. From the very first day, I knew it was going to be home for me. Or I was hoping it would be. I miss home, but this became my home."

What's racing like in Venezuela?

"It was great. The structure of the racetrack was beautiful but unfortunately like everything in the country, it's declined. Just to be around horses and ride races was a dream come true. I couldn't establish a comparison because that was the only place I had been. I loved it, I thought it was beautiful. But the beauty was shattered once I came here. I would never want to change it."

Are you a hero there?

"I wouldn't put it that way. I'm fairly well known in the horse industry because I've done pretty well here, but I'm not a hero by any means."

What did you think of Ryan Fogelsonger's move to California?

"I had a talk with him before he left. I thought it was something very good. It's so easy to leave any place when you're not doing good, but for him to leave when he was doing so well . . . . you have to give him credit. I told him, 'You're so young, you do not have anything to lose.' He wanted to give it a shot, I didn't think there was anything wrong with that. I told him, 'Go with an open mind and hopefully things will work out for you. If things don't go well, you better believe that everybody's' going to say, 'You weren't ready, you shouldn't have gone.' Only you know if you're capable or not.' It obviously didn't happen for him, but he can say he gave it a shot."

Are there a lot of experts telling you what to do?

"If you do well, everybody says, 'He was so good, I told him he should have gone.' If you don't do good, everybody's going to point fingers and say 'I told you not to go.' It's a no-win situation. If you think in your heart you want to give it a shot, you have to go for it. I give him credit for leaving. He's back because it wasn't his time at that moment and hopefully he'll have the opportunity to go again and do better next time."

Shug's 32 Flavors

was having a hard time getting her sorted out. When I brought her back to sprinting, she won her Grade I."

5

Lion Hearted, by Storm Cat out of the Grade I winner Cadillacing, was bred to be a champion though he never realized such potential. In 18 starts, he won four times, finished second six times and earned $191,630.

"He's a stud now in Maryland (at Northview Stallion Station). I think he'll be a great stud. He was a great big, good looking horse who had a wind problem.

"When he ran his races, he was good. He was a great second to Is It True in the Riva Ridge. I thought maybe he was going to win and he got stopped and finished second. He's already had a stakes winner in his first crop. Got my hopes up for him."

Coronado's Quest was a brilliant – if unpredictable – colt who flashed briefly into the 1998 Triple Crown picture even though he didn't run in any of the three races. Stuart Janney's son of Forty Niner won 10 of 17 career starts including the Wood Memorial, the Dwyer, the Haskell and the Travers, and earned $2 million.

"I breezed him out of the gate right before I brought him up here and Mike Smith said, 'Take him anywhere you want.' He went down the backside here like a Quarter Horse, went in :21, :44 and won. The next time I ran him here against Grand Slam, he pitched a fit in the paddock but he won. So I did some work with him and ran him in the Hopeful and he finished fourth.

Society Selection

"Forget those numbers, I'm going back to their names."

– Overheard from a bettor in the crowd

The horse trainer stopped...

...and looked at the toteboard, nodded thanks a couple of times, wiped his brow, fought back tears and began a long steady walk from the paddock chute to the winner's circle.

Now it's Saratoga – H. Allen Jerkens has won a stakes.

Society Selection, owned by Marjorie and Irving Cowan, came from well back in the 12-horse Test to put The Chief in the Saratoga winner's circle again. The 75-year-old Hall of Famer had done the unorthodox again.

Just over a month ago, Society Selection was hammered in the 1 1/8-mile Mother Goose. She finished nearly 15 lengths behind Stellar Jayne. Jerkens regrouped for the 7-furlong Test. He turned out Society Selection in her pen and tried to get her "light on her feet." Jerkens sent the daughter of Coronado's Quest for four breezes in the 14 days leading up to the Test: three furlongs in 35 3/5 seconds, four furlongs in 49, five furlongs in 1:02 and four furlongs in 46 1/5.

"If you have a gut feeling that what they did won't get it, you just have to do something else. But whatever you do doesn't have to work," Jerkens said. "You're so worried about it, you never get used to it. Even though you did everything you could do to win, you don't know if it's going to come off."

Society Selection made sure it came off with a devastating run past the field. Forest Music scorched the first fractions and turned for home with a clear lead but Prado had Society Selection bearing down like a state trooper. She collared Forest Music for a 6 1/4 length laugher. Bending Strings came from well back to finish second while Forest Music held on for third. Society Selection bled in the Mother Goose so Jerkens put her on Lasix for the Test.

"They said she bled a couple of drops but it wasn't enough to make her stop like that," Jerkens said. "We were going to Saratoga and going back years, horses bleed a little more up here for some reason so I figured might as well put her on it. And this race is generally a big race with big speed. That's what she does best. When it works, you look smart."

Jerkens has looked smart since his first $100,000 stakes win with Beau Purple in 1962. He's stood the test of time. Like always, he plays it all down.

"Number one, you don't know anything else. Number two, you play polo and do things that use up all your money so you have to keep working," Jerkens said. "You just get to where you like to compete, you like horses and that's why you keep trying. You have to be lucky. There's a lot of guys who try hard that can't get lucky. You also have to be lucky enough to do it every day. It's an every day game.

"You can't play it once in a while, you have to play it every day."

Shug's 32 Flavors

6

"He was a handful. I thought I had everything all straightened out and we took him over for the Cowdin. He froze in the paddock, threw the jock and this and that. I told Stuart, 'We're going to have to cut him.' About five minutes later, he set the track record. I said, 'I guess that's out.'

"So we fiddled with him some more and ran him in the Nashua. Same thing, he didn't act right. He won, but he didn't run that good. Then we changed a few things and I ran him in the Remsen and God Almighty, he acted perfect and he ran perfect. He was in front the whole way and won easy.

"When I went to Florida, I said, 'We got the nuts here.' He's speed, he's run around two turns. We ran him in the Hutchinson and he came up out of the paddock and we had to stop. When he stopped, he got to acting up. The people hadn't seen him before so they all started running at him, the outriders went at him, he got worse and worse and worse. I think if it was at Belmont or Aqueduct where the people knew him and everybody would have settled down he would have been fine. He finished second.

"He ran a pretty good race in the Fountain of Youth, he was second to Lil's Lad. Going into the Florida Derby, I thought we were going to be in pretty good shape and Mike got hurt about two races before. Robbie Davis rode him and he didn't know him. It was just one of those days.

"Then we did a myectomy on him and brought him back and he won the Wood. Robbie rode him. We were going to take him to the Preakness, he was the favorite in the program. I was going to ship him

Shug's 32 Flavors

down early that morning. Then Friday, he came up with something in his back foot. After we did the myectomy, he was much better. You had to think it had something to do with (the behavior). He could have been anticipating that he couldn't get his breath.

"Then he won the Riva Ridge, the Dwyer. Then we took him to Monmouth and he won the Haskell in a great race. It was a race that I never won before and I remember I was really thrilled to win it. Then he came here and won the Travers going a mile and a quarter. Then Mike got hurt and that was pretty much it. Mike could really ride him. It was hard to explain to other people how to ride him.

"People don't realize what goes into (training). They think they just show up over there in the paddock. My mother was that way. She'd think, 'Oh yeah, that's nice when they show up in the paddock.' Yeah, you don't know that I've been up since 2 o'clock in the morning worrying if he was gonna get to the paddock."

7 ***Seeking The Gold*** won the Dwyer, Super Derby, Swale and Peter Pan in 1988. The son of Mr. Prospector just missed winning the Haskell and Travers, failing in photos to Forty Niner. Out of the Buckpasser mare Con Game, the Phipps homebred earned $2.3 million.

"The day after Christmas I flew back from Florida. Personal Flag was in the Widener and Seeking The Gold was making his first start, he was a 2-year-old. Personal Flag won the Widener, and they used to have a press conference up in the press box. I said, 'I gotta wait, I run this horse in the last. I'll come up afterward.' It was about half dark and he won from here to

Wayne Lukas ran through the clubhouse,...

....his black pinstripe suit blowing as he ducked past the Chipwich cart and around a cooler being towed by a man in a Hawaiian shirt. Lukas reached the gate of the paddock chute and talked to Pat Day about a $35,000 claimer running in Sunday's last race.

Mission accomplished, Lukas composed himself and walked to the box seats to watch Boston Brahmin compete in the 6-furlong nightcap.

"One thing's for sure, this horse cannot ruin my day," Lukas said.

No, it would take nothing short of a natural disaster to ruin Sunday, Aug. 1, 2004 for Lukas, who performed another vindication act when two-time champion Azeri erased her first three-race losing streak by winning the Go For Wand Handicap over 10-race winner Sightseek.

Pat Day let Azeri hold court in typical style, on the lead in a Grade I. Day kept Azeri well off the rail while the other two major contenders, Sightseek and Storm Flag Flying, tried to keep her honest. Fractions clouded the honesty as Azeri lobbed through the first quarter in 24.33 seconds and a half in 47.75.

AZERI

Jerry Bailey cued Sightseek to inch closer to Azeri and the two distaff stars were inseparable as they turned into the stretch; Sightseek on the outside, Azeri on the inside but still well off the rail.

Sightseek began to wilt under Azeri's prowess to her inside and the 2002 Horse of the Year finished 1 3/4 lengths in front of a game-to-the-end Sightseek. It was only two lengths back to Storm Flag Flying.

The $150,000 paycheck moved Azeri past Spain (also trained by Lukas) to the top of the filly-and-mare earnings list with $3,569,820. It also vindicated Lukas, who took over Azeri's training in the off-season when owner Michael Paulson took the daughter of Jade Hunter away from Laura De Seroux. She won the Apple Blossom in her first start and then was handed three straight defeats, one worst than the next. There were calls for her retirement – not that Lukas was listening.

"I've been lecturing Mike Paulson. I said, 'Mike, don't worry about those guys. They're non-horse people, analyzing something from downtown New York or Iowa somewhere. They have no idea what we're doing,' " Lukas said. "This was a big one for Michael. He took a lot of heat. He's getting all the e-mails – I don't even have a computer, I don't get any of that stuff. He reads them. I told him, 'Michael, just throw them out. The good ones, the bad ones, throw them all away.' I never open them."

Throughout his career, Lukas has unapologetically done it his way. A former basketball coach, he's always in a full-court press. There are no easy days, no playing it safe. When it goes wrong – and sometimes when it goes right – lightning bolts come from the fans, the press, other trainers. When Azeri hit the skids, it was hammer time.

"When I was coaching I did what I thought I should do and didn't worry about it. I've always been real callous. You know my history down through the media. During the seventh race, I said to Michael, 'Do you know what's happening right now?' He said, 'What?' I said, 'All the members of the press box are sharpening their pencils getting ready for the barbecue. They're just tipping back in their chairs saying, 'Well, this will be a field day.' I said, 'We'll take them right out their game, you watch.' "

Azeri's performance squelched any doubters. The champion was back and possibly better than ever. She set a stakes record while beating one of the best mares never to be a champion, Sightseek. Azeri bled when she flopped in the Ogden Phipps Handicap June 19 and she hadn't been around two turns since winning the Apple Blossom. Both Day and Lukas thought the Belmont surface might have been the main culprit. The Go For Wand became the testing ground for Lukas and Paulson's sticktoitive-ness.

"I corrected her bleeding problem; the two-turn race and the change of surface was significant," Lukas said. "I felt comfortable . . . you're never overconfident when you run against the class of horses we hooked today, but I thought we had an excellent chance to win and I was anxious to get her back around two turns. Very comfortable. We had a few doubters. Actually we had a lot of doubters, I never saw anybody pick her but I felt good about it."

Azeri was in control from the start and would not be denied when Sightseek took a booming shot at her turning for home.

"There's a lot of reasons why she bled and you get a thousand theories. My theory is if they strain and stress a little bit more than normal, you might get that problem," Lukas said. "I didn't know she had any history of being a bleeder or anything before. I'm getting her cold. When you get a horse from a disgruntled trainer, you don't get the manual with them. They just say, 'Screw you, here you go.' So you find out things the hard way. We're on track now."

Boston Brahmin certainly wasn't – he finished last in the finale. But Lukas was right again –

– his day wasn't ruined.

"You've got a better chance at getting in Tom Durkin's booth than getting a ticket from me."

– West Point Thoroughbreds' Rich Cristiano
on Whitney accommodations

Shug's 32 Flavors

that house over there. We went up to that press conference and nobody cared about Personal Flag. They all just wanted to know who he was.

"He won his first four starts. (Randy) Romero was riding him and he kept telling me how easy he was winning but it was taking him awhile to get over his races. He won the Swale and I brought him back here and ran him in the Gotham against Private Terms. He got behind and the dirt started hitting him in the face and he finished second. We ran him in the Wood and finished second again to Private Terms on an off track.

"I didn't know anything about the numbers then, but these guys come and say, 'You gotta run him in the Derby. He ran a 1 on the sheets.' We ran him in the Derby and he just wasn't ready for it. He legitimately should have run in it, Private Terms was the 8-5 favorite and we had just been second to him twice. I thought with a little bit of luck, he could have won (he finished seventh).

"Then he went on to be a nice horse – 110 percent. I put Pat Day on him after that, he won the Peter Pan and everybody wanted me to run him in the Belmont. I said, 'No, we're not running in the Belmont, he won't run that far.' We ran him back in the Dwyer and he won, then we took him down there for the Haskell and Forty Niner beat him a nose.

"I'll never forget it, I was sitting there in those box seats and Indian Charlie was standing there, he had those binoculars. They hooked up at the five-sixteenths pole and he looked at me and said, 'Shug, these horses are fixin' to do some running.' He was right.

"It was 100 some degrees in the paddock at Monmouth, we put them on the van and brought them

Smarty Jones

SMARTY JONES

So, Smarty Jones retired.

I would have done it too. And so would you. I know, I know, sacrilegious, a blasphemous statement but come on – think about the money.

Sure, Roy and Pat Chapman are old, they aren't exactly poor, they're living a dream with Smarty Jones but the money is still at the apex of any decision they make.

The Chapmans can change the entire path of the family tree. If my parents, grandparents, heck, cousins, owned him, the conversation would go something like this:

"Son, we can run Smarty Jones and try to win around $3 million or we can retire him and make, ah say, a guaranteed $7.5 million for the first year. What should we do?"

"Well, gramps, it's like this, my kids can either go to Harvard or watch Smarty Jones try and win the Breeders' Cup in November. Let me think about it for a minute . . . give me Harvard."

It sucks. But it's the way it is and we're not changing it. Until purses can somehow compete with stud fees then it's a moot point trying to discuss whether Smarty Jones should keep racing. It's impossible. Nobody less wealthy than Warren Buffett would or could keep the horse in training especially when soundness becomes even a remote issue.

Smarty Jones fell prey to the rigors of the Triple Crown. He's jammed up, racetracky as we might say. So, he needs time away from the track which would jeopardize a fall campaign.

If he was a claimer, he'd keep going. If he was a gelding, he'd get a rest. Trainer John Servis could give the horse a proper break, say four months, on a farm somewhere. Maybe dare turn him out in a round pen to do his mind and body good. Then start a long, slow, legging-up process to ready him for his 4-year-old year.

It's all about risk and reward.

If you've ever been around horses, you know that it could be lights out at any moment. A garbage truck rattles a dumpster . . . an exercise rider has a bad morning . . . a blacksmith gets a nail too close . . . a vet misses a shot . . . a race doesn't fill . . . a track gets too hard . . .

Now, let's say you're Michael Paulson with Azeri. If he retires her and breeds her to say, A.P. Indy, for $300,000. Two years later, if the foal is correct and healthy, he can sell it for millions. But still, nothing like the realm of Smarty Jones. Paulson was brave by keeping Azeri in training. She's the blue hen but Smarty Jones is the cash cow.

Fans get screwed, yup, you're right. We need a star.

This spring, I visited a school in Loudonville, N.Y. All grades from kindergarten to sixth, they knew two horses, Funny Cide and Smarty Jones. Not one other. So, that's how we reach fans, with horses like Smarty Jones doing things like he did in the Triple Crown. It would have been good for racing if he stayed in training like Funny Cide.

Funny Cide, of course, is still running but if he was a stallion, he would be gone too. Look at him. Sackatoga Stable would have been crazy to keep him in training after his 3-year-old year. What's he made this year? A couple of hundred thousand, maybe close to a half-million. Add the expense and risk of keeping him in training and compare it to the relatively safe life of a stallion and it's simple math.

Math all of us would have done.

Shug's 32 Flavors

back up here. The next Saturday or Sunday, Woody (Stephens) works his horse five-eighths in 59. I said, 'I got this son of a bitch now. No horse can stand that.' I went a half the next Wednesday or something in 52. The next weekend, here Woody goes again, fast.

"In the Travers, he outsmarted everybody on that deal. He told (Chris) McCarron to drift out a little bit and let Pat Day get there, then shut the door. That's what he did, and we came around, we got beat that far.

"They always told me he wouldn't get a mile and a quarter. And I always said, 'He'll get a mile and a quarter if I can get him to where he'll wait on his rider.' Two times he ran a mile and a quarter and got beat a nose in the Travers here to Forty Niner and he got beat a neck to Alysheba in the Breeders' Cup Classic.

"To get him, with his pedigree, to run a mile and a quarter in top-class company was pretty satisfying. I was disappointed that he got beat those two times, but I wasn't disappointed in the effort."

8

Mining won six races and $264,000 during a career spent mostly sprinting. He raced at ages 3 and 4, taking the 1988 Vosburgh.

"He was a very good sprinter, who didn't get to the races until late in his 3-year-old year. Won his second start and then a little stake at Aqueduct in January. Took a chip out of his ankle, brought him back and got him ready here. Ran him in an allowance race at Belmont – he won that. Ran him in the Vosburgh, Grade I, and he won that – beat Gulch. He was favored in the Breeders' Cup (Sprint) in Louisville, he didn't handle

QUOTES

"Gordon Richards said that Fred Darling had to be the best because he treated owners terrible and he still won the (English) Derby seven times and had a barn full of horses his whole life."

– Allen Jerkens, talking about famous trainers

"My confidence is always the same. If the horses are going to run, they're going to run. If they show up, it's going to be good for me. If they don't show up, then it's bad for me."

– Jockey John Velazquez

"This is one that wakes you up, not one you wake up for."

– Jockey Aaron Gryder, on the way to track at 6 a.m. on a head-strong horse

"I don't want that guy. I want the baseball guy."

– Gryder's son, Christian, after his father gave him an Edgar Prado Bobblehead instead of a Derek Jeter Bobblehead

This is Manuel Azpurua's third trip to Saratoga.

He hopes it's his first trip to the winner's circle. He has two good vehicles.

The veteran trainer runs Weigelia in today's Amsterdam and has Gold Dollar for the Forego Sept. 4.

Azpurua bought Weigelia after he won a maiden claimer by nearly 10 lengths in September.

"I liked the way he do it," Azpurua said. "The first time I ran him, he finished fifth. I thought I made a big mistake. You know, everybody can make them."

Azpurua followed his father into the training business; he began helping out in 1938. He started in his native Venezuela, and after a stint at a military school in New York, he returned. Azpurua moved to the United States for good in 1978.

"I just love this country. I learned a lot in the military academy and I decided then, when I get lucky, I would come back," Azpurua said. "I've been here a long time already. You miss a lot of things but when you decide to do something, you have to look up front – don't look back, that's history. You have to live today, you don't know what's going to happen tomorrow. You try to know and try to see and you try to figure out what's going to happen but you have a lot of surprises, Senor."

Azpurua trains 24 horses at Calder. He won 25 races last year from 229 starts. He's planning on staying the meet with his two-horse Saratoga string.

"Being a trainer is not easy. You have to understand them and try to do the right things, sometimes you miss," Azpurua said. "I just love horses. I understand them, I talk to them. Most of it is understanding what they want or what they need. And what you have to do. That's the way, Senor."

Azpurua is 75 and going strong.

Manuel Azpurua

"Seventy-five is easy to say but it's a long way," Azpurua said. "You see a lot of things....

....Some beautiful days and some really sad days."

Shug's 32 Flavors

the track at all. Then he went to stud at Glencrest Farm.

"Very, very talented horse who was very unsound. Big body, heavy Mr. Prospector horse who could really run. I got more out of him than I thought I would but not as much as I would have liked."

Polish Navy only ran 12 times but he made them count, winning seven including the Cowdin, Champagne, Woodward and Jim Dandy. He was by Danzig out of the Tatan mare, Navsup. His second dam, Busanda, was the dam of Buckpasser. Polish Navy came along in McGaughey's first year as the Phipps' trainer, and delivered.

9

"I was nervous. Nervous, but I had some confidence in myself because I had done pretty well in the Midwest with what I had. I'm sure I was still guessing, a lot. I mean, you always are, but . . . I remember when I took this job, I told a friend of mine, 'You know, if I take this job I might have a chance to win the Champagne and the Frizette.' We won them in a week. Polish Navy won the Champagne and Personal Ensign won the Frizette. I said, 'Well, we accomplished this.'

"He got ready in a hurry. Ran early in his 2-year-old year, must have gotten some shins and we gave him some time and brought him back. I was pretty psyched about winning the Champagne, then I took him to California for the Breeders' Cup. That didn't work out that well but then he came back and had a pretty good 3-year-old year. He won the Jim Dandy here, then was third in the Travers to that good horse

Around the Allen Jerkens barn breakfast is never in short supply.

Success means gifts – food. Inside the office sit three dozen doughnuts. Saturday was an excellent day. Bob Frieze and Gary Gullo, agents for Edgar Prado and Jorge Chavez, have made early drop-offs. The help was unhappy that Prado's agent delivered doughnuts for Society Selection's Grade I Test win. "Doughnuts? That win deserves ham, egg and cheese sandwiches for everybody," says a hotwalker who's adhering to his Atkins diet.

No time to fret. They are readying Smokume for his stakes engagement in Saturday's Amsterdam.

Smokume is tall for a sprinter. "He's got a powerful hind end," says foreman Bill Higgins. "His stride is long like a route horse."

At 8:15 a.m., the procession begins. Shannon Uske on Smokume, Higgins on "Clint" the pony, assistant trainer Fernando Abreu chugging alongside on foot. Jerkens waits in his silver Ford pick-up. "I hope security lets me in over there," says Jerkens.

"We'll go out the back door," says Uske as the trio heads down the shady path toward Oklahoma. "You know how Oklahoma got it's name?" asks Higgins. "It's like walking out west to Oklahoma."

The plan is to breeze five-eighths off the pony after the renovation break. Timing is important. "We've never worked him over there," says Abreu. "The Chief thinks the surface is better over there, heavier . . . and he wants to mix it up."

It's 8:20 a.m. The pony and Smokume walk quickly. Abreu breaths louder than the horses. "At the pace we're going I'm not going to make it," he says. "My belly is kicking in – you guys have to slow down."

"Too many doughnuts," remarks Higgins.

Uske lovingly smacks Smokume in the rear. "He's awake today," she says. "He knows when we put the racing bridle on . . . we're going for a spin. He's not like one of those easy horses. I spend a lot of time with him in the afternoon on his shank. He loves to roll around in the pen, just jump around and be a horse."

Smokume walks and nibbles on Clint's neck and Higgins knee. "The pony is his lover," says Abreu. "As long as he's with Clint he's happy."

Uske smiles, sitting tall on Smokume. This is her big horse. Lilah, Chilly Rooster and others are resting on the farm. "My mom is coming up next weekend to watch him run," she says.

At 8:27 a.m. Smokume splashes through puddles and crosses Union Avenue. He stops traffic. The walk is a warm-up and he's more on his toes with each step. Abreu is soaked in sweat. He takes off his Old Navy hat and wicks the beads off of his forehead.

Higgins is jeered by "Griff," one of the NYRA helmet police. "He threatened to give me a ticket the other day," says Higgins. "Yeah, he yelled at me at Belmont for having my vest unzipped," adds Uske.

At 8:30 a.m., the Oklahoma track is within sight. A lazy Jack Russell splashes across the path. "That old dog better get moving," says Uske. "He'll run him right over him." The dog plays chicken with Smokume.

Smokume arrives at the Oklahoma gap. Abreu identifies The Chief from 150 yards out by his signature cap. He's leaning on the rail in front of the clockers' stand. Smokume and Clint jog onto the muddy track. Uske can sense he's ready. "He grabs the bit and arches his neck," she says. "His body language says 'OK, let's go.' "

After the turn Smokume breaks from the pony. Abreu's stopwatch beeps. A quarter mile later he says, "23 and 3". The assistant trainer walks toward the clockers' shack as the work unfolds. Smokume turns the far corner and reaches out. "Sometimes he bears out on the turn so he runs with a bit burr on the right side," says Abreu. "He took the turn well."

Smokume gets bigger and bigger as he nears the finish line. Uske urges mildly. He flies by. The watch beeps – 59 and 2/5 seconds.

Jerkens turns and asks the clockers what they had. "59 and 1," says Freddy the clocker. "I've been up here since April and that's the fastest workout I've seen."

"Only believe half of what you hear from Freddy," says Uske's agent Ralph Theroux.

"What'd they do? Rake the track?" asks Jerkens.

His question goes unanswered.

Shannon Uske and Smokume

Shug's 32 Flavors

of Mack Miller's (Java Gold). Then he came back and won the Woodward as a 3-year-old, he beat Gulch, Cryptoclearance, some good horses. Then we ran him in the Marlboro Cup and he was in front and he finished third. Then we retired him. He was pretty good, probably the first good horse."

Born in 1983, ***Personal Flag*** was one of McGaughey's first horses for the Phipps Stable. A son of Private Account, he won eight races for over $1.2 million while winning the Suburban, Widener, Nassau County and Queens County Handicap.

"He was a big horse, had some funny looking knees. I can't remember what he won but he must have won

10

something for me to take him down to the Haskell. Wise Times, that horse of Phil Gleaves, beat him in the mud. Then we came up here and we caught the mud. Not taking anything away from Phil's horse, but (Personal Flag) might have been the best horse that day. Jorge Velasquez was riding him, he had him down on the inside and he had to check him out of there at about the eighth pole. He looked like he was going to win, he came around and came running but he just got beat.

"Then he came back as a 4-year-old and he was a pretty good horse. Won the Suburban. Ran in the Breeders' Cup. He must have been 3 when I got there. I can't remember if he had ever run with (McGaughey's predecessor Angel Penna), probably hadn't. I really liked him in the Jockey Club Gold Cup. Caught mud and that horse Waquoit was in there and he loved the mud. He got in front and we couldn't catch him."

Editor's Note: The Special's Quint Kessenich is covering the West Virginia Derby for ESPN. He will be back in Saratoga in time for Sunday's races.

I'm covering the West Virginia Derby for ESPN today. Like the entrants in the nine-horse field, I'm not the high-ranking runner in the talent stable. I've got to prove myself in lesser events. The future doesn't exist. Run well and move on. Screw up – and they throw you in the trash heap. In television there's always another know-it-all, pretty face or smooth-talker who's angling for your job. It comes down to performance and trust. So you prepare. That's all you can do.

I've been to some cool events this year – the NCAA Wrestling Finals in St. Louis, the Derby and the Preakness, countless basketball, football and lacrosse games. But interviewing John Servis in the paddock after Smarty Jones' win was the most exhilarating moment I've had on TV. Did my 10th NCAA Lacrosse Final in Baltimore for ESPN; 45,000 fans and nearly 1 million viewers at home. Next year I'll do somewhere around 60 events for a wide assortment of outlets, but like training horses – nothing is guaranteed.

Off to West Virginia on Friday morning. I ship from Saratoga to Pittsburgh, via Boston – and then drive 45 minutes through country roads. My rented Ford Taurus has a gun rack. Taxidermy signs are popular. Hunting and fishing shops dominate every town square. Toto, we're not in Saratoga anymore. Christophe Clement warned me. He said, "Be careful." Like I was going somewhere really, really scary.

The Mountaineer Race Track and Gaming Resort is a slots casino, with a hotel and racetrack across the parking lot. Located in Chester, W. Va. it has 3,400 slot machines. It's 4:30 p.m. on Friday and the parking lot is full. The plates in the lot are equally divided between Ohio, West Virginia and Pennsylvania. Ninety percent of the cars are American. The hotel's not bad – except the business center doubles as a coat closet and the computer is down. No internet. It takes three repair men and two hours to fix it.

I steam in the OTB watching the races from New York and then see that P.G. Johnson passed away. He was the first trainer I talked to at Saratoga in the summer of 2002. Sean and The Special set it up to get me comfortable. It worked. His voice and toothpick were captivating. His secret was that I always felt as if he actually liked me.

But it's time to focus on Saturday's race. My job is to entertain, inform and enlighten. I'm not the story. The story is the story. Our segment is very short – I'll set the race up, specifically talk about the two favorites (Pollard's Vision and Sir Shackleton) and interview the winning trainer or jockey in the winner's circle afterwards.

Jeff Medders hosts the show from Saratoga with Kurt Hoover and Jeannine Edwards. They will bring viewers the Amsterdam and Whitney – two races I wrote about this week in The Special. The Jerkens' barn let me behind the scenes for Smokume's final workout and let me tell you something – that horse is razor sharp. I also interviewed Murray Johnson this week as he walked Perfect Drift for 45 minutes. How can you not root for Johnson and his gelding?

I've got a decent line on the West Virginia Derby – Pollard's Vision or lack thereof. Sir Shackleton has to answer the question of distance. Ecclesiastic will run closer to the pace with blinkers. Nine horses who've raced at seven tracks in their most recent start. But who's T.D. Houghton, Joseph Ambrosia, Eric Guillot and how do you pronounce that name?

Announcer Dave Johnson and our on-site producer Melanie Wignall will be arriving around sunset Friday. Our director, Mike Foss will fly from Washington Saturday morning. We'll meet and hammer out the details. I'm eager to walk the backstretch and get some good tidbits.

My first summer in Saratoga I needed an alarm clock. Now I'm so jacked that I need sleeping pills. At the Kentucky Derby, sleeping was my hardest assignment. They tried to break me with 4 a.m. wake-up calls, meetings until 10 p.m. but if the Clancy brothers can't break me . . . nobody can.

Outside my window, clouds roll over the hills. Across the grounds they'll run the 35th West Virginia Derby tomorrow. I'll be back in Saratoga on Sunday before noon – tired, but anxious to watch the Jim Dandy and then find someplace quiet to sit down and reflect about P.G.

QUOTE:

"I've got to go to work to get some rest."

– Jockey Richard Migliore, on raising four kids

Shug's 32 Flavors

11

Born in 1981, ***Vanlandingham*** was McGaughey's first champion as Handicap Horse of the Year in 1985. Owned and bred by Loblolly Stable, he won 10 times in 19 starts for earnings of more than $1.4 million. He was out of the money only three times, and won three Grade I stakes – the Suburban, Jockey Club Gold Cup and the D.C. International on the turf.

"Mr. (John Ed) Anthony sent me Vanlandingham as a 2-year-old. He won his first start at Churchill Downs going a mile. I remember people kept saying 'he's by Cox's Ridge, you can't run a first-time starter a mile,' but he was a great big long-striding horse and he won. I brought him to Aqueduct and I ran him and he finished second, then I ran him back at Aqueduct in January and he won way off.

"I took him to Oaklawn and ran him in the Rebel and won that thing really easy. And he got a clot in his eye. The vet kept saying he was OK, but I could see it was bothering him. So I got a human opthomologist to come and look at him, and he suggested changing the medication, and from then on he started turning the corner. He took a culture and it wasn't back yet, but then I worked him, it kinda weakened him enough, just kept bothering to where he spiked a little temperature on me. He'd have been 3-5 in the Arkansas Derby, maybe even less. So I didn't get to run him.

"Then we brought him back. The spring of his 4-year-old year, when I was bringing him back, and Doc Lavin was kinda advising Loblolly Stable and looked at the X-rays and threw his hands up and said 'Where do they hold the Eclipse Awards?' So I ran him at Churchill in an allowance race and he won. I ran him back in a stake at Churchill (the Stephen Foster) and

The saying is the game goes on without you.

P. G. Johnson

P.G.

The game will go on without Smarty Jones. It will go on without The Saratoga Special. It will go on without slots. And now it goes on without P.G. Johnson.

On Friday morning, the Hall of Fame trainer died.

The training chart was made up with every set; the condition book for the week was already marked with entries and jockeys.

Assistant trainer Ocala Cedano trained P.G.'s horses in the early morning. Port Chester finished fifth in the fourth; daughter Karen Johnson came to the races. P.G.'s friends mourned.

P.G. had not been in great health for the last couple of years. His wife Mary Kay died in May, and he knew there was little sense continuing on without his mate of 59 years. He needed a rest.

P.G. had been battling with his health for too long. It was difficult to watch a strong man wither away. His mind was sharp until the end, but someone decided it was his time to go.

I called the house this spring and asked Mary Kay to ask P.G. if I was doing the right thing with Volponi's half-brother Gentle Nudge. P.G. had sent me the horse in hopes steeplechasing might salvage something from a horse who seemed more like a dinosaur than a Thoroughbred. I couldn't decide if I should sell him for what I could get or give him time. The hope was Volponi could show up in his brother's lumbering stride.

"I'm sure he will tell you he trusts you," Mary Kay said. "And that he knows you'll do the right thing."

Mary Kay then heard P.G. from the other room and relayed my question.

"I won't tire my voice, Sean," Mary Kay said. "He said what I thought he'd say."

They were some couple.

After Mary Kay died, I knew I had a letter for P.G. in me – just to say how well the Johnson family treated me since I galloped horses for them in the summer of 1994. But I never got around to writing it. Now, I'm trying to pay tribute with some words in the back of today's paper. P.G. loved the The Special.

It's a shame in life that everybody doesn't see you the way some do.

Well, I guess that's how we make friends and enemies, isn't it? P.G. ruffled plenty of tackrooms around the racetrack but he never ruffled mine.

He got in a much publicized spat with Bobby Frankel last year. "The Big Horse," a book about his life, came out this year and Johnson is quoted unfavorably on many occasions.

I still don't know why P.G. talked so straight all of the time. Sometimes I think he thrived on being outspoken. Perhaps he felt like he had to live up to that feeling. I'm not sure he believed a lot of the stuff he said, though.

As far as I knew, he was a straight-shooting, loyalty-driven old timer. Boy, he had his ways and his opinions. He was as old school as they got, complete with hard 2-mile gallops, breeding for distance and sticking by your guns.

He would help anybody. He sent me horses to sell – and then gave me the money.

People would go to work for Johnson and never leave. Like Ocala, for 30-plus years.

By 10 Friday morning, Ocala had finished the morning work. He stood in the courtyard of the barn. His eyes said it all.

"He died happy because he died training horses," Ocala said. "He told me a while ago, 'I'll deal with the owners and all that, you deal with the horses.' "

So Ocala trained the horses and P.G. dealt with the owners and all the rest. Just like he said. Only thing was he was always better with the horses.

Gentle Nudge was eventually sold this summer for a little more than a board bill. I kinda wish I kept him now.

Just to keep P.G. around a little while longer.

Shug's 32 Flavors

he won that pretty easy.

"So (Mr. Anthony) wanted to bring him to New York and run him in the Suburban and I wanted to take him to Chicago and run him in something that was going to be easier. He insisted on running him in the Suburban. So I worked him there one morning seven-eighths of a mile, Larry Melancon on him and he went like 23 or something. I had never had a horse go like this. This jock comes back and his eyes . . . he says, 'I never been on one that worked like this before either.'

"I was concerned he worked too fast. I brought him up here and Pat Day couldn't come ride him, he was riding in the Stars and Stripes that day. (Don) MacBeth rode him and kinda had a big following and some of my buddies and stuff came up from Kentucky and they all bet on him, and he won the Suburban pretty easy. Beat Lord At War.

"Then we brought him up here, ran him in the Whitney, and finished third. He didn't have the best feet and this racetrack kinda got to him. We ran him back in the Jockey Club Gold Cup, on an off track – he was in front the whole way and won that. Mr. Anthony wanted to supplement him to the Breeders' Cup at Aqueduct, so we took him over to Aqueduct. He put up like $360,000 and he didn't run any good.

"He came back, it was half dark, Pat Day jumped off of him and looked at Mr. Anthony and said, 'Just was not his day.' Mr. Anthony looked at me and said, 'For $360,000, I wanna hear a little more than that.'

"He comes out of it good and (Anthony) said 'What about running him in the (D.C.) International on the grass?' I said, 'That's a wild thought – let me work him on it.' So MacBeth worked him on it, and he said, 'Man, he worked good.' So we took him down

Most Saratoga race goers probably don't know that one of the greatest riders of all time is still working in their midst each day at the track.

As the assistant clerk of scales, Hall of Fame jockey Braulio Baeza quietly goes about his duties of weighing in the jockeys before each race. Clad in a suit, his appearance today belies his legendary past. But the mark Baeza left on the sport is still evident.

"No other rider would have won it other than maybe Shoemaker or Braulio Baeza." That was Bobby Frankel just the other day, speaking of Pat Day's ride in the Schuylerville. Why is Baeza so respected? He's earned it.

In a career that spanned 17 years, he won 4,013 races and rode 24 champions. Nine of his mounts have been inducted into the Hall of Fame, including Dr. Fager, Buckpasser, Shuvee, Wajima, Arts and Letters and Damascus. Five times, he was the leading rider ranked by earnings, and he twice took home the Eclipse Award. Known for his sportsmanship, Baeza – the consummate gentleman – received the George Woolf Memorial jockey award from California turf writers in 1968.

There was more to Baeza than just figures. In a foray to Europe, he handed English champion Brigadier Gerard his only loss with a canny, race-stealing ride aboard American-trained Roberto. He was dubbed "The Sphinx" for his coolness in the saddle. There seemed to be a stopwatch in his head. A smooth finisher, he usually spared the whip in the stretch.

QUOTE:

"It's like crack, people are shivering waiting for it."

– West Point's Josh Cooper, on The Special's delivery in the morning

BAEZA

"I was never fond of the stick," said Baeza. "I used it only when it was necessary. I wasn't one of those riders that whipped a lot. I didn't believe in it . . . A lot of horses resent it – being hit – when they're doing their best, and you're trying to hit them, trying to make them do more than what they can."

Asked to choose a favorite horse from the many stars he rode, Baeza was diplomatic.

"It would not be fair to pick one of them. Dr. Fager's one of them. Buckpasser, Arts And Letters, Roman Brother . . . Shuvee, Cicada, Primonetta, Bramalea."

Of the many races he rode, one that is still fresh in Baeza's mind is Dr. Fager's record performance in the 1-mile Washington Park Handicap at Arlington while carrying 134 pounds.

"When he set the world record – that had to be one of his most impressive races. He did it so easy. He won by a city block. There was no need to ask him to run because he was so far in front."

Dr. Fager was known to detest the whip, throwing his tail straight up when struck during a race. So, Baeza's free-riding style fit the horse like spandex.

"Dr. Fager resented being hit because he was doing his best with no urging. So he resented when you hit him, sort of telling him to do more than what he could."

He split four races with his arch-rival Damascus. Baeza explained the deciding factor in their storied match-up.

"Anytime Damascus beat Dr. Fager it was because of the rabbit, Hedevar (entered by the connections of Damascus). It was a tactic – just tactics. They knew that Dr. Fager resented being rated, and he didn't want to see no horses in front of him. So, that was his downfall . . . Whoever went with him could never beat him at the end because he always outran them. In a match race, they couldn't beat him."

– Brendan Wilmot

Shug's 32 Flavors

there. MacBeth rode him, and he won. We were pretty thrilled. And we kinda backed off him – he was going to race him as a 5-year-old.

"I ran him in the Canadian Handicap on the grass at Gulfstream and he won that and equaled the track record. I didn't think he would ever run good on the dirt again. And (Anthony) wanted to take him to Santa Anita and run him in the Santa Anita Handicap. So we packed him up and took him out there, and he finished in the middle somewhere. Brought him back and I ran him in the Razorback (at Oaklawn), he finished second. He was a short-priced favorite and he pulled up bad. And that was the end of his racing."

Party School was the first stakes winner trained by McGaughey.

"I trained him for a stable which was Doc Lavin and a guy named Henry Meyer and their families – Mjaka Stable. He was just an older horse, an older gelding that I inherited, ya know. He'd run around there, win

12

an allowance race, be third in an allowance race and I ran him in a stake at Churchill Downs (the Kentucky Stakes on May 29, 1982). He won that with (jockey) Bill Gavidia. So it was a thrill. He pulled up bad in the race and to my knowledge we never figured out what was the matter with him. He never ran again, he was turned out on Henry Meyer's farm in Louisville in the front field for years, but he was just kinda one of those old hard-knocking horses that I'd love to have now. He was by Ward McCalister who stood across the street. He ran so good that day and never ran again."

Saturday, August 7, 2004

It's 5:14 a.m. I pick up 600 copies of The Special and a duffle bag of clothes from my brother's porch on York Avenue. His wife, Sam, saved my day and did my laundry. I change into clean jeans right on the street. Today's paper route is underway. To the sales grounds, Kip Elser's house, Ken Ramsey's house, the Oklahoma side and the main side. I need gas and my right rear tire looks low.

It's 6:51. I chase Mark Hennig down for an interview about Eddington's chances in the Jim Dandy. He tells me the horse has appreciated the break in training and hopefully he's a better horse for it. Eddington still is as pretty a horse as any on the grounds.

It's 8:02. The backside finally has some numbers. Nothing like years past but at least the sales people have come out to drink coffee and watch horses. The air is as Saratoga as it gets.

It's 9:32. I have a microphone in my hand for the first "Breakfast with Champions" at the Prime Hotel. Pat Day, Richard Migliore, Terry Finley and Dallas Stewart sit on a panel that would make Oprah proud (assuming she likes horse racing). We chat about smart horses, kicking the dog and pressure.

It's 11:42. The NTRA PAC Brunch is underway in the tent at the Reading Room. Tim Smith tells us how important it is for all of us to get involved politically. We eat crab-salad croissants and drink coffee.

It's 1:03 p.m. Rolled Stocking catches Forget The Judge to win the first. Nothing like a good claimer on the grass at Saratoga.

It's 1:07. We're trying to build an ad from nothing. We have no ideas, no art and no more inspiration.

It's 2:04. I walk to the track on North Avenue. The alleys in Saratoga must have some stories to tell. Imagine what they've seen. A tennis game is underway in between Union and North, deuce in the second set.

It's 2:39. Good Night Shirt wins the fourth at Pimlico. My hunch horse is no longer a maiden. There is nothing like watching your horse win a race. When I rode, I couldn't understand how owners got such a thrill. Now I know.

Saturday, August 7, 2004

It's 3:55. The sales grounds are quiet. John Ward, Steve Asmussen, Mike Ryan and a few others look at horses while the sky darkens. River Belle wins the sixth. It's pouring.

It's 4:03. The mail-room awning has been designated as shelter from the rain. I offer a kid $10 for his umbrella. He won't take it.

It's 5:12. Bwana Charlie comes from last in the Amsterdam to win the sprint stakes.

It's 5:18. Steve Asmussen stops and gets his picture taken with some random fans who swear they're related. He laughs and goes to the Trustees' Room.

It's 5:43. The Whitney field is being loaded into the gate. West Point Thoroughbreds' Terry Finley takes a deep sigh and readies to see if it's time. Seattle Fitz's Whitney goes up in smoke in the first furlong. Finley is deflated but stoic.

It's 7:48. I finish the first of my four stories that need writing before the night's over. The Jim Dandy preview goes to Jamie Santo for editing.

It's 9:07. Words on the Whitney are coming slow. The feature story is lurking in my brain. Somewhere.

It's 11:09. Our handicapper Pete Fornatale wants to go for a beer. He's at Chez Sophie celebrating his birthday and Good Night Shirt's win at Pimlico this afternoon. I used to go for a lot of beers at Saratoga. The Saratoga Special killed my drinking habit. Now I'm drunk on words, ads and distributing papers. I can't decide which has a worse hangover.

It's 11:26. "Please help – very tired – long day. Be back noontime on Sunday." It's our senior writer Quint Kessenich, who wants us to edit, proof and lay out a West Virginia Derby story. He works for ESPN on his off days for The Special. Now there's a resume.

It's 11:33. My brother Joe tries to transmit files to Staffield Printing. Our computer system has stopped quicker than Yessirgeneralsir in the Whitney. Computers are like part-time hotwalkers – they only work when they feel like it.

It's 12:46 a.m. About time to get the next batch of papers off the porch, at least, I have my laundry.

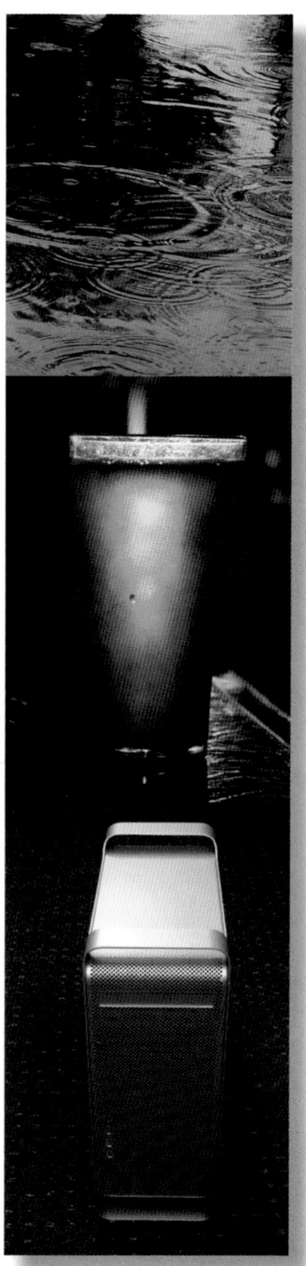

Shug's 32 Flavors

13

Try Something New, owned by John A. Bell III, was McGaughey's first Grade I winner. The daughter of Hail The Pirates won nearly $500,000 including two stakes at Keeneland.

"She kinda knocked around, took her four or five starts to break her maiden, she got it together and won an allowance race. Then she caught the slop at Keeneland, and they used to run the Bewitch Stakes at Keeneland on the dirt. She won. There was some horse in there that was the heavy favorite, she kinda stopped and we circled the field and won easy. And then I brought her up to New York and ran her in the Shuvee and she finished second. And I brought her to the Delaware Handicap and she got beat the dirtiest of noses to May Day Eighty, Calumet's filly.

"Then I ran her in the Beldame, and she finished third. I was kinda disappointed, then I took her to Keeneland again and she won the Spinster, that was my first Grade I winner.

"That was a huge thrill, to go back home and win it for a local guy, whose family were friends of mine. There were a lot of friends there that day, and that was quite a thrill. Not the biggest one, but there haven't been any bigger."

Champion older mare of 1991, Emory Hamilton's ***Queena*** won 10 of 17 lifetime starts, including separate winning streaks of four and five races. She earned more than $565,000 in her career.

"She never ran until she was 4. She never showed anything, she was a bad tie-up horse. And she got real sick the summer of her 3-year-old year. Had to send her to the clinic, with colic, and the chance of maybe

Dave Carroll worked for Shug McGaughey during the glory days of Easy Goer, Personal Ensign, Seeking The Gold, Personal Flag, Rhythm.

He worked an important horse for an important race and messed it all up.

McGaughey asked him one question.

"Dave, what were you doing this morning at 2 o'clock?"

"I was sleeping, Shug."

"Well, you know what I was doing?" McGaughey said. "I was thinking about this breeze. I was thinking about where this work was going to take

this horse. I could have slept. I wasted my time."

Tough love. McGaughey taught the Frank Whiteley way – teach by example rather than explanation. He wasn't warm and fuzzy; he just wanted to train horses.

Carroll learned enough to go out on his own and train horses like Fire Slam, who will go for the King's Bishop later in the meet. Carroll came up this weekend to see McGaughey be inducted into the Hall of Fame.

"He wasn't one that would point things out to you but you would learn by observation. It was like osmosis, you just soaked it up. Once he realized you wanted to learn and were there to work . . . he was a tough man to work for but fair," Carroll said. "Those years were unbelievable, every weekend we were going for something. It was maybe his best years collectively. The depth of the stable. I was just glad to be part of it."

Carroll worked for McGaughey for six years, galloping Easy Goer and learning the trade.

Twenty-five years since his first trainer's license, McGaughey enters the Hall of Fame as a first-ballot honoree.

There will be plenty of supporters. Former pupils Phil Hauswald, Tony Reinstedler and Carroll. Friends like Steve Young and Charlie Boden. Clients like Dell Hancock and the Phipps family.

McGaughey's been working on his speech for months. He's nervous about it.

But if it goes anything like his horses, it will be smooth sailing. McGaughey has trained eight champions – Easy Goer, Heavenly Prize, Inside Information, Personal Ensign, Queena, Rhythm, Storm Flag Flying and Vanlandingham. He won five stakes on Breeders' Cup Preview Day at Belmont Park in 1993. The list of horses he's trained goes on and on and includes Lure, Furlough, Coronado's Quest, Adjudicating, Dancing Spree, Finder's Fee, My Flag, Personal Flag and Versailles Treaty.

Not bad for a man who discovered he liked the sport when his parents took him to Keeneland and then got his first hotwalking job with David Carr. His breakthrough came with the Phipps job in 1985 but he had already trained Vanlandingham to a championship season and sent out graded stakes winners Lass Trump and Try Something New.

"I'm not sure I was ready for some of the things that happened," McGaughey said. "Taking Personal Ensign down for the Molly Pitcher and Personal Flag winning the Suburban a half-hour before. The six in a day thing. Two Breeders' Cups in a day. Seeking The Gold going down for the Super Derby when it was a million dollars."

Thoroughbred racing's Hall of Fame allows for a strange dimension – the inductees can still be in action. McGaughey runs three horses on the day he achieves the ultimate individual recognition offered in the sport. His plaque, like so many others, will need updating because he's far from through.

"There's always times when you get disappointed, you get down when you're maybe not as competitive as you want," McGaughey said. "It bothers me when I look up on big race days and I'm not more competitive than I am. I got to get used to that in a way because I don't have as many so I have to concentrate and try to do the best I can with the ones who come through here who are pretty good."

There will be plenty of concentrating. The Phipps breed to race and have lines and lines of strong pedigrees. Ogden Phipps died but his son Dinny has kept the stable going strong. The grandkids, let by Daisy, will make sure McGaughey has a full training chart.

"I enjoy them every day I'm around them. I miss Mr. Phipps but Dinny, Andy, Cynthia, I'm around Daisy and Ogden more than any of the other grandkids. They're a lot of fun, I consider them friends. I know I'm an employee and I treat it as that...

...but when we're away from here, we're friends."

losing her. They got her straightened out and we got her going again. She ended up breaking her maiden as a 4-year-old (in 1990) and she won a stake that fall, the First Flight. Then she came back, she won races like the Vagrancy and then she ran up here in the Ballerina and a horse passed her and she came back and won, that was a little bit of her trait that she would do. Then in the Maskette, same thing happened, and she won. Got passed and came back and won. Then we took her to the Breeders' Cup (Distaff) and she drew the outside post and it was at Louisville. They load her in there and didn't even shut the back doors so she didn't break good and finished fifth.

"I had her the whole time. I had just about given up on her. And (Emory Hamilton) the girl that owned her, she just kept telling me, 'Aw, don't give up. Maybe she'll come later, maybe she'll come later.' And you know, she did come later. When she won the First Flight I was tickled to death because I just never thought she'd ever win a stake. But with the pedigree she came in with, she was difficult. She was about as bad a tie-up horse as I've ever had. It runs in the family."

14

Versailles Treaty captured the Alabama, the Gazelle, the Test and the Ruffian among her nine career wins and $1.2 million in earnings. The daughter of Danzig finished second in back-to-back Breeders' Cup Distaffs (1991 and 1992).

"She broke her maiden in her first start the fall of her 2-year-old year at Aqueduct and then kind of went along and I think she was second in the Beaumont at Keeneland, then I brought her back there and went

John Servis quickly became the most publicized – and scrutinized – trainer in America during Smarty Jones' rise to stardom earlier this year.

It was, to be sure, a stage he had never been on. A hard-knocking Philadelphia-based trainer, Servis enjoyed success before Smarty Jones entered his barn, but Pat and Roy Chapman's son of Elusive Quality elevated that success to an astronomic level.

While he's visited Saratoga in the past (remember Jostle, winner of the 2000 Alabama Stakes), Servis' presence this year has been great. At the opening session of the Fasig-Tipton sales, he purchased a Grand Slam colt for $240,000. The Special's Sean Clancy caught up with Servis at the sales grounds yesterday, talking about Smarty, yearlings and life.

How much different is life this year? "Not a lot – it really isn't. I've had a few people come up to me that I didn't know, thanking me and telling me how much they enjoyed it and everything, but it's really not that different.

When you go look at horses, do people treat you differently? "It's funny, since Jostle, I noticed a difference then, but since then everybody's been really kind to me, everybody knows me. It's a little easier when they know you."

What did you learn on the Triple Crown trail? "I had no idea how vigorous it was. How tough it was, from the beginning of the year on . . . I really had no idea. The one big thing is when you do it, you've got to have fun, and we did – we had a blast. My wife, my family. My wife is more upset about this horse retiring than anybody and she didn't really get involved in the business. She did the book end of it and that was it; she rarely came to the barn. She comes to the barn all the time now. Her and her girlfriends will go to the barn in the middle of the night, 9 o'clock at night, and check the horses which I used to do. It's great. She's got a couple of 2-year-olds she really likes. The biggest thing is to enjoy it because you never know when you're going to get back. Have fun and enjoy the ride.

People talk about having a horse of a lifetime – how do you improve upon that? "I don't think about that. I don't believe that's it. The chances of me ever having another Smarty – guess what – probably never will. But you know what, I used to dream about going to the Derby and the chances of that . . . I thought, 'What shot do I have to get there?' I got there and won it. It can happen, it can happen. I got good clients that will spend some money and the guys that breed their own send me some good ones. Even the Pennsylvania-breds like Smarty, they send me some nice horses. I feel like I always got a shot."

You always acted like you knew you would get there . . . "I felt pretty good. I made a comment to Bob Yeats, who writes for the Arkansas Gazette or Democrat whatever it is (Arkansas Democrat-Gazette), after the Southwest when everybody was down on the horse. I said, 'Bob, this is strictly off-the-record, but in three months they'll be talking about this horse like he's the next Seattle Slew.' He said, 'Get outta here.' I said, 'You just watch and see.' After the Derby he said, 'Can I print that now?'

John Servis

I said, 'Yeah, now you can print that.' He's that good. He worked in 10 and change before I ever ran him. He's a super, super fast horse. The big thing was getting him to settle. That was my main concern all along. If I could get him to settle I knew he was a good ride."

Do you look at yearlings with him in mind? "Some . . . not really. He's got a lot of things I like but he was never the kind of horse that would blow you away. Until you put that bridle on him, he was just an average horse. When you put that bridle on, he would get to swelling up. Chappy asked me one day, 'If that horse was in the sale, would you have bought him? You'd have never have bought him.' I said, 'You know what Chap, I'd have bought him – if I could have gotten him for the right price.' I wouldn't paid more than a hundred (thousand), I'll tell you that. He's a good looking horse but didn't sweep you off your feet."

Did he change your life? "I can't go to the grocery store and be out of there in 10 minutes. My wife went to the grocery store the other day, and it was two hours to go to the grocery store. People see you . . . even my wife. People recognize her and they stop and talk. It's great, don't get me wrong. I've had people come up to me for my autograph and they're like, 'I'm really sorry . . . ' I say, 'Are you kidding me?' I love it because a year from now, people will walk right by me and not know who the hell I am. Right now, it's different to say the least. Even my friends, we go out to dinner and people notice me, they love it. They really love it – it makes them feel like they're sitting with someone important. My one buddy who we go to eat with quite a lot, whenever we call for a reservation, he always makes sure they know who I am, so we get right in. I said, 'We've got to stop this.' "

It's got to make you feel good. "It does, it really does. I don't know if I should tell you this or not, but the one thing my wife and I talked about early on was that if we get to the Derby I'm going to do my best to try to make it everybody's race. I'm from Charles Town (W. Va.). I quit college after one year. This business has been so good to me. I just want to give something back. Right now, it's tough, it's a struggling business. And I told my wife, 'The more people we can get involved, the better it's going to be. If this is my once chance I have to do it. . . ' I worked at it. What you saw was me, but I worked at getting everybody in on the ride."

Do you see the game in a different light after all this? "Not really. I'll tell you one thing. A few years back, I was training for Rick (Porter). Things were OK, but I just got bored with the business, I really wasn't happy with the way things were going. I didn't like the way things were going and I didn't feel comfortable. I talked to my wife a couple of times about getting out. She said, 'What are you going to do?' I said, 'I don't know, maybe I'll take a jock's book or something.' So every Sunday we'd go to mass and I'd pray to show me a sign, because I didn't know what to do. And that was the year I came up with Jostle. Then it was like, you know what, this is what I was meant to do. If you believe in that, then it was strong. Really strong. For me, from that point on, instead of grinding, grinding, grinding and trying to make it, now I have fun. Now I go in there, I train my horses, I enjoy it. It put things in perspective. You know what, this is what I'm meant to do. You sit out here and the sun come up . . . Who gets to work like this? Gets paid for this? It taught me to take the lows a whole lot better."

How did you handle Smarty's retirement? "It was rough for me, I'm sure it's going to be rougher when he leaves the barn, but I understand it. Under normal circumstances, he could come back next year and tear the industry up, just kick ass everywhere he goes. But when you have that kind of money hanging over your head and you got people who invested the kind of money they did and they're not getting anything back until he goes to the breeding shed, I can

Shug's 32 Flavors

through her conditions. I remember about the end of June, (Angel) Cordero rode her and she was 3-5 in a three-other-than. He was kind of laying back there and he made a run in the middle of the turn. Then he just sort of took her back again and I thought, 'Uh-oh.' Then he circled the field and came home – he was schooling her. She came back here and she won the Test pretty easy, and then we ran her back in the Alabama, going a mile and a quarter, and she was much the best and won easy. Then she won the Gazelle. And then we ran her in the Beldame and she finished second. I think she got into trouble that race. I was livid at Cordero, and I didn't say a word to him. In his retirement speech, he said 'I rode her terrible, the guy never said a word to me, I could tell he was steaming mad.'

"Then we went to Kentucky and ran her in the Breeders' Cup, and she was second to Dance Smartly. Then she had a good 4-year-old year, she won the Ruffian. We took her to Florida and ran her in the Breeders' Cup down there and she finished second to Paseana. Then she was retired, been a bit of a disappointment as a broodmare. Most of the things just kinda were OK. Then Saarland, who was a decent horse. Probably didn't give his all all the time. But she's got a Rahy yearling (Supreme Council) that could be OK, so I'm hoping she'll pick it up from there."

15

A bay colt by Mr. Prospector out of Dance Number, ***Rhythm*** won six of 20 starts and $1.5 million while being named champion juvenile of 1989. He won the Breeders' Cup Juvenile, and the Travers at Saratoga.

"A very aggressive 2-year-old. I ran him here in his

understand that. Steve Crist ripped them for it, but I know if it was his horse, he'd have done the same thing. From an economic decision, you had to do it. It didn't make any sense not to do it. From the racing decision, I think, everyone wanted to do it (keep him runing). Robert Clay, the Chapmans, and myself all wanted to race him. But when you sit down and write on paper the pros and cons, you can't. You can't. You're taking a huge risk. If you want to take that risk, that's fine."

What's the future? "I've got a couple of 2-year-olds I'm real happy with, so I'm shifting it over to them. Hopefully one of them carries me somewhere."

Is the Servis family now set financially? "Well, I wasn't bad off but I'm certainly in good shape now. It gives me the opportunity to do some things I wanted to do. I invested in some real estate up in the Poconos a few years ago. I think I'm going to take some money and invest in Florida so when I retire I can do the Poconos in the summer and Florida for the winter. I have a breeding right to Smarty, I think I'm going to buy a mare and breed her. Things I was never able to do. I always had a horse or two here or there but that was going to Timonium and buying a horse for a dime. On top of everything else, my kids can go to school wherever they want. That's a good feeling."

Have you talked to Smarty Jones about it all? "No, I haven't. I haven't had time – he hasn't had time, I should say. This poor horse, he's going to be tickled to death to get out of there for some peace and quiet. You can't even imagine. Every day, from 7 until 10, I get four or five calls. People calling that want to see the horse. People drive off the road, pull into the stable gate – don't know anything about the stable gate – they say, 'We're here to see Smarty Jones.'

Well, the guard calls me and says so and so are here to see the horse.

I say, 'Who are they?' 'So and so.'

'Well who are they with?' 'What company are you with, sir?' 'Oh, we're not with a company, we just came to see the horse.'

There are so many people. The head of security at Philadelphia Park, a guy named Lance Morell, he's done an outstanding job, he really has. He's called me here probably 10 times. 'This is what we've got set up. 9 o'clock, Glamour magazine's coming, 1 o'clock, ESPN's coming . . .' I had a guy, a photographer for Vogue magazine. A guy named Bruce Webber.

He called, and wanted to do a layout, was trying to get him on the cover. I said, 'Why?' He said, 'I just fell in love with this horse.' I said to call me in a couple of days. That afternoon I'm in the bathroom and my wife has a Vogue magazine. On the cover it says in bold print across the bottom, "Photographs by Bruce Webber." I say, 'Wow, this guy's legit.' It's a shame, if he could have raced another year and the NTRA really would have got their heads into it, we could have moved this industry ahead 30 years.

Soundness wise, what was he like? "He was good. When we did the nuclear scan, the vet was shocked that his wheels looked as good as they did for what he had been through. He ran every three weeks from the Southwest and two weeks for the Preakness.

Did he look different when you brought him back? "Yeah, he just wasn't reaching. Wasn't nodding, but he wasn't reaching. He'd get a little better and we'd turn him around and he just never reached. I bet I didn't gallop him five days since I brought him back.

Was that a surprise? "Yeah, you almost get to the point where you think he's invincible. When we started him back and I saw how he was, I thought, 'Well maybe it's just because he hasn't done anything for a while.' I jogged him for three weeks before I finally turned him around then it was like, 'What's going on here?' I couldn't really find anything. His feet had nasty bruises, that was the truth. We put glue-ons on him. And it didn't matter. We decided to block his feet, he got a little better. We blocked his ankles and he got a little better but still not enough. When we did the scan and all four ankles lit up, there was one hind sesamoid that lit up. That was like, 'Thank God we did this.' "

If it wasn't Smarty Jones, what would you have done? "Kicked him out for 90 days. Any horse. I probably would have given him 60 days, re-scanned him and if he looked good, I'd probably give him another 30 days just in case and then go on with him.

The more time you give them, the better off you are."

Shug's 32 Flavors

16

first start probably going 5 1/2 (furlongs), and he disappointed me. Finished third. But then I ran him back and he won, and I ran him in the Champagne in an entry and he was training really, really good and he finished second, probably should have won, to his entrymate (Adjudicating). We got him to Florida, and he did magnificent while the horse that won the Champagne, got down there and did terrible.

"And I really thought Rhythm would run well in the Breeders' Cup (Juvenile), which he did. He got a perfect trip, got through on the inside with (Craig) Perret and was able to beat a pretty good horse (Grand Canyon).

"Ended up being a champion, and he came back and his first start back was in the Fountain of Youth and he didn't run any good. Had to do some work on his wind. Then he kind of got it together later on that summer; he won a stake (the Colin) on Belmont Day. He was third in the Haskell, and I was a little disappointed so when he came here for the Travers we decided to change our strategy a little bit and just let him drop way out of it and come running and he was able to win. And when he trained up to the Breeders' Cup he trained as good as a horse can train and I really thought going into that race he would be double-tough. He kind of made a run around the turn like he was going to do something then flattened out and finished eighth.

"Rhythm was very good as a 2-year-old for about two months, and he was good when he got here; he was good in the summer of his 3-year-old year . . . Besides that, he was OK."

Shug's 32 Flavors

Dancinginmydreams. Bay mare, foaled in 1988. The daughter of Seeking The Gold and Oh What A Dance earned $64,600 in her short-lived career. She won her debut and finished second in the Matron.

"This is the filly that hurt herself. A great big thing. She won her first start up here. I ran her in the Matron

17

because an allowance race didn't go. She came running and just got beat to one of those good fillies Mark Hennig had (Raging Fever). Then we ran her back in the Frizette and she broke her leg in the race. There was a question of whether to save her or put her down back at the barn.

"The veterinarians didn't think she had much chance and Dinny Phipps said, 'Do you think you can get her to New Bolton without putting her through too much?' They thought they could, so Dr. Selway and Dr. Hunt rigged up some kind of magical bandage to put on her leg. They put her on the van and hooked her up to IVs and stuff. Got her to New Bolton and they started putting her together that night. They called me the next morning and she had gotten through that operation fine and she woke up in the swimming pool. That guy said her bone looked like you shot a shot gun off in a tin can and it hadn't come through the skin. It was in a hundred pieces.

"She spent 13 months at New Bolton, numerous operations for different things. Now she's out on a farm in Kentucky. She's got a yearling colt by Rahy and a filly foal by Forest Wildcat. She's turned out with other mares. She's got a big back ankle on her. Right there is a miracle of a horse still being alive because 9 3/4 out of 10 people would have walked away. We weren't going to do anything to hurt her but we wanted to give

So I needed another column idea. It was getting desperate.

It had to be past 8 p.m., with a long day behind and a long night ahead. I had stopped and started more times than a flooded-out Vega. Now there was nothing left in the tank. So I asked around the sales for anything. Just an idea to get me going. When in doubt, let the readers decide the direction.

"Don't ask me," Bates Newton said

"Gossip, everybody loves gossip," suggested Tom Ludt.

"That's why you're the writer," The Special's Dave Martin said.

Funny, I don't feel like one.

But leave it to an Englishman to come through in the clutch.

"Hip 84. Giant's Causeway. He's already had two important winners in England. Mick Kinane dropped his reins in the Breeders' Cup, I was on the table screaming. This colt could be the sales topper. That's what I want to read about tomorrow," said Tom Goff, bloodstock agent from across the pond.

Then I saw him – the keg-kicking walk, the impeccable shoulder movement, the head swing like a Gatling gun. Click, click, click, he looked every person in the eye. The manhole cover met his gaze – an easy sidestep – and into the walking ring. Elvis is alive.

Hmmm, Tom, you might be right.

The horse walked into the ring and stared at his kingdom. Awesome.

Walt Robertson asked for a million dollars. Spotter Tom Biederman whipped round with a $700,000 call. The race was on. Eventually it was Barry Irwin on the aisle, Stan Fulton's Fleetwood management nearby and Roger King on the loop. Theatrics from King, professionalism from Fleetwood, stoicism from Irwin. The hammer fell at $1.85 million. Barry Irwin of Team Valor got the prize.

Thirteen hips into the second night, the sale had a new colt in the yellow jersey. Lance Armstrong never looked so good. The horse exuded everything you'd want from a horse. His demeanor was cool. His pedigree imposing, with two blacktype siblings on the page. His conformation was sculpted by a commissioned artist having a good day.

Of course, all I had to do was ask Michael Hernon, Neil Howard, Brian Graves or Jonathan Thorne of Gainesway. They would have told me all about the horse when he arrived on the grounds. Or even months ago when Graves was keeping tabs on the horse back on Dr. Chuck Kidder's farm in Kentucky.

Maybe I could have gotten into the action that was taken at Barn 6 West before the sale. Hernon, Howard, Graves and Thorne put their money where their horsemanship was and bet $50 each on the final price.

Hernon predicted $100,000 more than the final price. Howard was $100,000 too low. They were both closer than the youngbloods who had to reach into their pockets after Fleetwood folded, King walked out of the pavilion and the slip came to Irwin.

"In this case, we take the money from Brian and Jonathan," said Hernon, his delight verging on smugness. "I'm sure there will be future bets."

Is this a great game or what? A horse goes through the ring for millions of dollars while $200 is on the table of the consignment team. It's like an owner betting on a horse.

Every day with a horse is a gamble and still you push your money through the betting window for some added thrill. Like an $88 exacta will improve upon a six-digit winner's check. And what about when they lose? A double play, you've lost your pocket money while your horse investment is going up in smoke.

As for Hip 84, he had Barry Irwin bowling earlier in the week. The Team Valor leader kept coming to Gainesway's shedrow. And it wasn't for the wooden benches in the shade.

The horse kept talking to him and Irwin kept thinking it was impossible. He was the kid in the candy store counting his change, the window shopper on Rodeo Drive hoping there was space left on the Visa. He didn't think he'd ever get the horse, so he went bowling with his girlfriend to take his mind off the swaggering bay colt. Bowling couldn't have been all bad as Irwin came to the sale with one thing on his mind and $2 million in his holster. He sat coolly while the increments climbed. He was buying into the poker game with $2 million, no more – even if it was the best horse he's seen in years. The horse who could take him to the Triple Crown. His luck held. Irwin parted with $1.85 million.

Graves and Thorne . . . $50 each.

Shug's 32 Flavors

her a chance.

"She'll probably make a great broodmare. The only way she made it was because she was a great patient. Everybody around her fell in love with her. I know there have been some lectures by surgeons who have used her as a subject. A bunch of them who took care of her went out to the farm to see her.

"I didn't know what to think (when she got on the van), this is the crapshoot of all crapshoots. At least we got her on the van and away she went. Then she made it. She's down there, happy as a lark. She looks great. It's remarkable she's alive today, being a broodmare and being that good of one."

Dancing Spree. Born in 1985, Dancing Spree won 10 of 35 career starts and earned more than $1.4 million for McGaughey and owner/breeder Ogden Phipps. Dancing Spree won three Grade I stakes, the 1989 Breeders' Cup Sprint and Suburban and 1990 Carter.

"You want to know the story on Dancing Spree? He's by Nijinsky (II) out of Blitey, never showed anything.

18

At any time, any place. I couldn't make him do anything. Good looking horse, sound. Popped a splint. I said, 'Well maybe that's it.' Took care of that. And started back – nothing, nothing, nothing, nothing. Was gonna give him away. Called Auburn – 'Yeah, we'll take him.' Then they called and said, 'We can't pay his van bill,' I said, 'Aw, to heck with it.' So I start him going again, and we're at Gulfstream and a friend of mine said, 'You got anything to go a quarter of a mile?'

"I said, 'Quarter of a mile? We're at the races, man.'

Brent Johnson couldn't find anywhere in Saratoga to hear Prince.

The piano bar at Siro's wouldn't even play his songs for crisp $100 bills. Until he walked into the Spring Street Deli Saturday morning. There it was – Prince – loud and clear.

"It's going to be a good day," Johnson said. "Somebody's playing Prince."

Boy, was it a good day. Better Talk Now, owned by Johnson, Karl Barth and Chris Dwyer under the banner Bushwood Stable, came from off the pace to upset the Sword Dancer Invitational.

Favorite Balto Star went to the lead, as everybody knew he would in the soft turf. B.A. Way (Better Talk Now's half-brother) kept the pacesetter honest to his outside. Second-choice Request For Parole pulled hard while in third. Silverfoot and Rochester came next.

Ramon Dominguez anchored the head-strong Better Talk Now in last. Fractions ticked by, plenty fast for the 1 1/2-mile distance and yielding turf, while Better Talk Now bided his time. By the stretch, Better Talk Now was in full flight while Request For Parole was going after a faltering Balto Star. Better Talk Now lugged in slightly, which he's known to do, but had plenty left to win by 1 1/2 lengths. Request For Parole finished second, with Balto Star third.

Trained by Graham Motion, Better Talk Now won his first Grade I stakes and provided the first Grade I for Bushwood. Johnson was elated.

"We've never even run in a Grade I," Johnson said. "Who thinks they're going to get here? You hope . . . That's what the game is all about, taking your chances and hoping for the best. This one has worked out great."

Bushwood purchased Better Talk Now from Diane Perkins about two years ago. He's now earned more than $650,000. Motion schools the high-strung gelding at Fair Hill Training Center in Maryland. He shipped up the day before the race.

"We always were impressed with him but he's not a nice horse to be around. It's not like you could fall in love with him. We gelded him last year and he's settled down," Motion said. "He's basically an easy horse to train. He's thrived being at Fair Hill. I couldn't believe how relaxed he was today. He had a tendency to be pretty keen early and I was worried about him getting the trip. He's actually maturing and settling down a lot."

Dominguez knows this better than anyone. The first time he rode Better Talk Now, the horse smoked off with him on the front end and faltered. Since that learned lesson, he's tried to ride him from well off the pace. The horse is so strong, Motion scratches

Better Talk Now

PRINCE FOR A DAY

him if he draws an outside post. Daylight seen from the outside is his undoing. From the inside, Dominguez can get him covered up to save his electric final kick. On top of being rank, Better Talk Now tends to lug in when the race reaches its final stages. Motion went with an extended blinker on his inside and a more severe bit.

"The blinker was kind of a desperate measure but it's made a difference. He was really leaning on horses in the stretch. It cost him races," Motion said. "I don't know how much of it's maturity and how much is the blinker but it's helped. We had to do something serious because it was costing him necks and noses."

Better Talk Now's career best was a win last fall in the Knickerbocker Handicap at Aqueduct. This year, he floundered in his first two tries but came back to run two strong seconds. He was second to Arlington Million winner Kicken Kris in his latest, the Bowling Green Handicap.

Johnson owns an investment-advisory firm in Fairfax, Va. Motion was his first choice of trainers even if it meant taking a while to get it done.

"We were looking to claim a horse, just to get our feet wet and we were told by the racing people in Maryland that he wouldn't talk to us," Johnson said. "We waited about a year and then started buying some young horses. Once we thought we might have the stock that would work, we went and talked to him."

Good thing. Motion now trains eight horses for Johnson's three partnerships.

Shug's 32 Flavors

"He said, 'We'll, I've got one.' I said 'Wait, I've got one.'

"Breezed him, breezed pretty good. So, I've nothing else to do with him, just go on with him. And kept on going. Got him to Keeneland, won his first start. He was 3. Piddled around with him, piddled around with him. By Nijinsky – got to run him long on the grass. He'd be third, fourth, third. Run him long on the dirt, same thing, be third.

"(Angel) Cordero said 'Let's try blinkers on him." So we put blinkers on him, be the same thing. He'd be up in the race, but as soon the horses try to get away from him, he'd get lost, be third. So I'm walking out of there one day and I'm thinking, 'What can be wrong here?' So I say, 'I'm gonna shorten him up a little bit.' So I said something about a mile and a sixteenth and somebody said, 'Nah, nah, shorter than that.' Shorter than that? So, that's kind of what happened. I shortened him up, he started running good, I ran him in the Churchill Downs Handicap, he won that. Came back, and Cordero talked me into running him in the Metropolitan Mile, he got beat two noses, was third (to Proper Reality and Seeking The Gold). Then I ran him in the True North, going three quarters, in June, and he won that.

"Cordero said, 'Let's run him in the Suburban.' Mile and a quarter. Ran him in the Suburban going a mile and a quarter in the mud, and he won. Now, he won because I think he ran a sprint race and then the rest of the way Cordero carried him. And he won. I brought him up here and I ran him in the Forego and he finished second to that horse Sidney Watters had that used to win here every year, Quick Call. Just got beat. Lost him the Sprinter of the Year, too.

"So Mr. (Ogden) Phipps said, 'What are we going to

Have you heard the one about the German, the Englishman and the American?

It goes like this:

Englishman makes a questionable decision which affects the German that then nearly kills the American. All are questioned.

The Englishman, let's call him Jamie Spencer, says: "Oh, blimey . . . I did nothing of the sort."

The German, let's call him Andrasch Starke, says: "Wuh? Bump, bump. Ugh."

The American, let's call him Kent Desormeaux, says: "I was far and away the best. He's a superlative who exclamations a zest for life. It cost me the world."

I'm all for freedom of speech, democracy and the rest, but why do stewards talk to jockeys when there's an inquiry or foul claim? In what other sport do participants get to talk to umpires – without risking an ejection – when a rule is violated.

Yesterday the Arlington Million ended in controversy (again) when Spencer angled in on Powerscourt, which shuffled Epalo and Starke over, which shuffled Kicken Kris and Desormeaux into Arlington Park's inside rail. Powerscourt roared off to win on his own while Kicken Kris righted himself and finished a determined second. Magistretti rallied to catch Epalo who ended up fourth.

Of course, the inquiry sign lit up immediately. All the experts (myself included) bandied opinions around quicker then after a political debate.

Powerscourt was disqualified and placed behind Epalo. Kicken Kris was awarded the win with Magistretti second, Epalo third and Powerscourt fourth.

It was a tough call, I won't argue that. And I'd rather be a manhole cover than a steward, but what's the sense of talking to jockeys? Stewards' decisions are always a matter of interpretation. That's not going to change, nor should it, but doesn't it ruin the objectivity of the stewards when they speak to the riders? How can it not? This is not the stewards fault; it's a simple fact.

In the Million, they talked to an Englishman who doesn't know the nuances of American stewards; a German who can't possibly speak the language or understand it as well as his counterparts speaking their native tongue; an American who's ridden in this country in front of these same basic stewards for his whole Hall of Fame career.

Isn't Desormeaux at a huge advantage?

I'm not saying this is why Spencer's horse came down, just that the formula can't work. With all the Latino jockeys in the jocks' room now, aren't they at a clear disadvantage when speaking to stewards? Listen, I interview them all the time and the truth is I understand Jerry Bailey, Richard Migliore and Pat Day better than Edgar Prado, John Velazquez or Jorge Chavez. It's nobody's fault. But Bailey, Migliore, Day – all American-born jockeys – get their point across better than their Spanish colleagues.

Could the benefit to the stewards of gaining whatever knowledge they gain ever outweigh the chance at pre- or misconceptions? And why do the guilty get to plead their case in what has to be an open-and-shut case to work.

It's like a hockey game where a man cross-checks an opponent into the boards and the ref blows the whistle, then asks both players if it was a foul, if it cost him the goal, if it was intentional. Now make one of those players a veteran or a fellow countryman, and make the other a rookie or a Swede and it can't work. Ask for a lie and you'll get it.

In the Arlington Million, stewards talked to an Englishman, a German and an American. Then they made a decision. Ridiculous.

The Englishman doesn't know the system here. He doesn't know what to say or how to say it. How are the rules interpreted? Is crossing over a reason for disqualification? What if you're much the best, do they take that into account?

The German, you might as well ask him to name the American presidents. How can he help his cause by trying to explain what happened? The Arlington stewards would need an interpreter.

Now that I think about it some more, it's not just when one jockey speaks the language and another doesn't. Some people can spin a tail better than others. Some can lie to your face and make you feel good about it. Some can't articulate their point with a speechwriter and a dictionary.

But riding races is about riding races, not speaking about races.

Let the jockeys ride and let the stewards decide.

Leave the explaining to the rest of us.

Shug's 32 Flavors

do now?' We're going to take him down and run him in Florida. I got him down to Florida, I'm telling you, this son of a gun trained like a bear. You know, I mean – whew. That was the same year Rhythm was down there. And I ran him (in the Breeders' Cup Sprint at Gulfstream) and that horse of Lukas' (On The Line) got in that wreck, and he got through all the way and beat Safely Kept right on the money. Won by a neck. That was in his 4-year-old year.

"Then he went to stud over in France. He was pretty good. He probably should have been Champion Sprinter that year (in 1989), Safely Kept was."

19

Lass Trump produced McGaughey's first Saratoga stakes win when she took the Test in 1983. She also accounted for the Revidere that year and the Ballerina in 1984.

"I had come back from Chicago in 1983. No, 1981. She was a yearling then. I had a couple of horses, one of them belonged half to me. I went to a barbecue after a Kentucky football game and a friend of mine was there named Joe Brown Nicholson and he told me he had bought a yearling filly for an airline pilot with Tiger Airlines named Alan Samford. The guy had come to him and had $30,000 to spend. They spent $18,000. She was by Timeless Moment. The guy just liked horse racing. I took her and she had some hock problems at 2, we got her to the races and she won at 2, she won at 3. I brought her up here to run her in the Test. I brought six horses up here that year.

"I ran her in the Test, Pat Day. She won, came from the back and won. Then they had a little condition stake on Travers Day called the Revidere Stakes, it

Society Selection

DOUBLING UP

Four days into the meet, Society Selection swept down the stretch to win the Test Stakes.

It was another Grade I victory for The Chief, Allen Jerkens. Society Selection sat 7 lengths off a half-mile in 44 seconds before closing to win the 7-furlong stakes.

After the race, Jerkens contemplated stretching Society Selection out for the 1 1/4-mile Alabama three weeks later.

"They'll probably want me to," said Jerkens referring to owners Marjorie and Irving Cowan. "I might. See how she is, see how she works. Give her a mile breeze. They won't go a half in 44 in the Alabama."

Three weeks later, there was Jerkens with a freshly stamina-laden Society Selection going for the 10-furlong classic.

The field broke in front of the stands. Yearly Report and Susan's Angel took the lead with 1-2 shot Ashado finding a solid spot in third. A Lulu Ofa Menifee shuffled back while Cornelio Velasquez had his hands full with Society Selection who was fussing with her head while between horses.

Down the backside, it was Yearly Report and Susan's Angel with Ashado in a comfortable spot to their outside. On the turn, the two pacesetters retreated and it looked like a rematch of the last two major 3-year-old filly stakes in New York. Stellar Jayne hooked Ashado and the duo turned for home with nothing but the sloppy going in the way of their grudge match. But Society Selection was still moving resolutely on their outside. Inside the eighth pole, the other two started to feel the furlongs while Society Selection, fresh off a mile breeze Aug. 16, stayed on to pull out the victory by 2 1/2 lengths. Stellar Jayne finally got the better of Ashado, but that was for the lesser prize. This day belonged to Society Selection, who took home her second Grade I of the meet.

"She went into it good," Jerkens said "She galloped and had a nice mile work with Shannon (Uske) and she went a half about two days ago. She won so it worked."

Society Selection produced a chart line a jockey would be proud of – eighth, seventh, sixth, fifth, third, first. It was the third Grade I score for the daughter of Coronado's Quest.

"Every horse is different. Horses are so hard to figure out. It amazes me when they win and it amazes me when they lose. Too much excitement for an old man. I thought for a second I was going to pull a Walter Brennan, remember that movie?" Jerkens said. clutching his heart. "It's like that commercial, 'It doesn't get any better than this.' I'm proud of her, and how. The girl that works her, the guy that rubs her, Fernando . . . I'm too old to do so much."

Assistant Fernando Abreu was there to see it all.

"She was training great but he didn't know where to go, the Ballerina or here," Abreu said. "He worked her a mile and he said if she worked good then he would come here. She worked a mile in 1:39, you couldn't ask for more. He was on go after that. He kept thinking of November Snow. She did the same thing."

After a glass of champagne in the Trustees Room, Jerkens made his way out the Nelson Avenue gate when he saw a girl selling roses.

"You gotta buy a rose now," Jerkens said, reaching into his deep pockets for his money roll.

"How many do you get for $10?"

"Two."

Jerkens handed the girl a ten-dollar bill.

"How do you like that?" Jerkens said carrying two roses. "They cost $3.75 each and she sells me two for $10. You can't beat the racetrack."

Or Allen Jerkens.

Shug's 32 Flavors

was non-winners of $50,000 or more. I think the Test was $50,000. She won that.

"Then I took her to Belmont and she was second in the Gazelle. Then she just kinda went through the motions. We ran her as a 4-year-old and she was doing fine, we brought her up here for the Ballerina and she won that. She loved Saratoga and this hard track.

"The (owner's) whole family would come here, they were just a Midwestern blue-collar family. He'd bring his mother and father here, they saw her win as a 3-year-old, then the same thing as a 4-year-old. They'd have a big time. When I left the Midwest, I lost track of him. I don't know if I ever saw him again. He got Lou Gehrig's Disease at an early age and died, he wasn't 50 years old. I don't know whether his parents are around, he was really a nice guy. He flew all over the world as a co-pilot for Tiger Airlines. He brought me two gold Rolex watches one time. I said, 'Boy, look it here.' I wore 'em about a month and the gold started coming off. They were fakes, got them over in Africa or something.

"It was a very exciting time. This guy was so excited and to catch lightning in a barrel like that, it doesn't happen that much. To come up here and win the Test, it was my first Saratoga stake too."

Finder's Fee earned over $700,000 by winning such stakes as the Matron, Astoria, Acorn, Cicada and Gallant Bloom. The dark bay mare was born in 1997 and is a half-sister to stakes-placed New Way and Treasure Island.

"Finder's Fee. Storm Cat out of Fantastic Find, kind of a little blocky filly, got ready quick. Thought she'd have a ton of speed, ran her the first time going five-eighths of a mile, dropped back to last. So I'm sitting

Mike Freeman was injured in a stable accident earlier in the meet.

The 75-year-old trainer fractured his shoulder and last time I heard was still in Saratoga Hospital.

Boy, you get too busy in this world. It happened Aug. 9 and every day I say I'm going over to see him. Haven't made it there yet. Forgive me. For now, here's a letter which will never replace a visit but here goes. Will someone make sure he gets this? Better yet, I'll take it there myself.

Dear Mr. Freeman,

You gave me a job in 1990. It was my second year at Saratoga. I was 20 going on 40, and boy, did I have all the answers. I rode three and walked three and walked over with every sixth runner to the paddock and hotwalked them back at the barn. It was old school. I was taking home $235 a week. My friends were making more than me, and I'll admit I almost quit. Then I called my dad at home and said I didn't like hotwalking and I wasn't riding enough. I'll never forget what he told me.

"Sean, you can do whatever you want but the Freemans (Mike and wife, Iris) are good people. They're good to know. They will treat you right and you'll be glad to know them for the rest of your life. Like I said, you can do whatever you want but you would be leaving them in a bind and that's not right. I think you should stick it out, it will be worth it in the long run."

So I stayed. Wow, am I glad I stayed. You and Iris have been some of my greatest supporters since that day I walked in your barn. You put me on Hodges Bay when I was 23 and didn't deserve the shot on a millionaire flat horse running over jumps. I lost three races on him at Saratoga. He was even money or less in all of them and I somehow or other messed up each race. You never got excited, you never got mad, you believed in me with all your heart. I wish I could have ridden Hodge once when I knew what I was doing, but he taught me so much when I needed to learn it.

Later, when Joe and I started Steeplechase Times, you and Iris jumped in with advertising and subscriptions. When I wrote Saratoga Days, you bought countless copies out of my backpack. When we started The Saratoga Special, you were there to sign up, to get us off the ground. You're one of the few advertisers that was here for Volume 1, Issue 1 back in 2001 and you're still here in Volume 4, Issue 23. The paper wouldn't be where it is today without both of you.

Along the way, I've met so many people who are friends of yours; they thought more of me for what you had told them. That means the world.

And like every job or experience, the people (and horses) I met made it worthwhile too.

There was Lou, Boot, Pete, Kathleen, Phil and faces that I can remember even if the names escape me. Lou now works in licensing; he was just as easygoing then as he is now. Boot was the quintessential groom, gruff with the people and sweet with the horses. Pete galloped Hodges Bay like he was a pony. Kathleen could clean tack faster and more often than anyone I've ever seen. Phil gave me daily lessons, on topics from Father Bill Daley to how to make a horse drink. He was the oldest exercise rider I had ever seen, but even then I knew I could never ride like him. There was the tall guy who rubbed Closing Bid . . . I've never met anyone who wanted to be following the Grateful Dead while walking the Appalachian Trail more than him. Where is he now?

And the always-mentioned Apples who stayed at Belmont that summer; no one had more stories about him than Apples.

I'll never forget the horses (though I may forget how to spell them): Oldsquaw, you demanded she train in cotton ear plugs. She'd shake them out all the way to the track but I figured it kept her occupied. Bat Prospector, who was ridden by a young jockey and future friend Mike Smith. She ran on the grass. Closing Bid, the chestnut stakes horse who was coming back from an injury. Joe's Dollar, he could fly. Wild Disco, she lugged in with me one day I thought I was going to hit the canoe. Majesterian, big and black, he ended up third in the Molson Million if I remember correctly. Of course, Hodges Bay, I galloped him one day, I can still feel the buck he gave me at the five-eighths pole. And my favorite, Bee's Prospector. He was the only horse in the barn I could gallop worth a darn. I stayed until the last day to see Angel Cordero ride him in his comeback race. He finished third. And I hotwalked him back at the barn.

I was glad I stayed then and I'm glad I stayed now.

Get better, Mr. Freeman. There are some young kids who should get to know you.

Sincerely,

Sean Clancy

Shug's 32 Flavors

there, 'Look at this.' Got a hole to open up, Mike Smith rode her, here she came. So of course I'm happy with the result but I'm buffaloed a little bit about the running style.

"Ran her back in a little stake in June, she was probably the favorite. Same thing. Dropped out of it, came running, finished second. Mr. (Ogden) Phipps was livid over the ride, but that was the running style, I just didn't realize it.

20

"And then ran her back in the Astoria in July and she won that. Brought her here and ran in an opening day stakes, and she didn't run a jump. So I couldn't figure it out, and she came out of it fine, and I took her back over there and same thing. Third or fourth or something. Pretty perplexed over it.

"Took her back, and Mike Lakow tried to talk me into running her in the Matron. I said, 'I've got to wait a little while.' And he said you better run her in there, and she won, with Herbie Castillo. So now I'm going to really get smart, we're gonna put (Jerry) Bailey on her in the Frizette, and she didn't run any good. And I worked her, I was still going to take her to the Breeders' Cup, I mean she won the Matron. She laid up a little too close in the Frizette, I think the track might have been a little bit off too. I worked her and I came back, they said she'd made a noise, so I scoped her and she was entrapped. So I brought the guy in from Ohio State, Dr. Robertson, he operated on her in the stall, and I thought, 'Well, we've got this taken care of.' But it took her a long time. I took her to Florida to run in the Breeders' Cup, but I couldn't get her to get over it. So I didn't run her. As a 4-year-old I ran her in a stakes when we came back from here, and I think

Shug's 32 Flavors

she finished third or something, Mike rode her and kind of put a little bit of a knock on her. Ran her back in the Gallant Bloom and she won. And that about took care of her career, but she's got an A.P. Indy foal now that's really a nice foal, so she should come back and make a great broodmare. Good race horse, not great, but pretty hard-knocking, was always sound. Just had the little breathing problem, which Storm Cats have."

21

My Flag. Bred to be a champion, she proved her own worth with a Breeders' Cup Juvenile Fillies victory and an Eclipse Award in 1995. She earned more than $1.5 million and won six of 16 starts.

"My Flag came in and, of course, she was by Easy Goer out of Personal Ensign so we had tremendously high hopes for her. It took a while to get her off the sides of the barn at Belmont, but she could run. She won her first start, came from way back, and (Jerry) Bailey rode her. And then we ran her up here in an allowance race and she was really tough in the paddock and I think she finished fourth.

"Then we took her back to Belmont, she finished third in the Matron. So we were pretty happy because at least now we got some black type on her. Then I ran back in the Frizette and she was second. So we went to the Breeders' Cup, you know, we had pretty high expectations for her. And it was at Belmont, came up an off track. She came from the back and she was able to get up in time to win the Breeders' Cup as a 2-year-old.

"That was pretty exciting because her mother had won, and now the daughter had won. Especially with

Last week Sean Clancy asked me to write a guest column about a trip I took recently to Del Mar. It was my first visit to that great track – the racing was terrible but I liked the environment.

I was all set to put my Del Mar thoughts on paper until I had breakfast with a dear friend of mine, John Bounviaggio, a retired New York City sanitation worker and a man I respect like few others in my life.

John is 62-year-old horseplayer, a carpenter, and most importantly, a real man. He's a guy who walks the walk and talks the talk. We met when I was in college and have stayed close since. He knows West Point Thoroughbreds is doing pretty well these days, but is more interested in how I'm doing as a father and a husband.

We talked about the losses the racing world has suffered over the last several months including the death of Phil Johnson and the tragic deaths of Mark Reid's and Kip Elser's young sons.

I confided in John that I frequently feel guilty because I'm so devoted to and passionate about the racing business that I sometimes lose sight of my most important job – being a father and husband. I know I'm no different than a lot of people in the racing business – the train gets going and never seems to slow down.

Races don't fill, clients need to be cooled out, horses get hurt – the list goes on and on. There is so much to think and be concerned about in our business. This crazy industry we're in really is consuming.

John had a solution – write my family members a letter (using paper and pen and not e-mail) to let them know exactly how I feel about them.

Let me tell you – I felt absolutely wonderful after sending the following to my 13-year-old son. Try it with your son or daughter – I'm betting you're even money to feel the same way.

Dear Ryan:

I am very proud of you. You know you are the apple of my eye. The last 13 years have flown by – I know in five years you'll be going off to college and on the road to a career and family of your own. Just the reason I turn off the Harry Chapin song Cat's In The Cradle when I hear the first note on the radio.

I'll always cherish the memories of playing ball, reading at bedtime, talking baseball, going on vacation each year and all the other fun things we did as the years went by (way too quickly I might add).

You know I'd like to make the years we have remaining together as enjoyable as possible. I promise to turn off the damn cell phone when we are riding in the car together. I'll stop checking e-mail after dinner and cut out all the other distractions that take my mind and attention off of you, my main man. My career in the racing world is important but not nearly as important as my job in helping you become the best man you can be.

You know I've harped on you about my pet peeves, namely having a strong handshake and always looking a person in the eye when you speak to them.

Make sure you follow your passion. There is no substitute for passion in your work and personal life. Whatever you do as a career, make sure you look forward to going to work in the morning. Hopefully,

Terry Finley

you'll find a career that offers you a chance to meet people like Angel Cordero and Randy Romero and Buzz Chace and so many other interesting and passionate people I get a chance to interact with in my career.

Always know there is no substitute for hard work. You won't get anywhere in this world without working hard each and every day.

Don't let money dictate your life. I know people worth millions of dollars who don't have an ounce of class and others who literally scrape by but exhibit class in every aspect of their lives. A real man is defined by what's in his heart and soul – not what's in his stock portfolio.

Be nice to people – it doesn't cost any more to be warm and friendly than it does to be a total idiot.

Make sure you always look for solutions. You'll be presented with many, many challenges and problems over the course of your life. Don't whine about problems – bring solutions to the table.

God knows we have enough people in this world who are expert problem identifiers but never seem to come up with any solutions.

Take time to smell the roses. Too many people in this world (me included at times) are always looking at what's going to happen tomorrow or next week or next month or next year. Enjoy today. Cherish the time you have with your friends, family and your environment. Really savor your good report cards and breakaway goals and tough scoops at first base.

Always do the harder right over the easier wrong. You know we talk about how much tougher it is to regain someone's trust then it is to gain it.

Ryan, I could not have asked for a better son. I am so proud of you. Let's make the next five years the best ever.

Love, Dad

(Terry Finley is founder and president of West Point Thoroughbreds.)

Shug's 32 Flavors

a filly with that kind of pedigree, to win a race of that significance. Then we gave her a little bit of time in the winter and I brought her back and I ran her in the Davona Dale and she finished second. I ran her back in the Bonnie Miss and she won. And then she won the Ashland and I took her to the Kentucky Oaks and I'm sure she was the favorite, and didn't run a jump over that track. Easy Goer wouldn't run over it either. I don't think Personal Ensign particularly liked it, even though she won, that was not her best race.

"And then Mr. Phipps wanted to run her in the Belmont which I didn't really have a problem with. She ran credible, she was third (to Editor's Note and Skip Away). And then ran back in the Coaching Club (American) Oaks and she won that, pretty handy, too. I was kind of looking forward to that, going a mile and a half . . . I'd skipped the Mother Goose cause it was close to the Belmont, and brought her up here and ran her in the Alabama and she finished third, kind of got in a tangle. She was big, and from where she came from she shot into trouble and couldn't get her going again. So, we were disappointed, kind of had a bit of a reason. Then we ran her back in the Gazelle and she won that.

"She was a mix of both (parents). She was big, she looked more like him color-wise and stuff, but she was bigger. Sort of had both their running styles, coming from the back. Natural distance horse. She really wanted to run a long way. Still was pretty rough to be around, she was big, but she got better the more we raced her. Took her to Canada and ran her in the Breeders' Cup, she finished fourth. I was hoping she'd do better but when you look back on it, it probably wasn't that bad of a race. And then her 4-year-old year, she didn't run much, she had some ankles

Shug's 32 Flavors

on her and I guess they were probably bugging her a little bit. Then we retired her, and for her first foal, we bred her to Storm Cat, and her first foal was a filly called On Parade that had her running style."

On Parade. By Storm Cat out of My Flag, On Parade started just four times, but earned a win and a Grade III stakes placing before being injured and retiring to the breeding shed.

"She won her first start as a 2-year-old in the fall (of 2001) and I ran her back, I think I was trying to run her in an allowance race that never did go, so I ended up running her in a little sprint stakes at Thanksgiving time (the Valley Stream) and she finished third to two fast fillies. And that was fine. It was a good race, thought we'd go into the winter. Ran her at Gulfstream, finished second going seven-eighths. I ran her back going long, she finished second again. Didn't really give her any excuse, and she came out of that race and she had a knee. Sent some X-rays to Dr. (Larry) Bramlage and he said we needed to go in and take part of, it was kind of like a slab fracture, and shave it down. So I said, 'Well, if we do that, how's she going to come back?' And he said she probably won't come back and be as good, because of the support factor in the knee, so we sent her home and bred her and she's got a Pulpit yearling colt right now (Parading) that's an outstanding looking colt. And I think she's got a Rahy foal."

22

Storm Flag Flying. by Storm Cat out of champion My Flag, she earned the 2002 Eclipse Award as champion juvenile filly and won the Personal Ensign

The first raindrop fell at 5:57. The seven Travers runners went in the gate at 6:21 – in virtual darkness.

Rain pelted down, the skies were Ichabod Crane-dark, the infield fountain was blowing sideways.

And 2:02.45 later, the Belmont Stakes, run 12 weeks earlier, suddenly got a lot easier to take. On that day, Birdstone upended Smarty Jones' Triple Crown bid. Everyone and everything, from rival jockeys to Smarty Jones' exuberance, were blamed for upsetting the coronation. Rarely, if ever, was it considered that it was Birdstone himself who deserved credit.

Well, he just won the Travers, pushing his record to five wins from eight starts, with three Grade I victories. Believing yet?

Edgar Prado engineered the Belmont and the Travers. He's a believer.

"I told you, the Belmont wasn't a fluke," Prado said after the Travers. "I was very confident. He was training good, he was looking good. He ran his race."

And what is his race? A perfectly executed plan of stalking the pace and getting a jump on the closers. Favorite Lion Heart went to the lead like he always does. He managed the first quarter-mile in a reasonable 24.48 while Jim Dandy-winner Purge kept watch just off his tail. Long-striding Eddington found a spot on the inside third. Sir Shackleton and Birdstone, both from Nick Zito's barn, came next with longshot Suave and Zito's third ace, the late-running The Cliff's Edge, in last.

As they went down the backside, a half-mile mark of 49.15 came to pass with Lion Heart and Purge rolling along on the pace. Rounding the turn, shading 6 furlongs in 1:12.82, Lion Heart was retreating. Purge was hanging. Eddington was paddling. Birdstone was rallying. The Cliff's Edge was looming.

Purge had nothing to counter the resoluteness which propelled Birdstone to the lead. Shane Sellers implored The Cliff's Edge to the edge of contention but he couldn't find another gear. Birdstone had not just extra gears, but overdrive.

"He gave me three gears today. One when he ran out of there, one when I called on him down the backside to keep position and one in the stretch," Prado said. "As soon as he gives me a burst, he'll come back to me. That's class. Good horses have two gears, he has three. You're in a position to hold your spot and be able make your move whenever you want. He will do that and then relax. Some horses will give you a burst but you have to fight them to slow back down, not him – he's always there for you."

Birdstone has always been there for Zito and owner Marylou Whitney. The small but smart-looking colt won his debut by 12 1/2 last year, right here at Saratoga. He failed in the Hopeful, finishing 6 1/2 lengths behind Silver Wagon. The son of Grindstone then won the Grade I Champagne in his final juvenile start. It's been stop and start for the Kentucky-bred in 2004. He won a second-level

BIRDSTONE

No, Smarty Jones is long gone and Birdstone is solidly atop the present 3-year-old crop. The Cliff's Edge had every chance to run down Birdstone but didn't, though he put in another solid effort. Lion Heart stopped like he'd been lassoed. Purge was dynamic in the Jim Dandy and soft in the Travers. Eddington has yet to keep it on boil. Suave and Sir Shackleton are a notch below the best.

And Zito completed a training 10. From his Saratoga base, he produced Birdstone for the Travers off works alone.

"When we brought him back to Saratoga I noticed a change in him," Zito said. "I told John (Hendrickson) and Marylou, 'Let's forget about those prep races, let's just go for the big one because I have a feeling that he's going to fire.' He's got such a big heart that he's going to fire on the right day, on the right time. And that's what he did."

The Travers capped off a five-win day for Prado. His 10-percent commission for those five winners came to $84,060.

"I'm very thankful for what I have, every day. I come in and do my job and don't think about the money. It's nice when you win a race and there are people behind you, happy for you. When you win a race and nobody says anything, they walk away from you, that's bad," Prado said. "If you put a smile on someone's face, everybody high-fives you, the crowd is cheering for you. That's the biggest victory. When you earn the respect of everyone. I go home and enjoy my family. It doesn't matter if you sweep the whole card of the Breeders' Cup if people don't respect you."

It was only 1999 when Prado came to Saratoga as a Maryland phenom trying to crack the jocks' room. He's come a long way fast.

"Saratoga is a very political place to be. You have to go out and do political things," Prado said. "When you go home and enjoy the family, that's the best thing. There is no price on that. I'm happy to have this great day but I'm more happy for having a nice relationship with everybody."

Most especially Birdstone.

allowance at Gulfstream in his 3-year-old debut. The Lane's End and the Kentucky Derby were flops. The Belmont was a triple gainer with a twist. And the Travers was better.

"When you ride those kind of horses, you have to ride with confidence," Prado said. "In the Belmont, he kept on trying, trying, trying. Today he showed me all the gears that he has. He impressed me."

During the Belmont, questions dominated Prado's mind.

"In the Belmont, he was going against an undefeated horse going for the Triple Crown – there wasn't that kind of horse in there today. In the Belmont, there are all these questions. 'Can he get the distance? If I move too early am I going to come up empty? If I wait too long . . . ?' A mile and a quarter, it's a different story. And there's no horse that's undefeated today."

Shug's 32 Flavors

in 2004 at Saratoga.

"We liked her and she ran everywhere up here that day when she broke her maiden, but I wasn't really worried about that. She was really difficult, she'd freeze in the barn, freeze on the race track, might do anything. I wanted to run her in an allowance race and it didn't fill – so I ran her in the Matron and she won easy.

"Between the Matron and the Frizette I had a really, really difficult time training her. She just wouldn't do anything we wanted her to do. We'd get it done, but it was difficult.

"And I really didn't know how she'd run when I took her over for the Frizette after that. Come race time, she did everything professional. She come away from there and laid right off the pace on the outside and when (John Velazquez) called on her she won going away by three or four lengths, pretty handy. We had to ship her to Chicago (for the Breeders' Cup Juvenile Fillies) and I didn't know how that was going to go, so we went right on top of the race. We went in on Thursday. I took her to the track in the dark on Friday morning, just to get her around there once, she did fine. Schooled her in the paddock that afternoon and she was really pretty good. When we were leaving there she really got mad because she didn't get to run, she was raising some hell, but she settled in.

"She went over that day and she saddled fine, then all during the race she was looking around, the whole way. Johnny said, 'I had to kind of keep her attention the whole time,' because I made a mistake, I think, by taking her up there in the dark, because she hadn't seen all those stands, where they were, this and that,

23

It seems that you gain the most insight of something you truly love from an outside source.

Just when you think you know everything there is to know about your passion, it's sometimes best to ask someone who doesn't share your passion what they think.

Here's where I come in.

Six months ago, if you had asked me who Ten Most Wanted was, I would have responded with a confident – that new rap group? (note the confident question mark). How about Funny Cide? Well, it could be a sequel to that once immensely popular comic series Far Side, but I gather not.

Now, give me a picture of a horse and ask me to make it look good in print and I'm your man. You see, for the past several years I have been a horseman in the small sense that I have the position of taking the pages of Steeplechase Times and The Saratoga Special and make them presentable in print. Page layout, graphic design elements, photo collages, choice of color, type – and that doesn't touch the tip of the iceberg when you consider that

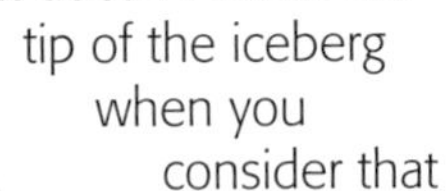

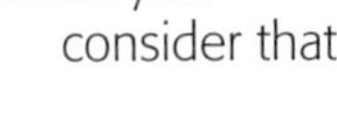

PASSION

when the paper is put to bed it has to be readied for the printing process. EPS-ing, PDF-ing – it's a whole other language that we speak.

I remember as a youngster, my clique of friends and I would come up with alternative ways of speaking to others our own age so that our parents couldn't understand what we were saying. It was called "Avaglavish." The printer's world embodies the same soul.

More to the point, when I was invited to become part of the grandiose machine called The Saratoga Special, I was about to be exposed to a horse-racing phenomenon I could never explain without having experienced it first hand.

Yes, it's that way with most things you are passionate about.

My passion is bicycling and I live it. I feel most comfortable when I am on the saddle, spinning down a smooth macadam road, a constant sweat being wicked-away in the cool morning air as my heart pounds a constant 170 bpm. That is my bliss and I partake consistently. Ask me for tips on saddle adjustment, nourishment requirements or post-ride muscle maintenance and I'm right there with you.

Although brief, my time in Saratoga showed me why the small New York town, that when mentioned in casual conversation, brings a gleam to the eye of every horse lover. It really does take the sport of Thoroughbred racing and boil it down into an intense love and it shows in everyone involved. The passion is there in the early mornings at Oklahoma, it throbs as the horses take the track and run the wide path of sand and dirt against a backdrop of the slate-covered spires of so great a grandstand. It's a photographer's dream. It begs to be brushed on a canvas.

It's as if God said "Take horses and race them in a place." So man chose Saratoga Springs. And God said "It is good."

I still don't know much about the trainers, jockeys, owners, the ins and outs of wagering. But here's some insight from an outside source. If you are passionate about horse racing and want to immerse yourself in it – the look, the smell, the feel....

....there's only one place to go. Saratoga. But then, you already knew that.

(Kevin Titter spent a week with The Special this summer, and writes from his home in Elkton, Md.)

Shug's 32 Flavors

so she was looking all batty. He said he thought in the turn she'd pull herself up, so she made the lead probably a little sooner than we wanted her to, and then he said she just threw her ears up, and he said he was waiting on a horse to come to her. He said, 'I knew I had more, but she wasn't going to give it to me then. I didn't want to reach back and hit her.' So Composure came to her and got by her, then she just put her ears back and went right back to running. People asked me 'Were you nervous?' I said, 'No, it happened so quick.' I could see her ears up so I felt like, that if she got something maybe to run at, she'd have it. So she came back."

24

Personal Ensign. Few horses captured the public's attention the way this daughter of Private Account and Grecian Banner did. Unbeaten in 13 starts, Personal Ensign was champion older mare of 1988 and earned $1.7 million, including victories in eight Grade I stakes. Her career finale, a come-from-behind victory over Winning Colors in the 1988 Breeders' Cup Distaff, is a race for the ages. At Saratoga, she beat males in the 1988 Whitney and is honored today with the Grade I Personal Ensign Handicap. As a broodmare, Personal Ensign has produced champion My Flag and Grade I winner Miners Mark, and was named Broodmare of the Year in 1996, an honor her dam earned in 1988.

"She was a career maker. For her to win [the 1988 Breeders' Cup Distaff] and the way she won it, that wasn't training, riding or anything else. That was sheer determination. For her to win 12 in a row and get beat, it would have been anticlimactic. For her to win, it put the period at the end of the sentence. It made everything worthwhile."

Shug's 32 Flavors

Easy Goer. By Alydar out of the Buckpasser mare Relaxing, Easy Goer was voted 2-year-old champion in 1988. At 3, he won the Swale, Gotham, Wood Memorial, Belmont, Whitney, Travers, Woodward and the Jockey Club Gold Cup. Easy Goer was inducted in the Hall of Fame in 1997.

"He gave me the opportunity to go into the Triple Crown with a really hot hand at a young age. He was the favorite for two of them. It's fun to run and compete in those races, but to go in there with one that's going to be even money, well, that's even a lot more fun.

"After the Derby, even though I felt like he hadn't handled the track that day, it was a question mark if (Sunday Silence) was that much better. Then we got to the Preakness and got beat a nose, I knew we were probably the best horse that day, but I also knew that we could compete with him.

25

"When we went to the Belmont, he had come out of the Preakness so well, I had a lot of confidence after what had happened in those three weeks. It was a great gameplan and everything went right on how to get him into the Belmont. I knew he loved that track, I knew a little more about Sunday Silence then, and I don't think everything went right with them during those three weeks.

"After he won the Belmont, we ran him in the Whitney and he was able to win that. Then he won the Travers. Won the Woodward and the Gold Cup. I maybe made a mistake running him in the Jockey Club Gold Cup. I knew going a mile and a half would probably take a little sting out of him coming back going a mile and a quarter (in the Breeders' Cup Clas-

Practically by definition, Saratoga suspends reality.

People rent out their homes to strangers for six weeks. Some businesses open only for the racing season. Others count on the 42 days to make – or break – the budget.

And that's what makes it so tough when real life gets involved. We aren't always prepared.

Sean and I sometimes joke about what would happen if one – or both – of us got hit by a bus. He wouldn't know what to do about computers, advertising placements, printer issues, layout and such; I would have as difficult a time talking to jockeys and trainers the way he does. Thankfully we haven't had to deal with life outside Saratoga to that extreme, but others have.

Gary Handfield's father died last week. A longtime "ponyboy" at NYRA racetracks, Frank Handfield was pictured in The Special's Aug. 10 edition alongside champion Vanlandingham. The next day Gary, who works in the racing office and is a placing judge, let me know about it and told me how much fun it was to go back down memory lane. His father, retired and living in New Jersey, appreciated the recognition as well. Gary didn't say his father was ill, just that it was nice to see his photo in the paper. Ten days later, Frank Handfield died. He was 76. I didn't know Frank, but ached nevertheless when Gary told me outside the racing office the morning after it happened. I guess I knew Gary Handfield had a father – everybody does – but now I feel like I knew him.

Dave Harmon's mother is ill. Our photographer, Dave went to New Jersey to see his mom Tuesday. She wasn't doing well, he told me Sunday. Somehow, Dave didn't miss a day of work, though we would certainly understand if he did.

Gary and Dave each must feel like he's been hit by a bus full of reality. Real life can be scary, especially when you're trying to suspend it for a while. Gary and Dave are in Saratoga, doing jobs that matter. Family crises don't occupy much brain space beforehand, but they hog it afterward. Friends call with problems. Your sister needs someone to talk to. Your mom would love you to call. Your dad just wants to say hello. Have you got the time? Probably not enough – not during Saratoga anyway.

I'm a husband and a father. My wife Sam, and the three boys Ryan, Jack and Nolan spent about four weeks in Saratoga and went home Tuesday. I've got more newspapers to build so here I am – balancing the reality of a family with the fantasy of a deadline every night far from home.

When they left, I told the boys I would see them soon and did my best to explain why I had to stay. Jack was emotional. Ryan was mad. Nolan seemed realitively oblivious. Sam is in her fourth year of this nonsense and seemed to understand, though she'd prefer to have her husband. He'd prefer to be with her, too.

I worried about the drive to Maryland – they made it – and wished I was at the wheel. I worried about the first day of school (sixth grade for Ryan, third for Jack, pre-school for Nolan), and longed to

be at the bus stop. I'm still worrying about everything else – last year, Jack nearly got pneumonia in his first week back from Saratoga – though I know I can't do much from here.

So far there haven't been any crises – though I did get an angry telephone call yesterday when they couldn't find me in the paddock during ESPN's telecast of the Travers Day stakes. Ryan was not impressed when I told him I covered the Victory Ride.

At the Hall of Fame induction, Wayne Lukas spoke about being brave and taking chances in life. Hall of Famers, he said, tested their personal lives to chase greatness, uprooting families, working long days and traveling to all corners of an industry that demands much of its participants. Some Hall of Famers probably damaged their personal lives in the process, but the point was made – hard work, a little risk and talent can pay big dividends. I read a great quote from Kiaran McLaughlin about not going to Dubai to train anymore. He said his first job was to be a father and a husband, and training horses so far from home was no longer worth the impact to his family.

Everyone faces those sorts of decisions, whether Saratoga is involved or not. The reality is, nobody knows where life is going so you may as well do your best. Test your balance, reach a little, push your limits, hang in for another week at Saratoga. Just remember to tell Gary and Dave you're thinking about them....

– and keep an eye on the buses.

Shug's 32 Flavors

sic). I thought he could probably beat those horses easy enough. I'm not sure it really did, I remember at the post position draw, we drew the inside and (Charlie) Whittingham drew the outside and he said then, I might have got the advantage then. We got beat a head. We broke to the inside and he broke sharp from the outside, it could have taken a little bit away from him. But it was a great race, he got beat a head by a great horse.

"It was fun because Whittingham made it fun. He was a great guy and he had fun with it. He wasn't pointing fingers and trying to jab about this young guy, 'he doesn't know what he's doing' or something like that. He was always complimentary. He would say, 'Well, maybe we were best in the Derby because we liked the track better.' When we went to Pimlico, we stayed in the same place. And he and his people were always cordial. So that made it fun. Plus, competing in those kind of races you have to make it fun or it's nerve-wracking. That's what you were doing it for.

"He was easy to train, he just wasn't very sound. When he broke his maiden here, his shins got sore. They were asking me if I was going to run him back in the Hopeful and I felt like if I could train him over this soft track and get him back to Belmont, I might be able to hold his shins. So we didn't run him in the Hopeful, I took him back there and ran him an allowance race, he ran a fifth of a second off the track record. Then he won the Cowdin and then the Champagne."

Cat Cay. A foal of 1997, she was by Pleasant Colony out of Cadillacing, as a racehorse she won eight races (three stakes) and earned $488,000.

"She didn't run at 2, and won her first three starts at 3.

Shug's 32 Flavors

Then we ran her in the Mother Goose and we were going to like her a little bit. She made a little bit of a run around the turn and finished fifth. Disappointing. She came out of the race banged up and I backed off her. She had a

26

bad back. She was kind of arthritic, so we just had to warm her up some. She was a big, good-looking thing by Pleasant Colony out of Cadillacing. You'd have thought she wanted to run long, but she had more traits of her mother in there.

"She was a come-from-behind sprinter, and she'd win the races when they set up right for her. You had to time it right. I was really happy with her when she won at Keeneland (the 2001 Thoroughbred Club of America). She liked that track, kind of hard and flat.

"We sent her home and bred her. She's got a Forest Wildcat foal and she's in foal to Storm Cat. She'll probably make a great broodmare – it's a pretty good female family down there."

Country Hideaway. A 1996 foal of Seeking The Gold and Our Country Place, she won 10 races and earned $762,000 with victories in the First Flight, Vagrancy, Bed O' Roses. At Saratoga she finished second twice in the Ballerina.

"Country Hideaway is the first foal out of a mare that Mr. (Ogden) Phipps bought (Our Country Place). Bought her as a yearling, a half-sister to Sky Beauty, he loved that family. He wanted to buy Sky Beauty all the time. The price was too high, so we ended up buying a Pleasant Colony half-sister to her. Out of Maplejinsky. Bought her as a yearling, privately, she never ran. Sent her home and bred her to Seeking the Gold, got Country Hideaway. She didn't run as a

Tommy Kelly had $50,000 of Leonard Sasso's money to spend on five horses at the Saratoga yearling sale.

It was 1959, when $50,000 could buy five promising yearlings.

Sasso's plane was late for the sale. In the meantime, Kelly fell in love with a yearling by Heliopolis. His eye, his walk, his demeanor. An imported English stallion and sire of winners of almost $10 million, Heliopolis had died that April after leading the sire list in 1950 and 1954. He produced stone-cold runners such as High Gun, Helioscope, Summer Tan and Princess Turia.

Kelly had been around some of his offspring and knew they were mean. He rubbed one for Man o' War's trainer, Lou Feustal. The horse would knock Kelly around for sheer sport. Turn your back and you were on the ground. The colt for sale, a half-brother to Nail, would go in his stall and sleep after every showing. Lie down like a dog at his master's feet. Kelly was sure this had to be the best colt Heliopolis ever had.

Kelly couldn't help himself – didn't want to help himself – and kept bidding well past the budget set forth by Sasso. He bought the colt for $80,000.

Now, how to break the news to Sasso. Kelly met Sasso's plane and cleared his throat. Sasso spoke first.

"You bought me five new horses, huh?"

"No sir, I only got one," Kelly said. "For $80,000."

"Only got one?" Sasso asked. "For $80,000?"

"Well sir, he's a nice colt . . . " Kelly stammered.

Yearlings back then were selling for $5,000. The $50,000 he was budgeted for would have bought five promising youngsters. Only later was Kelly informed that $80,000 was the most a yearling had ever sold for at the sales. Sasso wasn't impressed.

He wanted to send the horse back. Kelly was scrambling for his life; he would have bought the colt for himself if he had any money. He believed in the colt, just a gut feeling. He couldn't imagine sending him back, even if the sales company would take him back.

Kelly was in a full-court press trying to convince Sasso to take the risk. Dinner came and went, with drinks aplenty in attempt at softening the deal. Kelly explained the colt's quality, the look in his eye, the fact that Heliopolis had died and this was the last chance to get a horse of such lineage and quality.

Owner and trainer went to the Reading Room at the corner of Nelson and Union Avenues and continued the one-way dialogue.

"Blams" were going around, and Kelly was pleading for Sasso's faith, when there was a knock on the door.

"Gentlemen, I know what's been going on for the last two hours. I'm going to take Tom Kelly's side and I've got my checkbook to prove it. If you don't want the horse, I'll buy him right now."

Kelly nearly fell off his chair. He was off the hook. The savior – Christopher T. Chenery. The horse – Globemaster.

Chenery, of Meadow Stud and future Secretariat fame, bought a quarter interest in the horse that night. The utilities tycoon would be partners with Sasso.

Two years later, Globemaster won the Wood Memorial and finished sixth in Carry Back's Kentucky Derby. Globemaster opened up four lengths under Johnny Rotz in the Preakness before Johnny Sellers got Carry Back rolling to catch him in the last jumps. Carry Back failed in the Belmont but Globemaster ran another blinder, finishing second to Jacob Sher's Sherluck (Braulio Baeza up) who paid a then-record $132.10.

Globemaster won several stakes and certainly improved upon Sasso and Chenery's investment. Kelly made it to the Hall of Fame after training 65 stakes winners and one champion.

The moral of the story? Always answer the door.

Shug's *32 Flavors*

2-year-old, and then as a 3-year-old won five times, her first stakes win was the First Flight. And then at 4 she came back and she won the Vagrancy at Belmont and she was second here in the Ballerina. Then she went on, she won the First Flight that fall on Breeders' Cup Day, and I ran her back in the Top Flight, and she was second. Brought her back at 5, and she won the Bed o' Roses, and I was really pointing her to the Ballerina. She kind of made the lead at the last part and that one filly of (Allen) Jerkens' kind of beat her on the inside, just right on the money. Shine Again, I think. Then she sort of tapered off after that. Retired with 10 wins, earned $762,000. She's got an A.P. Indy yearling filly (El Coyote) and she's got an A.P. Indy foal and she's in foal to Dynaformer, so not only was she a great racehorse but she has a chance to be a good broodmare. Didn't want to run long, probably never ran her on the grass, which was a mistake. I was really disappointed that she didn't win a Grade I; she's a young mare with a ton of pedigree."

27

Dispute: A 1990 foal, she was bred by Ogden Mills "Dinny" Phipps. By Danzig, out of Resolver, she won four Grade I stakes: The Kentucky Oaks, Gazelle, Beldame and Spinster, and more than $1 million.

"Dispute broke her maiden in the fall of her 2-year-old year. She was a great, big, beautiful filly. And I remember walking back through the tunnel (at Belmont) I told Dinny, 'This is what we're looking for here. Not only for a racehorse but as a broodmare, too.' And then we took her to Florida and she won the Bonnie Miss, beat Sky Beauty. I elected to pass the Ashland and I took her to the Kentucky Oaks and she beat Eliza

Shug's 32 Flavors

. . . was in front the whole way, (Jerry) Bailey rode her. It was a great thrill. I won three stakes that day, she made the third one. Then she kinda backed off a little bit. But then she won the Gazelle and the Beldame on the 'five-in-a-day' day.

28

"I took her to California for the Breeders' Cup, and she finished fourth. Then her 4-year-old year, she won an off-the-turf race, in the mud, then she won the Spinster. Then we took her over to the Breeders' Cup, it was at Louisville, and she got an abscess in her foot, and that was the end of it. I couldn't get that thing healed up, and I sent her home. She's been a terrible disappointment as a broodmare. I sold her at the November sale last year. I thought she'd have been as good a broodmare as ever lived. She won over a million dollars, four Grade Is. She was a good horse. She would have been really, really tough in the Breeders' Cup that year (1994)."

Fantastic Find. A 1986 foal by Mr. Prospector out of the Riva Ridge mare Blitey. Unraced at 2, she was second here in the Test at 3. At 4, she won the Hempstead at Belmont, a Grade I stakes now named in honor of her owner and breeder, Ogden Phipps. Produced Finder's Fee, winner of five stakes including the Grade I Acorn and Matron.

"Really well-bred filly, beautiful. Won like her first three starts. Brought her up here and ran in the Test, which was Opening Day – kind of a handful in the paddock. Finished second, was disappointed, but the winner was Safely Kept. So as you look back on it, it wasn't quite as bad. She was pretty flighty and I didn't get a chance to get up there and get her schooled,

What if Todd Pletcher trained steeplechasers?

Think about it for a moment. Would he still win as often? How about Allen Jerkens? Society Selection at 2 miles over national fences, anyone?

The horses are the same breed (despite a few misconceptions) so why not? In honor of today's New York Turf Writers Cup, a Grade I, $100,000 hurdle stakes, flat trainers are talking jump racing.

"I've had some horses that were pretty one-paced that would be good candidates for steeplechasing," Pletcher said on Wednesday. "It would be interesting to give one a go someday. When it's the first race, it's tough for me to get here but I watch the stakes and if the TV's on I'll watch it. I watch it with interest."

Pletcher's former boss, Wayne Lukas, laughed out loud when presented with the possibility, but knew immediately what he would want in a steeplechaser.

"A lot of bone. I would think I'd want a big, rugged one because that's got to be pretty strenuous on them."

Mike Hushion thought breeding.

"You'd want a distance pedigree, but an agile horse," he said. "They look like they have to be pretty athletic and able to do different things. I used to train Vintage Class (fourth in Wednesday's jump race) – he's run well twice up here."

Allen Jerkens, who actually rode steeplechasers as a young man, has given the game some thought recently.

"If I had my health and some years, I'd like to train some jumpers again," he said. "They say you have to train them light. I want to train them hard – I'd like to work them a mile and a quarter to see how good they are. You take a horse with a lot of natural speed and teach him to jump, you'd have something – it would be like cantering to him between the jumps."

Mark Hennig has trained several horses who moved on to steeplechasing, and sometimes entertains offers from jump trainers looking for prospects.

"I probably wouldn't train him much differently than I would a flat horse – I'd start out that way, anyway," he said. "Dabble in it and see what happens. I think it's like anything else, if your horse is fit to go three-quarters then he's fit to go a mile and a sixteenth if he's got the pedigree and the style to do it."

Thanks guys, that was fun and apparently you've got the right idea.

Jumpers do train like flat horses. They jog a mile and gallop a mile. They gallop 1 1/2 miles. They work

between races (Mulahen, who starts today, went 5 furlongs in 1:01 4/5 Aug. 26). They blow out (morning-line favorite Praise The Prince went 3 furlongs in 38 and change the other day).

"You don't even train the horse that different than a flat horse," said trainer Tom Voss, who trains both flat and jump horses. "You probably put a lot more bottom on, that's the difference between a flat trainer and a jump trainer. You spend a lot more time before you breeze them."

How about a Hall of Famer?

"I'd get him damn fit, that's the first thing," said Lukas, still smiling over the proposition. "I'd get him fit and then take him out there and hope he could jump. I'd have to get somebody on him who knows what they're doing, because I wouldn't have the first clue how to make one jump."

It's really not that difficult. Horses are natural jumpers, say the steeplechase guys.

"A good pupil can do it in two months," said Voss. "We start with logs on the ground. They walk over them, trot over them, and let the horses tell me how fast they go from there."

Voss said the best steeplechase horses often aren't the fastest learners. They think things through, and really learn to jump – in-stride, out-of-stride, fast, slow, behind horses, in front of horses, side-by-side, whatever it takes.

"You've got to be careful with the early part," said Voss. "If you scare them, you have to start all over again. A lot of horses aren't as good as they think they are. If it's too easy for them, that's not the way I want it. You've got to make it hard for them, make them make a mistake and learn how to get out of trouble."

Like good flat horses, quality steeplechasers come in all different sizes. The stereotype is a big, strapping specimen with a stride as long as the admission line on bobblehead day. That's not always the case, and good jumpers often mirror the criteria given by trainers for good flat horses. The keys are athletic ability, conformation and temperament.

"You want a horse that's going to stay and a horse that's going to come off the bridle a little bit," said Pletcher. "Your first reaction is to find a bigger, scopier horse but that probably falls into the category of the other two things – staying and coming off the bridle – but it doesn't always have to be that way. I'd say an athletic horse is more important than size. I've had some big horses that might be a little too clumsy to do it."

Mr. Pletcher, move to the head of the class.

Voss can rattle off steeplechase characteristics faster than the Elias Sports Bureau can move baseball statistics.

"Mid-sized. I don't want a real big horse or a real small horse. Fairly short cannon bone, not too long a back, a nice deep shoulder and a very good hind leg. All the best horses have big, strong gaskins (the upper part of the hind leg). If you can put all of those things together, you are very lucky, but I'll take three out of four any time."

Most of those characteristics are on the list of "wants" for any trainer looking for any racehorse – flat or jumps. So what's the big deal?

"Once they've run a couple of times, you don't train them any differently than any other horse," said Voss. "And once they've learned and have run a few times, I try to school them as little as possible. Would you keep taking a 2-year-old to the gate after he's gotten OK? No, of course not. You don't have to be a rocket scientist."

You just have to be a trainer.

Shug's 32 Flavors

all that kind of stuff. Then we ran her in the Gazelle and she finished third. And then we kind of put her away. She came back as a 4-year-old. They used to run a bunch of stakes on Belmont Day, and she won the Hempstead that day, which was a Grade I, which was big for her. We won three races that day, Adjudicating won the Riva Ridge and Rhythm won (the Colin). Then she came up here, she was second in the Ballerina, Grade I, she was second in the Shirley Jones (at Gulfstream). Retired after her 4-year-old year, she was the dam of three stakes-type horses, the best one being Finder's Fee, who was a Grade I winner. She's in foal to Forestry, she's got a 2-year-old filly who won her first start this summer, hurt her stifle a little bit, put her away for a couple of months, named Dream Time. Should come back and be a good horse. Got a foal by Giant's Causeway. She's been kind of a big addition to the Phipps stable as a racehorse, as a broodmare. You know, Finder's Fee, her daughter, should be a great broodmare.

"I thought she would be a great broodmare. She was a beautiful filly, probably the prettiest filly as ever was through here. I used to go down and just stare at her. I'd take Mr. Phipps down and look at her some too. Especially, you know, after she won her first two starts by way off. Sometimes I'd take Mr. Phipps down there, say 'Just go down there and look at her.' So we felt like she'd go home and develop into a really good-looking mare and have good-looking foals, and she has. Treasure Island, who was by Danzig, finished second in the Peter Pan, in maybe his first stakes start. Then hurt himself, hurt a back sesamoid, kind of getting ready for bigger and better things. I thought

Shug's 32 Flavors

I had him set up perfect when he hurt himself. That didn't work out. Then a couple of fillies, you know, I think Dream Time really can be good, she should be a stakes-type horse."

30

Pine Circle. A 1981 foal, by Cox's Ridge out of Gallant Man mare Gaebale. He earned $598,191, including the Grade I Widener at Hialeah. He was second in the Belmont, Arkansas Derby and Travers and third in the Secretariat and Brooklyn.

"Pine Circle won his first start, then I ran him in like an allowance race at Keeneland. Ran him in the Hawthorne Juvenile – he won that, took his number down. Put another horse up, of course. That horse's test came back positive. So, those people, they claim that the test that came back bad was Pine Circle's test and not their's. So anyway, we went to court where we ended up winning, got the money . . . six months later.

"Sent him to California for the winter of his 3-year-old year because we had a couple of other 3-year-olds going to Oaklawn. Didn't do any good there. Brought him back. Were gonna run Vanlandingham in the Arkansas Derby, got sick, so we ran Pine Circle in it. Comes flying at the end finishes second to Althea. So now it's kind of on to the Kentucky Derby. Ran him in the Derby, kind of finished up strong, finished like fifth or sixth. Took him to the Preakness – same thing, came finishing at the end, finished fifth or sixth. We go to the Belmont, and think, maybe he's got a pretty good chance in the Belmont. We knew Swale was in there, he'd won the Derby, didn't run any good in the Preakness, but . . . We finished second in the Belmont

It was victory number 62 for John Velazquez – eclipsing the meet record he set last year.

Daily Racing Coverage

Saturday, September 4, 2004

The SARATOGA Special

Trainer Subscriptions to The Special compliments of SALLEE HORSE VANS

Price: $1

Year 4 • No. 31

62

John Velazquez breaks his record

It was number 34 for Todd Pletcher – one away from the meet record he set last year.

It was Saratoga victory number one for Willard Straight, a 4-year-old colt by Lion Cavern owned by Lawrence Goichman.

It happened in the Troy, a stakes restricted to horses that had not won an open sweepstakes on the turf in 2003-2004.

Velazquez rated Willard Straight in the back of the nine-horse field and let Battle Won and Voodoo lead the way. By the head of the stretch, it was a typical Saratoga turf race. Horses stacked up like a dagwood sandwich at the eighth pole. Little Jim opened up but couldn't hold off the flying finish of Willard Straight.

"I hit him and he was like a

gun out of there. It was a great feeling," Velazquez said. "I thought he was going to be 10 lengths behind (early) but he was right with the bunch."

Little Jim held on for second and West Point winner Golden Commander rallied for third. The win was the sixth career tally for Willard Straight who was making his first start since finishing seventh in the Grade III Mervin Muniz at Fair Grounds in March.

"This race was the only thing he was really eligible for in this condition book. When the book came out we zeroed in on this and that was it," Pletcher said. "This horse won a restricted stakes, with these kind of races you never know who might show up. But we knew it was the right distance, he was fresh and we know he runs well fresh. It was just a matter of pointing to it."

Pletcher pointed Willard Straight like he's pointed his other 33 winners at the meet. A winner of one restricted stakes (the King Cugat) last fall, Willard Straight came up with a stifle problem after the Fair Grounds trip and spent time at a farm in Kentucky before rejoining Pletcher's string. The trainer put him on a long slow road to Saratoga.

"If anything, I was a little worried about going over the top. We backed up his work schedule a touch, just to make sure we didn't have him ready two weeks ago," Pletcher said. "There was a period where instead of working back in six or seven days, we gave him 10 or 12. He had a couple five-eighths and we backed up to a half in the next one. Just to try to buy some more time. The worst thing sometimes is to have one ready and nowhere to go. You have one you know is ready and when you finally get to the race they're not as good as they were two weeks before. That's no good."

Velazquez leaves the training to Pletcher while Pletcher contributes to the race strategy. They have changed the game in New York.

"We are pretty much on the same page. He has more marks on his Racing Form than me," Velazquez said. "I mark every horse, every race. I went to see his Form and it was worse than mine. I think that's what makes it easy for both of us. I go out there with a plan, he has a plan and we compromise a little bit. He gives me a lot of confidence to go to plan B, C, D."

Willard Straight stayed with Plan A which secured the record for Velazquez with three days still to go. He's out of town on Monday but any victory now is stuffing. Not that Velazquez is counting. Records are for the press to ask him about and for his agent Angel Cordero to shoot for when he's booking mounts.

"I don't look at the numbers. If it happens, it happens. I just want to ride well, keep my people happy, ride winners and the numbers follow," Velazquez said. "It's all a cycle. If you ride well, you get better horses and it will continue. Who cares about the numbers? I like winning and I like pleasing my customers, that's what counts."

What does the record mean?

"A winner is a winner, it doesn't matter how many numbers. I like riding well, I push myself to ride well. I like winning don't get me wrong but first is riding well....

....Ride the winners, and the numbers come after."

Shug's 32 Flavors

to Swale. So we bring him up here and run him in the Travers and I thought everything was going good then. Swale had died, so Pat Day's riding Pine Circle, and he's finishing up, Track Barron's in front of him and he stops. And Pat had to check him just enough to give Carr de Naskra time to jump on him and finish second in the end, but he ran a really good race. Then we took him out and ran him in the Secretariat on the grass, and he finished third. We took him to Hialeah that winter and he won the Widener.

"Then he sort of retired and went to stud over in Australia, never heard any news. At one time, in his 3-year-old year he made between three and four hundred thousand and never won a race. So kind of a funny little horse to have around. But he came from the stars . . . I was surprised he won the Widener, but he liked running around a small racetrack, and it was about a 14-horse field, there was a lot of action that kind of kept him in the race a little more so he didn't drop way out of it that day. His kick was good enough to get him there."

31 ***Aldiza***. 1994 foal. By Storm Cat out of the Alydar mare Aishah. She earned $496,394 and was out of the money only three times in 19 starts with six wins, including the Grade I Go For Wand.

"Beautiful, beautiful mover – made a terrible noise. Nothing we could do really to help her but she could run enough to where she won. Gary Stevens rode her in the Frizette and she was able to finish third. We won a little stakes with her as a 3-year-old, up here, kind of a conditioned stakes, so she was a stakes winner with all this pedigree.

Pierre Bellocq, known to the racing world as PEB, has provided charming, entertaining and relevant sketches for the Daily Racing Form for 50 years. The Special's Adrian Bacolo recently spoke with Bellocq about his life, his work. An exhibit of Bellocq's most prominent work can be viewed at the National Museum of Racing through Dec. 31, 2005.

When you do portraits of people, how do you choose who you draw?

It has something to do with the actual events, of what's going on in the racing world. I choose the people that are in the news. For instance, when I do a sketch for Page One of the Racing Form, of course the people involved [are] the most prominent in the race. Also, I always try to keep my file up to date with caricatures – I don't do portraits, I do caricatures – so when I go to the races I try to choose a prominent apprentice, a bugboy that has a great future, the jockeys, the valets. The jockeys tell me, 'Well, you should sketch this guy, because he's going to make it.' Also, if I am in New York and jockeys or trainers are coming to New York for a big race, I will make sure to sketch them instead of going to Texas, or other places.

What's the distinction you're making between a person's portrait and a caricature?

There's a wide difference. A portrait is somebody making a portrait of somebody, is something to bring the beauty or the elegance or the charm of the person. What I'm doing with the caricature is to bring the character of the person. It's much more an inside thing than an outside thing. A caricature is not just to make somebody [ridiculous] or ugly or funny, but something to bring up the inner self of this person into simple lines. It's exactly the opposite of a portrait.

What do you look for in a person when you decide to make a caricature? What do you like to emphasize?

Ideally, I have to know the person a little bit. Again, it's not only the superficial feature of the face – it's what emanates from the person, you know his character. Then I emphasize an expression; it's not just to draw the line of the face of the person, but it's to bring up the expression of the face of the person. If the person is jolly or sad looking, I have to show that in my sketch.

Of all the people you've drawn, who has been the most expressive or colorful?

If I do Bob Baffert well, it's really unique because you can bring out a lot of his expression; he's a very charismatic man. It's really exciting to draw him. It used to be Eddie Arcaro, for instance, in the good old days. Arcaro had a very strong feature. People like [Nick] Zito are interesting to draw. He is a handsome guy, but he has lots to show in a caricature. Jockeys, you have fascinating faces, like Edgar Prado, for instance. Edgar Prado reminds me of a jockey who I used to admire in France a long time ago, when I was a teenager. His name was Ray Johnston; he was an Australian but his father was from Japan. He has this very similar attitude that Edgar Prado has: very cool, very serious and also extremely professional.

Looking at the cover to "Stars of the Turf," the difference between somebody like Prado, who is standing there smiling vs. somebody like Angel Cordero Jr., who looks pretty aggressive . . .

You asked me to name a few characters. He's another one – Angel Cordero – that has such an elastic or rubbery face. All kinds of expression going out of his face, so that was a joy to draw.

What sort of response do you tend to get from people once they see their caricature?

I think people are pretty happy about seeing their caricature, in general. The only adverse reaction comes from wives [laughs], wives that object, 'It doesn't look at all like my husband. I know him better than you.' [Laughs.]

You've really heard that before?

Oh, yes, yes. In the back of that, the person came to me and said, 'I like my sketch. Don't worry about my wife.' And, of course, ladies themselves when I draw them, sometimes I get some reaction.

Well, how do you explain it to the people who don't appreciate the caricature?

I don't. I really don't explain because when I came to this country, caricature was almost, not unknown, but it was not popular. There were cartoons; but caricature was something that developed a lot since the '50s when I came here. I didn't see too many in the press except a very, very few geniuses, like Al Hirschfeld, for instance, in The New York Times. But today it's blooming, it's really a great thing. In a culture, there is always evolution of something. Fashion, also. In the early political days of America, you had a lot of great caricaturists. And then it died, maybe for lack of talent – I have no idea. There was a rebirth of it: today you have great caricaturists.

Would you say caricature is a fashion statement?

It's fashion today. You get caricatures in almost every magazine. For me, I was influenced early in my life by great French caricaturists. One was Sem [born Georges Goursat], and Sem was my idol when I was a kid. Sem was a man from the belle epoch. I think we can see his sketches even today; Maxime's, the restaurant, all the menus are still covered with his sketches. When they have a big Hollywood movie like "Moulin Rouge," you have all kinds of sketches by Sem.

You've worked for the Daily Racing Form for 50 years. What is it that first interested you in horse racing? At one point you made a professional decision to stay with horse cartoons, not political cartoons.

It was my heritage. I was born into the sport of racing, in France. Three generations of my family were involved . . . At the time my father was a jump jockey, and I grew up among racing people. It was natural. When I was a young teenager, I was always in the midst of my father's friends and jockeys. I had some talent to draw and naturally influenced by what I saw outside. And I lived in Maisons-Laffitte, which is the maker of horse racing, it's a training center near Paris. And then it was, at the time of the German occupation. There was nothing really to do but wait and wait for the liberation of the country. At the time, I was just sketching away, whatever I could, and it was mainly horsemen and people in the racing business.

How old were you at that time?

When the war started I was 12, when it finished I was 17.

Do you remember your very first caricature?

Yes, as a matter of fact, I remember. I saved it and I framed it. It was never published. It was a neighbor of my father, a jockey; he was struggling to keep his weight down and my father would go to have a drink with him and he was in his sweat box. I always saw that man in a sweat box, by the way, sweating like a pig. I have his sketch, with his jockey's cap and everything else. I keep it as a lucky omen.

Looking at that drawing and looking at something you may have done, say, this morning or yesterday, what's gone on in between?

This is exactly what the curator at the museum of Saratoga wanted. They came to see me in my studio about a year and a half ago, and when they talked to me about an exhibit I thought it was just a regular kind of thing where you align frames and

Shug's 32 Flavors

"And we kind of raced her around, she would be second or third, it was a shame because of just the wind getting in her way. Then we brought her back up here the next summer and ran her in the Go For Wand and she hooked up with that good filly of (Bill) Mott's, ended up winning the Breeders' Cup that year . . . Escena. They hooked up and she was able to win. So she'd won a Grade I, that was a big thrill, to be able to get her to go a mile and an eighth and do that. That was just one of those days where everything sort of went right with the breathing once she got into a rhythm.

"Mike (Smith) said she kind of let her air out around the three-eighths pole and sort of took it from there. And then we ran her in the (John A. Morris Handicap), but she didn't run very well. So then we backed off, ran her in the Spinster and she finished third and we retired her after that. Probably, if she'd been able to catch her breath, there's no telling how good she could have been, as good as I could have ever had. You know, she's going on now, she got Alchemist, who's fine. We had another full-sister to her who got hurt.

"She'll be a great broodmare, but if she'd been able to get her air, she would have been a great horse. She was a beautiful big filly, beautiful mover, and she was a Grade I winner. Her foals have been fine. We bred her to A.P. Indy. They've all be fine . . . A little bit fiery, being out of a Storm Cat mare. But the breathing, nothing's wrong.

"I think we (operated) along the way somewhere, but it didn't help a whole lot. Like I say, a couple of days she was able to fight through it. Why, I don't know. She liked it up here. She won a stakes as a 3-year-old here and she won the Go For Wand as a

sketches on the wall, people look at them and enjoy them. What they had in mind was completely different. They wanted to explain to the visitors exactly what you asked: what happened in my style, in my career since the sketch to the last one. When I looked at it with a visitor's view, I am very, very grateful to the curator, [Lori Fisher], because she did a professional job with this thing. She started with the very first sketches published in France and it goes along the way to what I do today.

Now that you have this exhibition up, how does your career look to you?

I am extremely happy that I made the decision of staying close to the racing world, because it provided me freedom of doing what I really enjoy to do. The other side of it, doing 15 years of political cartoons, was a great challenge because I was in America and I really wanted to express my inner feeling about political situations. I was very grateful that a prominent morning newspaper [The Philadelphia Inquirer] would do that; it was a great deal of excitement for me, the ambition of doing something like that. It was obsessive because when you do a political cartoon you have to be immersed with everything that is happening in the world. I would have probably continued to do political cartoons if the people that wanted me to continue left me leeway to do, from time to time, some horse-racing cartoons. I was told it was either one, I couldn't do both. So that's when I made the decision. [the Racing Form] suggests dates, important events I'm supposed to illustrate. They leave me alone about the choice of subject, the choice of ideas. This is what I appreciate so much about it.

Do you have a favorite piece of work you've done for the Racing Form?

One sketch that is at the museum was probably one of my favorites because the inspiration was so spontaneous. It was the sketch I did at the occasion for the Travers a few years ago. The sketch was done at the same time when [former President] Bill Clinton was doing his televised confession about, you know, he was a bad guy, he was trying to be better now. And I linked it to an actual race with Coronado's Quest – a horse that was erratic in the spring and became a little more manageable at Travers time. I linked the character of the horse with Bill Clinton, and it came out to be a very funny sketch.

With your time in Saratoga, what have you been able to take back to your studio, in terms of inspiration?

I have been very much involved in this summer's events because of my personal link with them, for instance. My oldest son was an assistant trainer for Patrick Biancone, and of course they had this Lion Heart. It was supposed to be a favorite in the race. What I take back is a lot of emotion and a great deal of gratitude for the people in Saratoga.

If there was some way you could personify Saratoga in a human being, in a caricature, what would be some of the features you would spend time on?

The feature that I always come back to is the town, this whole place comes alive, greatly alive in the summer months – but it's a unique experience every time because you have a phenomenom of this incredible crowd. Also, the town is looking back to a beautiful past of American life, when things were more gentle, more charming. I think it was created earlier in the century by very well-to-do persons that wanted to get away from New York, that wanted to spend some time on vacation, doing a little bit of gambling, a little bit of sports – and these ingredients are still there, and uniquely. You don't find that in too many places in America. You find something of charm that doesn't exist anymore. This, to me, what I find so exciting about the place. It doesn't diminish. It's still there.

Hard to believe one year ago I was in the car on my way home reading a copy of The Special when I saw an e-mail address for Sean Clancy.

I decided I would write him when we arrived home, maybe he'd let me write an article. I had no idea the newspaper would become such a big part of my life.

Over a month after my first article, I realize what a month it was. For the first time, I was a part of Saratoga. I could wake up and walk to the races (my real home is over an hour away), I could talk to trainers, meet jockeys, enjoy the paddock every day.

The memories and experiences are endless. My high-school English teacher always told me that lists are boring, but cramming 36 days of horse racing into one story is difficult. Recalling the most memorable moments is not.

Nearly every morning I would wake up and walk down Union Avenue and cut through Congress Park to Broadway. I would sit down and have breakfast at the same restaurant. The food was good and affordable (college budget), but one day I decided to buck the trend and try Uncommon Grounds.

While waiting for my sandwich, I looked over and saw John Servis. We had just published an article on him, so I introduced myself, shook his hand and told him how much I enjoyed the story. He thanked me and we went our separate ways. But minutes later he came back over and started a conversation. I would have never thought I would talk with the trainer of Smarty Jones at breakfast. Only in Saratoga.

Auctioneering at a benefit dinner has opened doors I never thought I'd pass through. And it was fun too. It was the largest crowd I've ever auctioneered to, quite intimidating just three months removed from auction school.

Our photographer Dave Martin allowed me to watch the morning routine of a Thoroughbred. It was early, I remember almost falling asleep while leaning against the bales of hay in the shedrow, but it was great. Horses are beautiful, and have a powerful presence that too many don't appreciate.

I attended my first auction (for horses) at Fasig-Tipton. I was expecting a mere congregation of people in the pavilion, some bid-calling and that was it. I was wrong. I felt like I was at the Oscars, the only missing component being the red carpet. I ran into a high-school teacher – one I would preach to how I would be involved in horse racing someday. Showed her a copy of The Special, and how proud I was.

Unbridled's Song, one of my favorite horses (I watched him break his maiden in person and later win the Breeders' Cup) had his sons and daughters in the sale. I got to stand within inches of them before they entered the ring, reminiscing how he was a horse that forged my love of the sport. Maybe someday I can auctioneer a future son or daughter of the horses I saw this summer.

Interviewing trainers was a new thing to me, and just a couple of weeks into the meet Sean called me on my cell phone and asked me to cover the stakes. Talk about pressure. I enjoyed every minute of it though and would do it again without hesitation.

I took my 7-year-old brother, Tanner, to the rail for the Test Stakes. He's an emulation of myself at that age; loves the game, wants to be a jockey, calls races while running around our house, all that stuff. I put him up on my shoulders as Society Selection lowered her head and dug deep right in front of us.

Finally seeing Funny Cide was awesome too. I had felt all day it was the largest crowd ever at Saratoga. I took Tanner upstairs to the clubhouse to watch the race and after it was over, a disgruntled bettor murmured some unpleasant thoughts about the gelding. I explained to my brother how tough his trip was, stuck wide through fast fractions, a scenario many horses are unable to cope with. Funny Cide fought until the end, however, and Tanner appreciated that. At dinner he learned forward and said, "I don't understand why people don't like Funny Cide. He was almost a Triple Crown winner just like Smarty Jones and everybody likes Smarty Jones."

Shug's 32 Flavors

4-year-old here. I don't know whether it's the clean air that helped or just some days she'd get into rhythm where maybe things were going her way. (The other days), it wasn't like she got checked or had a lot of horses in front of her, she laid up close to the pace . . . maybe those days she was there and didn't get any wind. It was a shame. I remember Gary Stevens jumped off her that day of the Frizette and said, 'What a shame this is.' She finished third. But she'll be a great broodmare. When we get it all right."

Shug's 32nd Flavor...

Somewhere along the line, Shug's 32 Flavors morphed into Shug's 31 Flavors. Ah, the beauty of daily publishing – we ran the same Here and There page two days in a row which in turn cut one of Shug's horses.

The good news is we were doing these interviews with Shug on the fly so all it meant was one less scamper down Shug's shedrow at the end of the morning looking for some insight about one of the cogs in Shug's Hall of Fame wheel.

Good thing, Saratoga isn't an eight-week meet.

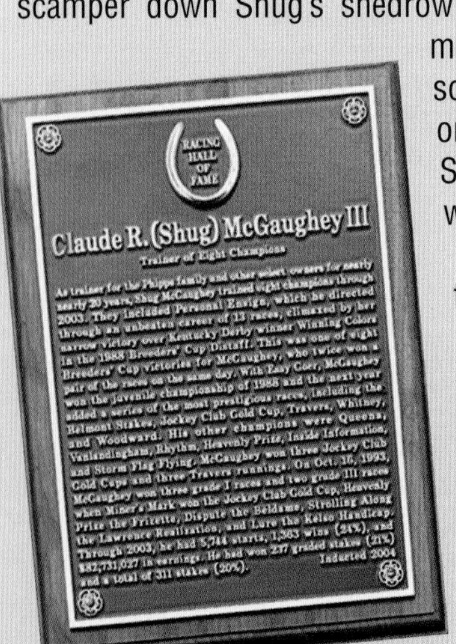

He has a hard time focusing on his spelling words, yet he'll dive into a sophisticated conversation about horse racing.

The feeling just before the Travers was electric, literally and figuratively. The sky was dark, the thunder looming and the rains coming. But all those factors were ignored and forgotten. Nothing could take away from the excitement of the Travers. I watched it from the winner's circle. The location doesn't get much better than that for my favorite race.

Speaking of the Travers, should I ever become czar of the world, it would be mandatory to start college after the Midsummer Derby. Unfortunately, I did have to leave Saratoga early this year, and while limited to what my friend Tim wants to do (he has the car), I alleviate the stresses of homework with thoughts of Saratoga.

I know someday I'll drive to the gates at Saratoga, settle into the announcer's booth, look down after the feature and see Sean in the winner's circle with his tape recorder handy, realizing that I would not have made it without his help.

At that same moment, I know back at the office Joe Clancy is resisting the temptation to throw his monitor out the window; PDFs are great, but they take too long to make. Jamie Santo meanwhile is flipping between the day's results and the Miami Herald on his computer. The Dolphins will have their year soon enough, Jamie.

Tod Marks and Dave Harmon will be photographing the winner of that feature race, while Dave Martin searches for the song that will alleviate the stresses of a deadline. Adrian Bacolo is thumbing through national publications, seeking new ideas on layout design while Quint Kessenich updates his stable mail and writes a story. Hopefully before this is all done, "mad amounts" of papers were sold.

It was the greatest summer of my life, and I'm sad to see it end. The list of thank yous is endless. The windows into the sport they've opened are priceless.

As I write this in my dorm room, I look around and see piles of laundry, schoolbooks and garbage. I would do anything to have that Saratoga feeling back.

There truly is no greater place on earth.

– SUNY Oneonta student Travis Stone spent his first summer with The Special.

And then there were none.

Thirty-two issues have been crossed off. This is the final page of the final issue of the 2004 season.

As my father would say, "I hate to leave, but I really must go."

For the first time since we started this paper in 2001, progress is palpable. People are beginning to follow.

Like Willie Nelson said to a fledgling band, "Build a house of quality in the woods and the world will beat a path to your door."

Beating a path to our door might be a stretch but followers have at least learned that the newspaper is a daily, it's worth reading and we're here to stay. Come to think of it, that last one has been a learned lesson on our part too. The first year, tomorrow's issue was always in doubt – up to when we saw it on the porch in the morning.

Now, we invent the John Velazquez's 62 Winners cover at 7 the night before it's to run, mess with it for an hour or two and in the morning people are asking us for commemorative posters (we'll see what we can put together).

Saturday morning, Barclay Tagg rode up on his pony while I was holding my usual post at the Morning Line Kitchen. He thanked me for writing the paper.

"You like horse racing," Tagg said. "It's nice to read stuff from someone who likes the sport."

Thank you. We like horse racing, that's why we write this paper. You like horse racing, that's why you read it. It's working. But sadly for the fourth time in four years, six weeks of momentum gets cut down at the end of the meet. It's like reaching for the tape at the top of the gym-class rope and being told to come down. Or getting rained out while you're on deck in the ninth.

We need a week off but then we could go again. Alas, it's Saratoga and it has its time frame, its short life span. That's what makes it so special. It's as bittersweet as biting into a chocolate-covered aspirin tablet.

Saratoga raises everyone's expectations, hope springs eternal and nowhere does this happen with more pressure. Desperation and euphoria are stablemates here. Some barns packed up last week, tail firmly between their legs, heading home to regroup and try to balance the checkbook. Some barns have rolled through glorious stanzas at the meet, they're sad to see it end. Jockeys have felt both sides of the equation, owners too. For that matter, fans, gamblers, management, newspapers, anybody who knows Saratoga has lived the spectrum. It's day-to-day for 42 days.

And now it has an official close.

The Saratoga Special, just like Siro's, the Fasig-Tipton salesgrounds and the Jim Dandy bar, gets shuttered for the next 10 1/2 months. Rest.

We've probably averaged 7,000 words a day for 32 issues. Whew – 200,000 words – we just wrote a novel.

Some days it's been "War and Peace." Other days, "Tuesdays With Morrie" (well, "Shug," anyway). And still others, it's bounced between a Marvel comic and an Elias Sports book. As long as you're reading and enjoying it, then we'll do our best.

As for me, it's time to get some sleep, pay some bills and to stop eating pizza six nights a week. We'll see you next year. As I labor for an ending to six weeks of writing, Red Rooster plays a song on my head phones. I listen to the words for the first time:

"I didn't see you drifting away . . . You left me on Labor Day with no work to do and having conversations with pictures of you . . . I was happy before we met and I might be happy again but it ain't come yet . . . I been home sick and hungry and hard up . . . Summer left me behind . . . I got September on my body and August on my mind . . . "

Fade out.

Pat Day
Lost In The Fog
Bellamy Road
Flower Alley
Ashado

Saratoga 2005

And then there were five.
Wow, half a decade of publishing.

Deadlines were getting smoother, the staff was getting more professional and the papers were streaming off the printer. Don't blink or it'll change.

Flower Alley swept the Jim Dandy and Travers. Ashado and Shadow Cast split Grade I stakes for the girls. Lost In the Fog came and conquered. Henny Hughes and First Samurai did their part for future stardom. Edgar Prado upset John Velazquez while no trainer could match the ammo of Todd Pletcher.

As for the Special, here's to another five years. Ah, make it 50.

It's a family affair. For Charlie Barringer, more commonly known as "Saratoga Charlie," Opening Day is more than just the start of a six-week racing season, it's the perfect day for a family reunion.

"This Opening Day is fantastic," he said. "I have all of my family here. I haven't had any winners, but I don't need them. I'll get them. I'm just having a great time with my friends and family."

Barringer, a Clifton Park resident, has been to Opening Day at the track for 54 consecutive years, and his family has gathered in the same spot for the last 40 to commemorate the start of the racing season. With 14 grandchildren, seven children plus spouses and many friends and partners from the Castle Village Farm, the area is full of activity.

"The whole family just comes for Opening Day," he said. "This is our big thing."

Barringer arrived at the track with his son Chuck at 6:30 a.m. to reserve the same area the family occupies on Opening Day every year. In the far corner of the Big Red Spring area, next to the paddock fence, the family sets up camp for the day. With close to 60 people gathered around picnic tables covered with food and coolers full of drinks, the family spends the day at the track.

It wouldn't be a family reunion without pictures. Posters covered with photos of the family and Barringer's racehorses are hung from the trees, and a photo album from last season's memories decorates the center of the table.

Cousins Samantha and Alyssa Barringer both said the best part about the day is being with the family.

"My favorite part is going to the race and sitting here with all of my cousins," Samantha Barringer said. "I also like all the junk food."

The Barringers were not the only people there as the sun was coming up to reserve that sacred space. Jay Pittman arrived at the gates to race to his picnic table at 6:15 a.m.

"We always sit right here around this carousel," he said, referring to a backyard group of televisions shaded by an umbrella. "And thank God they didn't make us wait until 7 o'clock to get in."

Pittman said he has been to Opening Day for 34 out of the last 35 years, and always sits in the backyard in the shade.

"It's our local track," he said. "It's history so I come back every year. Today you get a lot of people who really don't care about racing, but it is like a regional holiday. So everyone comes out."

Everyone did come out. From the young to the old, the veterans to the novices, the racetrack buzzed with excitement as bets were placed and winning tickets cashed.

With a newspaper in his hand containing the picks for the day, 99-year-old William Hurley sat in the shade and waited for the races to begin. He has been to Opening Day between 35 and 40 times and looks forward to seeing familiar faces each years.

"I like to see the people," he said. "I have a lot of friends who work here and also come here every day. I knew most of them from Belmont."

Like Hurley, Martha Pristupa has been coming to Opening Day for 35 years, but now she can finally call herself a Saratoga resident. Just last year she moved to Saratoga Springs from Long Island.

"We love the town and we love the races," she said. "And it's better because we live here now."

Not everyone who comes to the track on the Opening Day is a seasoned veteran. Bill McCue traveled up to the track from Newburgh to get his first taste of Opening Day. He said he comes a few times every year, but today just seemed to be an opportune time.

"I love the horses and I'm a bettor so it doesn't get any better than this," he said.

Barringer and Pittman follow the tradition of securing the same seat every year, McCue doesn't want anyone to wish him good luck. While each has his own customs and superstitions, everyone has the same goal: to win and go home with more money than he came with.

The track provided an exciting atmosphere for all 25,818 fans, and despite the hot and humid weather the backyard and all of the picnic tables were full as the 137th season began at Saratoga Race Course.

"You can go see a show and you are there for an hour, but you're at the track all day long and I don't think I've ever had a bad day," said "Saratoga Charlie" Barringer. "It's always a great time."

– Christine Paska

HENNY HUGHES

Gary Stevens cantered Darley Stable's recent purchase Henny Hughes back to the winner's circle after the 100th running of the Saratoga Special.

The horse slowed to a walk and his connections swarmed the son of Hennessy. With a big grin on his face, Stevens told Darley's Jimmy Bell, trainer Patrick Biancone and anyone in earshot one thing.

"I don't know what he paid for him, but you can tell his Royal Highness, that he stole this horse."

After Henny Hughes' flawless route in the Grade II Saratoga Special, Stevens might be right.

Recently purchased by Sheikh Rajid bin Mohammed al Maktoum, son of Darley's Sheikh Mohammed, for a reported $4 million-plus price, Henny Hughes lived up to the billing (and the bill) with the easiest of victories.

Henny Hughes hopped down the lane with his ears pricked and Stevens simply letting his hands follow his motion. The margin was 3 3/4 lengths – with a nudge it could have been double digits.

"No exertion down the lane. None at all," Stevens said. "I just snugged my reins up a little bit at the quarter-pole. Of all the good horses I've ridden, at some point during the race, maybe at the eighth-pole, I've chirped to them just as a reminder. This horse I've ridden him twice and I have not chirped to him yet. He's just doing this with his ears up, cat-and-mouse."

A big cat with a bigger future. Darley likes to race and they like to make stallions. They just bought one with huge potential in both areas. The breeding business loves 2-year-old success and Henny Hughes has the secret. People buy yearlings for millions, Darley took a shot and bought a horse who was already 2-for-2 and quickly became 3-for-3 and a graded-stakes winner.

"The decision is a lot easier after watching him run," Bell said. "He showed a lot of precocity. Based off his two previous races, you get excited. You look for potential and he took a step further in showing that today. At the end of the day, you'd like to think that (a stallion career) can happen but there's a lot of stops to make between now and then."

So far, Henny Hughes has made the stops better than an ice cream truck at the neighborhood pool.

"I'll move a finger, maybe a sixteenth of an inch, and he jumps on the bridle and waits for me," Stevens said. "Like, 'What do you want me to do? What do you want me to do?' It's almost if he knows the day's going to come when he's tested but he's saving it. He doesn't even know how fast he is."

Stevens rode Henny Hughes' sire, Hennessy, as a 2-year-old in 1995. He was a chestnut dynamo who won the Hopeful, Sapling and Hollywood Juvenile Championship and finished second in the Breeders' Cup Juvenile. Trained by Wayne Lukas, Hennessy made nine starts as a 2-year-old, winning four of them.

"Believe it or not, if somebody were to send me back in time 10 years, I would have thought I was on Hennessy," Stevens said. "That was a special group of 2-year-olds – Honour And Glory, Hennessy, Unbridled's Song – and he reminds me so much of Hennessy. It's been a long time since I've been on a 2-year-old that's as precocious. It's a lot of fun. These are the kind that keep me around. Riding one like him is worth five months for me."

QUOTE:

"What kind of angel are you?"

– Four-year-old Cole Stewart, son of trainer Dallas, to jockey's agent Angel Cordero Jr.

"She worked fine and it happened when she was galloping out, the rider said she took a funny step," said my friend about a filly he trains at Laurel Park.

The 2-year-old filly shattered her leg in five places.

It was just before 9 a.m. Wednesday when my phone vibrated and I saw my friend's mobile number. I almost screened it – I was sitting in my golf cart, talking with a group of trainers, just beyond the outside rail of the Oklahoma training track. The renovation break had just ended and the fresh track had beckoned fleets of horses. It was a glorious morning at Saratoga.

Six hours away in a barn at Laurel, there was disaster.

The filly was standing in the stall, sedated out of her mind, vets had X-rayed the leg. It had snapped in every direction, like a grenade had landed in her joint.

She cost $12,000 at a 2-year-old in training sale, her pedigree was modest at best. If the surgery worked, and that was a big if, she could be a cheap broodmare or a lawn mower, that's all. A sore horse swatting flies in a dusty paddock is no Munnings painting.

The owner said put her down. The groom wanted to save her. The vet said it was my friend's call.

He asked me what he should do.

"I was OK before I called you but now I'm getting upset," he said. "I don't want to put her down but what am I going to do with her? If it was Ruffian, you might do the surgery and it still probably wouldn't work. The groom keeps looking at me, asking me to save her."

My buddy owns a small farm near Laurel, it's full of horses. Old and young, sound and sore. He's saved a lot of horses since I've known him. Any profit he makes from training horses usually goes right back out when a horse needs a home.

But this was different.

"If you think you need to put her down, for her sake and everybody's sake then you need to put her down," I said. "You know, the only reason you or I or anybody can save the ones we do is because we don't save them all. It's brutal and it's not supposed to feel good. If your gut says put her down, that's your instinct and your knowledge talking, then put her down."

That's what he did.

A day later, I watched Society Selection, Roses In May and Request For Parole breeze. I watched Wonder Again go to the track and snort and jig like a yearling. I buzzed back to my office after a sharp, energetic morning on the backside.

Switching instantly from racetrack to office, I checked my e-mail.

"Sean, we are so sorry about Succeed. I watched him peacefully lay down and go to sleep. I am sure he is now in 'horse heaven' without pain and running around with Winterking and Virge. In the short time I knew him it was easy to see how special he was and why you loved him so. Kate and I send our love."

– Buddy

Then I cried.

Over the years, readers of The Special have gotten to know Succeed, a horse I retired five years ago after a largely unsuccessful career as both a flat and steeplechase horse. Once part of Harbor View Farm's storied program, he came to Saratoga as my pony a few years later and he lived a pretty good life. He was turned out in a field more often than he was in a stall – his coat either faded from the sun or standing on end because of the cold.

This summer, the firm ground aggravated his tender feet and old injuries. He got lamer and lamer. At 11 and needing constant care, his body was falling apart. I called in my 70-year-old father who knows more about horses than he knows about himself. When I left for Saratoga, I knew Succeed was not coming around. God played a cruel joke when he made horses – so strong yet so fragile. I fed Succeed a handful of carrots before I left, patted him on the neck, knowing he probably would be gone when I got back.

The note I received was from a great friend of mine who helped out in the clutch.

My father – me still being his youngest boy – hasn't told me yet. It's been a long, sad day for him, just like yesterday was a long, sad day for my friend.

I'm going outside to call both of them and think about Succeed.

SAND SPRINGS

John Velazquez sucks in his chest and makes like he's going deep-sea diving without an air tank.

Then he holds it – one-one thousand, two-one thousand – like a dare on a third-grade playground.

That's how he rides the aggressive-running Sand Springs, winner of yesterday's Diana Handicap.

"I don't even breathe," Velazquez said afterward. "On the backside, I take my first breath. I don't move very much on her, pretty much the same hold the whole time; tight a little bit, give a little bit, tight a little bit, give a little bit. Tight enough where she doesn't (throw her head) because if she does that, you lost her. She's one horse, I don't do anything."

For jockeys, sometimes doing nothing is doing everything. Velazquez has been doing nothing, anything and everything over the first four days of the meet. The 33-year-old banged out 10 winners in four days, well on his way to last year's record 65 victories which topped his record 61 from the previous year.

Velazquez swept the Diana and the Jim Dandy on Saturday and took the Lake George on Friday. Whether it's sliding Ready's Gal off the speed in the Lake George or coaxing 9 furlongs out of the rapid Sand Springs or any of the other victorious rides during the week, Velazquez placed a brick on the accelerator when gates opened Wednesday. He rides favorite Ashado in the Go For Wand Sunday.

When Bailey opted for Intercontinental in the Just A Game, Hall of Famer Bill Mott didn't look far. Velazquez has now ridden Sand Springs twice in her career and won both. With a firm but delicate touch, Velazquez manages to filter some of Sand Springs' nerves while allowing her to still run the show.

"She's just a little aggressive," Velaquez said. "If you can get some control at the start, it helps. It was better breaking from the outside. I kept her out there and she came back to me a little. When we got to the backside and relaxed, I said, 'This is pretty good.' At the three-eighths pole, I said, 'Mommy, you're going to have to run now.' She picked it up and finished up."

With two key scratches to her outside, Sand Springs inherited the outside stall of the gate which made life easier for both horse and jockey.

"I wanted to be outside so I could get her comfortable and then come in little by little," Velazquez said. "After that it was pretty easy. I let her relax, then come back in little by little and then she kicks in. It works for me."

Like everything in Velazquez's world right now.

He'll pick up a check next week which would buy out most mortgages but he rides like he doesn't need the money; a perfect combination of patience, style, poise, strength and intelligence. Velazquez keeps emotions out of his decision making. Ocasionally, he'll get mad after a race, curse himself and march back to the jock's room but it's over quicker than it started. It's taken 15 years of constantly polishing and learning but Velazquez has solidified himself as the top jockey at Saratoga. Jerry Bailey has slowed his intake and talked about retirement and only Edgar Prado competes with Velazquez's numbers. Last year, Velazquez won his first Eclipse Award and a 2005 model seems well within his grasp. Although, Velazquez would never give it any thought; he doesn't allow himself to think about tomorrow (or even the next race). Only today

"It's a long meet, the hardest part is to try to keep it up," Velazquez said. "I stay focused on what I want to do. Race by race, day by day and try to concentrate on the horses I'm riding. I try to do my part, try to concentrate, try to not make any mistakes and hopefully things work out. But then again, I'm riding good horses. You got to ride the horses, you have to be in the game. I can ride as good as I want and it's not going to happen if the horses don't help."

So far at Saratoga, they've helped like a soup kitchen on a cold day in the ghetto. With help from the horses and trainers like Todd Pletcher, the mid 2000s at Saratoga will be remembered as the John Velazquez years. Not that he's buying any of that.

"I go day by day, race by race, that's it. You know me," Velazquez said. "I just try to ride good. If I ride good, I'm happy. If the horses run good, if they respond, and they win, it's a big gift. A big, big, big, big gift. I can't be perfect all the time and I will be critical, knowing that I screwed up. You learn from them. I ride for a lot of people that I can come back and say, 'I screwed up.' "

They don't hear that often.

Artie Schiller

Richard Migliore rode out of the paddock on Artie Schiller.

Reunited with his big horse, the jockey smiled and gave a glad-to-be-here pat along his arched neck.

"Like sitting on my couch," Migliore said.

One fast couch.

Timber Bay Farm and Denise Walsh's Artie Schiller wore down a stubborn Silver Tree to take the $150,000 Bernard Baruch Monday. Trained by Jimmy Jerkens, Artie Schiller drafted just off the controlled pace of Silver Tree in the five-horse Grade II stakes. The favorite and second choice made it a two-horse race within the first quarter-mile. Jerry Bailey and Silver Tree volunteered to take the lead while Migliore took no chances and placed Artie Schiller in an outside stalking position; second, never more than 1 1/2 lengths off the lead. A yawning gap spread with every fraction to Del Mar Show, Seeking Answers and America Alive.

Silver Tree eased into the final turn with Artie Schiller starting to come under pressure from a scrubbing Migliore. Turning for home, Silver Tree stole a half-length when Migliore switched a lane on Artie Schiller. The duo sprinted over the good turf in a two-horse duel that should have ended in a dead heat. They went the last furlong in 11.76 seconds with Artie Schiller managing to outkick Silver Tree by a neck. America Alive closed for third, 6 1/2 lengths back.

"As long as I'm within range of a slow pace, he can outquicken anybody. He kind of bobbled at the five-eighths pole, he let go of the bit and I was struggling just a touch," Migliore said. "I don't want to use him in increments – when I go with him, I go big with him. I've never inched, inched, inched on him. Even when I've been in front, I've held him up and when I ignite him, I ignite him all at once, and he blasts off."

If only NASA could master the same kind of blast off.

The Bernard Baruch filled out the 10th consecutive stakes line on Artie Schiller's chart. In those 10 starts, the son of El Prado failed to hit the board once, in last year's Breeders' Cup Mile. His 12th-place finish, a trip right out of a "You Need AAA" commercial, caused Migliore to lose his spot on the couch.

Migliore suffered a fall the Thursday before the Breeders' Cup. He took off his mounts that Friday and came to Lone Star Park knowing he was banged up but expecting to ride Artie Schiller to his first Breeders' Cup victory. Migliore tapped the brakes once going into the first turn and from then on Artie Schiller was playing a losing game of Frogger. Every gap came and went before he could get to it, he finished 12th. On Sunday morning, Migliore went straight from the airport to the hospital where X-rays showed a broken wrist and a broken rib in his back.

"All the people I've admired in my life are the people who show up and perform. They play hurt, they play sick, they get the job done. They don't take sabbaticals, they don't take vacations. They get it done," Migliore said. "My purpose was singular. I was going there to get the job done. It backfired; I wasn't Curt Shilling in the World Series."

No, just a middle reliever getting shelled as the game slipped away. Bill Entenmann of Timber Bay, Tom and Denise Walsh and Jerkens were miffed by the whole situation.

"Mr. E. was pretty mad after the Breeders' Cup," Jerkens said. "No one knew what to think, we never had an inch to run in the whole race so everybody was frustrated. We got absolutely no run for our money, not even a chance. Everybody was so pent up, so frustrated, Richie was the fall guy."

In March, Artie Schiller shipped north from Florida's Palm Meadows training center to Belmont Park. Migliore was there to greet him.

"I went over there and Jimmy said, 'I got bad news.' To be honest, I thought he got hurt and that would have been worst-case scenario," Migliore said. "He said, 'We're going to make a change and try somebody else. Everybody was pretty disappointed with the Breeders' Cup.' I said, 'Listen, I understand that – nobody was more disappointed than me in the Breeders' Cup.' I understood, I couldn't argue with their decision but I'm sorry, I went there trying to do the right thing but my desires got in the way of my common sense."

Edgar Prado hopped on Artie Schiller in his 4-year-old debut and promptly won the Grade II Maker's Mark at Keeneland. Rallying from off the pace, Artie Schiller sprinted clear to win by 2 1/4 lengths; it was an audacious effort. Six and a half months after the Breeders' Cup, Artie Schiller was as good as ever. Migliore wasn't. He rode the Maker's Mark, finishing far off the board.

"He warmed up by me. It was like looking at a girl you went out with or you were close to and you still have feelings for, now somebody else is out with her," Migliore said. "Then he won, I was genuinely happy for him but again, that 'I should be with him' feeling."

Prado rode Artie Schiller in the Dixie on Preakness Day at Pimlico; after losing his rhythm twice in the stretch, he failed to outfinish Cool Conductor, losing by a nose. The Manhattan came next. The 1 1/4-mile stakes might have been a stretch for Artie Schiller but as always he ran hard, just missing by a half-length to Good Reward and Relaxed Gesture.

The "Ride Migliore" banners were constantly paraded in front of Jerkens' barn; Tom Walsh, valet Karl Keegan and let's face it, Migliore himself, never stopped championing the cause.

"I continually made it known that I'd love the opportunity to ride him back," Migliore said.

"Edgar's a great rider and he's ridden him well but I just think this horse and I have a special connection."

So my nephews came to town Sunday.

Three boys for their fifth full summer at Saratoga. We just asked Ryan, 12, to go to the Spring Street Deli and pick up two chicken-salad sandwiches. He started to whinge about the job.

"Oh, man, I just came from there."

"How about five bucks?"

"What kind of sandwiches do you want?"

Five bucks or no five bucks, this seemed like work.

If he only knew.

Here he is in Saratoga for the summer, bedded down on York Avenue in the bottom floor of a house ("It'd be nice to live in the whole house, you know?" Ryan says.), walking distance to the track, kitchen full of food, central air, porch, friends his age.

Joe's wife, Sam, and the boys made the five-hour drive in a seven-seat Toyota Sienna minivan. Ryan shuffled through 1,437 songs on his iPod. Jack, 9, played some sort of Super Mario on his Game Boy. Nolan, 4, asked Jack questions and ate a Dunkin Donuts Munchkin for every mile traveled. Sam read the directions, drove the van and tried to keep three kids under wraps.

They arrived at 4 p.m Sunday. Let the games begin.

Sunday: "Sorta" put clothes away, cookout with neighbors (the ones who painted the sign saying "Welcome Back" on the front door); five adults, six kids, talk about playing zone. The cookout was at the neighbors' in-ground pool and the kids picked up where they left off in 2004.

Monday: Three bowls of Cinnamon Life cereal and then to the office to harass Joe into sending them to the races with copy chief Jamie Santo. Jamie spots them two bucks and they jump on Richard Migliore (who always gives them autographs and goggles) in the fourth. Mig wins, returns $10. They go for Chantal Sutherland (uh, Ryan must be growing

FAMILY

up) in the fifth at 54-1. They cross every available limb while the inquiry light's on, cheer once it's off, cash their $110 ticket and take direct flight to the Carvel Ice Cream stand. One vanilla cone with sprinkles, one chocolate cone with sprinkles, two cups of chocolate/vanilla swirl with sprinkles; they use dollar bills for napkins. At night, Jack and Nolan stay home and play with the neighbors. Ryan goes to the jockeys versus police softball game with a gaggle of 13-year-old girls; according to Ryan, they only want to talk and don't watch the softball game. Funny how that works.

Tuesday: Sleep until 9 a.m. Swim. Jack and Nolan go see a live performance of "Pinocchio" at the Arts Center. Ryan gets dropped off at the office and has done nothing but walk half a block to pick up two sandwiches.

Wow, what a difference a generation makes.

Back in the 1970s, the Clancy family used to venture to Saratoga. Yup, every summer, Dad, Joey, sister Sheila and Sean made the trek from Delaware to upstate New York. Mom usually had the good sense to stay home. This was "Bad News Bears" meets "Planes, Trains and Automobiles."

Hop in the minivan, er, the six-horse Imperatore horse van and drive to Saratoga. Leave at midnight (better for the horses) and drive through the night. No stops (better for the horses) and arrive at 6 o'clock in the morning.

Hot, covered in hay and horse, Dad tired and agitated because the horses are nervous and the stall man can't find his stalls – welcome to Saratoga.

That's OK, off to the hotel for a shower and a nap. Two choices – Lassie's or the Blue Spruce. My dad worked for a millionaire and wanted to save $40 a night in hotel fare.

The Blue Spruce wasn't too far out of town, say 10 miles. It was nothing and next to nothing. The water tasted like the Big Red Spring gone bad. The black-and-white TVs offered two channels on a clear day. Lassie's was farther from town than the Blue Spruce, the water tasted like water but the nothing hadn't even gotten out this far. Count cars for fun – three on Friday, two on Saturday, four on Sunday . . .

To the Annex in the morning. Sheila walks the horse, Joey mucks the stall, Sean washes the feed tub. Dad's horse Odd Man steps on Sheila's foot, Joey stabs his foot with pitch fork, Sean catapults into makeshift drainage canal after feed tub lip finally gives way. Sheila hates horses, Joey yearns to meet Stevie Cauthen and Sean tosses his doughnut wrapper and orange-juice bottle into the red can of steaming-hot water, Bubba from Burley Cocks' barn yells like we kicked his cat. Dad grumbles because horse won't eat, exercise rider is late and horse draws outside post in the 2-mile maiden hurdle for Wednesday.

To the races in the afternoon. Horse goes off at 5-2, jumps too high over first, too low over second . . . and we're back in the Imperatore by 7 p.m. Well, it's better than the Blue Spruce.

Ryan just returned with the two sandwiches.

"Keep the change, buddy."

"It's only four bucks. You owe me a dollar."

Seth Gregory paced around the grandstand as seven horses galloped to the start for the Cab Calloway.

Gregory gnawed on a piece of gum like he was mad at it. He went to the hot-dog stand for a napkin to wipe his brow. He stripped off his navy blazer and held it under his arm. He gulped deep breaths like he was being drafted. Finally, he gathered his family and nervously planted himself in front of the big-screen television in the grandstand.

This happens when a horse you bred and your father owns (and you still have the mare) has a shot in a $250,000 stakes at Saratoga.

"It's a lot easier when it's somebody else's horse," said Gregory, assistant to trainer Mark Hennig. "The past few hours have been rough."

Then in 1:53.09, the stress was gone and elation had begun. Gold And Roses, a son of Gold Token, tracked Galloping Grocer, reeled him in on the turn and earned a cool $150,000 for the Gregory family.

Seth's mother, father, brother, cousin and a few friends he bikes with started yelling, "Come on Token" before the field turned down the backside. Gregory started cheering on the turn, slapping his right foot on the floor like Keith Moon on a cymbal. Inside the sixteenth pole, Gregory and trainer Tom Bush jumped up and down together like a World Series winning pitcher and catcher.

He might not admit it but there was a tear in Seth Gregory's eye as he made his way to the winner's circle.

Seth Gregory will tell you, flat out, he's a cynic. Tell him it's a nice day and he'll tell you it's going to rain. Praise somebody and he'll bash them. He's as realistic as a tax form. He'll tell you he doesn't believe in dreams.

Then he throws pixie dust at a filly who needs a home. Won Perfect Rose won two races, got hurt and foundered behind. The owners had two choices – put her down or give her away. Gregory knew the filly, adored the filly and started dreaming.

"I just fell in love with her because she was so determined. I figured I'd see her run for the rest of her life and she'd go on to other things," Gregory said. "Then you take her home and she was in dire straits. I got the neighbors who train Standardbreds to pick her up, they brought a horse to the raceway and I went over there and helped them cool out their horse, then we threw her on the gooseneck behind the Standardbred and went home."

Home was two hours away, in Garrattsville, N.Y., where Henry Gregory owns a farm made up mostly of cows – never a foundered horse who needed serious attention just to live, never mind become a broodmare. Seth came home a few days later to change the packing in her hind feet.

"I drove home and you would have thought Muhammad Ali came home," Gregory said. "All my friends, not only my parents but my cousins, some of the neighbors were there, all wanting to see what we had to do to take care of this mare. You pretty much knew if Mom and Dad weren't around, you could call someone to take care of her."

Won Perfect Rose gradually flourished and gave birth to a filly by Signal Tap. Won Dozen Roses won seven races and earned black type when she finished second in the Niagara. Her second foal, a colt by Tomorrows Cat, never made it to the races and her third foal had Gregory pacing the grandstand yesterday.

Seth Gregory

"You always try to better your situation and over the years I've bought and sold a few horses," Gregory said. "I've always wanted a mare of my own, you look at the program and see a filly with a good pedigree and say, 'Gosh, I wish I had that money.' She just had a lot of grit. She was determined in everything she did."

Obviously, Won Perfect Rose passes that on to her offspring. Her two foals to race have both earned black type and Gold And Roses looks poised for an enterprising career.

"It's indescribable because I know how much we go through every day to try to get them there," said Gregory, on his way to the Trustees Room for champagne. "The high is unbelievable, you have so many lows and so many things can go wrong, so when something comes together it's very special. There were plenty of times when I said, 'I'm spending a lot of money and I've put a lot of faith in (Won Perfect Rose) and it's either going to go very well or very sour.'

Fortunately, she's rewarded us for giving her the opportunity to survive."

Late July 2000 behind the Saratoga jockeys' room.

Pat Day, all 4-foot-11 of him, commanded attention as he read aloud from the Bible. Around him stood jockeys, valets, a racing official or two. Collectively, they needed Day to get them past the recent death of jump jockey Jonathan Kiser. Individually, they needed that and more. A valet requested a prayer for his ailing mother. A jockey asked for safety on the course. An official suggested something for his brother, at home undergoing surgery.

That was five years ago, and Day delivered with all the finesse, timing, aplomb he used on the racetrack for 8,803 victories between 1973 and this summer. Yesterday, the Hall of Fame jockey announced his retirement – and left most of the sport digging up a wealth of Pat Day memories.

Unbridled. Seafaring Man. Cat Thief. Two Trail Sioux. Traditionally. With Anticipation. Easy Goer. Those Thoroughbreds and others felt the receiving end of Pat Day rides which were equal parts give and take, hurry up and wait, push and pull.

"My best memoires of Pat are when you put him up on a horse you knew exactly that you were going to get 100 percent," said trainer Carl Nafzger Thursday. "He rode a great style and if you knew his style and fit his style, you had something. He never did hurt a horse. He always helped a horse."

Nafzger and Day teamed up for numerous wins, none more sweet than the 1990 Breeders' Cup Classic with Unbridled, but the trainer singled out Day's perspective as much as his ability.

"The trouble with this business – trainers, breeders, jockeys, all of us – is we get thinking we can do something. We forget it's the horse that does it. The good horse takes us all where we're going. We all play an intricate part in him, but it's the horse that takes us and I think Pat never did forget that. Pat always remembered it was the horses who took him there."

And they took Day to amazing places – first in total purse earnings (nearly $300 million), fourth in total victories, the Hall of Fame in 1991, a dozen Breeders' Cup wins, five Preaknesses, three Belmonts, four Eclipse Awards and a Kentucky Derby. He started riding in 1973, but didn't progress to the national stage until beating addiction and embarking on a path of pious belief. Day credited God for his success, and paid homage after most every win. In retirement, Day will actively work with the Racetrack Chaplaincy of America.

Day the jockey starred on racing's biggest stages. The human being went beyond that, touching people in every corner of the industry. His retirement did not really surprise many, but still left a void.

"I'll miss him, miss his riding, but I think he felt like it was time to go in a different direction," said trainer Shug McGaughey, who frequently teamed up with the jockey. "I'm sad to see him go, but I'm happy for Pat. I'm sure he thought long and hard about it and not just in the last few days."

McGaughey easily recalled rides aboard Easy Goer (such as the 1989 Belmont), Heavenly Prize and others through the years.

"We had a horse, Traditionally, who was kind of funny – he wanted to run off with you a little bit – and Pat ended up winning the Oaklawn Handicap on him," said the trainer. "Pat wasn't going to out-muscle one at all. He just kind of out-talked them."

Hands, patience, sense of pace, timing. They all describe Day's riding style. He could wait, and make one run that often finished on the correct side of a photo finish. He could perch in the irons while nursing a horse through quick fractions, repelling challengers with an effortlessness that belied the jockey's motives.

Trainer Jonathan Sheppard put Day aboard With Anticipation in the 2000 and 2001 Sword Dancer at Saratoga, but Thursday Sheppard singled out another Pat Day ride as one of his most memorable.

"I watched the last big race he won, the Fleur de Lis at Churchill Downs June 18, just happened to see the simulcast of it," said Sheppard. "He went to the front and sat still as a mouse on the filly (Two Trail Sioux). He let them catch up to him turning for home and one horse maybe even got a half-length or a neck in front – then all of the sudden he gets down and rides and wins by 2. A typical, masterful Pat Day performance and I'm glad I saw it now."

Like many, Sheppard's first reaction to the retirement news was sadness.

"He's a part of our organization, a part of racing," said the trainer. "He's one of the greatest riders that ever lived and all of the sudden he's not

going to be there anymore. I'll miss him."

Trainer Wayne Lukas wasn't surprised by Day's decision, and praised the jockey for it.

"Most professional athletes don't go out on their own terms, they don't know when to quit and he's definitely going out on his terms," said Lukas. "He knew when he felt it was comfortable for him, but he's always made the right decisions. He's very good about that. He hasn't made many bad decisions with his life."

Lukas singled out Day's ride in the 1999 Breeders' Cup Classic aboard Cat Thief as a personal favorite, but paid credit to the jockey's ability to ride any horse.

"I don't think he rode horses, he just stayed out of their way," said Lukas. "He had an unbelievable knack for pace and an ability to not hinder horses. He didn't do anything that got them beat. A lot of guys maybe think they have to ride every horse. Pat took the philosophy that the horse was the key and that he was going to do as little as he could to hinder his ability. And when he fit one, he really fit it."

Trainer Dale Romans won hundreds of races with Day in the saddle at Churchill Downs and other tracks, and marveled at the partnership.

"There were too many horses to talk about," Romans said. "He would always get there, but I told him he was shortening my lifespan by getting up by a nose all the time. He never got around to riding (2004 Turf Champion) Kitten's Joy – I always wanted him to because they would have been a great match, but circumstances just never worked out."

Regardless of who you talk to, no one can discuss Pat Day the jockey without getting around to Pat Day the person. He impacted people beyond the stable area or the outside rail. He reached. He preached. He set a good example.

Nafzger put it best – "He did some great things, but being who he was was greater than what he did."

Amen.

On Pat Day:

Jockey Mike Luzzi:

"When I went to Kentucky, I had ridden with him here but I had never ridden with him on his turf. I won the Bashford Manor on Boston Harbor and we're galloping out. He says, 'Man, jock, what were you doing? I gotta claim foul.' I said, 'Pat, what did I do?' He said, 'You got me good, you like to drop me.' I galloped around and the race is official, then I watched the replay, there wasn't a horse around me the whole race. He said, 'Welcome to Kentucky, jock.' He was one of the best that ever did it. God bless him."

Jockey Jerry Bailey:

"The first Breeders' Cup Classic (on Wild Again) had to be the best. I don't think people know how hard it is to come down the stretch head and head in any race, even on a horse who doesn't respond that great from the stick, and not hit him just once. Much less for $3 million. That's as cool as it gets. He's a guy you couldn't follow. If you were following him hoping to get through at the eighth pole after he did, it wasn't going to happen. He would wait long enough for him to get through and for him to win, it wouldn't work for anyone else. You almost had to bail out early because he was just too patient, it was OK for him but not for you.

"He was in my corner, he always used to tell us he loved his job. 'I love my job.' It could be six feet of mud, pouring down with rain, getting beat on a bunch of favorites and I'd ask him, 'Do you still love your job?' And he'd say, 'Yes, I still love my job.' He had a passion for the game and it couldn't help being infectious. It gave me a better perspective of how blessed I am to be able to do this.

"I'll miss riding with him, I'll miss him in my corner. He was just a very positive influence. I try and think I'm pretty well grounded but he would, daily, give me a better outlook on life."

Jockey Robby Albarado:

"It's the end of a book. It's like you were reading a book and you just finished it and now you have to find another book. Riding-wise, I learned patience. Around the jocks' room, professional for sure. He joked when he wanted and was serious when he needed to be. He had that air about him. People watched what they said around him. He made you a better person. It was like Michael Jordan walked in the room or the principal came in the room. Not in a lecturing way. He would do the prayer session sometimes, if the chaplain couldn't make it. You listen to the chaplain but you don't really listen. When Pat did it, you listened. He'll be missed."

Valet Eddie Brown (Day's New York valet for 26 years): "When he was inducted into the Hall of Fame, I was filming the whole thing. I had never seen him choke up when he was talking, he choked up, the next thing I knew I couldn't see through the viewfinder, my eyes were swelling up with water. Just a classy guy and a great rider. Patience and love for other people, one class act. Before he turned to Christ, I saw him want to tear up the room. He was one tough little guy. It was night and day. We've been friends for a long, long time."

I was a kid in the Saratoga jocks' room.

A young, fledgling jump jockey with less confidence than a toddler on his first walk. I felt out of place, looked out of place, was out of place.

There was Angel Cordero Jr. and his plaster-rattling salsa music. Mike Venezia and his quiet, quiet way. Chris Antley and his cocksure exterior. Eddie Maple. Randy Romero, Richard Migliore, Jerry Bailey, Jose Santos, Robbie Davis, Jean-Luc Samyn, Craig Perret, Jean Cruguet, Herb McCauley, Frank Lovato Jr., Julie Krone, Don Brumfield. And Pat Day.

I rode a bad race on a jumper who came off the bridle a mile into the 2 1/16-mile race. He fell apart, I fell apart. It felt like I had never ridden a horse. I was mortified when I saw myself in the replay, looking like Kareem Abdul-Jabbar in a washing machine. It felt worse.

After scanning every corner in the room, I finally got the nerve up to ask Pat Day (the most approachable jockey) what happened out there in the blur that others called a race.

"Uh, Mr. Day, I fell apart out there. I guess my horse got tired, I tried to finish on him and it felt like I had never ridden a horse. He came out of the bridle and then I came out of the bridle, I couldn't change my cross, couldn't switch sticks, my reins kept getting longer, I couldn't do anything. What do you do when this happens?"

"Wait for another day," Day said.

So Pat Day.

That year, 1988, Day won the Adirondack on Pat Copelan for who else, Wayne Lukas. He took the Diana on Glowing Honor for Mack Miller and Rokeby Stable. He copped the Forego on Quick Call for Sidney Watters Jr.

I wanted the key to success and Day gave it to me (although it took years to understand) in such a concise four-word statement. He made it so simple.

Horses only run as fast as they're able to run. You can help them but the biggest help you can give them is stay out of their way. That was always Day's way. Cordero was all muscle, daring horses to lose. He had a whip arm that could win the sledgehammer contest at the Schuylerville Fair. Day would bide his time, usually arriving so late dinner was already cold. While both successful, Cordero knocked spots off horses, Day couldn't knock flies off horses.

"Wait for another day."

Love his riding style or hate his riding style, he etched his Hall of Fame plaque years ago and continued to ride at a furious pace until hip surgery curtailed his riding last year.

Robby Albarado fought for elbow room with Day on the Kentucky circuit.

On a hot day last year, Albarado was in the middle of riding 10 races at Churchill Downs. Feeling tired, Albarado heard himself saying, "Man, this is brutal, I'm riding 10 today . . ." then he walked past Day's scorecard – a sheet pinned to his locker. Day, 20 years older than Albarado and already squarely in the Hall of Fame, was booked for 10 rides as well.

Albarado likes to inform anyone who will listen that born-again Day could trash-talk better than Deion Sanders.

Day nailed Albarado in a photo one day at Churchill, and as they galloped out Day went to bantering.

"That right there is why I still do it, to outride young punks like you."

Last year, Albarado took a break from the trash talking and asked Day why he was still riding.

"Pat, you have nothing else to prove, you've ridden the best horses in the world, you've won the best races in the world," Albarado said. "Why you still doing it?"

"You'll see," Day said. "You'll see."

Again, Day had another jockey thinking.

Pat Day was back.

A month into his return from hip surgery, the 51-year-old jockey put Two Trail Sioux under a "Pat Day Spell" to eke out the Fleur De Lis Stakes June 18 at Churchill Downs. Trained by Wally Dollase, the 4-year-old filly was rank early, then settled, then came late to win by a length.

It was Wild Again in the 1984 Breeders' Cup Classic. Summer Squall in the 1990 Preakness. Cat Thief in the 1999 Breeders' Cup Classic.

"They came to us at the top of the stretch," Day said. "She gathered herself and gave every indication there was more left in the tank and I was able to keep her contained until late in the stretch. I called on her and she responded and got the job done."

But there was a big problem.

"It was a great race, a great effort and coming to the wire I should have been filled with joy, it should have been a joyous occasion, it gave every indication that I was certainly back," Day said. "I knew in my heart I rode a good race and played a major factor in the outcome. All those things that should make you feel good as a rider but the joy of the victory was decidedly missing. That started me searching, asking, looking."

Day searches, asks, looks in only place. The Hall of Famer went on a retreat and searched for God's answer.

"I got away and first I pled with God," Day said. " 'Please, fan the flame of my competitive fire. I can do this, yeah I'm 51, but I'm healthy, I'm happy, I'm light, I'm ready. I can do this a couple more years but I can't do it if I don't have that competitive fire.' I got no fanning of the flames."

Retirement from anything is a daunting notion. Retiring from riding races, as we've seen time and time again, is tougher to grasp than space. At least until it's the right time.

"I spent three days with the fellowship of the Lord. Quiet, alone, searching the scriptures, praying," Day said. "Sunday, I took a drive, about 3 o'clock, 4 o'clock, while I was out driving around, I said to myself, 'It's time.' At that moment, it was like a cloud lifting off my shoulders, immediately followed by a sense of joy and peace and contentment."

The sport creates a natural dependency in jockeys. Ride 10,000 races and each one has its own nuances. Ride champions and the rush will last a lifetime. The desire to ride races, the thrill it provides and the money that goes with it makes it a tough gig to cancel. Retirement?

"That very question will be faced by one and all at some point in time, it won't be easy for them," Day said. "My prayer is that they would all be faced with that question and answer it affirmatively and they don't wait until something tragic happens that puts them on the sidelines. When that happens and they don't dictate when they retire from the saddle, it leaves a bitterness, a feeling of no closure. The ones that I've talked to who have had to go to the sidelines because of injury, there hasn't been closure, they didn't answer that question in their terms. Nobody wants to have to retire."

Day returned to Saratoga yesterday, the first time he didn't head to his bench in the jocks' room, first time he didn't mark up his Form with notes for future rides, first time he didn't head to the paddock to ride a race. Eddie Brown, Day's valet for close to 30 years, began to organize Day's equipment.

"We'll disperse some of his stuff," Brown said. "Give it to some kids who aren't doing any good."

For Day, the timing of his retirement couldn't have been scripted any better. With a scheduled Racetrack Chaplaincy meeting and the 50th anniversary of the Hall of Fame, he had his going-away party in style Monday.

At the Hall of Fame inductions, he received an ovation worthy of a king.

"Before I was out of my seat they started clapping," Day said. "I can't explain the feeling, I got a little weak in the knees. It was . . . it was . . . indescribable. Emotional. A good moment, a good moment."

Two Trail Sioux's going to miss him.

Steve Asmussen ran 11 horses at five race-tracks Friday....

– only one competed in a graded stakes at Saratoga. Forest Music came through with a win in the Honorable Miss Handicap. The victory ticked Asmussen's career odometer to 3,000.

Three thousand victories for the 39-year-old trainer from Texas.

Not that he's counting. When you send out more than 1,300 runners and win more than 275 races in nine months, counting takes too much time.

"I promise, I found out yesterday in the paddock at Arlington when I won a race, they said it was 2,998. I had no idea before then," Asmussen said. "The weird thing about it is we went past 2,000 and I didn't know it. Nobody said anything."

CINDERELLA MAN

They are talking now.

Asmussen became the 25th trainer to win at least 3,000 races.

Focused, introspective, professional, Asmussen combines horsemanship, numbers, supportive owners and good help to run a corporation which wins races anywhere. Equally fond of $5,000 claimers as he is Grade I stakes horses, Asmussen vowed to scale down his operation after breaking the single-season win record last year with 555.

"We still have a lot of horses but our numbers have dropped a lot since last year. Absolutely trying to set the record, for the vain reason that it really is, I had a lot of horses last year that I don't have now. January, February and March, my numbers were way up but it was just carryover. You didn't just get to January 1 and say pick them up. Now we're probably down 50, but the bottom 100 swapped for the top 100, way-better horses. Opportunities like (Forest Music) – what a good trade-in she was for 10 others."

"Trainer's 3,000th Win" will be inscribed on Forest Music's win photo from the Honorable Miss. Sure beats a $7,500 claimer at Retama.

"Awesome. Freaky awesome, 3,000 at Saratoga, in a stakes," Asmussen said. "I think I've won 20 races lifetime at Saratoga and you get to put that on your picture like it all happened there....

....I am Cinderella."

Four-year-old Nolan Clancy's Worth Repeatings:

"I don't follow the rules."

When asked why he's not going miniature golfing with his two brothers.

"Get out, I'm driving."

To his uncle Sean as he took the wheel of the golf cart

"I can't see because this pole's in my way."

As he stood at the eye-level rail of the Oklahoma training track

Saint Liam / Commentator

Nick Zito has been tinkering with his Hall of Fame speech for weeks now.

Known to be glib, natural, open, Zito wanted to write it all down to be sure he includes everyone he needs to thank but he also wants to be himself, let it be natural, conversational, don't read it like a script.

After the day Zito had Saturday, you can be sure he went home and made some notes in the margins of his white legal pad.

Ugh, Noble Causeway eases . . . In The Gold breaks horribly . . . entry two-three in Test . . . then Commentator . . . in Marylou's Whitney . . . for Tracy Farmer . . . talked with Kim about wanting a good weekend before the induction . . . the ups and downs . . . told Stevens he was his kind of horse . . . guts on the lead . . . signed autographs . . . high-fived crowd . . . press talked to me . . . kissed Kim on the way out . . . walked back to test barn . . . the game . . . that's the game.

It will be some speech come Monday.

Commentator saw to that with a stoic and determined victory in the 78th Whitney Handicap. Ridden for the first time by Zito's fellow Hall of Famer Gary Stevens, Commentator broke sharply, securing the lead from favorite Saint Liam. Swingforthefences found a comfortable spot in third while the closing duties were split between Sir Shackleton, Limehouse, Pollard's Vision, Eurosilver and Wiggins.

On the backside, Commentator looked like he had strung Christmas lights across an orchard as the field dissipated behind his scorching speed. After a half-mile, it was a 15-length spread from Commentator to Wiggins. After 6 furlongs, it was 32 and counting between Commentator and the retreating Pollard's Vision.

Edgar Prado gave favorite Saint Liam every opportunity, keeping him close enough to Commentator to have a chance when the frontrunner's burner ran down. Commentator fanned the flame all the way to the wire, bravely repelling Saint Liam by a diminishing neck in the $750,000 Grade I stakes.

Owned by Tracy Farmer, the New York-bred son of Distorted Humor pushed his career tally to seven wins from eight starts. The chestnut gelding made his debut last summer at Saratoga. He rattled off five straight one-turn victories before faltering in the 1 1/8-mile Hal's Hope in January. Zito sent him to the bench for nearly six months and he returned bigger and better; drawing off to win a 7-furlong allowance/optional claimer at Belmont by 16 1/2 lengths.

Zito thought about sprinting Commentator, opted for the Whitney and in return got the pole vault he wanted for Monday's induction.

"This is probably the most important victory of my life, going into the Hall of Fame Monday. It's a special day for me and we're going in the right way," Zito said. "I was happy when that wire came. It was unbelievable. He's an amazing horse, but it's a hard style. I always say, play the game, play the game."

Nick Zito

Zito had played the game Friday but the game had done nothing but shove the 57-year-old trainer. Noble Causeway, who was a vet scratch in last Saturday's Jim Dandy, pulled up in the third race. Zito's favored entry Hide And Chic and In The Gold finished two-three in the Test with In The Gold forfeiting all chance with a bumbling start. Zito was 0-for-5 on the day and needing a jolt.

"It takes a lot out of you," he said. "But it's like when they asked me after I had all those horses in the Kentucky Derby, I said, 'When you think about what happens in life, you know, this isn't that bad.' No matter how up or down we get, we get a shot to play this great game. The Hall of Fame is a career, maybe this is the best race of my life. We're going into the Hall of Fame on the greatest note you could possibly have, winning the Whitney and Sir Shackleton was third."

Also owned by Farmer, Sir Shackleton finished nine lengths behind Saint Liam. Swingforthefences stayed well, but couldn't muster a rally and finished fourth. Limehouse, Eurosilver, Wiggins and Pollard's Vision rounded out the order of finish behind a 1:48.33 final time.

Stevens knew Zito wasn't having his best of days, or meet for that matter, and was glad to help roll out a red carpet.

"I hadn't said anything to Nick about the Hall of Fame. The last couple of weeks for him were a little tough. Started out the meet a little slow, then with Noble Causeway being scratched the other day and pulling up today, his chin was dragging a little bit," Stevens said. "People don't realize, getting inducted into the Hall of Fame, you want to keep a good form going into the Hall of Fame so you can say, 'Yeah, I belong here' because it's kind of hard to believe. All I told Nick down there was he belongs in Hall of Fame, 'Enjoy it and I'll see you on Monday morning.' He got a big smile on his face and I know it picked his head up a little bit."

Zito doesn't need a history lesson or a set of name tags to understand and respect where he's going Monday.

"It's been a long journey, it's a great, great honor. Seeing Mr. Whiteley, Mr. Mack Miller, Mr. Nerud, Mr. Jerkens who I talk to all the time, all those great Hall of Famers," Zito said. "Going into the Hall of Fame, this is the way you want to do it. What a way, to go into the Hall of Fame, the right way."

Now about that speech.

"I started on a legal pad and then typed it up but like everybody says, you're not supposed to just read, I gotta have some notes because I don't want to forget the people who took me there," Zito said. "A lot of my friends and people I'm close to, they really want me to talk the way I talk to the press, that's what people like. Of course, you have to write something because there are a lot of people you have to thank but I'm going to say a few things. I've written it myself, if it comes out bad, no one's to blame but me....

....I'll say what I have to say and I won't disappoint you."

It was one of those car rides where the parents are one scream away from pulling over and running.

Like any good parent, Steve Mitchell resorted to bribery on his youngest daughter.

"We're all in the car and she's in a bad mood," Mitchell said. "The kids are there, we're trying to calm her down. We just bought this filly. I said, 'Look, if you behave you can name this horse.' She said, 'Leave me alone!' My other daughter said, 'That's the name of the horse.' "

Leave Me Alone, a California-bred filly by Bold Badgett, won four of her first seven starts before taking a swing at her first Grade I in Saturday's Test. She blasted to the lead, hung an opening quarter-mile of 22.42 seconds and a half-mile in 45.46, then streaked home by 7 3/4 lengths. Owned by Steve Mitchell's Mitchell Ranch and trained by Eric Kruljac, Leave Me Alone toyed with a competitive group of 3-year-old fillies.

Favorite In The Gold broke slowly and was quickly last, in a double-digit hole while Leave Me Alone outsprinted anyone around her. Maddalena gave futile chase before fading to fifth. Her entrymate Sense Of Style never got into contention while New York-bred upstart Acey Deucey spun her wheels near the back of the field.

Ridden by Kent Desormeaux, who travelled 3,000 miles for the call, Leave Me Alone finished the 7 furlongs in 1:22.76.

It was a joyous 1:22.76 for Mitchell and Kruljac, who had just teamed up for their first Grade I victory.

"I'm unbelievably excited about her. She's the best one I've had," Kruljac said. "She's a biomechanical machine. She's so balanced, she's a Michael Jordan with four legs."

Kruljac picked out Leave Me Alone as a yearling, purchasing her for $35,000. She had a gash on her forehead and was barricaded in her stall with plywood.

"I asked to see her out and once she got out I saw the way she moved. There are things I look for when I buy yearlings and I don't spend a lot of money. It was all looks," Kruljac said. "She's by a very, very consistent, useful sire who stood in California for most of his life for less than $2,000. They don't know who their parents are – they're a direct result of a genetic lottery. This filly caught all the good things in her second and third generation."

Whatever she caught, it was fast. The Test pushed her career earnings over $500,000. She made her debut on the turf, finishing 11th in a Hollywood Park maiden sprint. Taking advantage of the California-bred program, Leave Me Alone won her next two starts before finishing second in the Santa Paula. She stretched out to 1 1/16-mile in the Melair, winning by 4. Freshened for two months, Leave Me Alone returned in the Grade II Hollywood Breeders' Cup Oaks where she finished fourth. After that, Kruljac started booking flights for the chestnut filly.

Leave Me Alone battled hard on the lead at Calder in the Azalea Breeders' Cup July 10, winning the Grade III by a nose. She jetted back to Santa Anita for two breezes and then landed in Saratoga Friday afternoon.

Mitchell was enjoying Leave Me Alone's victory in the Test, at least until Kruljac whipped around from his seat and tried to celebrate with Mitchell. He knew better. The owner and trainer had been here before.

"When she won the Melair, Kruljac turned around and said, 'You got a racehorse,' and he picked me up," Mitchell said. "If you've seen Kruljac, he looks big and strong. Well, he's a lot stronger than he looks, he picked me up and gave me a bear hug. I couldn't breathe and I'm yelling, 'Leave me alone.' He let me go. Today, he turned around and tried to grab me and I said, 'No way, and don't touch my kids either.' "

Mitchell's oldest two kids, Sam, 15, and Danielle, 12, made the trip to Saratoga. The youngest, "Leave Me Alone" Johnnie Grace, 4 1/2, stayed at home in Phoenix.

"Angel, do you remember Joe A . . .?"

Angel Cordero's eyes lit up like only his can, he stopped in mid-sentence and scurried over.

"Do I remember? The best of the best. Mr. Joe," Cordero said. "How are you, Joe? You look great."

Joe Aitcheson

Cordero turned to jockey Chantal Sutherland (and anyone within earshot) and told about Joe Aitcheson, the greatest steeplechase jockey who ever lived.

"He did the jumps," said Cordero, who shared the same valet with Aitcheson. "He'd come in busted, bruised, neck wrapped up, shoulder strapped up. I'd say, 'There's no way this guy's gonna ride today.' Then he'd go out and win."

He did it 440 times, more than any American jump jockey in history. This is the Laffit Pincay of jump racing. Joe was a boxer in the Marine Corps and started riding jumpers at 28, about the time most jump jockeys are starting to think about retiring. His first year, 1956, he rode 10 races, fell four times, broke his collarbone twice. Doctors pinned it the first time and gave up the second time. Five years later, he won his first championship. He went on to win six more titles before retiring in 1979.

You don't get good at something if it's a lark. Joe was singlemindedly determined, like a dog after a ball; all that mattered was riding winners. Joe retired because of too many falls, but only after he had made more comebacks than Larry Holmes. At 77, he still gallops a few horses during the week at Laurel Park and wouldn't mind getting back on a jumper. Recently he moved into a retirement community, insisting on a room on the top floor so he could stay in shape by walking up and down the stairs.

"I could still ride a race all right," Aitcheson said to National Steeplechase's Bill Gallo. "I would need a few months to get fit, but I could do it."

Every child had one. An idol. Most picked a slugger who was on television every night. I chose Joe Aitcheson. When teachers asked, "Who do you want to be when you grow up?" it was his name I wrote down. So when he called asking where he should stay in Saratoga, I made instant room in our two-bedroom (three-person) house.

Inducted to the Hall of Fame in 1978, Joe wanted to come to Saratoga for the Hall's 50th anniversary. His navy sport coat was ready to go, he had his Amtrak tickets already booked and he wanted some numbers for rooms.

Joe, you're staying with me.

So last night, a Hall of Famer came to town. Elbow deep in three columns, I sent Travis Stone and my nephew Jack to pick up Joe from the train station.

"He looks like a jump jockey," I said. "Black hair, fit, a little on the old side but a great guy."

They saw one of the first guys to get off the train and asked him if he ever rode horses and if his name Joe.

"No, sorry, I'm not Joe," he said.

Nearly the last passenger off the train, Joe ambled along the platform.

"We knew it was him right away," Stone said. "You can tell he was something big."

They stopped for ice cream at Stewart's. Joe insisted on paying.

Joe and I hopped in the golf cart Friday morning and went to the track.

"I don't know anybody in the game anymore," Aitcheson said. "I haven't been up here in a long time."

We parked in front of the Morning Line Kitchen and the receiving line started.

Scotty Schulhofer, Barclay Tagg, Ralph Theroux, Bill Gallo, Tommy Walsh and some people neither Joe or I knew stopped and chatted. Joe ate a corn muffin and watched horses train.

"I'm really glad I came out this morning," he said. "I didn't think I'd know anybody any more. Boy, I didn't think they'd remember me. I didn't know Angel Cordero even knew who I was when I was riding with him."

When you're the best of the best, they know.

Back then, they saddled horses under the trees in Saratoga.

Wide open, without a fence, without anything between horses and fans. It was bucolic and good for the soul, of course there weren't lawsuits and liability insurance back then either. Each horse had a separate tree, right where the picnic area is today. They'd literally walk through the crowd to get

to their trees. For the fresh, there were covered saddling stalls where the paddock is today.

No worries, horses were meant to be saddled under trees with the crowd milling about, jiving with the grooms and rubbing elbows with the owners, trainers and jockeys. Gravel, grass, horses and trees.

On Aug. 4, 1973, four horses for the Whitney Handicap were saddled on the turf course, the last time it would happen in Saratoga. With an overflow crowd expected to flood the place; all there to see the great Secretariat, it was decided to keep the horses out of the trees and on the turf course. Secretariat, Onion, Rule By Reason and West Coast Scout were fitted with tack on the infield grass. Only True Knight was saddled in the enclosed paddock behind the grandstand. Back then Saratoga's infield was open, and trainers would congregate there to watch races.

Secretariat, Triple Crown winner, had returned from his 31-length Belmont romp to take the Invitational at Arlington Park. Five weeks later, the Meadow Stable colt came to Saratoga as a living legend. Syndicated for a then-record, $6,080,000 and winner of 13 of his first 15 races, Secretariat was sent off at 1-10 by the 30,119 on hand.

Allen Jerkens, working hard on his "Giant Killer" nickname entered Onion, who four days earlier set a track record going 6 1/2 furlongs. Jacinto Vasquez put the Hobeau Farm homebred on the lead, skipping along in 47 4/5 for the first half-mile. Secretariat and Ron Turcotte gave chase through three-quarters in 1:11 1/5.

Chase and chase and chase. Onion, by Third Martini out of the Beau Gar mare With A Flair, kept running, widening under the wire by a length in a 1:49 1/5. It was all Secretariat could do to hold off 6-year-old Rule By Reason for second money. The great champion lost for only the third time in his career.

Secretariat wasn't at his best that day and it was up to trainer Lucien Laurin to put out the fires after the loss. The trainer tried to explain his 1:34 mile workout a week earlier, the horse appeared listless after the race, maybe the move to the deep rail cost him the race, perhaps the race went up in smoke when he charged the gates, causing them to open before the start.

Jerkens cried after the race. Laurin wanted to.

Later that day, Jerkens went back to his barn on the Oklahoma side and brought out the football. Known for legendary touch-football games, Jerkens hung his coat and tie on the saddle stand and started throwing passes to hotwalkers, friends, foremen.

Onion, still jazzed from his 15 minutes of fame, disagreed with the commotion. His hotwalker walked out into the middle of the game of football.

"Chief, you're stirring up the horse," he said. "You got to stop playing."

They kept right on playing.

After the football game and after Onion was settled deep in his bedding, Jerkens headed home; he couldn't bear seeing any more people. He never liked the attention, and in a way felt bad for the great Secretariat. All the trainer wanted was some peace, quiet and a good meal.

"I just want to get out of town and not see anybody," Jerkens said to his wife.

They decided on Barney's, a falling-down place in a falling-down town outside of Schuylerville. They drove there to get away from it all.

Jerkens ambled up the walkway, opened the door and the first person he saw was Lucien Laurin.

Disclaimer: I was 3 years old and wearing seersucker overall shorts when Onion saw the steal sign and upset Secretariat. I watched it from the five-sixteenth pole with my family. All I remember is my father getting excited to show his kids the great champion Secretariat, who even ambled over for a pre-race photo. This story was told to me second hand, I hope I got close to giving it justice. If any of the facts are wrong, hey, it was just a story about an era gone past.

The Fasig-Tipton Select Sale gets underway tonight at 7:30 at the Humphrey S. Finney Sales Pavilion.

Traditionally held over three nights, this year it was shortened to two sessions. With 153 yearlings in the catalogue, numbers are significantly less this year. Major consignors like Lane's End, Three Chimneys Farm and Stone Farm decided to stay at home this year.

The Special caught up with Fasig-Tipton President Walt Robertson Sunday afternoon and talked about the state of the Select Sale.

What's the mood two days before the sale?

"We absolutely love our horses. We've been through all the horses and I'm really, really happy with the way they look. Sometimes you'll have some come to the sale less than you would hope for, but this year is as strong across the board as we've had it."

Are there years when you're worried about the quality of horses?

"Hell, yeah. This isn't one of them, this one will be fine, I don't know what the market will be, nobody does. It's usually about the horse and if that's what it's about, we'll be fine."

What was the cause of the decrease in numbers?

"Your guess is as good as mine. I hope it's a short-time thing. We were just down 50 horses from what we've been. We've been as low as 175 before and as high as 210, 215. We had to hold our standards to where we've been and that's what we've done."

What changed this year?

"It could be any number of things, a lot of people wanted to sell at our sale in Kentucky, the competition gets their share. This year we lost a few consignments, hopefully they'll be back next year."

Is there more pressure this year?

"No, I don't think there's any more pressure. I'm not feeling any more pressure because I like my horses so well. You go in and see several horses you're not fond of, that's pressure."

Did you expect the low numbers?

"No, we didn't see it at all, but we held our standards and I'd like to think we've got a better horse here. We'll know more about it Wednesday."

You could have filled the catalogue?

"You can always fill it, absolutely. But what you have to do to do it is not good for the horse sale. People come up here expecting a certain kind of horse – we damn sure better deliver it."

Is the July sale easier to put together than this sale?

"This year it was. This year a lot of people wanted to come to July, we had 150 more than last year. That varies from year to year and who knows how it's going to be next year?"

Do you set out to have more horses in one sale than another?

"No, we don't set out for any horse sale, to say, 'OK, we've got to have 500 horses' or anything like that. We want as many horses as we can possibly get here until our stalls are filled – of the right kind of horse. Same thing with Kentucky."

Are the lower numbers an anomaly or the start of a trend?

"I'm not saying it's a trend, you can't call one year a trend. It's my aim to have more horses next year. But, it's also our aim to take the right horse and hold our standards. Maybe in past years, our standards have been relaxed a little bit. After looking at these this week, they haven't been. They've been pretty stringent and the right horses have shown up."

Have you, yourself, seen every yearling in the Saratoga catalogue?

"I've probably seen 65, 70 percent of them. There are six of us who look and we go out in pairs. I've seen the majority of them."

Is this sale ever in jeopardy of being discontinued?

"This is an important sale for us. It's also an important horse sale for the whole game. The industry needs this horse sale, we need this horse sale. Good horses have come out of this sale....

....It was here a long time before I was here and I fully expect it to be here a long time after I'm gone."

We had this grand idea of creating a John Velazquez Watch.

After two straight years of setting and breaking the record for most wins at the meet, we thought we could design a Velazquez-o-meter which would track his victories during the meet. We even had our graphic artist create one, a graph of miniature horses and we'd fill in each one as Velazquez kicked home another winner. All the way to another record.

Boy, the fans would have loved it. Johnny would have hated it.

Especially now that Edgar Prado has moved within one of Velazquez at the top of the jockey standings. Velazquez opened up with a bang, doubling and tripling during the first week. The title race looked over. Then Prado started winning races Velazquez-style, and has climbed within one victory of the lead.

Funny thing is neither Velazquez nor Prado is counting.

Sure, they know it's close and they both yearn for the title, but you don't get to the top by doing the math on the way back to the jocks' room after every race.

When Velazquez won the Statue of Liberty last week I mentioned that Karakorum Splendor made the same amount of money winning the restricted stakes as Ashado earned for winning the Grade I Go For Wand.

"She did?" Velazquez said. "You know I don't look at that stuff. I just try to ride winners."

And so they do.

Prado and Velazquez split divisions of the De La Rose yesterday. Velazquez stealing the first with the Todd Pletcher-trained Path Of Thunder and Prado engineering a green-light-only trip from Cloakof Vagueness in the second half.

Velazquez went home after finishing fifth on La Reina in that one, while Prado went out to ride the last, a New York-bred maiden going 5 1/2 furlongs. He rode a first-time starter for Richard Dutrow and took all the money. Stephanootz broke a step slowly and ran evenly to finish a disappointing fourth.

Prado stripped off the sub silks and watched the replay.

"She didn't break," Prado said to nobody in particular.

He watched the replay, then waited for the head-on angle, then cursed when it wasn't shown. Another long and prosperous day was over, with two wins including the De La Rose and another spot gained in the Velazquez chase.

Not that you're going to get any trash talk from Prado.

"We're working, we're working," Prado said. "Three more weeks to go, I won't be here Saturday or Sunday. Johnny will only be out there Saturday."

Well, he knows where his enemy is anyway.

Prado flies to Arlington Park for the ride on Kitten's Joy in the Arlington Million while Velazquez picked up the ride on Better Talk Now. They do battle in the Grade I Beverly D with Prado on Wonder Again and Velazquez on 3-year-old filly phenom Melhor Ainda. Jerry Bailey (third in the Saratoga standing with 14 wins) will be in Arlington too. At least the boys give the Saratoga jocks' room a break for a day.

"This year it's spread out so it's wide open for everybody," Prado said. "You have three more riders this year, Ramon (Dominguez) is here, (Eibar) Coa is here, unfortunately (Rafael) Bejarano got hurt. It's always been tough. The thing is, when Johnny and Pletcher get hot, they make it tough for everybody. This year it's been Jerry and Billy Mott, it seems like every time they run on the grass, they're very tough."

Prado took his only Saratoga title in 2002 and Velazquez has run away with the last two.

"It's whoever gets hot and who's riding for them. I have (Richard) Dutrow, luckily, but he doesn't run many against Mott and Pletcher. Then we try get business from all the other little guys, one piece from everyone," Prado said. "I try not to worry about, I try just to win and then go to the next race and on and on and on. If you start worrying about it, you start riding differently. I try to ride the race according to the horse."

Velazquez, Prado, Bailey all say the same thing when it comes to chasing titles. They respect the quest, they respect their competition and they fight the urge to get emotional about an unemotional exercise. Horses run better when jockeys don't over-try. They run better when jockeys don't press. They run better when jockeys aren't riding with another mission. The best jockeys learn this early and then capitalize by knowing it.

"I don't want to change anything, I'm going to do my best and if it's meant to be, it's gonna be. That's the best way to look at it," Prado said. "I don't want to press and start looking for other riders and watch them. I'm going to go out and if I have the best horse and the best trip, I win the race. You don't want to worry too much, all you have to worry about is yourself and your horse, that's it."

Get out the Prado-meter.

QUOTES:

"Didn't he want him?"

– Trainer Kiaran McLaughlin's daughter, Erin, after John Ferguson bailed out on a $3.1 million yearling Wednesday night

"What, do you think I stay up on my porch all night?"

– Trainer Rick Violette, asked if it rained last night

"This right here is what you call the goods."

– Fasig-Tipton's Terence Collier as Hip 98, a colt by Fusaichi Pegasus, walked into the ring before going on to sell for $1.1 million

"Good call, good call on the gate."

– Trainer Todd Pletcher, after a security guard opened one of the Union Avenue exits to let fans (and the leading trainer) out after Thursday's seventh race

"I'm not a valet kind of guy."

– Trainer James Bond, walking to his car after a Fifth Avenue cocktail party Thursday

Clinton Potts visited Saratoga Aug. 5.

It was a working vacation for the Delaware Park-based jockey, who rode longshot Umpateedle in the Honorable Miss. Up and back, Potts was out of town before happy hour was over at Siro's. But the 34-year-old jockey got a quick look around and thought about how much he'd like to return and really see Saratoga.

Nine days after his first visit this summer, Potts was back.

"I was up here to ride that race and I thought it was real pretty," Potts said. "So I thought I'd come up and get around and see it."

But everything had changed.

Two days after Umpateedle couldn't keep up with Forest Music in the 6-furlong sprint stakes, Potts was riding the first race at Delaware Park, a seven-horse field of $16,000 claimers. Four-year-old gelding Pete's Pantherskin raced in mid-pack in the 1 1/16-mile dirt route.

The horse shied at something – maybe a lost shoe off another horse or a flying rock – and jumped to the right. Potts was off balance instantly and Pete's Pantherskin shot to his right again when he landed. Potts spun in the air, did a 180 and hit the ground backward, thudding into the dirt and snapping three bones in his neck.

Potts was back in Saratoga because he had nothing else to do. Out of work and in a halo brace screwed to his skull. Potts' doctor predicted six to 12 weeks in the brace which constricts all movement from the neck up. Herman Munster had more pivot.

"I stood up right away, walked to the ambulance, got in the ambulance, sat down and told them where I was having pain. They put a neck brace on me and laid me down," Potts said. "When you're injured like that, your body goes into shock and adrenaline takes over – until you sit down and your heart slows down and you mellow out, then you start feeling the pain. I knew right away something was wrong because I was seeing stars and lines and I broke out in a profuse sweat. I've been injured enough to know that something's broke."

Clinton Potts

Jockeys measure time by injuries. This was the third major injury of Potts' 16-year career. He had a horse go down with him at Penn National; he broke his right arm, four or five ribs, his right leg in two places. Two years ago, a horse flipped over with him at Delaware; he broke both his collarbones, some ribs, punctured a lunge, fractured his pelvis.

"I've had my share of catastrophic injuries," Potts said. "I know what to expect, I know how to handle it, I know what to look forward to, I know I'll have the opportunity to ride again."

Potts knew whom to call after doctors placed him in the halo brace – basically a box that's attached around his torso – which keeps his head still. Laffit Pincay's been through injuries like a cow goes through cud. In a four-decade career, the all-time winningest jockey had pretty much been the poster child for aches and breaks. Pincay was placed in a halo brace when he was 55. Potts is 34.

"I asked him if he went through the same issues – he said everything I'm going through, he went through," Potts said. "Your body is so fit and all of a sudden you're stuck in this thing and your body's crying out to go do something and you can't go and do anything. You're put into this small little space, like your own personal prison."

Potts has been repeating Pincay's advice – "You just have to concentrate, you know you have your legs and you know you have your arms, you can walk around, you can move. One day, you're going to ride again or at least have the opportunity. You're going to live, you have a long life in front of you."

For Potts, his long life in front of him will continue to include riding races. He's a jockey; he makes good money being a jockey, money he couldn't make anywhere else. Even with four screws drilled into his head and a metal brace holding his neck and head in solitary confinement, he's still a jockey.

"The doctor says you shouldn't ride, you could break your neck again, you could be paralyzed. Well, that could happen with a good neck. I still have my strength and my youth," Potts said. "When to stop, I guess, is personal, when something clicks in your own head. It's different for everybody. The first time I got banged up would have been enough for some people. It's like playing golf for some people, football players playing football. It gets in your blood and you really want to do it. I love doing it. And I love the horses."

As Potts spoke about returning to the saddle, he constantly fiddled with the brace. He pulled it from his chest, he squirmed like a child at the ballet.

"It's very constricting, I can't move my head up and down or side to side," Potts said. "It's entrapping. I'm very claustrophobic and at times when I'm laying still I feel like I can't catch my breath. It's better than the alternative – the doctor gave me the option to have surgery or wear the halo. I didn't want surgery so close to my spinal column, one slip of the knife and that's that. So I chose to wear this for however long it takes."

Knowing Potts, it won't be for long.

Bill Mott leaned on the open door of his silver Toyota Avalon and finally said it....

...."It sounds crazy, but I never thought she'd get beat," Mott said. "I quietly had a lot of confidence in her."

It was nearly an hour after Kinsman Stable's Sweet Symphony decimated her six rivals in the 125th Alabama Saturday. Mott had talked through rolls of reporters' tape, done an ESPN interview, celebrated in the trustees room, walked to the parking lot with his family, been told the Yankees' score three times and been hailed by parking attendant Felix Huertas (who dropped to his knees in mock worship).

That's what happens when you send out a 3-for-3 filly and she comes back 4-for-4, in the Grade I Alabama, no less. The homebred daughter of A.P. Indy made her debut May 12, winning a maiden by three-quarters of a length. She followed that with an effortless spin going 1 1/16 miles in a Belmont allowance, then made her next condition going 1 1/8 miles at Saratoga July 28. Those three races set her up perfectly for her stakes debut in the $750,000 Alabama. Mott added Lasix for the first time and gave Jerry Bailey a leg up – his horse did the rest.

Sweet Symphony got bounced around going into the first turn and had one horse behind her as the field turned down the backside over the good going. Ashland winner Sis City took them along through splits of 24.31 and 48.86 seconds while Sweet Symphony gathered momentum leaving the backside after 6 furlongs in 1:13.43.

Turning for home, Sis City was faltering on the rail while favorite Spun Sugar made the lead and Sweet Symphony kept R Lady Joy bottled up in fourth. By the stretch, it was over as Sweet Symphony blew past Spun Sugar to win by a convincing 6 1/4 lengths. Spun Sugar held on for second with R Lady Joy third. Sis

Sweet Symphony

City finished fourth with Dance Away Capote fifth. For All We Know and Ready And Alluring eased under the wire to wrap up the seven-horse field.

Twenty-three days before the Alabama, Sweet Symphony toyed with three rivals in a two-other-than allowance at Saratoga. For Mott, it was an Alabama prep. For Bailey, it was simply a sign of things to come.

"I told him after the last race that he could go hunting for any kind of company he wanted," Bailey said. "I knew the Alabama was fairly close but I thought she could take a step up because she was doing everything so easy. If you have the right horse you can tackle them any time you want, whenever it's right for them."

The Alabama was certainly right for Sweet Symphony. Not one to make audacious moves with his horses, Mott went into the stakes brimming with confidence, even though Sweet Symphony was spotting experience to every filly in the race. That's what good horses will do for you.

"It's unusual to see one come along – one, two, three and then to make that step and win that impressively. It wasn't an accident. I believed in her," Mott said. "She makes it pretty easy, it wasn't the most spectacular training job. She's straightforward, easy to handle. She's just always been wait and go. From the very beginning, she's been so cruise control. You don't come up with them like that very often. None of them."

Sweet Symphony arrived from owner George Steinbrenner's farm early

this year. Mott never asked why she didn't come in as a 2-year-old and they never told him. He just went about training the filly with the great walk and beautiful head about racing. She picked it up like an honor-roll student and it's been as connect-the-dots as training horses can be.

"She trained up to her first race and ran so good going seven eighths, she's just sitting there going along waiting for you to ask," Mott said. "With a lot of horses, you're hesitant to do it; usually you run them a couple of times and they get too anxious and you're trying to slow them down, horses want to run off so now you're working to get them back and wait on you. There's never been a problem with her. She is so professional."

For Spun Sugar, the Alabama marked her third Grade I start in the last two months. For Sis City, it was her ninth-straight stakes start since September. It was Dance Away Capote's 10th-straight stakes appearance since September.

"She's pretty fresh, what she lacked in experience, she probably made up with not being worn out," Mott said. "It's different for all of them, you're never in the same circumstances with any of them."

As any baseball fan knows, Steinbrenner can be tough on managers. Mott finds "The Boss" easy to deal with when it comes to training horses.

"The connections never pushed me, never told me where to run, they let you do your job – they don't want to lose, but they let you call your own shots," Mott said. "This was my idea and they figure if you want to do it, just make it work. As long as you win, there's no pressure. They are not backseat drivers."

And yes, that was Billy Martin turning in his grave.

Of course, even Martin didn't have the speed and slugging percentage of Sweet Symphony who beat older fillies and mares in her first three starts and now has a Grade I score on her record. Mott couldn't help thinking about what's next. The Breeders' Cup?

"She's so forward, I don't see why not," Mott said. "One more race, you base it off of that; you go to the Beldame and four weeks later you've got the Breeders' Cup. If she runs good in the Beldame, give it a try. You'd be stepping up against older mares but that's what we did with Ajina....

– she was second in the Alabama, was second in the Beldame and won the Breeders' Cup in California."

Jerry Bailey was having an odd Saratoga.

Plenty of winners but no stakes victories; the opposite of what he's been known for over the past couple of seasons.

After 21 racing days and 24 stakes runnings Bailey had yet to win a featured race. At a meet like Saratoga where he usually wins stakes with alacrity, the Hall of Famer had the duck when it came to black type. The duck had never roosted in Bailey's camp before.

After 20 issues of The Saratoga Special, I had talked to him once and that was for a quote about Pat Day's retirement.

Love him or hate him, Jerry Bailey is a great interview. Just have your thoughts and questions ready because where it takes one guy 50 words to get his point across, Bailey can do it in five. He has a race so broken down that he can explain it to you in less time than it takes for a reporter to push record. So far this year, he hadn't had the opportunity to give his sometimes terse but always accurate assessment of a race.

He came close Friday when he rode My Typhoon in the Lake Placid but he messed it up – he'll tell you that. The Todd Pletcher-trained Ready's Gal possessed lone speed and awesome recent form. My Typhoon could sit anywhere but was the one horse who had the tactical speed to soften up the favorite. The Christophe Clement-trained Naissance Royale looked like the benefactor if they went too fast in front.

Bailey went after Ready's Gal, never backing off through demanding fractions; setting the table for Edgar Prado and Naissance Royale who edged My Typhoon by a head. If you think you were mad when you lost your money or you had something to do with Ready's Gal and My Typhoon, you should have been Bailey.

"I overestimated Todd's horse and underestimated Clement's," Bailey said. "That's frustrating to me because I try not to make those errors. I try to be very precise in those areas and I was frustrated with myself on that one."

With a Hall of Fame plaque, nearly $280 million in purses earned, close to 6,000 winners, Bailey could afford to let one roll off his back. Not likely.

"I've tried to make the most of every opportunity I've had in stakes and I think I've done a pretty good job with the exception of Friday," Bailey said. "I've been beaten in some photos but I don't think I could have done anything different. Friday I could have."

Bailey thought about the Lake Placid when he went home that night, he thought about it at dinner, he thought about it when he went to bed and he was still thinking about it when he got up.

"Until 9 o'clock (Saturday) morning, I was pretty frustrated," Bailey said. "Usually I would have kicked myself all the way to the first race but I kind of let it go this morning, there's nothing I can do to change it."

Going out and winning the Alabama for My Typhoon's trainer Bill Mott would help. Bailey gave the undefeated filly every chance in the Grade I stakes, she came through with a huge effort and Bailey was suddenly back in front of the reporters.

"It's good to have it come right on the heels of yesterday and in a race like the Alabama, it kind of smooths things over a bit," Bailey said as he walked to his car after the Alabama. "I've realized that I'm not mounted quite as well as I've been in other Saratogas and it's been kind of strange, numerous wins but no stakes. I've come close a lot of times, with a little luck I could have won a couple of them."

Now ask Bailey about Bill Mott and Sweet Symphony and it's the same old Jerry Bailey we almost began to miss.

Question: How good is Sweet Symphony?

"All you can do is beat who they lead over to you and she's certainly done that every time."

Next: How was your trip?

"She was a little confused, she got put in tight around the first turn but only for a step or two then she figured it out. Once she knew what was going on, she handled it really well, then she was a very professional horse."

Next: Can she get better?

"She'll improve. Fairly laid back, professional, she was keyed up today, I think Billy had her really tuned up, she was game-ready today."

Next: What's it like to ride for Mott?

"They're going to be fit and they're going to be as ready as they can be when he leads them over. Sometimes I have to pull the trigger a little early, I can do it with his, knowing there's enough air in the tank. Sometimes the race dictates you're going to have to move a bit early to take advantage of a situation, you're not worried with him."

Welcome back Jerry.

For a moment, the stretch run of the Personal Ensign sounded just as it should have. "Come on, Ashado. Come on, Ashado" resonated everywhere.

Then when you listened more closely, when you stopped and really heard it, there was no A, as in Ashado, the champion and favorite in the 1 1/4-mile stakes. No, this was "Come on, Shadow. Come on, Shadow."

And the chorus was straight from trainer Neil Howard's crew in front of the clubhouse's big-screen television. Led by assistants Joe DeSantis and Annie Finney, they pleaded for their 4-year-old filly to hold off Personal Legend in the Grade I stakes. After a long, sustained rally from fifth in the six-horse field, Bill Farish's Shadow Cast held sway over Personal Legend with frontrunner Two Trail Sioux in third. Island Sand and Ashado finished in a dead heat for fourth.

As the "Come on Shadow" dissipated and the crowd checked their programs to see who it was that beat the champ and why they missed it, one voice could be heard above the occasional shriek.

"I knew she'd win today. I knew she'd win today," said DeSantis, mostly to himself. It wasn't boastful, arrogant or loud, just straight and honest. Walking to the winner's circle he joked, "I almost bet $20 to win on her and then I said, to heck with it."

After Shadow Cast had gotten her picture taken, DeSantis and Finney followed the Smart Strike filly back to the test barn and explained why they knew Shadow Cast would win her ninth career race and push her earnings to $923,751.

"When she trains this good, she runs this good. Isn't that right, Annie?" DeSantis said as Finney nodded her head. "She trained the best she had ever trained coming into this race. Color. Coat. Eating. You name it. The way she worked the other day, she did it so easy and on her own, we had a good feeling coming into today. Without a doubt. She loves it up here. She loves this racetrack."

Ridden by Robby Albarado, Shadow Cast took her usual spot in the back row while Two Trail Sioux opened up a quick 6 lengths. Ashado found her typical spot, tracking in second while Island Sand sat just off her flank. Personal Legend crept closer going down the backside while longshot A Song In A Minor gave chase in last.

By the final turn, Two Trail Sioux started to feel the steady fractions (23.02, 46.84, 1:11.23) while Shadow Cast gunned past Island Sand, Personal

SHADOW CAST

Legend – and Ashado. About then, Neil Howard and his wife, Sue, knew.

"Neil and I just turned to each other, we didn't say a word," Sue Howard said in the winner's circle after the race. "You just know when you see a move like that, and one thing she doesn't do is hang."

Shadow Cast gunned past the furlong pole to score by 2 3/4 for her first Grade I victory in a career that began when she won her debut at Churchill Downs Nov. 29, 2003. Bred and owned by Bill Farish (son of Lane's End Farm owner and former ambassador William Farish), Shadow Cast lost by 6 1/2 on the grass in the Diana on the first Saturday of the meet. Before that she was fifth in the Fleur De Lis, she won the Louisville Breeders' Cup on Kentucky Oaks Day and was beaten less than a length in the Apple Blossom at Oaklawn Park

"She's been a very nice filly, I would have said she was going to run well today because she could not look any better, could not be training any better," Howard said. "She worked in 13 and change out here a week or 10 days ago and the way she finished and the way she looked, that's when I called Bill and decided to go. But you're just looking to be second or third behind Ashado."

Shadow Cast would have none of that as she put away Ashado with ease and then stayed through 10 furlongs in 2:02.07. Last year, she won four races including an allowance at Saratoga. She had never tried 1 1/4 miles, but this time everything was right. Finney, DeSantis, Howard, Albarado and Farish all knew this was her day.

"She's got a little bit of a problem tying up. I ran her in the Fleur De Lis, three days after tying up a little bit," Howard said. "I'm ashamed to say I screwed it all up. I told Bill, we decided to go ahead and run, her blood came down, everything seemed OK. But with these fillies they can't overcome like those big 1,200 pound colts. She hadn't thought about tying up since. I don't know what it was but it was an unbelievable change since the Diana. With fillies, they can go back and forth."

In the Personal Ensign, Shadow Cast was only going forth. Albarado went into it confident, thanks to Howard and Shadow Cast's actions before the race.

"Neil never says much," Albarado explained. "He said, 'I've got two horses who are training unbelievable.' They both won today, Alumni Hall and Shadow Cast. I could feel it in the post parade, she pranced to the gate. Usually they prance away from the gate, she pranced toward the gate, wanting to do it."

Going against the likes of Ashado and recent Delaware Handicap-winner Island Sand, Shadow Cast went off at more than 14-1. Two Trail Sioux stumbled at the start and then put pressure on anybody close while cranking along on the lead. Shadow Cast picked off her rivals with ease.

"When I went up to Ashado and Johnny (Velazquez) started riding, I said, 'This will be be fun from here,' " Albarado said. "I thought it was going to be tougher task, she's the best filly in the house, Johnny was grinding on her . . . I won't say I knew I was home free but I knew they would have to run to beat her. She never loses if she's in front at the eighth-pole. And Neil had said in the paddock....

'See you in the winner's circle' and he never says that."

Todd Pletcher waited by himself.

He stood just on the other side of a phalanx of photographers, at the mouth of the paddock chute where the seven Travers contenders would enter. After three consecutive stakes and no action, Pletcher was ready to put the tack on Flower Alley and get the 136th Travers on its way.

Pletcher is a horse trainer. He wasn't thinking about the prestige of the Travers, about winning the $1 million race or about not having a runner in the first three stakes on the card. The meet's leading trainer was thinking about his horse.

"My biggest concern was how the horse came into the paddock," Pletcher explained. "I didn't like the way he saddled in the Jim Dandy, he was charged up. Obviously it didn't affect his performance but I thought we got away with one that day."

If Flower Alley got away with the Jim Dandy then he ran away with the Travers. Owned by Melnyk Racing and ridden by John Velazquez, Flower Alley was flawless in the paddock and in the race, winning by 2 1/2 lengths over Bellamy Road. Roman Ruler held on for third.

When Nick Zito opted to run Bellamy Road in the Travers, he did more than just add intrigue – he simplified the strategies of everyone involved. For Bellamy Road, the beaten favorite in the Kentucky Derby, brought lone speed to the Travers. Off since the Derby, Bellamy Road drew the 1 hole and was going to the lead.

After that part of the puzzle was set, it looked like Flower Alley would be the bridge between the electric speed of Bellamy Road, the tactical speed of Haskell winner Roman Ruler and the late runs of Reverberate, Andromeda's Hero, Don't Get Mad and Chekhov (in that order).

The race unfolded like the Sunday paper.

Bellamy Road and jockey Javier Castellano took the field into the first turn, Flower Alley and Velazquez followed. Once there, it was a matter of when Velazquez wanted to chip away a few stones from the pacesetter's wall. This is where Pletcher knew he'd be, where Velazquez knew he'd be and where every jockey in the race knew he'd be in the 1 1/4-mile stakes.

After a quarter mile in 23.54 seconds and a half in 47.43, Velazquez went to his tool belt, letting out a notch and easing to Bellamy Road's tail. Castellano could feel his chances slip at that moment.

"He was just galloping, like when you go to the pole working a horse, nice and easy, 23 and change for him is like 25," Castellano said. "I saw the shadow next to me and I said, 'That's Johnny.' When Johnny put the pressure on me, I felt like I didn't have as much horse as Johnny."

Velazquez knew it too.

"He gave me so much confidence today it was unbelievable. He was just going so well the whole time," Velazquez said. "As soon as we got to the backside, let's go and put a little pressure on Bellamy Road, we drew away from the whole field. Then I sat back again and gave my horse a chance. I wanted Bellamy Road to work, I'm not going to give him anything easy."

Bellamy Road stretched away from Flower Alley through 6 furlongs in 1:10.92. Velazquez checked on Roman Ruler once, twice, three times and knew he wasn't a factor. It was only Bellamy Road.

The duo turned for home and Flower Alley gradually put away the gallant Bellamy Road. For a moment, he fought back. But the 1 1/4 miles and the 3 1/2-month layoff combined to tone down his run, allowing Flower Alley to draw away and finish in 2:02.76.

Perhaps Pletcher worried about Flower Alley's paddock behavior because that was about the only concern he could conjure.

"I felt like we had everything right, a mile-and-sixteenth race in the Dwyer, a mile-and-an-eighth race over the track and we had 28 days between races," Pletcher said on the way to the trustees room. "I felt like we were getting the best of it from Roman Ruler because we had a little more time. We were getting the best of it from Bellamy Road because of a little less time. And I was hoping we were just better than the other ones. Everything fell into place. I was confident the horse was doing really well and we were in the right place at the right time."

That's been happening all meet for Flower Alley. The $165,000 yearling purchase easily won the Jim Dandy by 5 1/4 lengths. Two 5-furlong works went routinely and then it was up to racing luck and ability in the Travers. The Grade I score was the fourth career victory and third stakes win for the son of Distorted Humor.

Flower Alley finished third in his debut in December at Calder then won two in a row this spring including the Lane's End at Turfway Park. Sent to Oaklawn Park, he finished second to Afleet Alex and then ran hard in the Kentucky Derby finishing ninth after pressing a rapid pace. That's when owner Eugene Melnyk and Pletcher made a critical decision that would eventually help the horse sweep the two key Saratoga 3-year-old stakes.

"He ran a great race in the Derby, he had a rough trip, chasing a fast pace, got stopped behind a rabbit a couple of times in the turn," Pletcher said. "It wasn't an easy choice (to wait) but it was one of those things when I talked to Eugene and we were feeling each other out a little bit and he said, 'You know what, I don't really want to run in the Preakness.' I thought, good."

Pletcher started working backward from the Travers and chose the one-turn Dwyer at Belmont Park and the 1 1/8-mile Jim Dandy as preps. Roman Ruler upset him in the Dwyer, besting him by a half-length.

Then the two set out on different paths, with Roman Ruler going for the Haskell

at Monmouth Park and Flower Alley taking aim at the Jim Dandy. They both won, but Roman Ruler gave away eight days of rest to Flower Alley, which was perfect in Pletcher's mind.

"For me, four weeks is always better than three and three is always better than two, it's that simple. Four weeks seems to work better and I can't pinpoint why," Pletcher said. "I don't know if our horses run well fresh because of something I do or don't do or what, but statistically it seems to work that way. Maybe with more time, they run big and then they need more time to get back to that same kind of race."

Flower Alley needed a month to better his Jim Dandy performance, dominating the Travers to give Velazquez and Pletcher their first victories in the Saratoga classic.

"Good horses make you do a lot of things that other ones will not let you do," Velazquez said. "This horse, let him run, slow him down, let him run, slow him down....

....A lot of horses would not do that. Special horses do that."

If a horse trainer can do a home-run trot, Todd Pletcher was Kirk Gibson (minus the limp) after the Travers.

The usually subdued Pletcher roared into the winner's circle like a tornado to a coastal town. He hugged anyone from his father J.J. to agent and exercise rider Angel Cordero to valet Tony Milan to owner Eugene Melnyk. He picked up Cordero like he was a traffic cone on the street and hugged him like he was home from the war.

At about the same time, friend and first-call jockey Velazquez rejoiced in his own way, cantering back to the winner's circle on Flower Alley. When he got to the winner's circle, Pletcher was still circling the bases.

"I couldn't believe it," Velazquez said. "He never shows any emotion. Never."

With that, the jockey fulfilled the first half of my assignment.

One part of a writer's job is to seek out answers. The second, and more difficult, part is to seek out reasons for those answers.

So I asked Velazquez why Pletcher was excited. Sure, I know why, but the writer in me needs Velazquez to say it. And Velazquez responded just like he always does but this time the jockey got on a roll. The reasons flow easier when you're asked about winning the $1 million Travers for a friend and longtime teammate.

"Why? It's special. It's not the money," Velazquez said. "It's the prestige. The hard work. The honor. This guy works for so many years

since he was a little kid. He knows about racing. His family. It's the honor to win one like this. Look at me or Jose (Santos), coming from where we come from, it's not about the money, it's about the prestige and the honor to win something like this. The money comes and goes."

Winning the Travers stays. Velazquez has thought about the Travers since he heard of it after moving to America from Puerto Rico.

"It's something special to live this kind of life," he said, "and you get to appreciate everything. It's special. You see other people doing it and you wish one day you'll have it. Working and getting the opportunities I get, you've got to be proud of it. It's special. It's special."

Velazquez already owns two riding titles and the record for most wins in a season at Saratoga. Those are all well and good but this was the Travers.

"This tops winning the title," he said. "You have so many winners and don't have a Travers, you feel like you haven't accomplished much. Everybody would love to have one Derby, one Travers. Now I can say I won one. I can look back and say, 'I won one Travers.' You have so many ups and downs in this business. You're great one day, the next day you suck. Maybe I'm being hard on myself but that's the only way I can do it."

Velazquez has learned to temper his temper when it comes to losing but his frustration over stupid mistakes will never go away.

"There are some things you can do to avoid mistakes when you ride horses," Velazquez said. "Things happen in races, some things you do are stupid, it's like, 'Why did I do that again?' You definitely have to feel how the horse is going, you have to anticipate all the things that can happen. When I do something stupid, that's when I'm hard on myself. If the horse runs OK and I don't think I did anything wrong, I can take that, but I'll be the first person to come back and say I really (screwed) up."

Not that he expected to say that about the Travers.

"I knew my horse was ready, (Angel) said he's been working real well. He was going well enough that he was giving me the confidence that he could put pressure on Bellamy Road," he said. "If I didn't have it then I couldn't have done it. The horse gives you the signal that he can do it so you take it. That's what makes horse racing."

Bellamy Road and Flower Alley made this year's Travers, sketching a blue print for tactics. Velazquez went after Bellamy Road on the backside and put the cards in his hand instead of Javier Castellano's.

"He went in 23 and 2, almost 24, If I let him back up to a 49 and change and a 1:12, then it's going to be hard to catch up with him," Velazquez said. "I didn't want him to do that. I said, 'Make him work, make him do something.' "

Bellamy Road did more than he wanted to early in the Travers and Flower Alley did exactly what he had to do late. Velazquez wasn't counting the money when Flower Alley galloped out but he was feeling the moment.

"It was unbelievable, goose bumps. I don't know, just emotional," Velazquez said. "Just pure emotion. I was galloping out, I feel that air or something through me. Wow. I can't believe it. I got tears in my eye coming back, I'm not going to lie I got tears in my eye. The emotions you get from this business, it happens. It's a rush. A title, it's constant, doing this, doing that. This is one of the most important races there is and all of sudden it hits you. The Breeders' Cup, the race in Dubai and this one, they got to me. I might not show much emotion but I feel it. This year, I feel it more than ever. I don't know why."

Now, maybe we do.

NAME OF THE DAY:

Breathalyzer, ninth race.

– The 3-year-old filly is by Cozy Drive out of Wine Connoisseur.

Greg Gilchrist stood in the Saratoga Race Course trustees room, a smile all over his face. The television replayed the last race over and over, and the trainer sipped his champagne and watched in awe.

Each time, the result was the same – Lost In The Fog won.

Which sums up the horse's whole career.

The 3-year-old won his ninth race Saturday, but this victory was special for his connections. This time, it was a Grade I stakes. This time, it was Saratoga. For Lost In The Fog, it was just like any other race.

"He just doesn't look like he's going that fast – but then you look up at the clock," said Gilchrist. "It's the sign of a good horse, because that means all of his action is not going up and down, he's going forward with everything he does."

The $250,000, 7-furlong stakes began a little like a Quarter Horse claimer for the inside starters. Breaking from the rail, Fusaichi Rock Star stumbled, then ducked out and knocked into Social Probation, who then slammed Lost In The Fog and his jockey Russell Baze. But Baze remained patient and waited for his mount to regain his composure.

It didn't take long.

Lost In The Fog found his stride and the lead before the field left the chute. He covered the opening quarter mile in 22 seconds, entered the far turn in control and approached the stretch, lengthening his advantage all the while. Baze wanted to wait, Lost In The Fog wanted to go.

"On the turn, he switches leads and opens up," said Baze. "It's a natural thing for him, I don't have to do anything. He makes my job very easy."

Gilchrist knew they were winners entering the stretch.

"I saw Russell kind of look under his shoulder to see where everybody was at," said Gilchrist. "I've watched Russell Baze ride for 25 years now, when Russell takes that peak under his shoulder, and he's three or four in front at the quarter-pole, the rest of them are in a whole lot of trouble."

The Daddy and Storm Surge tried to make-up ground but sputtered. Social Probation and Better Than Bonds rallied to finish a non-threatening second and third, respectively. Lost in the Fog was 4 3/4 lengths clear at the wire.

"He's gone from a decent horse, to a good horse," said Gilchrist. "I don't want to use the

word great because that might be a little premature, but he's sure moving towards champion status."

The itinerant son of Lost Soldier has crossed the United States six times, won at seven racetracks and shows no signs of slowing down. Gilchrist, like his trainee, takes it all in stride.

"I still think the thing that impresses me most about him is he travels," said the trainer. "Just think if we could stay at home and have them come see us, which is not going to happen. That impresses me so much, that the horse can go ahead and do that and still perform each time. He's an incredible animal. That's not my training, that's his make-up. He's that kind of horse. There are a lot of guys that can train a horse like that, good horses make good horse trainers, and he's damn sure a good horse."

Baze and Gilchrist are down-to-earth horsemen. Gilchrist's sport coat and jeans wouldn't make the cover of a fashion magazine, but for him, they were right. Even a little press about an orange T-shirt (which he said is his favorite) worn during Lost In The Fog's schooling session didn't change his attitude.

"We do have good clothes," said Gilchrist with a laugh. "We're kind of in a relaxed mode today, we clean up pretty good on occasion."

Baze dresses for every occasion in the bright orange silks of owner Harry Aleo, but like Gilchrist, is humbled by the attention.

"They wouldn't know who I was if I wasn't lined up with this horse," said Baze. "I think it's the catchy name, that and the fact that he's obliterated most of the fields he's run against, but people love him. I feel like a groupie. Everybody knows the horse, nobody knows me. They're just following a good horse."

With nine wins and counting, Lost In The Fog figures to take Gilchrist and his team even higher.

"It's getting to where that win streak weighs on you a little," said Gilchrist. "I've been doing this a long time, there's always somebody better out there. I'm not saying that he's going to get beat, they seem to all get beat sooner or later, there are formidable foes out there. I will prepare him to the best of my ability and I will always do what is best for him. If he's not ready to go over there, then he won't go over. It won't matter if everybody in the world expects him to be there. If it's not in his best interests, he won't show up."

It's hard to picture Lost In The Fog losing, and Gilchrist doesn't trouble himself with the possibility.

"I don't know if and when that does happen how I'll accept it, but I'm sure you've got to take the bad right along with the good," said Gilchrist.

"We certainly have a lot of good and I hope it continues."

QUESTIONS, We've Got Questions

Trainer Kiaran McLaughlin's daughter Erin works the ice cream and water stand right outside the racing office at the track. She's been keeping track of the sights and sounds (and questions thrown her way) throughout the meet. A "best of. . ." list:

Where can I buy cigarettes?

Where can I buy beer?

Where can I buy lighters?

Where can I buy Carvel?

Where can I buy straws?

Where can I buy coffee?

Where can I buy milk?

Where can I buy ice?

Where can I buy Ben and Jerry's?

Where can I buy a saddle?

Where can I buy frozen lemonade?

Where can I buy peanuts?

Where can I buy Red Bull?

Where can I see the race?

Where can I find an ATM?

Where can I touch a horse?

Where can I find a bathroom?

Where can I see the leash put on the horse?

Where can I find the paddock?

Where can I find the paddock pavilion?

Where can I see the horses?

Where can I buy a bagel and cream cheese?

Where can I rent a car?

Where can I buy a silicone wrist band for the track?

Where is the Big Red Spring?

Where can I find the blankets?

Does the sun move and what time will I be in the sun?

Where did I come in?

Where's the gate with the big fountain?

Where can we see David Cassidy without paying for the clubhouse?

Where's the padlock, you know, where they walk the horses around in a circle?

Do the jockeys where the same colors for each race?

And our favorite:

– a man watched the replay of Pomeroy winning the Vanderbilt, thought the horse won twice and wanted to cash his ticket again

Doug Fout smiled, steered his family toward the winner's circle, shook hands with a litany of well-wishers – and then he took a moment.

A MOMENT

"It means so much to me that I can't explain to you how much it means," the trainer said. Then he paused, crunched back a few tears and sighed deeply. "This horse got hurt in the A.P. Smithwick, things didn't go his way and he got beat – then I lost my dad."

Fout's horse, Hirapour, ran down Three Carat in the stretch to win Friday's New York Turf Writers Cup 25 days after finishing third (and needing six stitches to close a gash behind his right knee) in the A.P. Smithwick. Fout's father, well-known steeplechase and flat trainer Paul, died Aug. 16 at 78. Call it emotion, stress, whatever. Doug Fout let it out while waiting for his champion to return from the Grade I victory.

"For this horse to come back and do what he did today . . . and the fact that my father won this race in 1975, it means a lot," he said.

Winning jockey Matt McCarron, who broke his arm in a fall here Opening Day and had surgery to get back in time to ride the Turf Writers, echoed the sentiments.

"I don't think Charles Dickens or anybody could write a better fairy tale," he said. "It was unbelievable, a dream come true on a true champion. He won the race, it had nothing to do with me. He's a brilliant animal."

Owned by Eldon Farm, Hirapour won the 2004 steeplechase Eclipse Award and seems poised to do so again after scoring his second Grade I win of the year in the Turf Writers. The 9-year-old Irish-bred pocketed $95,520 for the effort as the 6-5 favorite. Three Carat stayed for second with Party Airs third.

Not that it was easy.

The Turf Writers looked to be full of early speed, but turned into a tactical nightmare for the late-running Hirapour. Say What You See set a tepid pace while expected company Mauritania and Party Airs backed off to leave the second spot to Praise The Prince and an unsettled Paradise's Boss. Hirapour raced eighth of nine early and was still there with a circuit remaining the 2 3/8-mile race.

Before the eighth of 10 fences, McCarron moved to the outside; Hirapour responded by moving to fourth behind Praise The Prince, Paradise's Boss and Three Carat.

"They weren't going near the gallop I thought they would," said McCarron. "Paradise's Boss was swinging up there and my horse was struggling a bit. I was starting to second-guess what I had done, but when I pulled him out down the back just to give him daylight, to let him know it was time to go, he took me there."

Smithwick winner Paradise's Boss tried to stretch them out again, taking over the lead going into the final turn; he was quickly joined by Three Carat and an ominous Hirapour in the two-path, under urging from McCarron. Three Carat, carrying 18 fewer pounds than the eventual winner, took a brief lead on the final turn while bidding for an upset.

"From the three-eighths pole I was off the bridle and riding," said McCarron. "I had him in a spot where he was up on heels, but I didn't want to go three-wide at that point and I still wanted to keep my position. I could almost hear him say, 'Dude, what are you doing? They're in my way. Not yet.' As soon as I pulled him out, even though I thought he didn't have another gear, he found that gear."

Hirapour drew even at the last fence, and drew off to score by 3 3/4 lengths. The son of Kahyasi improved to 10-for-17 over jumps and stayed on a pattern of winning every other hurdle start going back to November 2003. In nine American jump races, he owns five wins, three seconds, a third and $467,650 in earnings.

The extra 2 1/2 furlongs, and Hirapour's ability to relax early, were the difference between a third in the Smithwick and a win in the Turf Writers.

"When you get him at a distance and he can run horses down like he did today . . . if he can chase horses he will not give up," said Fout.

"I don't care if he's on three legs or two legs, he will give you everything he has."

KIDS At The Track:

We received an e-mail from a friend yesterday that summed up the experience of taking kids to the track:

We've taken no real vacation this year, but took Jake and Casey up to Saratoga Springs. The first day, Casey spends betting trifectas (pick first three horses in order of finish). That night I asked why he always made that bet. He says that if he picked a horse to win and got it right, he may win $20. I would just make him pay for his own bets from then on. If he hit one of these bets, he would get a couple of hundred dollars and he could buy a Playstation. I say, 'but you are making bets that you have no chance of winning; you are just throwing away money.' He says, "Why do I care? It's your money."

That comment got under my skin and I decided I would change the rules the next day. Instead of paying for each bet as made, I give them each $40 and say they now have to risk their own money. Again he surprises me. He never places a bet all day and walks home with a $40 payday.

This kid can really play me for the sucker sometimes.

When the gate crew loaded May Night into her stall for the P.G. Johnson Stakes, another eight 2-year-old turf fillies still had to load. So Robby Albarado, aboard May Night, let his thoughts wander.

"I had this feeling, 'You know, it ain't that bad what I'm doing. I'm riding, I'm still making money, my life hasn't stopped one minute, one hour,' " Albarado said. "It's up to me if I let it bother me when I ride, obviously it doesn't because I know everybody close to me is safe – I just feel bad for the whole city."

New Orleans, dear New Orleans.

Born in Lafayette, La., Albarado has made a life in New Orleans. He's ridden at Fair Grounds since he was a teenager, winning over 1,000 races. He owns a house there. He calls 10 restaurants his regular joints, in a city that serves some of the best food in the world. His friends there are policemen, firemen, lawyers, doctors, hotwalkers.

Hurricane Katrina devastated The Big Easy this week. New Orleans, as Albarado or anyone else knew it, is gone.

Robby Albarado

NEW ORLEANS

"It's the most I've thought about it all day," Albarado said of the post parade on May Night. "It puts some kind of spirit in you, like, 'I'm not that bad off.' I'm watching it at 1 in the morning, seeing the same thing over and over but it's like I can't believe it's happening. I can't fathom having nothing, like these people."

New Orleans is suddenly the setting of Lord of the Flies. The city is under water. Looting is rampant. Levees have broken. People are stranded on rooftops. Bodies are floating in pools of floodwater. Lafayette, roughly 140 miles to the west, wasn't touched. Baton Rouge, the state capital which lies between the two cites, wasn't touched. The evacuation from New Orleans to Baton Rouge took nine hours. It's usually a 45-minute trip.

"The best picture I saw that describes the fear in people is of a 20-year-old kid driving a school bus," Albarado said. "He just jumped in and started picking up people on the highway and drove it to Houston. He's 20 years old, he looks like a 12-year-old kid behind a steering wheel, he drove 300 miles in a school bus to get out of there."

Albarado, like fellow horsemen Al Stall, Dallas Stewart, Neil Howard and Lenny Pike, sits helplessly watching his city drown. Albarado's only family member in New Orleans, his sister, fled to Houston long before the hurricane hit. His wife and kids are safe and sound in Kentucky. His house in New Orleans is probably gone, some win pictures destroyed, the furniture molding. But he's a lifetime away, riding winners in Saratoga.

"I can't imagine sitting on a highway right now, the only thing I own is what I have on, no direction, no job, don't know when I'm going to get a job, with my kids sitting there, two or three months before they get to any kind of school, don't know where they're going to go to school," Albarado said. "Some guy jumped off the roof of the Superdome. It would be easy to bail out."

It's the Chicago Fire, the San Francisco Earthquake of our lifetime. It looks easier to bulldoze what is left and start over again – when the water recedes – than it does to repair what's there.

"It's the worst thing I'll probably ever see, I thought the Trade Center was bad but I think New York City stopped for a couple of days and everything was back moving again, shaken, but moving again," Albarado said. "This, this will be months before anything gets moving. Months before electricity is turned on at the biggest buildings. I've never seen anything so wide-spread tragic. It seems like it will never be the same in New Orleans."

Albarado is one of the fortunate ones with ties to New Orleans. His house, near the broken levee, was his secondary home. He has a job that he can do anywhere in the country. He has money in the bank. He's riding stakes winners at Saratoga (May Night won).

"There's so much history, so many monuments and buildings there. You ever ride in one of those carriage rides? They'll tell you all about the history, places that have been there for 100 years and they won't be there any more," Albarado said.

"They say it's worse than any war, worse than any bomb you could drop. It will never be the same again. You'll say the old New Orleans."

QUOTE:

"Next time, no jeans."

– NYRA security guard to trainer Bobby Frankel, on his way into the paddock Wednesday

Saratoga's Daily Newspaper on Thoroughbred Racing

The SARATOGA Special

Year 5 • No. 6

Ashado Knows

Year 5 • No. 23 $1

WEEK 5

Turning The Corner

Ashado

COMPLETE SALES RESULTS INSIDE

Saratoga's Daily Newspaper on Thoroughbred Racing

Wednesday, August 10, 2005

The SARATOGA Special

Trainer Subscriptions to The Special compliments of SALLEE HORSE VANS

Year 5 • No. 13 $1

Fusaichi Pegasus filly brings $2 million to drive standout first night

Saratoga's Daily Newspaper on Thoroughbred Racing

Monday, August 8, 2005

The SARATOGA Special

Trainer Subscriptions to The Special compliments of SALLEE HORSE VANS

Year 5 • No. 11 $1

Hot Lick

Santana Strings rocks early while speeding to stakes win

...n takes 2nd stakes in 3 days

THE AMSTERDAM

thought they were going to cheapen him up. How dumb I was."

Tomillo did nothing but increase Santana Strings' value. In his next next four starts, Santana Strings finished second in the Spectacular Bid, flopped going long in the Arlington Washington Futurity, won an allowance race at Hawthorne and finished second in the Sugar Bowl at Fair Grounds. Finally, Asmussen had seen enough and the deal was made for Ro Parra's Millennium Farms to purchase the Florida-bred who originally cost $8,000 at OBS August 2003.

"I had run with him, I'd seen him, he's just a good racehorse. He was second to Storm Surge in the Sugar Bowl, we were third with Razor who's won about three stakes, so we pursued him," Asmussen said. "We needed him. He's a perfect example of what we're trying to do. Ro Parra, we had claimers for him before and now he's concentrating on better horses."

He's got a good one in Santana Strings even if it took a while for Asmussen to get it right with the chestnut colt.

■ See AMSTERDAM, page 3

Inside

Nick Zito leads 2005 Hall of Fame class

Wednesday, August 31, 2005

The SARATOGA Special

Trainer Subscriptions to The Special compliments of SALLEE HORSE VANS

$1

Bailey 29

Velazquez 34

Prado 38

POMEROY (Forego – Saturday)

WEEK 6

Season's final stretch features steeplechase Grade I, top sprinters, 3-year-olds on the turf, and a four-way race for the jockey championship

FOREST DANGER Saturday

PARADISE'S BOSS (N.Y. Turf Writers – Today)

Thursday, August 18, 2005

The SARATOGA Special

Trainer Subscriptions to The Special compliments of SALLEE HORSE VANS

$1

...e Yaddo

Kate Winslet (Richard Migliore) gets a pat after her win.

■ See KATE WINSLET, page 5

On The Bus drives through for Roma...

BY SEAN CLANCY

■ See ON THE BUS, page 4

Saratoga's Daily Newspaper on Thoroughbred Racing

The SARATOGA Special

Year 5 • No. 22

Sweet

Mott, Bailey team up for Alabama score with unbeaten Sweet Symphony

BY SEAN CLANCY

And then there were none.

Thirty-two issues have been crossed off. This is the final page of the final issue of the season. And, yes, I'm going to be contemplative and maybe even hokey as the curtain falls on another Saratoga meet. As my father would say, "I hate to leave, but I really must go."

OK, that was the lead to the final Cup Of Coffee from last year.

Yup, this is the Farewell Column. Cue the band, The Saratoga Special is heading home.

The first thing we'll be asked when we get there is, "How was Saratoga?"

How much time do you have?

Exhilarating. Exhausting. Stressful. Frustrating. Hot. Cool. Rainy. Sunny. Emotional. Drunken. Sobering. Short. Long. Testing. Amazing.

Saratoga is the ultimate test in racing. For us, it's the ultimate test in publishing. We've completed our fifth year.

My brother Joe and I drove the company golf cart around the backside Saturday morning. We looked at a horse for sale, stopped by the Annex and were treated to the Samyn & Voss Comedy Hour, got some advice from Richard DePass, bought some peanuts off the fruit truck and meandered from one side to the other and back. We didn't do a thing for this issue of the paper. No interviews, no ad sales, no editorial strategizing. Nope, we were in a different mode.

Once you start packing, the trip is over.

"We've gotten no sleep, been away from our homes for six weeks, stressed our personal lives and here we are with one more issue to go to complete our fifth year," I said to my older brother. "You know, Joe, this would be perfect if we had just made $200,000 at the meet."

"I'd settle for $50,000," Joe said while cracking open another peanut.

It's not about the money or we'd be doing something else.

One thing you sometimes forget when you make a living in this game is how much you enjoy a day's racing. Just a day at the track. Most of The Special's staff will get two of those – Sunday and Monday – before heading home.

A few afternoons to put up our feet and put off our worries.

Joe Clancy will be the one half-happy for one final day at the track and half-wishing to be home with his wife and three kids.

Pete Fornatale will be the one worrying about today's handicapping rather than tomorrow's for a change.

Jamie Santo will be the one shaking the urge to start circling typos in the Form and trying to find a winner in it.

Travis Stone will the one wishing for another week and hoping for a job in the industry, come graduation from Oneonta in December.

Dave Harmon, Tod Marks and Dave Martin will be the ones without cameras for the first time in six weeks. Well, you know photographers, maybe they won't put the cameras down.

Jim Mulvihill will be the one contemplating how he can make this his permanent gig.

Shelly Chase will be the one stretching her arms after carrying papers for six weeks and wishing for her bed at home.

I'll be the one watching the races and NOT looking for a story angle in there somewhere. The one not thinking of how to get the jockey and trainer to open up. The one not noticing the early fractions, where the winning horse was bred or where he's going next.

All of us will be the ones hanging at a picnic table between the Big Red Spring and the paddock. Heckling trainers and jockeys and trying to pick some winners for shipping money.

We'll be the ones with pockets full – OK, half full – of betting money and heads full of memories from Saratoga 2005.

No one ever called my brother even-keeled.

For the fifth consecutive year, Sean just stomped out of a Saratoga Special office with a sigh and a resigned "I've got nothing, nothing. Nothing."

He was speaking for all of us as we close Issue 32 of Year 5 of a summer racing newspaper that would test the patience of Mother Theresa. The Special is a project born of an idea. A company our size shouldn't do a newspaper five days a week for six weeks, but here we are. We survived another summer, made friends, won over more fans and managed not to strangle each other. The office joke is "Hey, what are you doing Tuesday? You want to hang out?" Yeah, right. We will go our separate ways, at least for a while. There are no new stories, no new jokes, no new ideas. We left them all here.

For me, the meet revolved around special moments – most having to do with the creature God called a Thoroughbred. That large, four-legged beast brings people to Saratoga like a mountain stream draws salmon.

Bill Mott stopped training for a half-hour one morning and talked about horses with me. All I wanted was a preview of the Bernard Baruch. I got a lesson, a funny story or two and a great morning. Like all of us, even Mott marvels at the process of training horses at Saratoga or anywhere. "What we do as trainers is fix things. You train and you fix. You train and you fix. You're looking and you're trying to repair. Sometimes the repair work gets moved to the back burner because you're busy getting one to the detention barn or running a lot of horses or dealing with people distractions." I left with the impression that Mott would train horses even if there were no races.

A few weeks later, Mott handed me the quote of the meet: "I was thinking about the Alabama before the two-other-than." He was talking about his 3-year-old filly Sweet Symphony. The next day, she won the Grade I easily in her stakes debut and fourth career start.

When jockey Pat Day retired, I talked to trainers Wayne Lukas, Dale Romans, Carl Nafzger, Jonathan Sheppard and Shug McGaughey. They all paid homage to Day's riding ability but went beyond to describe a person who meant something to them.

Journalism sages will tell you not to get too close to your subjects, but sometimes there's nothing you can do about it. I picked Matt McCarron up at the surgical center in Albany after he broke his arm. The steeplechase jockey needed a plate, eight screws, and a ride back to town. I talked to trainer Doug Fout about holding his father Paul's hand after turning off the ventilator. In seven minutes the son lost his dad.

Seventeen days after Paul Fout died and 37 days after McCarron broke his arm, Hirapour won the Turf Writers for the trainer and jockey.

I will miss chances to talk horses with John Velazquez – he compared Ashado to Serena Williams. When he's done riding, he could take up writing. I will miss my morning coffee and conversation at The Saratoga Sleigh. I will miss the banter in the racing office. I will miss my neighbors on York Avenue. Tom Voss and John's Call. The power of having a horse like Hirapour look at me instead of the other way around. Talking horses with Richard Migliore. The magic of a staff – Shelly, Jamie, Pete, Travis, Christine, Dave, Tod, Dave, Jim, Kevin, Emily (though we never met), Barbara, Sheila, Mary Beth, Shelly's mom, Shelly's grandmother, Jan, Dave, Jeff and the team at Staffield Printing in Clifton Park. It wouldn't have happened without you.

For almost two weeks, I've missed my family. Sam, Ryan, Jack and Nolan spent the middle part of the meet in Saratoga and we did at least a few things on our list – gambled, met people, strolled the sidewalks, went to our favorite restaurants, swam in Saranac Lake, got up early and watched workouts, drove the golf cart. The boys started school and have – quite normally – tested the patience of their parents (especially Sam). I snuck home for a day last week, surprised everyone other than Nolan (who simply said "oh, hi dad" when I walked into the kitchen). I'll be home in Maryland for good Sunday night or Monday morning, soaking up normalcy again.

I won't soon forget the racetrack performances – Lost In The Fog, First Samurai, Leroidesaminaux and Flower Alley made Travers Day worth savoring. Chowder's First's late charge to win the John Morrissey won't soon be forgotten and neither will Commentator's wire job in the Whitney. Sand Springs, Ashado, King's Drama – great stuff.

Two days ago I got asked for an autograph. A man standing on the clubhouse apron, just beyond the gate to the winner's circle called to me.

"Joe, Joe Clancy, come here."

I was waiting for a complaint about not handicapping the jump race properly but he pulled out the first edition of The Special – ever – and had me sign it. The headline that day in 2001 read, "Ready, Set, Go." Not sure if we were ready or set, then or now, but we have sure been going. We met another fan, J.R. from Boston, the day before. He talked about racing, computers, what being here means to him. He vowed to someday spend a summer in Saratoga, following the horses he would normally follow at home via television or other means. This year, he finally did it. He did Saratoga, but at the end of the meet there's a price to pay. His credit card bills will be huge and, as he put it, "There are dragons to slay at home."

May they fall easily.

INDEX

ARTICLES AND PHOTOS

INDEX

ARTICLES AND PHOTOS

Photos by Tod Marks, Dave Harmon and Barbara Livingston